University Library

Administration

Rutherford D. Rogers

University Librarian, Yale University

David C. Weber

Director, Stanford University Libraries

University Library

Administration

The H.W. Wilson Company

New York   *1971*

UNIVERSITY LIBRARY ADMINISTRATION
Copyright © 1971
by
Rutherford D. Rogers and David C. Weber

International Standard Book Number 0-8242-0417-4

Library of Congress Catalog Card Number 75-116997

PRINTED IN THE UNITED STATES OF AMERICA

To
E. M. R. and N. M. W.
silent but indispensable partners
in all our work
and especially this

PREFACE

This volume is designed to provide librarians and other academic personnel with a current treatment of the more important issues in the administration of a university library. It is hoped that library school students will find the work useful, and with this in mind we have been somewhat more explicit in spelling out abbreviations and explaining terms (e.g., NPAC and residual hypo) than would be necessary for the more experienced reader. The book is written from the point of view of the Director of Libraries, which means that the details of operation of an acquisitions department or of a circulation department, for example, are considered only to the extent that there are major policy issues or particular problems that must concern the Director and with respect to which he must play a central role in decision making. The issues and problems dealt with are those which, in substantial degree, affect the economy of the library operation, its service to its clientele, the securing of adequate financial support, the impact of various matters on the staff, and external relations both on and off campus. Obviously, no detail of operation will be without interest to the Director. He may be concerned with minutiae as seemingly inconsequential as signs. Yet it is equally obvious that a director's time is so limited that he must single out critical issues for his special attention. These are the focus of this volume.

Under most topics there is treatment of such points as the justification of programs, policy determinations, staff requirements, communication of problems and their solution, budget and fiscal control and accounting, legal concerns, and matters of relevant emphasis among different aspects of the library program. This is not an historical study of the development of university libraries; it concentrates on the problems as seen during the late 1960's and as anticipated in the 1970's and 1980's. At the same time it is a practical document, and thus a number of specific statements of policy or regulations have been included as examples from a variety of universities.

This is not to say that historical background and the existing published literature are not of value. Indeed, a research library is an organization which is singularly based on all previous experience, and its most expensive instrument — the catalog — is an accumulation of records prepared over decades; rare today is the institution which can start its bibliographic records *de novo* with a computer-based book catalog or other more modern techniques. Consequently, one who attempts to treat of the range of administrative problems in the university library must recognize his indebtedness to the large number of authors who have recorded in library journals and in monographic literature their experiences, their philosophies, their problems and proposals. There are classic works such as those by Randall and Goodrich (1936 and 1941), by Guy R. Lyle (1944, 1949, and 1961), and the standard text by Wilson and Tauber (1945 and 1956), as well as the publications of library associations, library schools, individual university libraries, and the Federal Government.

Although the authors have benefited from numerous items in the published literature, they have relied most heavily on their own personal experience at the Rochester Public Library, the Grosvenor Library, Harvard, Columbia, and Yale Universities, the New York Public Library, the Library of Congress, and Stanford University. To that extent this volume can be regarded as a personal document. Yet the authors would be forgetful indeed if they did not, in this inadequate fashion, register their recognition of the stimulation and contributions to their thinking that they have gained from colleagues in dozens of research, public, and special libraries, and from faculty and university staff with whom they have worked at Harvard, Yale, Columbia, and Stanford.

It is our pleasure to acknowledge specific help from or permission to use and quote from documents of the following: Association of American Colleges; Association of Research Libraries; Brown University Library; University of California Library, Berkeley, Los Angeles, and San Diego; University of Chicago Libraries; Columbia University Libraries; Columbia University Press; Cornell University Library; Harvard University Library; University of Illinois Library, Urbana; University of Kansas Library; University of Michigan Libraries; University of Michigan Press; University of Minnesota Library; University of Pennsylvania Library; University of Pennsylvania Press; Princeton University Library; Rice University Library; Stanford University Libraries; University of Texas Library; University of Utah Library; Washington University Library; and Yale University Library. We thank ARL members who sent bookplates.

Each author has zealously read, edited and rewritten the other's work so that the final product may be accurately represented as a fully joint undertaking which, in its gestation, proved to be a pleasant and stimulating experience. It is hoped that the results will prove useful to colleagues here and abroad.

R.D.R.
D.C.W.

May 1970

CONTENTS

Contents

Contents

Contents

Contents

Contents

Contents

Contents

Contents

Contents

PHOTOGRAPHS

Photographs

Photographs

All photographs courtesy of the respective universities.

INTRODUCTION

A university library is both a collegiate library and a research library. It is collegiate in its provision of books and other documentary records to support the students' program of instruction and to encourage the habit of reading and the use of libraries. As does the college library, the university library must also provide materials for use by the faculty members in the preparation of their courses of instruction and by the staff of the institution in the performance of their administrative and executive responsibilities. However, the university library differs from the college library in offering a wider range of undergraduate programs, offering graduate instruction beyond the Master's level, and usually offering advanced professional programs in a number of fields.

A university library is also a research library in that it provides collections in depth. It is this characteristic which requires not 100 but 200 volumes per student — collections which number in most instances from 400,000 to 4,000,000 rather than from 40,000 to 400,000. Not only basic treatises, primary source materials, and the major journals are collected for its fields of instruction — as is the case in a college library — but the university library must also collect the secondary and tertiary sources, the background materials, the compendiums, the annotated and revised editions, the commentaries on commentaries, publications in remotely related fields, analyses from faulty as well as sound points of view — in short, a very substantial portion of all of the relevant thought on all subjects of interest to the university's young scholars and their mentors.

In this second sense, the university library is a research library in the manner of the Library of Congress or the Reference Department of the New York Public Library. It is a research library which is typically a congeries of special libraries, rather than merely a major collection on a fairly circumscribed area or subject, such as are the Huntington, Folger, Linda Hall, Pierpont Morgan, or Newberry libraries. In such a comparison, a university library follows the former rather than the latter pattern; and whereas other re-

1

search libraries are likely to be noncirculating and highly centralized, the university library tends to decentralize according to major academic disciplines or departments, and readers may borrow from a substantial segment of the collection.

Users are more homogeneous in a university setting than in the pure research library, possibly a little more possessive and demanding of "their library," and likely to participate in its development as members of a faculty-student advisory committee or as individual consultants on collection building. As a consequence the director of a university library is likely to be closer to his clientele and more intimately answerable for the success or failure of his enterprise than is the director of a nonuniversity research library. The staff, likewise, is more uniform in both its professional and nonprofessional ranks with heavy reliance on resident students, and faculty and graduate student wives, factors that assure high turnover and, occasionally, sensitive administrative problems.

The university library fulfills such functions as these:

1. The selection of materials to be acquired and their procurement by various methods; materials may include books, periodicals, manuscripts, microtexts, films, sheet maps, and other graphic materials.
2. The organization and catalog listing of these materials via a complex of bibliographical records to aid in their location.
3. The marking, bookplating, and tagging of materials to show their ownership, location, source of funds from which purchased or the name of the donor.
4. The binding and protection of these collections to assure, within reason, their availability for future generations of students.
5. The circulation of materials, some under various degrees of controlled access, in order to make the materials as widely accessible as possible to members of the university community.
6. The provision of assistance to readers in the use of these materials, by means of publications, individual instruction, group instruction, and other instructional means designed to facilitate their use.
7. The provision of study facilities in a useful variety of accommodations and locations, so designed as to be conducive to scholarly work.

8. The relations with other libraries and institutions having library collections so as to benefit the scholar elsewhere who needs occasional use of the university's items and, conversely, to benefit the university's scholars who occasionally need access to items in other libraries.

The place of the library in the university community is partly academic and partly nonacademic. It operates as an intellectual activity yet it has many aspects that are of a purely routine or business nature. Its place in the university is usually defined by a statute of the Board of Trustees. Such a statute may be brief, as is Harvard's:

> The University Library consists of all the collections of books in the possession of the University. The Director of the University Library shall be *ex-officio* Chairman of the University Library Committee and of the Committee on the Library of the Faculty of Arts and Sciences. The University Librarian shall be *ex-officio* Vice-Chairman of these committees. Both the Director and the University Librarian shall visit and inspect the libraries comprising the University Library system and be *ex-officio* members of their library committees. The librarian of each library shall annually make a report to the Director of the University Library. The general control and oversight of the Harvard College Library and of the other libraries comprising the University Library system are committed each to the appropriate Faculty of the University.[1]

On the other hand, the statute may be quite explicit on a number of topics, as is that of Columbia University:

> §80. DIRECTOR OF LIBRARIES. There shall be a Director of Libraries appointed by the Trustees, on the nomination of the President, who shall be the general executive officer of all libraries under the control of the University. It shall be his duty, under the direction of the President, to see that the Statutes relating to the Libraries are properly enforced; to give continuous study to the needs and conditions of the Libraries; and from time to time report his findings and recommendations to the President.
>
> §81. ADMINISTRATION OF THE LIBRARIES. The Director of Libraries shall appoint all needed assistants and subordinate officers and fix

---

[1] Statutes, number 14, pp. xxiii-xxiv, *Harvard University Catalogue,* December 1967.

their titles, duties, and compensation, provided that the total amount shall not exceed the appropriation of the Trustees for that purpose; he shall be the custodian of all property of the Libraries and shall have charge and control of the buildings and rooms containing it; he shall make and enforce by suitable penalties all needed rules relating to the Libraries, library readers, subordinate officers, and employees.

§82. LIBRARY STAFF. Officers of the Libraries shall consist of librarians and such additional persons as may be so designated by the Trustees. The designation "librarian" shall apply only to an officer appointed as such to serve instruction and research through assembling, organizing and furthering the use of books, periodicals and other records available through the Libraries. Officers of the Libraries will rank with officers of instruction or officers of administration with respect to University privileges.

§83. ACQUISITION OF BOOKS. All books, maps, charts, and other printed matter given to the University or purchased from funds appropriated by the Trustees or given for that purpose shall be deemed a part of the Libraries and shall be marked and catalogued as such; and all such purchases shall be made by the Libraries except that similar material needed continuously in administrative offices and laboratories may be deemed a part of the equipment of departments and purchased, paid for, and cared for under the rules governing departmental equipment. No less than three copies of all reports and other matter printed by authority of the Trustees, except such as may be printed for their exclusive use, shall be deposited in the Libraries.

§84. USE OF THE COLLECTIONS. Rules governing the consultation and borrowing of materials from the collections by officers, employees, registered students, and others will be prescribed by the Director of Libraries with the approval of the President.

Students who fail to comply with rules governing the care and use of the collections, including the proper charging and return of books, may, after review by the appropriate dean or other officer, be deprived of good standing in the University.

§85. GIFTS. All gifts of money to the Libraries shall be paid to the Controller, who shall disburse the same, subject to the approval of the President, for the purpose, if any, specified by the donor, without special vote or appropriation; and such gifts made without conditions shall be used for purposes recommended by the Director of Libraries with the approval of the President.

§86. LIBRARY STAFF COUNCIL. There shall be a Library Staff Council, drawn from officers of the Libraries in a manner directed by the Vice President of the University, which shall have the duty of advising the Director on matters relating to the internal operation and administration of the University Libraries.[2]

The past decade has witnessed major developments — or departures — in university libraries. Perhaps the most notable factor has been growth itself, which has brought with it problems of bibliographic control and physical facilities as well as those problems associated with business management: personnel administration, scientific budgeting, financial administration, and planning. Great advances have been made in constructing more functional and attractive buildings that reflect greater concern for the comfort and working ambience of staff and readers. Private faculty studies within the library abound. The general reading room with phalanxes of large reading tables has given way to diversity as expressed by lounge chairs, individual carrels, carrel-clusters, and divided tables — all more strategically placed in relation to books.

The prodigious growth in collections has been characterized by both greater bulk and greater variety of formats. Taken together, these two forces have exerted rending stresses on traditional methods of bibliographical control. More and more research libraries are abandoning decimal or home-made classification systems for that of the Library of Congress. Greater standardization, talked about but largely avoided for decades, seems to be coming speedily and with ease, encouraged by the Public Law 480 program and the National Program for Acquisitions and Cataloging.

Microtext has failed to solve space problems to any significant extent and has begotten a plethora of largely inadequate equipment with a host of maintenance problems. Nonetheless, at some future time there is sure to be a far greater impact from microtext than at present, and all libraries must follow developments in this field.

The greatest technological force in the next two decades is likely to be the computer. As yet largely unproved, it is being vigorously applied to library processes large and small. Success in the application of machine techniques to such routines as ordering, fund accounting, cataloging, circulation, and serials control seems certain provided universities can absorb the substantial costs involved.

---

[2] Columbia University. *Charters and Statutes, with amendments to April 6, 1959.* New York [1959]. Chapter VIII, "The Libraries," p. 13.

Introduction

These internal applications foreshadow related user benefits in the form of remote access, speedier searches, greater mastery of burgeoning literature, and improved search strategies. At least one generation into the future is the digital storage of any significant segment of the intellectual content of a large research library.

The forces that have expanded research libraries require, as their counterpart, greatly enlarged and more highly specialized staffs. Personnel administration has had to become more scientific and professional, as has bibliographical control. Advances have been recorded in position classification, salary plans, performance ratings, communication, training, fringe benefits, and status.

As we look to the 1970's and beyond, a clear need is discernible for a more adequate supply of librarians; linguistic, subject, and area specialists; and computer experts to keep university libraries as vital components of campus information systems. In fact, some universities are taking faltering steps toward integrated information complexes that will draw together computation, library, and related facilities. It may be expected that in many instances the library and its director will constitute a principal force in such enlarged activities. These trends have already produced salaries for university librarians (meaning all "professional" staff members) that approach faculty salaries, and it is to be expected that this trend will continue with the library staff gaining increased recognition in terms of salaries and status.

Greatly augmented expenditures for books, staff, and buildings have imposed strains on most university budgets. Federal funds, through the Higher Education Facilities Act of 1963 and the Higher Education Acts of 1965 and 1968 do not, as yet, constitute major elements in university library funding, but potentially these could be significant factors in future support of university libraries. The Federal Government has already made immense expenditures and commitments in support of research. Federal action has brought to the fore the importance of recorded data in the dissemination of research results and in supporting related research efforts. This awareness has resulted in additional burdens for research libraries, but it has also been accompanied by a recognition of the significance of libraries in the national information picture. It is not too much to expect that there will be an intensification of this awareness and that university libraries will be recognized for what they are — in-

6

dispensable resources for research within their own institution and equally indispensable components of the national research patrimony.

There is already Federal legislation bearing on "networks for knowledge," and there is certain to be unrelenting pressure for a more rationalized system of sharing resources that will heavily involve university libraries. The relatively elementary efforts in computer technology will come of age. It is predictable that MARC II tapes will be the catalyst that will bring about greater standardization in procedures and a greater awareness and sharing of resources. Abortive efforts, to date, in facsimile transmission will someday prove economically feasible on an attractive time scale. Vexatious problems of copyright must be solved if information is to be freely and rapidly available to the research scholar, but this, too, is inevitable in a sufficiently long time span.

As the predominant manifestation of the research library genre, university libraries have, in the words of a university vice president, become "big business." This is true by several applicable measures: volume of purchasing, size and specialization of staff, use of resources, diversity of formats, extent of physical plant, and total funds involved. Once upon a time, the librarian could be a scholar, even a dilettante or an ivory-tower recluse. It was then fashionable to deplore the librarian who was only a manager. Perhaps we have reached a new level of maturity when the library director needs to be knowledgeable in the book world, scholarly in his interests, catholic in his reading, *and* a practical business manager skilled in personnel administration, budgeting, and financial management, as well as thoroughly versed in the extremely technical issues of library and information science: classification and subject analysis theory, computer applications, microphotography and microtext readers, facsimile transmission, and copyright.

The foregoing provides a picture that is anything but two-dimensional. University libraries have become extremely complex mechanisms demanding a great deal of those who direct their activities and who participate in their operation. It is hoped that the reader of this book will approach it with the zest that such an enterprise merits and not regard university libraries or their direction and management as unrewarding or unchallenging. They are quite the opposite.

1. THE LIBRARY PROGRAM

It is axiomatic that any institution should define its goals and that those who work in the institution should grasp the far-off objectives and also realize the speed with which goals can be attained. To presume that the objectives of a university library are determined by curricular specialization or higher administrative fiat within the university would be gross oversimplification.

The director of a university library has, as a primary responsibility, the task of educating others in the university about library problems, including, for example, the library costs attendant upon academic venturing into new fields, the realities as well as the implications of computer applications to libraries, the inexorable requirements for space that a given level of acquisition may demand, the advantages and disadvantages of decentralizing collections and services, the wisdom of a separate undergraduate library, the economics and service impact of in-house versus commercial binding, the desirability of the curatorial system in building collections, the degree of emphasis merited for special and rare collections at a given stage of development of the library, the quality of staff and the costs thereof required to operate a first-class library, the aspirations of staff for recognition and appropriate status, and the relative effectiveness of various methods of acquiring publications, e.g., blanket orders, exchanges, foreign purchasing missions, and on-approval plans.

It is decisions in a multiplicity of areas such as those just enumerated that determine the nature and goals of a university library. There must be leadership within the library to recognize and isolate such issues, to bring them before the proper people, to press for discussion, to present advantages and disadvantages, to "sell" certain courses of action, to make decisions, and to communicate such decisions within the library and the university. Such responsibility will find its center of gravity in the director's office, but many library staff members, students, faculty, and general administrative

9

Humanizing of interior spaces: the open-shelf periodical room beneath ground-level skylights — O. Meredith Wilson Library, University of Minnesota

officials must be brought into the decision-making process. The extent of involvement of any one group will depend upon the issue at hand. The director and his staff must be aware of the mechanisms that may be potentially effective (e.g., committees, advisory groups, bulletins, memoranda) and the constituencies that may have an interest in a given problem.

More fundamental still, there has to be in the midst of a sea of complex issues someone who harbors a general vision of where the library is headed and attempts to shape individual decisions toward a long-range target. Such target may be the aspiration to move a third-rate library into the first rank in size and distinction with all that this implies in collections, buildings, and staff; or the target may simply be to maintain excellence in a library of distinction, a task that may be as difficult as striving for excellence if one is surrounded by complacency.

Targets that are more narrowly defined but which may lead to ultimately broader achievements might include such things as (1) adequate study room facilities to accommodate faculty members who rely heavily on library materials, in order that they work effectively and in comfort, either singly or in groups; (2) building an economics collection that is characterized as "ragged" or "uneven" until the lacunae are filled and a new level of excellence is attained; (3) gradually rationalizing a branch library system that is extensively decentralized in relatively weak units into fewer centers of strength; (4) recruiting librarians on a national rather than local basis, seeking more advanced specialized preparation, and building a salary scale that will not only attract but hold such people; (5) increasing the ratio of clerical support to make more effective use of professional staff and thereby stimulating an improvement in the general level of individual performance with accompanying operational and service improvement; or (6) undertaking a phased broad-scale automation effort.

PROGRAM PLANNING BY THE LIBRARY STAFF

In the formulation of specific goals, the library staff, its quality and collective attitudes, is certain to be a primary factor. This element may be positive or negative. An old-line staff in a rapidly developing institution may lack the capacity to face new issues or may resist change through ultraconservatism or fear of the personal implications that radical developments may bring in the way of increased responsibility or competition from an enlarged staff. If this is the case, a change of course may require adroit and patient maneuvering internally before other groups are approached. However, long-term staff members can often prove surprisingly receptive to change, for they may recognize that they can never be anything but frustrated employees if they are working in a second-class library within an institution that has moved or is moving to a new level of excellence. The director should make it the first order of business to know his staff well enough to identify such pockets of strength. In making key appointments, persons should be selected who offer both solid preparation and desirable personal qualities but who may add a fresh dimension to the staff that will prove useful in attaining longer-range objectives; for example, an acquisitions librarian with a considerable background in computer applications may be appointed even though no automation has taken place or is immediately anticipated. More will be said on this in the next chapter; but to assure staff support in a rapidly changing library, every effort should be made to identify and recognize abilities within the existing staff.

It has been said that individual decisions must be shaped toward a long-range target. Problems that seem misleadingly simple, such as the question of changing classification systems, may have major impact on library services, staff, and costs for decades to come. The change from the Dewey Decimal to the L.C. classification is a problem that should be studied and discussed extensively at the staff level before a definite decision is reached. The director may know that the change is unavoidable, but rather than proclaim his decision, he will weigh the disruptive effect that such a decision will have on established routines and the complexity of the solution: Should there be complete reclassification of the entire collection? should there be partial reclassification of very active branch or main reference collections or of serial sets? should the new classification be applied only to new acquisitions or to publications after 1970 except in literature? how will users be affected? what are the cost implications? what has been the experience of other libraries? what is the relationship of such a course to automation? how would partial reclassification affect deployment of collections and general space needs? how will the individual cataloger be affected? By the time

11

these issues are discussed and clarified, the faculty may be enthusiastic about the prospect of adopting a new classification and the staff may have found effective ways for an immediate change.

PROGRAM PLANNING WITH FACULTY PARTICIPATION

This brings us to a second constituency that should be involved in such a decision, namely the users. Since faculty and students are the primary users of a university library, their needs must be of paramount concern to the library in setting general goals and short-range targets. The fact that a university, to a greater extent than other library jurisdictions, contains a preponderance of people who depend on recorded knowledge in their daily work is one of the joys and strengths of university librarianship. This dependence can be translated into appreciation or criticism, and it is probably a pretty dull and lifeless institution that doesn't have a generous mixture of the two ingredients. Furthermore, it would be an unimaginative librarian indeed who could not turn valid criticism of collections or physical facilities toward greater library support. Vigorous faculty criticism has started more than one university library on the road to improvement. Few people who have not worked in a university environment can appreciate the power of an aroused faculty. The university exists to educate students, to conduct research, and to publish the results of that research. In a quite literal sense, the center of this effort is the faculty, supported by requisite library and laboratory facilities. When widespread faculty opinion can be brought to bear on a given issue, action is almost certain to ensue.

It is not surprising, therefore, to find mechanisms within every university to link faculty opinion with the library administration. This may be a loose *modus operandi* under which the university librarian consults regularly with the deans of schools or executive heads of departments of instruction about their needs, about budgetary problems, or about changes that will affect them. An intermediate or related device is the departmental library committee on which the departmental librarian may sit and to which, upon occasion, the director of university libraries may be invited. Perhaps the most common mechanism, however, is the Library Committee of the Academic Council or Senate or one appointed by the president or provost. Such a committee is likely to meet regularly, probably not more frequently than monthly but oftener than once a year. Such committees should be *advisory* rather than controlling; nonetheless, the library director who pursues goals directly opposed to faculty sentiment is probably in for trouble.

The faculty library committee can be an immensely useful group in an advisory capacity. The library will do well to measure faculty views on a myriad of library problems before taking steps that may arouse strong criticism of the library. The very act of consulting with the faculty informs them in advance of unpopular but essential actions and associates the faculty with the solutions adopted.

The functions of such a committee may be summarized as follows:

1. Selection or recommendation of a new director (unless a special search committee is assigned this responsibility).
2. Establishment of major operational policies such as circulation rules, regulations for use by outsiders, access to and publishing of manuscripts, and book-collecting emphasis.
3. Support for the total library budget, often with particular advice on the allocation of the book budget (if departmental allotments exist).
4. Advice on the selection and promotion of senior library personnel.
5. Advice on an extraordinary purchase of a book collection or acceptance of a major collection or endowment with "strings."
6. Concurrence in the creation of a new branch or combination of branches.
7. Support for and advice on a major library building program and specific significant design elements.
8. Counsel to the library administration and university administration on the general library program.

The faculty has specific contributions to make in each of these areas.

The faculty committee can be particularly helpful in determining budget priorities when there are likely to be strong elements of disappointment for some constituents. Also, the forceful backing of the faculty can win higher priorities for library programs within the overall university budget.

The faculty has a strong stake in new library buildings — not just in physical amenities that affect them directly but in program and policy considerations associated with buildings. For example, the

13

question of the establishment of a separate undergraduate library building contains within it far-reaching implications for academic experimentation as well as effective support of conventional teaching. Money devoted to the undergraduate library building and its operation, however, becomes a prior claim on total resources. The faculty can provide valuable counsel on the relative importance of such a step vis-à-vis an enlarged research book budget and expanded physical facilities for research collections. In a sense, decisions with respect to additional branch libraries are equally momentous because branches tend to grow and eventually require larger operating and capital budgets that profoundly affect the nature of the total library operation.

If there is to be a new central university library or a major addition to the central building, the faculty can be very helpful in determining the total number of faculty studies that should be available and the size and furnishings of the studies. They can contribute to even more momentous decisions on the extent of subject departmentation within an enlarged central building and the deployment of the research collections. A major central building program often results in prolonged "temporary" dislocations of services and collections. The faculty can be helpful in deciding which of several solutions will prove least inconvenient and can share in a decision that may be inevitable but is, at the same time, certain to be unpopular with some users.

There are numerous problems relating to acquisitions policy that are of great interest to the faculty and on which they can be of assistance. If the library maintains a departmental allotment system, the faculty endorsement of actual budgetary allocations can be a source of strength. Conversely, if the library wishes to terminate the allotment system, faculty support is very desirable and may be decisive.

A library with moderate resources may have a difficult time determining its policy on the purchase of rare books and manuscripts. The impecunious library, of necessity, will probably forgo such purchasing; the affluent library can purchase rare materials without retarding more general types of collecting. The faculty can display unusual good sense and balance in helping the intermediate library to arrive at a policy that will balance financial resources and research and teaching needs.

14

The faculty is also a party at interest in the acquisition of extensive microtext series. Faculty members, better than any other constituency, know the research significance and the vexatious difficulties associated with large bodies of microtexts. They can also help the library to weigh the wisdom of spending (or committing) tens of thousands of dollars on large-scale microtext programs which may, in part, duplicate conventional resources, as opposed to using lesser or comparable sums for selective acquisition of important individual works in the o.p. or reprint market.

The faculty has a large stake in cooperative acquisitions, whether with a neighboring institution or in a national program. Such programs involve both the use of funds and ease of access to materials. In either respect, the faculty will be affected sooner or later.

As a fine example of faculty involvement in acquisitions, the establishment of a curatorial system for selection is almost certain to create great and enthusiastic faculty interest. Such a program has implications for the quality of collection building and for the burden that the faculty must bear in the collecting effort. Curators associate more intimately with the faculty than do almost any other library staff group; therefore, the faculty can play a pivotal role in starting a curatorial program, even to the point of proving immensely helpful in recruiting curators.

There is a host of operational or service decisions in which faculty opinion is very useful. The question of switching to a new book classification raises numerous issues of faculty interest. Will older materials be reclassified? If so, what is the financial impact on other endeavors? If not, how will books with the same subject in two classification systems be housed in order to be readily accessible?

The question of the library's engaging in automation experimentation is sure to raise substantial faculty interest and comment. Undue optimism may have to be tempered, but support is almost certain to be available since the faculty see at first hand the intractability of the manual system.

Library service to local industry and nonuniversity users competes with faculty and student use. If the library plans to establish a technical information service to industry, the faculty will want to be certain that such a program provides for a preferential system to protect the university community.

Library hours and stack access affect the faculty as personal users and as teachers. They will want long hours, and they are likely to favor broad stack access because most faculty members are devotees of the browsing concept and wish to generate in their students this same enthusiasm for exposure to a broad expanse of the published literature of a field. Faculty support can be useful in a related operational detail: exit monitoring to assure that books removed from library buildings are properly charged. If such a program is new in a university, it is sure to spark some resentment. If faculty (and student) support can be marshaled in advance, the transition will be smoothed.

Finally, and most importantly, there is a hard-core minority in every faculty group consistently delinquent in returning books, whether for annual renewal, for use of another reader, or for reserve purposes. Librarians, unaided, cannot cope with such people, but backed by a strong faculty committee and by university officials, librarians can obtain compliance with reasonable regulations.

PROGRAM PLANNING WITH STUDENT PARTICIPATION

Effective student opinion on the library is much more elusive and less likely to be carefully considered. The university librarian can expect isolated complaints in letters to the editor of the student newspaper, and there may be reportage with or without benefit of consultation with library officials. The library will have to weigh its response or nonresponse on such occasions, but it should not be insensitive to valid criticisms when they are made.

Formal liaison with students will commonly take one of two courses. In the present mood of greater student participation in the affairs of the university, some faculty library committees have co-opted student members. This arrangement has much to recommend it because students thus get full exposure to library problems without the expense in staff time of a separate committee. However, there are some problems of so strictly student concern (e.g., noise in an undergraduate library) that a purely student committee may be advisable. Such a group may be appointed by the head of the student government. On important issues, committee members may be willing to canvass student opinion and be very helpful in setting policy. A separate student committee may be conducive to more relaxed and freer student participation than a mixed faculty-student group. Thus, under differing circumstances, both courses have merit.

PROGRAM RELATIONSHIPS WITH UNIVERSITY OFFICES

The director of the university library will probably report to the president of the university or to a vice president or to the provost, but there will be a wide spectrum of relationships with other university offices. And the cultivation of relations with trustees or regents can often be appropriate and useful to an understanding of and support for the place of the library in the university.

The controller of a university usually has within his jurisdiction all financial accounting and budgeting. This will involve the library in giving and receiving reports on salaries, wages, payrolls, book funds, and supply and equipment expenditures, and in an infinite variety of policy relationships on such matters as the transfer of funds from one account to another, year-end carrying forward of balances, and general administration and control of funds. Administrative data processing may also be under the controller, and the library will have to look to this operation for payroll checks as well as for periodic financial statements. Gift and endowment funds may be generated and invested by other departments in the university, but the controller's office exercises direct oversight over the use of such funds, and a smooth working relationship between library and controller staffs is most desirable to assure full communication and congenial disposition of numerous details.

The controller may report to a financial vice president who, because of his position, works more directly than the controller with the board of trustees on the raising of funds, on budgets, on long-range financial estimating, and on handling of the securities portfolio in a private university. The library director is certain to be involved with the financial vice president in these major areas; and when large, unanticipated sums are needed, for example to purchase a significant private collection, the financial vice president may be able to provide all or part of such monies or know donors who can be induced to contribute to such a project. The raising of gifts depends in part on offering a prospective donor a range of opportunities in the hope that one may have particular appeal to him. If

17

the library is to get its share of gift dollars, the director must keep this elementary fact in mind.

Anyone who has been around libraries for very long, particularly large libraries, will realize that they are confronted with a multitude of legal problems. Relations with donors raise numerous legal points in regard to evaluation of materials, varying testamentary or gift provisions, and disposition of property. Copyright can be a recurring legal problem, particularly if the library operates photocopying machines. *En bloc* purchases of materials should be on a contractual basis, and when tens of thousands of dollars are at stake, it is advisable to seek legal advice on the drawing of the contract. Large blanket order agreements are essentially contracts and should be subject to expert legal review. As will be explained more fully in Chapter 6, the library is usually the designated purchasing authority for books. As such, it deals in transactions that total hundreds of thousands of dollars annually. No business of this magnitude can function without legal advice, whether it concerns a damaged shipment of books or a major purchase. The legal staff will probably report to an administrative vice president or the university's business manager. The library director will do well to cultivate a solid relationship with the university's attorneys wherever they are located.

The vice president for administration or for business affairs is likely to have under his jurisdiction the business manager, the construction manager, the planning office, the purchasing office, the university personnel office, and the staff legal counsel. Several of these offices, in turn, may be subsumed under the business manager.

At a minimum, the business manager will be concerned with purchasing and building maintenance, both of which functions intimately affect the library. All nonbook purchasing (of supplies and equipment) and contract maintenance (e.g., of typewriters and duplicating equipment) will be handled through the purchasing office. The library will probably be authorized to make minor purchases through a petty cash system, but any major item of supply or equipment, whether purchased or leased, will have to be negotiated through the purchasing agent. This should be accepted as a desirable course of action because experienced purchasing staff know sources of supply and can procure items at favorable rates that make the library's budget stretch as far as possible.

18

Building maintenance, meaning all repair of buildings, equipment, and grounds, as well as housekeeping of the premises through a custodial staff, is likely to be under the business manager. The library constitutes a major item in the university's physical plant, particularly when there are dozens of branches and a large central building. The office of the director of the physical plant, sometimes called the superintendent of buildings and grounds, will be called almost daily on such matters as emergency repair of plumbing and locks, deficient cleaning of offices or reading areas, painting, leaking roofs, grounds upkeep, and all the endless problems that beset a large physical plant.

The planning office is the coordinator of all architectural work for new and renovation projects. Outside architectural firms may do the major design work, but the planning office articulates the university's wishes and interests, brings the user (e.g., the library) and the design talent together, and watches over the execution of the building contract documents. A senior planner is usually assigned to each project whether it involves relandscaping the rear of the main library building, the construction of a stack in hitherto unused basement space, or the designing of a multimillion-dollar building. The planner works with the library (and outside consultants) on development of a detailed program for space and equipment and on such details as interior decoration. There will probably be a separate construction manager who coordinates the solicitation of construction bids and the letting of contracts for buildings and whose staff oversees the day-to-day progress of construction, checking to be sure that construction materials meet specifications and that work is performed in exact conformance with drawings.

Finally, the general university personnel office will be a very active component in the library's intra-university relationships. The personnel office will be the major referral point for nonprofessional employees; will probably be the central office for personnel classification; will process new employees, seeing that they have explained to them the insurance and other benefit programs; and will place them on the payroll and have them execute necessary tax-withholding and other documents. The director of personnel or his staff can be of great assistance in dealing with serious personnel problems, in offering specialized training for library supervisors, and in conducting a recruitment program for nonprofessional library positions. The

19

director of personnel may also play a major role in setting salary ranges for library positions and in determining the status of librarians within the academic community. These matters impinge so importantly on the library that good working relationships between the library staff officers and the university personnel office are essential.

The budgetary support for the library and its negotiation are likely to be prime responsibilities of the office to which the library director reports, or the budget process will be carefully controlled by such authority. The entire library program can stand or fall on the soundness of this relationship, whether it be with the president, academic vice president, provost, or dean of the faculties. There must be careful explanation of objectives, and even of some of the subtleties of individual library activities. It is also at the presidential or provostial level that acceptance of the library director as a full and important officer of the university can be determined. If the director is regarded as the equivalent of a dean, he will be invited to attend meetings involving the deans and meetings of major officers that recommend high university policy. Too often university libraries that fail to get this level of recognition are caught short when completely unanticipated demands are thrust upon them. They are likely to be stepchildren in budget allocations and in staff salaries and status. Such a policy reflects abysmal short-sightedness on the part of university officials whose reward is likely to be inadequate functioning of a service central to research and teaching. However, the library director must earn their confidence and appreciation through his understanding of the broad problems and objectives of the university by bringing the library program into conformity with this larger framework and by demonstrating soundness, integrity, and imagination in administration of the library.

The director of the university library will be well advised to allot a certain amount of his official and social effort to maintaining good relations with the many university staff officers that bear in any important degree on the library's well-being. Acceptance of membership on university committees by senior library personnel is an important part of the job of liaison with the faculty and the administrative staff. Such general liaison reinforced by meetings on specific problems, an occasional luncheon at the faculty club, or other participation in the life of the university can be of inestimable value in communication and understanding.

Persons who work with budgets, procurement, staffing, physical facilities, and maintenance are impressed with standards or with objective measures. Unfortunately, research library operational standards are largely in the developmental stage, although formulas for physical facilities are now widely accepted. The university librarian must make full use of comparable statistics on cataloging costs, salaries, staffing, book prices, and acquisitions effort. Imperfect though these devices may be, they are likely to be accepted with reasoned explanations of why a local situation fits or fails to fit a general pattern.

The use of consultants or an outside survey team can occasionally be beneficial. It is safe to assert, however, that outside experts and consultants more often fulfill a diplomatic than a technical void. It is sometimes possible for an outsider to be more frank in regard to a library problem or to have his advice accepted more readily than that of a regular member of the staff. It may be beneficial to the university to have an "outside" study of cost of library service in order to strengthen the case for higher overhead on government contracts. There are also times when expert knowledge, particularly in building planning, does not reside in a staff, and it will be desirable to import such talent. There are also problems that can be handled with greater dispatch by bringing in specialized personnel. Consideration of a new photographic laboratory or of a reclassification project are good examples of this. The library director will have to weigh the real need for consultants and use them as wisely and as sparingly as possible. Full use of talents on the library staff, published literature from other libraries, and experienced personnel in local university offices outside the library can usually obviate most needs to use outside experts in most university libraries, whereas outside help can more often be justified in smaller libraries. (This subject is developed in Chapter 9.)

There is a widespread absence of specialized planning and operations research staff in university libraries. These functions tend to be performed by the director and his staff, including division and department officers. Occasionally a specialist can be brought in from the staff of the controller or the business office. Sometimes a faculty member may undertake research in a problem chosen from library concerns, for instance book storage alternatives. But as libraries become multimillion-dollar enterprises, thought needs to be given to the wisdom of investing staff and money in a sustained examination of goals and procedures. A few libraries have moved, or are moving, in this direction, and automation is forcing a detailed look at manual procedures. Needless to state, the director of the library must be heavily involved in any such planning or analysis.

In recent years the university library has begun to play a much more active role in the teaching and research effort of the university than it did in the past. The library administration must be alert to this trend and receptive to opportunities to further the library's role. The movement away from assigned readings and toward greater emphasis on undergraduate as well as graduate seminars, on reading periods, and on independent research bespeaks a greater reliance on libraries. The potentialities of computer applications in opening the resources of libraries, tying research libraries into a national system, and making remote access available to the professor in his study or laboratory suggest a different magnitude of usefulness of university libraries. These as well as the more mundane problems of staffing and budgeting have gained visibility on the horizons of the university librarian, and he must shape his vision of the library he runs with these responsibilities and opportunities in mind.

SELECTED REFERENCES

American Council of Learned Societies. *On Research Libraries: Statement and Recommendations of the Committee on Research Libraries Submitted to National Advisory Commission on Libraries, November 1967.* Cambridge, M.I.T. Press, 1969.

Association of Research Libraries. *Problems and Prospects of the Research Library.* Edwin E. Williams, ed. New Brunswick, Scarecrow Press, 1955.

Buck, Paul. "A Credo Reconsidered," in his *Libraries & Universities: Addresses and Reports.* Cambridge, Harvard University Press, 1964. pp. 147–63.

Clapp, Verner W. *The Future of the Research Library.* Urbana, University of Illinois Press, 1964.

Commission on the Humanities. "Libraries for the Humanities," in its *Report.* New York, 1964. pp. 31–45.

Downs, Robert B., ed., "Current Trends in College and University Libraries," *Library Trends,* 1 (July 1952), 1–165.
Especially the articles by McAnally, Swank, and McCarthy.

Licklider, J. C. R. *Libraries of the Future.* Cambridge, M.I.T. Press, 1965.

Lyle, Guy R. *The Administration of the College Library.* 3rd ed. New York, H. W. Wilson, 1961.

Randall, William M., and Francis L. D. Goodrich. *Principles of College Library Administration.* 2nd ed. Chicago, American Library Association and University of Chicago Press, 1941.

Rutgers University Graduate School of Library Service. *Studies in Library Administrative Problems: Eight Reports from a Seminar in Library Administration Directed by Keyes D. Metcalf* [David C. Weber, ed.]. New Brunswick, Rutgers University Press, 1960.

Wilson, Louis Round, and Maurice F. Tauber. *The University Library: The Organization, Administration, and Functions of Academic Libraries.* 2nd ed. New York, Columbia University Press, 1956.

2. PERSONNEL POLICIES

Administration has been defined as getting things done through people. No seasoned administrator will quarrel with the critical significance of finding the best possible person for every position no matter how important or minor. The key to successful administration in any institution rests on having reliable, honest, informed, and skillful persons in both major and intermediate positions. The chief of a unit who can be relied on to handle subordinate personnel fairly and to bring problems to the director at the right time, who is reliable in his reporting and honest in his demands, who is emotionally stable, and who has common sense and judgment as well as technical proficiency is a jewel beyond price. The director who has positions filled by persons possessing these attributes is assured of a sound operation and is free to devote himself to larger issues such as planning and university-wide contacts that are almost certain to be neglected if he must be constantly coping with personnel problems. Consequently, the selection of personnel becomes a matter of foremost concern to the library director. At a minimum, he must be able to delegate selection responsibilities to his staff officers with constant review of their effectiveness; at the maximum, he must himself participate extensively in the selection process.

SELECTION OF A LIBRARY DIRECTOR

The selection of the director of university libraries is of major significance to the future of the library system. The incumbent director will usually be asked for suggestions; but he should never participate in the actual selection process since, even if he is universally regarded with affection or has been regarded as a superior administrator, he is not in the best position to judge the needs of the next administration nor to interview candidates with these needs in mind. On the other hand, the incumbent should be absolutely can-

25

did in discussing the library and the university with any candidate who wishes to speak with him.

The director will need a broad variety of qualifications, including intelligence, leadership ability, some graduate education, an agreeable personality, an open mind, a keen interest in higher education, a knowledge of and a love for the world of books, health and energy, a degree of wisdom, good judgment of people, and hopefully a formal training and considerable experience specifically suited to prepare him for the responsibilities of directing a university library. He usually will be between thirty-five and fifty years old, and sometimes younger but seldom older, unless he is promoted from within the library system. He always should have had administrative experience with increasing responsibility.

It is not possible to prescribe an exact set of qualifications since the needs of any institution at one point in time will be unique. The director should hopefully be weak in none of the above qualifications; he should offer substantial strength in the areas of greatest need to the institution. His intelligence, judgment and personality will, in the end, be of more importance than his formal training and experience.

The above statement should not be interpreted to mean that a graduate degree in librarianship is not important. It is of very considerable importance, and every university would be well advised to make this a requirement, other qualifications being equal. But the M.L.S. is not an attainment of the greatest importance in the larger university libraries where a very strong team of associates and assistants with the M.L.S. can bring specialized backgrounds to bear on the substantial problems of a university library. The authors believe that the most important consideration in choosing the director is the quality of the man himself. Experience or academic degrees, whether the M.L.S. or Ph.D., are definitely secondary.

That point having been made, however, the advantages of a man with the M.L.S. should be stressed. First of all, the entire system of professional education is based on evidence that a man specially trained for a post is more effective than an equally capable man who lacks that preparation. Secondly, the university library administrator will need to be able to judge and decide on a host of matters requiring some specialized library knowledge, whether it be of acquisitions sources, classification, computer applications, or building

26

planning. This is equally necessary for budget management, the disposal of duplicates, the physical care of books, the handling of government documents and serials, or the creation of bibliographic instruments. The third and most important reason for choosing a man with the M.L.S. has to do with his relations with the librarians on his staff — his ability to converse understandably and sympathetically with the staff, his ability to receive the full confidence and support of the staff, his effectiveness in recruiting librarians to fill positions at all levels and their ability to take pride in his leadership in their professional associations. The administrative librarians on the staff of a university without such a director will probably find it somewhat harder to state their needs and to attract and hold a professional staff of high quality. The position of associate director is likely to be several times more crucial in such circumstances.

Although a professor or a man from another field of endeavor may make a special contribution to advancing the library program, a man of equal ability who has chosen academic librarianship as his profession and has spent years in studying the theory and learning the practice of librarianship is in the best position to handle the administration of the university library.

SELECTION OF DEPARTMENT HEADS

The most important appointments made by the director will be those of his chief associates, the persons to whom he delegates responsibility for administering the library program. He will unquestionably take a personal interest in their recruitment and make the final decision himself, in some instances obtaining the concurrence of the chairman of the committee on university libraries, or a representative group of the committee, as well as of a representative of the provost's office. The practice in universities will vary in this respect.

It is generally good policy for some two thirds of the appointments to be made by promotion from inside the library staff. On the other hand, a few senior officers should be brought in from outside to add leavening through breadth of experience and a fresh point of view.

The director should strive to build a team of senior officers with a wide variety of qualities and talents which can be brought to bear

27

on any particular library problem. This may be justification, in one instance, for giving consideration to a woman or in another instance to a man, to a foreign-born or foreign-educated librarian, to a person with a business or science background, and so forth. A good deal of the very important policy determination and long-range planning will be conducted by the director with this group of senior officers; so it is important to keep in mind that they not only will operate a department for which they must be specifically qualified but they also must be able to make a contribution to important staff deliberations in the director's administrative council.

The specific qualities to be sought in any department head will be a mixture of various characteristics. An essential ingredient is effectiveness in personal relations — the supervision of personnel, their organization and direction, work in committees, and relations with subordinates and superiors. This is of inestimable value; it is doubtful that any individual can serve as a department head without talent in this critical area. A second quality is certainly mental ability — the thoughtful, penetrating, intellectual or scholarly attributes which are necessary in a changing library world and are certainly useful in relations with faculty associates. Beyond these, no exact specification can be given for department heads as a whole. It is obvious that they must be competent librarians with a good formal education who have had appropriate experience of increasing responsibility and who have given evidence that they can perform at the level required.

The relations of the director of libraries with these officers should include mutual respect, close communication, and absolute candor. The director should have department heads who are sufficiently competent so that the director can concentrate on matters involving departmental policy and extradepartmental issues and can leave the departmental administration to the person assigned that responsibility. Each department head will need to know all of his department's operational details; the director needs to be familiar with them but must consider the specific processes only when a point of policy, a significant economy, or other major interest makes it necessary. Depending upon the personality and workload of the director and the rate of change in library procedures and policies, the director will in greater or lesser degree wish, or need, to delve into operational details. Involvement of the director in operating details will be more frequent during the first months a new department head holds his position or when a new director is trying to become familiar with his responsibilities.

The operation of any department must be based on a clear understanding by staff at all levels of its function, responsibilities, policies, and procedures. For this purpose a departmental manual may be useful. It is certain that any major decision must be recorded in a memorandum, with copies sent to the director and other individuals concerned. Not every action of a department must be so recorded, and the operation can be slowed down drastically if too much is committed to paper and there is other evidence of "red tape." Still, it must be kept in mind that department heads are candidates for even higher positions, and there may be an unforeseen illness, accident, or other reason that a person must leave his position; so an adequate record of important actions is essential if the organization is to operate smoothly when an administrative change occurs.

THE PERSONNEL OFFICER

There is a breaking point or optimum size beyond which there must be a delegation or sharing of selection and other personnel responsibilities. Based upon experience, the opinion is ventured that when the total staff passes one hundred, there should be some sharing of selection, perhaps along professional and nonprofessional lines. When the professional staff alone approaches one hundred, there is probably a substantial argument for a library personnel officer. However, even in the largest university libraries, there will be a major reliance upon a general university personnel office for recruiting and screening candidates for nonprofessional positions.

A full-time library personnel officer need not be a librarian, although there are advantages to having this kind of background if such an officer determines personnel classifications and handles professional recruitment. Judgment is the most essential quality a personnel officer needs to possess because the success of his effort depends so much on the exercise of this trait: in selecting employees, in determining appropriate salaries, and in judging the merits of complaints. He must also have the attitudes and personality that inspire employees to come to him with problems and accept his disposition of complaints. It is useful to have a person who has had some general personnel experience. If the personnel function is not a full-time assignment, an assistant or associate director who has had good supervisory experience can often function effectively.

In a sense, the library personnel officer functions within the library much as a general personnel officer functions within the university but within narrower limits of authority in several respects. By delegation from the library director, the personnel officer may give final approval to certain classes of appointments and may be authorized, again within certain limitations, to fix salaries and wages. The director or an assistant director will probably approve professional appointments and salaries, and higher-level clerical and specialist salaries. Professional interviewing and recruitment are likely to be shared by the director or assistant director, but the personnel officer may interview nonprofessionals in collaboration with unit supervisors. The latitude for establishing personnel policies will be limited in the library because of overriding university policies, but recommendations may emanate from the library for changes in such general policy as, for example, length of work week, night pay differentials, and holidays, because these are matters that intimately concern the library staff. The library personnel officer may handle many personnel problems, receive complaints, and adjudicate minor issues between supervisors and employees, but major problems including separation will be referred to the director or associate director.

STAFF SELECTION AND APPOINTMENT

In general, university libraries control the final selection of all personnel. The burden of professional recruitment is likely to fall entirely on the library with only occasional assistance from the university personnel office. The latter, however, will refer clerical and secretarial personnel to the library. In the best university personnel offices there will be preliminary screening of applicants, some testing of clerical skills, and even the obtaining of health clearance required for certain positions involving strenuous physical activity. If this practice does not prevail, the library will be well advised to establish its own program of testing, not only of typing and shorthand skills, but also clerical aptitude including such a pervasively necessary ability as alphabetization.

Personnel Policies

Universities have certain reservoirs of employment not available to other libraries, namely students, and student and faculty wives. This is not an unmixed blessing because it results in built-in turnover and presents, at least with faculty wives, certain delicate problems of library-faculty relations that are best avoided. If a faculty wife becomes a personnel problem, the effect on the library and the demand on the time of the director can be most unfortunate. Such employees present minimum risk if the individual is used on short-term projects, in the smaller branch libraries, or in a specialized assignment, e.g., in an art slide collection or as coordinator of residence libraries. However, if the labor supply is adequate, the library should carefully weigh the employment of people who may have a high "sensitivity" potential.

There is the related problem of hiring close relatives on the library staff. Long and not always happy experience has left the writers with the firm conviction that this is to be avoided. There will be times when a wife may seem an even more attractive employee than a husband or, *in extremis*, when the solution to a difficult recruiting problem seems to be acceptance of husband and wife or parent and child. When this mirage shimmers before the director or personnel officer, he should accept the axiom that one mistake in such an appointment may outweigh a dozen successes. Here again the risks may be minimized if assignments can be made that are geographically and administratively remote. The employment of close relatives in the same division or in a supervisory-supervised relationship should always be avoided.

In general, no one should be appointed to the staff who has not been interviewed by appropriate members of the library staff. The skilled interviewer can detect many (but not all) potential personnel problems. Excessive loquacity, undue dwelling on unimportant details, inability to fill out the personnel form accurately and completely, obesity, repeated avoidance of frank answers to legitimate inquiries (such as the reason for changing positions), lack of personal neatness — these and many other signs should not be lightly disregarded.

There are also times when an appointing officer will be so impressed by a candidate or under such pressure that he will be tempted to act immediately without checking with previous employers. This can be a perilous move and it is to be avoided. If haste is essential, a long-distance telephone call is a good investment. Telephoning is also recommended in cases where there seems to be a real question about an apparently good candidate; people will usually reveal more about a candidate by telephone than in writing. Reference checks are advisable even for former employees particularly if they have been at another library for several years. There are cases where once first-rate employees develop serious emotional or other problems while employed elsewhere, and reemployment without checking references can have unfortunate results that can be avoided. Each candidate should be entirely acceptable — hopefully, enthusiastically acceptable — not only to the personnel officer but also to the division chief or branch librarian for whom the applicant would work. If any of the three or four library officers who may interview the candidate have any real reservations, even "sensed" reservations, it is wise to look for other candidates.

Any substantial time gap in a list of previous employment should serve as an alert to the interviewer; also, beware the floater who changes positions frequently. Do not accept for a clerical appointment a person with an M.L.S. degree, and only in special circumstances offer a clerical appointment to one with any other professional degree or certificate. Think twice before hiring someone at a salary far below what he has received before. Even well-intentioned people who seem eager to work for less money just to be associated with your particular institution, or to switch from cataloging to reference, or to move to a more favorable climate will rapidly forget these reasons and feel inadequately compensated. As a general rule such appointments are not recommended.

Appointment to other than an entrance-level position always raises the question of promotion from within versus importing a special talent from outside. There are very strong arguments in favor of internal promotions whenever possible. Such actions raise the hopes of younger employees that they, too, may be promoted if they stay and if they perform well. It is also true that one has a fairly accurate assessment of someone already on the staff, whereas one is likely to get favorable rather than unfavorable details in regard to a person at another institution. Furthermore, the person already on the staff knows procedures, persons, and policies, and this will shorten the time in the new assignment before he begins to make major contributions. Also, experience in one place in the university library system can produce extra dividends in other library assignments.

Despite these several factors in favor of an internal candidate, the reasons for bringing in an outsider can be compelling. An outside candidate may offer truly superior qualifications; he may also bring collateral specialties that will prove useful on wider grounds than the immediate position. An internal candidate who is acceptable but not outstanding is often useful in an intermediate position but severely limited in more senior assignments. There is some danger of developing a monolithic staff when backgrounds of most employees have been built in one institution; even though such a situation may provide wider understanding derived from common experience, it suffers from the lack of diverse experience and ideas. There is no general prescription for any one appointment, but a mixture of internal and external appointments is probably healthy and is likely to be a natural consequence of a considered attempt to appoint the best available person in each instance. There are times when no suitable candidate appears to be available and the temptation is great to make an unwise compromise. Every appointment cannot be made with enthusiastic expectations, but this should be the objective. The writers are firmly convinced that the best policy is to postpone action before too quickly picking someone who seems a poor risk.

Appointment in an "acting" capacity in a position is sometimes necessary. It provides a longer time to seek and interview candidates, it bridges time between a departure and the time when the appointee may be able to arrive, and it may give a local staff member an opportunity to demonstrate that he has the qualities needed for the more senior post. Such "acting" appointments are not good for the incumbent or the library if drawn out. The incumbent lacks the full authority and is certain to feel frustration after a few months; the library program is bound to mark time until the appointment is settled.

In canvassing internal candidates, there is always the question of the technique that will best produce the desired results. If the staff is not too large, the director or personnel officer may simply run through the various possibilities and single out two or three candidates. The trouble with this method is that it doesn't give the person with an unexpected interest a chance to make it known. For that reason, many libraries have adopted a posting system which lists vacancies and invites expressions of interest. Under civil service, appointments may have to be made from the top three candidates ("the rule of three") on a civil service list, but this kind of rigidity is rare in university libraries. The posting system can serve a very useful purpose, but if improperly organized, it can also be a heavy burden on supervisors and appointing officials. It should be understood that there is no obligation to grant a personal interview to everyone who applies. If there is such an obligation, supervisors will find themselves going through the motions of interviewing obviously unqualified candidates or the perennial malcontents who apply for every advanced position. The system, properly run, can turn up some surprising solutions to vacancies and can give the staff a feeling that appointing officers do not consistently pass over internal candidates without at least considering them.

In the actual hiring of staff members, the terms of employment should be stated in a letter or an appointment form. A clear statement of grade and title, salary, duration of appointment, reimbursement (if any) for moving expenses, and some indication of assignment or duties should be included as a minimum, together with the effective date and the place and time of initial reporting. If a leaflet is not available describing conditions of employment and fringe benefits, some reference should be made to these and particularly to those benefits, such as vacations, in which there may be a variation depending on level of appointment or length of service.

BENEFITS

At one time libraries offered advantages in vacations or other fringe benefits in contrast to other enterprises, particularly industry. These advantages have largely evaporated as industry has responded to demands of labor for more liberal benefits. Insurance and medical programs in industry are frequently equal or superior to those in universities. As a consequence, universities have to stress environmental and cultural factors that are important to many individuals. A number of university libraries are able to offer time off (perhaps eighty hours per year) to audit university classes that will be beneficial to an employee in his work. In some institutions, such class work cannot be taken for academic credit without payment of customary fees. The wholesale availability of nonfee study could distort class sizes and faculty-student ratios, and create a need for additional faculty with attendant financial problems, not to mention the impact on the work of the library if many staff members were released for study.

Sabbatical leaves are becoming more prevalent for librarians. This privilege rarely extends to the entire professional staff but is beginning to be available for selected employees. Usually, the library director must endorse a request for sabbatical leave, the final decision resting with a vice president or provost. If a privilege of this kind is to have respectability, it must be based on a proposal sufficiently meritorious to justify the granting of the leave. Six or twelve months of foreign travel hardly qualifies. But a research project aimed at publication, a bibliographical project, advanced study, and other educational undertakings designed to contribute significantly to the librarian's intellectual growth and experience may be worthy of approval.

Professional leave for one month or less, depending on the purpose, may be granted by the director. Leave to attend conferences and institutes may be treated in relatively liberal fashion as long as the library can spare the individual. A less liberal policy would be followed with respect to leave requests for travel to make investigations of libraries in this country or abroad. On the other hand, extended visits to book dealers and agents in foreign countries for purposes which can be considered part of the librarian's normal responsibilities would be considered as time spent on the job.

As is the case with professional leave, the library has a right to demand that the librarian perform his university responsibilities with full effectiveness before he undertakes any outside professional work. Given this as a basic requirement, a librarian may be allowed to spend some small fraction of time on outside professional work just as professors may accept consultantships. At the level of assistant director or associate director this may be interpreted as reaching a maximum of one day per week, which is a common faculty rule of thumb. Below this classification level, the fraction would have to be determined and approved by the library administration.

Some institutions can offer to pay partial moving expenses for librarians who join the staff. If librarians do not have faculty titles, they may still be equated with faculty members of varying ranks and be entitled to commensurate assistance. Such funds are usually controlled by some central authority in the university, but payment for librarians can be established as a matter of policy. Actual disbursement would be contingent upon submission of receipted bills showing payment to a mover (or to REA Express, Air Express, or other firms that may handle shipments of books or other small items). Costs usually cover mileage for a personal automobile or, within the stated limits, fares on public carriers for members of the family. With considerable latitude for administration, a typical scale of payments follows:

Deans (including the library director)	Full expense
Professors (including the associate and assistant library director)	3/4 of actual expense up to $2,000
Associate professors (including senior divisional and departmental library officers)	3/4 of actual expense up to $1,600
Assistant professors (including assistant library departmental and divisional officers, curators, etc.)	3/4 of actual expense up to $1,200

These amounts may vary substantially depending upon the distance of the move, and whether the appointee is single or has a large family; and reimbursement may not be available for appointments to the junior grades. In hardship cases the eligibility or percentage limitation may be waived, and the decision may vary in some measure depending upon how strongly the university wishes to attract the individual.

CLASSIFICATION

Personnel classification, which was rare in libraries a few decades ago, is now widely applied in libraries whether under civil service jurisdiction or not. Largely through enlightened personnel administration in the offices of the largest employer of all, the Federal Government, the theory of classification has been refined to an increasingly sensible degree. Basically, position classification attempts to define the duties to be performed, the lines of authority above and below the position, scope of responsibility, and the qualifications, both personal and substantive, needed for successful performance. Although the concept has been somewhat modified, the focus of position classification is on the requirements of the job within an organizational framework. Stated another way, a Ph.D. degree does not necessarily make one a better filing clerk; in fact, it may make one worse because of a short-interest span in an inherently dull job. Within reason, there is at least a basic combination of skills needed to execute a certain mission, like cataloging or acquisitions work, efficiently and economically. This presupposes that there should be a balance among these skills and that everyone in such an operation cannot expect to progress indefinitely to a higher classification and pay scale.

Granted the basic validity of the foregoing, the fact remains that an individual can have an impact, either positive or negative, on a job. Through exceptional accuracy and speed, a filer, for example, may consistently turn out so much work that his ability should be recognized in some way. If there is a promotional channel as, for example, in bibliographical searching, an employee may be promoted. If no such promotional ladder is inherent in a job, there should be provision for rewarding outstanding performance. In civil service, it may be possible to give more than a single step-increase; in a private noncivil service institution, the merit principle can be followed and is highly recommended.

There is an increasing need in university libraries for those having specialized skills; linguistic, subject, and computer specialists are an indispensable part of a research library staff. Moreover, the difficulty of work and the range of knowledge, e.g., a working knowledge of several languages, prevails over a wider segment of the staff. This is a factor that can be lost in classification studies. If personnel classification is performed by a technician from outside the library, he may be tempted to lump bibliographical searchers and other library specialists with clerks elsewhere in the university. This can easily result in injustice to such staff members and may require special effort to remedy the situation.

Personnel classification is a constantly evolving matter because no progressive organization stands still; the classification scheme grows, becomes more complex and is reorganized, and any one of these functions affects personnel. As a consequence there must be a more or less constant reexamination of classification. This may be

37

the responsibility of the university personnel office, of the library, or of a civil service commission. In one way or another, formally or informally, this must be done; and however executed, the director of the library and key supervisors should regard this as a matter of major importance. The fairness with which the individual employee is treated in this respect is a matter of grave concern to him and therefore to staff morale.

Most libraries have a hierarchical system of classification titles that denote level of responsibility. In the Federal service there are grades GS-1 to GS-18: the larger the number assigned to the position, the more senior the position, the higher the salary scale. Some state jurisdictions and many private universities use a Roman numeral scale: Librarian I, II, III, IV, V, or Library Assistant I, II, III, IV. Others differentiate by words such as "Junior," "Senior," "Principal," or "First." Still others follow the faculty nomenclature and use Librarian, Assistant Librarian, Associate Librarian. The following are three examples from large universities:

Example A

    STUDENT ASSISTANT — a class for hourly (casual) employees

    LIBRARY CLERK — a class of positions requiring basic clerical skills

    LIBRARY ASSISTANT — a class of nonprofessional positions requiring special linguistic, subject, or technical competence

    LIBRARY INTERN — a class of preprofessional positions for persons with at least baccalaureate degrees who are preparing for careers in librarianship

    LIBRARIAN I — for beginning librarians with postgraduate library degrees and other persons of established professional caliber

    LIBRARIAN II — for experienced librarians and those in junior supervisory positions

    LIBRARIAN III — for senior supervisors and experienced librarians with considerable responsibility

    LIBRARIAN IV — for senior officers

Example B

	Page
Clerical Group A	Bindery Processor
	Duplicating Machine Operator

Clerical Group B	Desk Attendant Clerk (prefix department or function) Clerk-Typist Secretary A Secretary B
Technical Group	Typist Key Punch Operator Proofreader Binding Technician Binder Photographic Technician Driver
Bibliographical Group	Library Assistant Searcher (General) Bibliographic Assistant (General) Bibliographic Assistant (Special) Indexer
Administrative Group	Supervisor Administrative Assistant
Intern	Library Trainee
Librarian I-V	

Example C

Bindery Clerk	Messenger
Bookmender	Typist-Clerk
Technical Processing Assistant	Receptionist-Typist
Technical Processing Specialist	Typist
Subject Specialist	Mail Clerk
Shelver	Senior Clerk
Portal Monitor	Building Superintendent
Circulation Assistant	Senior Storekeeper
Library Services Assistant	Secretary
Library Specialist	Executive Secretary
Senior Library Specialist	Library Intern
Group Supervisor	Librarian I
Department Services Supervisor	Librarian II
Copy Machine Operator	Librarian III
Senior Copy Machine Operator	Librarian IV

Whether these scales apply to nonprofessionals or professionals, they imply a kind of distinction that is not always felicitous. Employees are rarely satisfied until they reach the top rung of the ladder. This is admirable, but everyone in a large system cannot progress indefinitely to the top. To combat this emphasis on ranking, some university libraries are using working titles such as "Cataloger," "Reference Librarian," or "Searcher," that describe the work performed rather than the level. A person may progress in salary to a very considerable degree within these titles, and supervisory positions carry distinctive titles like "Head of the Serial Section," "Chief of the Government Document Division," and "Supervisor of Microtexts." More and more university libraries are receptive to a salary policy that permits subject specialists without administrative duties to advance to substantial salaries in the conviction that this kind of competence is as valuable as some levels of administrative ability and should be so rewarded.

SALARY ADMINISTRATION

It is stated with valid reason that salary alone does not determine a person's happiness or lack thereof in a position. Nonetheless, salary is a very sensitive and important factor meriting the closest scrutiny at the highest level of any library. There is no such thing as complete confidentiality in salaries whether or not this is the stated policy. In a private or public institution, there is a natural curiosity on the part of each employee about other people's salaries in order to gauge the fairness of his own. Under civil service, there is likely to be little confidentiality except possibly within very narrow limits. In a private institution, many employees do not wish their salary to be public knowledge unless they choose to disclose the information, as many will do; but employees are entitled to know the salary ranges for their positions if there are stated ranges. If not, paid-rate minimum and maximum of ranges should be published.

Periodically, it is helpful to make distribution tables or frequency tables of salaries paid. The simplest form of such a frequency table is to list titles and the number of people falling within a range:

Title	Incumbents	Title	Incumbents
Librarian I	7	Librarian IV	12
Librarian II	30	Librarian V	2
Librarian III	25		

40

Personnel Policies

A more refined method is to prepare a scatter chart (as illustrated on p. 42) that pinpoints each salary in terms of years of employment. Those out of the clustering must be explainable as extraordinary cases.

A third method is to compare salaries for several institutions if the information can be obtained.

Ranges	Total of 7 libraries		No. of incumbents this university	
$ 7,000– 8,000	71		12	
$ 8,000– 9,000	150	72%	29	83%
$ 9,000–10,000	200		18	
$10,000–11,000	207		15	
$11,000–12,000	123		8	
$12,000–13,000	71		4	
$13,000–14,000	18		0	
$14,000–15,000	23	6.6%	2	3.4%
$15,000–16,000	12		1	

If analysis shows that one's own university departs from the norm, one should weigh possible reasons for such variation. In the third chart, immediately above, the local university library staff clusters toward the bottom of the scale. This may be explainable by an unusual number of younger appointees to a rapidly growing staff, but it may also be evidence of a substandard salary scale that needs careful adjustment as rapidly as financial resources permit.

In some libraries, salaries are adjusted on the anniversary of appointment dates, thereby spreading this work throughout the year. More commonly, however, salaries are adjusted at stated intervals with the possible exception of an adjustment, especially but not exclusively for clerical employees, in the middle or at the end of the initial training or probationary period. Annual or semiannual adjustments have the virtue of enabling responsible persons within the library to weigh alignment of salaries among employees of like or dissimilar performance within and between major organizational units. The importance of this cannot be overstressed. A university may follow one procedure for the faculty and a different one for other staff, and the library will usually need to follow these local patterns. For example, faculty and librarian salary scales for the next fiscal year may need to be set in the middle of the preceding academic year in advance of recruiting efforts whereas nonprofessional scales may be determined months later.

41

1968-69 SURVEY OF LIBRARIAN SALARIES
Librarians with an MLS (or equivalent) degree

Sample of the salary distribution pattern in one library (number of individuals represented by figures) when cast against the percentile curves derived from 903 librarians in a set of institutions participating in the study.

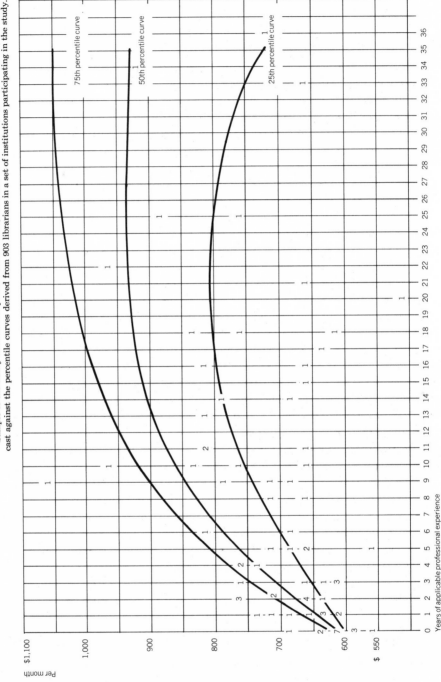

Personnel Policies

Whenever an appointment is made to the staff it presents the danger of over- or underpaying in relation to those already on the staff and thus can create extremely sensitive situations. It is essential that initial salaries be very carefully controlled if there is latitude for exercise of judgment rather than mandatory rates. The salary should be not more nor less than the candidate appears to deserve in relation to existing staff on the basis of the position, special responsibilities, previous education and experience, previous employment references, and even to some smaller extent the impression of personal qualities which was obtained during interviewing. The same rationale suggests the wisdom of a fairly early review or series of reviews of performance to test the validity of the appointment as well as the salary.

Following is a practical guide that has proved useful in adjusting beginning professional salaries in a library that is free to adjust entering rates:

Qualifications	*Salary and Salary Adjustments*
Basic qualifications: 2 languages and graduate library degree from an ALA-accredited university	Basic entering salary
Subject master's degree in relevant field	+ $400
Better than average reading knowledge in desired exceptional language(s): e.g., Slavic, Greek, Portuguese, Arabic	+ $200
High Grade Point Average (above 3.5) for undergraduate degree (also Phi Beta Kappa membership or National Merit Scholarship)	+ $100
High Grade Point Average (above 3.7) for graduate library degree	+ $100
Exceptional personal qualities	+ $100
Relevant experience: Teaching at college level — ⅓ to ½ value Subprofessional library work — ⅓ to ½ value Business experience — ¼ to ⅓ value	+ $300 per year for equivalent full-time work

∴ The actual initial salary is the basic entering salary plus all applicable upward adjustments. The total, however, should be moderated so as to be reasonable in relation to experienced librarians already on the staff.

ORIENTATION AND TRAINING

Persons in authority in research libraries tend to forget how very complex such institutions are in the eyes of the inexperienced staff member as well as the user. If there is no program to explain the relationship of departments and procedures, employees develop feelings of frustration and a sense that what they are doing is isolated and meaningless.

A reasonable investment in orientation is decidedly worthwhile. This may vary from two or three general meetings of one hour each at which the work of several departments is described to a more ambitious program of one-hour visits and orientation talks in a series of departments. Not only will this result in greater understanding, but it is almost certain to create a feeling of pride that the employee is associated with an organization that is larger and more important than he realized. The library staff association or other organization of employees often plays a useful role in orientation as well as in broader programs for new staff members. Some have welcoming committees that arrange temporary housing, assist new employees in arranging transportation to work, and otherwise help them to get adjusted to a new community. The staff association may arrange receptions for retiring or departing staff members, send condolences in case of death in the immediate family of a staff member, or send flowers to a hospitalized employee. All of these touches can bring a human element into a large group of people who might otherwise seem impersonal and remote.

Orientation is essentially generalized training but, beyond this, a large staff requires a great deal of training. No organization can function without on-the-job training whether formally or informally organized. This is usually the most practical and therefore the most useful training. A carefully developed set of staff manuals can be a valuable training device; and although such manuals are usually expensive to create and a nuisance to keep up to date, they can save a great deal of individual supervision and personal training as well as assure greater uniformity of information. But even with a good staff manual that describes procedures, flow of work, and relationships of functions, some personalized attention must be given to overseeing the new staff member, answering questions, and explaining subtleties that cannot be included in a manual.

In the larger libraries, more formalized training classes may be worthwhile where there is rapid turnover in a fairly large group of employees performing a reasonably discrete task. Classes for filers, bibliographical searchers, and stack personnel are examples where formalized training may be the most effective and economical way to assure qualified personnel.

Every library shares the national responsibility to recruit people into the library profession. A university library that, as a matter of course, employs dozens or hundreds of students is in an ideal position to identify those who have discovered that librarianship can be an exciting and rewarding profession. Experienced librarians should be alert to these opportunities and should be helpful in counseling anyone who expresses curiosity or interest. Close association between the library and the student placement office, career advisers, or counseling staff may lead to librarianship being suggested to a student who had not previously given it thought.

Some libraries are able to assure their student assistants employment upon graduation from library school. Others are happily situated close enough to a library school to permit combination work-study programs. One recruitment device that has been found effective at Harvard, Indiana, and Stanford is creation of the special personnel classification "Library Intern" for staff members with a baccalaureate degree who demonstrate professional capability and an interest in making a career in librarianship. This classification may carry a special pay scale commensurate with a senior clerical position, and duties should be correspondingly advanced, if possible into the area of preprofessional duties. To round out the program, a senior member of the library staff should be available to counsel the interns and to organize special development sessions, visits, rotation of assignments, and special training.

JOB MOTIVATION AND EVALUATION

The personnel goals of a library are job productivity, the individual's personal development and satisfaction, and overall library program advancement. These can be promoted through a program of personnel development grounded upon suitable training and supervision. This development is measured by formal performance reviews or achievement ratings.

45

Without able supervisors to train, direct, encourage, sympathize, and review, the best of policies have no effectiveness. These positions should be filled with the most experienced, capable and humane employees. It has been said with some truth that a good library could survive months without a director while no library could survive a week without such persons as the loan desk supervisor, the individual in charge of transfer and cancellation processing, the bookstack manager, the chief serial records attendant, the head of the binding preparations and finishing section, or the card catalog curator. The talent required in such crucial positions is not merely a thorough technical knowledge, although that is mandatory; it is also the ability to lead and motivate people.

Motivation of staff is not easy of attainment. It is, however, at least as important as salary and fringe benefits in enabling goals to be achieved. This is why volunteers help in churches and hospitals and are frequently available to assist libraries with art prints, sheet maps, or manuscripts. It has been widespread practice to fit people into rigidly defined jobs, whereas, ideally, assignments should rather be fitted to individual talents. Good personnel administration will seek ways of satisfying the employee's psychological needs, giving him a feeling of responsibility and accomplishment. A library that fragments jobs into minuscule tasks for the sake of "efficiency" or "streamlining" will find it has stifled interest on the part of the staff, for no one likes to feel that he is merely a cog in a huge machine.

The good supervisor will convey a sense of the "mission" of the library, will explain how each task is important to the overall effectiveness, will show interest in the individual's job problems, and will encourage suggestions for improving the organization. Participative-management theory states that employees are motivated by drawing them into the decision-making process so they can relate their personal goals and achievements to those of the organization. This philosophy is increasingly important in libraries as they become highly organized with hundreds on their staffs.

The contribution of the individual and his professional development should be regularly reviewed with the supervisor. The formal practice of evaluation uses forms such as the examples shown in Appendix I.

"Service reviews" or "performance ratings" may be regarded as a bother by those in supervisory positions who have to make them, but it is a practice that can save many headaches and morale problems if properly done. The performance rating or review is usually a more or less formalized evaluation of an employee's work prepared at stated intervals. It should be shown by the person preparing the review to the employee reviewed, and there should be opportunity for two-way communication. Misunderstandings should be ironed out in such conferences, and defects in training spotted. This should be an occasion to discuss with the employee his strengths as well as shortcomings and to explore ways in which he can make progress during the next review period. In cases of seriously deficient employees, the review may provide a warning that employment will be terminated if performance is not improved. An exercise of this kind lies at the heart of successful administration.

Employees want to know where they stand, and if honestly executed, the performance rating can be an invaluable device. In the absence of such a system, properly organized and used, inadequate or problem employees are allowed to drift until precipitate action may be taken, often to the legitimate amazement of the affected employee. It is essential that a supervisor perform such ratings with meticulous fairness. An unreasonably favorable review can have consequences that are disastrous if an employee has to be separated. In a civil service setting, he can make a strong case that the evidence does not justify the action. Since service reviews should have an important bearing on salary increases and promotions, fairness of reviewing becomes critical to the welfare of the library as well as the employee. In the early years of employment, there should be regular reviews, every six months or annually. Employees who have been on the staff ten or more years may receive reviews on a more relaxed basis, perhaps every three to five years, but this schedule should be accelerated if the employee becomes a problem. There are some who hold to the view that even older employees should be reviewed regularly. Many employees, regardless of their length of service, welcome regular reviews, and since supervisors change with some frequency, an incoming supervisor will appreciate a recent review as a basis for preliminary judgment of his staff. Furthermore, if the previous supervisor had a decidedly more favorable opinion of an employee than the new supervisor, it is well to know this in discussing the review with the employee.

Employees may want copies of performance ratings for their personal files. The employee may also want an opportunity to respond to criticism or to present his side of a sensitive point. Both desires are reasonable. The form should provide space for rebuttal, and the employee as a matter of course, or on request, should receive a copy of his rating. Ratings should be signed by the responsible supervisor and by the employee. It should be made clear that the latter's signature does not signify agreement with the rating but rather is evidence that he has been shown the review and that it has been discussed with him, a point that may subsequently be indispensable. Each rating should then be reviewed and signed by the library personnel officer and the director with comment as to any varying opinion and any action to be taken.

A staff committee has, in a few institutions, been used to review promotion proposals and recommend action to the director. There may be one committee for assistants and another for librarians below the department head level. Members of such a committee should make judgments only upon those at or below their own classification. The advantage of such a procedure is that it brings the staff into the administrative process, and morale may be improved by greater democratization. Experience also indicates that such a committee will not as a general practice urge promotion faster than would the director. A major disadvantage is that librarians cannot be judged on publications or public lectures, as can professors; as a result such a committee would need to evaluate supervisors whose performance ratings constitute one of the most important parts of the documentation. Further, it would be desirable to interview students, faculty, and associates — a cumbersome process at best. Promotion review by committee is likely to achieve greater objectivity through judgment by more individuals; but it is not likely to produce better value judgments of quality of work, or judgments on the value of the individual supervisor's recommendations and executive action, nor will it accelerate the rate of professional growth or provide a keener assessment of the importance of the individual to the institution when assessed against the nuances of the labor market. The time required for peer evaluation is not inconsiderable. A staff advancement committee, or committees, may in some instances provide useful advice for the director but in no degree can it relieve the director of the ultimate burden for personnel action.

48

Personnel Policies

A library director once remarked, not altogether facetiously, that as soon as a library grew to two staff members, personnel problems might be expected. In staffs that run into the hundreds, there are sure to be many problems. Some of these will be the result of unavoidable emotional difficulties that individuals sometimes develop; some will be the result of off-the-job stresses and conflicts that may render an employee temporarily or protractedly unproductive or a source of friction on the job. Other problems will arise because employees get bored with routine, become discouraged about prospects for promotion, develop conflicts with fellow workers or supervisors — or for a host of other reasons. There must be some chain of appeals through which an employee can share his troubles or appeal for counsel. This chain must extend through the organization to the director and sometimes beyond. Depending on individual circumstances, the employee may need advice from other university officers who can speak with authority on health, legal, or financial problems.

Libraries have a built-in problem because of the division of the staff into "professionals" and "nonprofessionals." This is a dichotomy that is often resented by the latter group. The library staff should try to avoid using this terminology, tempting and convenient though it is. Constant reference to "professionals" and "nonprofessionals" suggests a caste system that is not justified by actual working situations. Certainly in a large library, there are many persons without formal library training who play vital roles in the conduct of the library.

This is not the place to write a complete manual on the handling of personnel problems. There is a substantial literature on human relations, on supervision, and on personnel work in general. Almost any of these sources is likely to provide useful suggestions. The university personnel officer may be particularly helpful in difficult cases involving separation or the handling of emotionally disturbed individuals. The library director should try to operate with restraint, with patience, and with careful attention to facts. The more serious the problem, the more a responsible official should redouble his efforts to operate on facts — which often seem hard to come by in emotion-packed situations — and to make scrupulously fair and humane decisions.

49

Staff members may have some inclination to by-pass intermediate supervisors and go directly to the head of the appeals chain. Unless the trouble stems from friction with a supervisor, an attempt to resolve on-the-job problems should be insisted on at the working level. At the same time, the director and his office associates will find it rewarding to keep an "open door" for troubled staff who need advice. Written records, including service reviews, can be of great usefulness if it can be demonstrated that persons have had notice of shortcomings. Supervisors have a tendency to want to get rid of unsatisfactory employees in a surprising number of instances before adequate warning has been given and before the employee has had a chance to improve. Decency and fairness require that the head of the organization ensure that this not be the case.

Although written records are desirable, a record that is compiled *sub rosa* should be suspect. There may be times when one is justified, but they will be rare. Excessive tardiness or absences, falsifica-

tion of leave or production records, or faulty work (e.g., in filing cards or in cataloging) that can be documented should be openly challenged and made a matter of record between the supervisor and the employee, rather than being secretly recorded in the supervisor's black book.

References have been made elsewhere in this chapter to the close scrutiny of an employee's performance during his probationary period. This period is standard under civil service, and it should be a part of every appointment procedure except in very advanced appointments when the employee has an established reputation of excellence. Probationary periods can usually be extended by a written statement from the library in those cases in which there is justifiable uncertainty about the adequacy of the individual. The mere need to extend a probationary period, in the ordinary course of things, suggests that the employee probably should not be kept. Termination of an appointment is always painful and unfortunate,

Two circulation assistants at the Circulation-Reference Desk at the library entrance: an example of a departmental library within a large university library system — Harvard-Yenching Institute Library, Harvard University

but it is folly to try to build a strong staff while compromising at the entrance level. It is not always charitable to an individual to keep him in a position or in a library that may be beyond his ability.

The most convenient time for professional staff changes is the beginning of the academic year, although the summer may not be impossibly difficult. Since spring is the most active and profitable recruiting season for library school graduates, it is highly desirable that librarians give notice no later than March if they plan to leave in September. This suggests that six months should be the minimum notice period, and that notice of intention to leave in the late fall or winter should be even longer. By the same token the library should give at least six months notice to a librarian if it does not intend to renew his appointment, and, if possible, such notice should be given as much as nine to twelve months in advance. Terminations for cause may be shorter depending on the seriousness of the case. If the cause is extremely serious (drunkenness, physical assault, stealing) termination may be summary. If the library does not wish to have an employee around because of danger to other employees or threat to the integrity of card files or property, salary may be continued for a short period (four weeks) but the working relationship may be terminated forthwith. This is occasionally the safest, least expensive, and most painless way to deal with a serious problem.

A library must give, as well as seek, information about employee performance. Reference inquiries should be handled with fairness to the employee, past or present, and to the prospective employer. There is no conceivable justification for praising a poor employee in order to get rid of him. On the other hand, employees are rarely one hundred per cent good or bad, and honest reports on a person's good points should be offered as well as candid reports on shortcomings.

Tenure in the strict academic sense is not prevalent among non-civil service libraries. Tenure-in-fact exists in most libraries. In the latter instance, appointments tend to be renewed annually automatically, or are made "without limit of time," meaning that a person can be terminated for cause but is protected from capricious separation. Probationary periods for nonprofessional staff members are usually concluded within six months; for professionals, in from two to eight years. In some cases, university librarians are covered by the *Statement of Principles on Academic Freedom and Tenure* promulgated by the American Association of University Professors and the Association of American Colleges, which provides, in part, that

> the probationary period should not exceed seven years, including within this period full-time service in all institutions of higher education; but subject to the proviso that when, after a term of probationary service of more than three years in one or more institutions, a teacher is called to another institution it may be agreed in writing that this new appointment is for a probationary period of not more than four years, even though thereby the person's total probationary period in the academic profession is extended beyond the normal maximum of seven years.

ACADEMIC STATUS AND FACULTY RANK

There is increasing interest on the part of librarians in academic status or faculty rank. The former is fairly common and should be universal; the latter is less prevalent but exists in an increasing number of state universities. Academic status may mean a number of things: eligibility for privileges enjoyed by faculty, such as faculty club membership, reserved parking, Teachers Insurance and Annuity Association and College Retirement Equities Fund membership, and so forth, but not faculty tenure or rank. Faculty rank would encompass all of these things plus professorial titles and membership in the Academic Council or Senate. Sabbaticals, a call upon research funds, nine-month appointments, faculty salary scales, and some other perquisites may come with academic status or with faculty rank, or may not come under either standing. The arguments for faculty rank rest on such factors as full partnership in the educational enterprise and recognition of librarianship as a learned discipline, or on more mundane bases such as improved salaries or the fact that librarians would have clerical standing if not given faculty rank. There is still a considerable body of opinion that holds that the library profession can stand on its own feet without being cloaked in faculty titles, that the preparation for the preponderance of librarians does not go beyond the master's degree while the doctorate is the customary minimum for professorial status, and that careers in librarianship have their patterns of

53

training and advancement and marketability which are quite disparate from those of professors. If faculty status means that library ranks are to be determined by graduate degrees and publishing, these would not seem to be fair measuring sticks, and if strictly applied would redound to the disadvantage of most librarians. Each university library will need to determine which perquisites are appropriate given the situation in its institution. Gradual improvement over several years may be attainable in some cases while a drastic change of policy to a vastly improved status for librarians may be feasible in others. Timing and tactics may be the crucial determinants.

LIBRARY UNIONS

The history of trade unionism in American libraries goes back to 1914. Over a half century later the existence of unions in either public or academic libraries is not widespread, but the activity discernible in key libraries suggests that this may be a factor with which more academic library directors are going to have to be concerned in the future. Professional journal articles on the subject were extremely sparse in the 1950's and became reasonably numerous only in the mid-1960's.

Library staff members have been encouraged to move toward unionization because of more permissive state laws on the subject; the success of kindred professions, especially teaching, through unionization; the appeal of the philosophy of the labor movement; and the belief that belonging to a union is far more socially acceptable than it once was. Although library unions continue to be interested in wages and working conditions, they have widened their horizons to demand greater participation in decision making.

At the Conference of Eastern College Librarians in 1968, there was an extensive discussion of unions. One speaker with considerable experience in the public library union movement disparaged unions as self-seeking organizations that maintain an attitude of conflict with management despite library management's eagerness to do "what is right for the staff." Union negotiations were described as brawls, and it was alleged that unions pressed unreasonable grievances thereby consuming one third to one half the time of key administrators. Other speakers predicted the complete unionization of college faculties within ten years, and it was confidently stated that the day of the appointed library director was waning — that in the future library staffs would elect the director.

The two academic libraries most frequently mentioned in the literature of unionization are the University of Pennsylvania and the University of California at Berkeley. At the former institution in 1967, a group of library staff members formed a local chapter of the American Federation of Teachers with three principal objectives: to improve the conditions of employment, the library service itself, and relations between the library staff and the university administration.

The Berkeley staff appears to have been much more active. Approximately thirty Berkeley librarians joined a library chapter of Local 1474 of the American Federation of Teachers (AFL-CIO) in 1965. Among the first things to which the union directed attention were the definition of academic status for librarians and leave for civic duty. By 1968, it was reported that a third of the staff were union members.

The Berkeley librarians apparently saw a close correlation between economic and professional demands. They felt that true status and commensurate rewards depended upon the ability to participate meaningfully in professional activities. Although they were interested in the classic goals of better wages, shorter work weeks, and improved grievance procedures, they also wanted to build a better bridge between library administrators and other librarians. In 1968, they presented the newly appointed director with a "Library Improvement Program" that covered such matters as tenure, participation in policy decisions, a greater voice in evaluating and developing collections, recruitment of minority personnel, budgetary support for longer hours of service, improved security of library materials, access to research funds, sabbatical leaves, and time off to take courses with remission of tuition. More recently, the union has again been active in urging academic status for librarians.

These examples of union activities at two universities are given in detail because they probably foreshadow more accurately than mere speculation the shape and substance of the union movement. There are some people who see little or no relationship between staff aspirations for academic or faculty status and the union movement.

The evidence would seem to be contrary to this point of view. It is at least possible that unionization would strengthen the position of librarians seeking faculty status.

The director of a university library should keep several things in mind if there is a movement to unionize his staff. He should immediately seek the advice of both the university personnel office and university legal counsel. Collective bargaining is controlled by Federal, state, and sometimes local laws, and the nature of the institution (public or private, city or state) may determine the applicability of statutes. In a city or state institution, one may work with the Department of Labor.

It is often customary for a union to concentrate its first demands on payroll deduction for union dues and a much tighter grievance procedure in which union officials play a part. Demands may include giving union officials a voice in promotions and acceptance of the seniority principle in assignment and promotion of staff. The library may be asked to consider a commitment to perpetuate all desirable past "practices" with respect to staff handling and working conditions; unlimited staff time off to engage in union activities; union use of bulletin boards and internal mail services; library distribution of union literature to all new employees; and the right of the union to replace the staff association. Each of these demands has complex implications which should be carefully considered before being granted, if indeed they are granted.

Studies of professionalism have led some people to conclude that librarians have been slow to organize as union members because national and local professional associations have performed many functions of a union in recommending standards that relate to pay scales, vacations, tenure, and other aspects of working conditions or status. This may be true; a local staff association can effectively promote improved conditions and save its members most of the cost of union dues. There would seem to be other evidence that librarians are not insensitive to gains achieved by union members in the field of teaching as well as those in quite unrelated endeavors. The fact that the two university library staffs that have been most prominently mentioned in news about unionization have joined local chapters of the American Federation of Teachers is not without significance.

An unhealthy personnel situation in a library is likely to foster unionization; an active, responsive personnel program with ample communication between staff and administration is a discouragement to unionization. There is obviously no benefit to the library administration from the existence of a local chapter of a national union. On the contrary, a strong local staff association can promote better staff development and sense of participation, and the result can be a more satisfied and better caliber of library staff. Even so, it seems probable that the union movement is here to stay among college and university faculties, and the inescapable conclusion is that librarians will not be unaffected by this activity.

PROFESSIONAL ASSOCIATIONS

The degree to which librarians participate in professional associations will vary, but most libraries find their travel budgets inadequate to send to professional meetings at the expense of the institution all who would like to attend. Solomon-like decisions must be made that are almost certain to be unsatisfactory in the eyes of some staff members. Trips to conferences can be overdone, and some reasonable limitation, like one or two conferences per year irrespective of who pays travel expenses, may have to be imposed.

Some libraries pay partial expenses of all staff members allowed to attend conferences, thereby spreading limited funds evenly. Others are less democratic and pay full expenses for the director and certain heads of departments and divisions. It seems to the writers that there is much to be said for a system that canvasses all potential travelers at the beginning of the fiscal year and that, as a basis for apportioning funds on a sliding scale of reimbursement, permits consideration to be given to rank, the interests of the library, and official participation in organizations holding meetings (whether that participation takes the form of a committee assignment, panel discussion, prepared paper, or service as an officer of the association), as well as the professional development of the librarian which may be improved by selective attendance at professional meetings.

Many conferences may be so peripheral to the interests of the library that no representative need be sent. The person who is not a confirmed conventioneer but who is able to strike a sensible balance between his responsibilities on the job and general professional participation should be encouraged within available resources. It should also be kept in mind that the expenditure of some travel money for selected staff members to visit other libraries to observe operations and special items of equipment and buildings, and to discuss extraordinary problems, may occasionally be a better investment than travel to meetings.

SELECTED REFERENCES

American Library Association, Personnel Publications Committee. *Personnel Organization and Procedure: A Manual Suggested for Use in College and University Libraries.* 2nd ed. Chicago, American Library Association, 1968.

Branscomb, Lewis, ed. *The Case for Faculty Status for Academic Librarians.* (ACRL Monograph No. 33) Chicago, American Library Association, 1970.

"Collective Bargaining: Questions and Answers," *ALA Bulletin,* 62 (December 1968), 1385–90.

Downs, Robert B., ed. *The Status of American College and University Librarians.* (ACRL Monograph No. 22) Chicago, American Library Association, 1958.

Lewis, Robert. "A New Dimension in Library Administration — Negotiating a Union Contract," *ALA Bulletin,* 63 (April 1969), 455–64.

McNeal, Archie L. "Ratio of Professional to Clerical Staff," *College and Research Libraries,* 17 (May 1956), 219–23.

Mumford, L. Quincy, and Rutherford D. Rogers. "Library Administration in Its Current Development," *Library Trends,* 7 (January 1959), 357–67.

Smith, Eldred. "Librarians and Unions: The Berkeley Experience," *Library Journal,* 93 (February 15, 1968), 717–20.

Stewart, Nathaniel. "Library In-Service Training," *Library Journal,* 72 (January 1, January 15, February 1, 1947), 16–18, 146–8, 200–3.

Vosper, Robert G. "Needed: An Open End Career Policy: A Critique of Classification and Pay Plans for Libraries," *ALA Bulletin,* 56 (October 1962), 833–5.

Wilson, Louis Round, and Maurice F. Tauber. "Staff Manuals in College and University Libraries," *College and Research Libraries,* 2 (March 1941), 126–35.

3. LIBRARY ORGANIZATION
AND COMMUNICATION

A large university library is not an overgrown college library, nor is it closely akin to a big public library. Like research libraries generally, it is a conglomerate of highly specialized operations ranging from a wide spectrum of acquisitions techniques to cataloging in from thirty to fifty languages and dialects. This inherent complexity is intensified by two kinds of growth: first the ever-expanding flow of material that threatens to clog the operational pipelines because of both sheer bulk and diversity of formats and, second, the inevitable staff growth essential to coping with the workload. The halcyon age when research libraries were concerned almost solely with monographs and serials is a happy memory. A modern research library complements these traditional forms with technical reports, offprints, microfilms, microcards, microprints, microfiches, phonodiscs, phonotapes, educational films, computer programs, punched cards, digitally stored data banks, and so on. Staff growth, like the nature of materials, has been characterized by greater diversity and specialization. A degree of subject and linguistic competence never before approached is now commonplace. To this mass of specialized materials and staff have been added new techniques, including increasing mechanization, that have brought an accompanying complexity and need for specialists. A situation like this requires increased departmentalization and compartmentalization. It demands rationalization, coordination, and improved methods of communication.

DEPARTMENTAL AND DIVISIONAL ORGANIZATION

For the most part, university libraries develop their patterns of administrative organization in isolation. But reference to the accompanying organization charts reveals a surprising uniformity in number and identity of units. (Included for comparison are those for

A professional school library making use of a mezzanine to bring a substantial number of books in close proximity to reading areas — University of Chicago Law School Library (designed by Eero Saarinen)

Columbia, Michigan, Minnesota, Princeton, Stanford, and Yale.) First of all, there are major departments like Reference, Circulation, Rare Books and Special Collections, Catalog, Acquisition, departmental libraries (especially in the sciences), and an Undergraduate or College Library. In four instances there are several autonomous libraries not reporting to the director of the university library.

Within the major subdivisions, there is less identity of units but, even so, a rather remarkable similarity. The Government Documents department constitutes a major division at Stanford but its function is subsumed under the Reference Department at Michigan, Minnesota, and Yale. There is a different allocation of units between the Circulation and Reference departments (at Columbia the rubrics are Central Stack Services and Central Reference Room), but these differences of placement are relatively insignificant. A comparison of Catalog and Acquisition departments reveals that there are some variations in nomenclature, but a very great similarity in functions (for example, book ordering, exchange, gifts, and binding under Acquisition). The differing treatment of serials and searching is of interest, as are the formal Catalog Maintenance units that exist at Michigan and Minnesota.

These rather remarkable similarities suggest that there may be certain natural functional organizational patterns in university libraries. But some of the differences are worth analyzing to see whether they, too, are meaningful.

The second level of administration shows significant variations. At Columbia, Minnesota, and Princeton there is one Associate or Assistant; Michigan appears to have three; Stanford four; and Yale seven. The Director of University Libraries at Stanford appears to be somewhat more directly involved in oversight of major departments than at Minnesota or Princeton, yet organization charts are deceptive in this respect.

One of the most interesting differences is the separation of the acquisitions and cataloging functions and the lines of control, with all except Columbia using an Assistant or Associate Director to coordinate the two technical service departments. There have been much variation in opinion and considerable experimentation in this area in the last three decades without any conclusive evidence favoring one pattern or the other. At the moment, there are newer

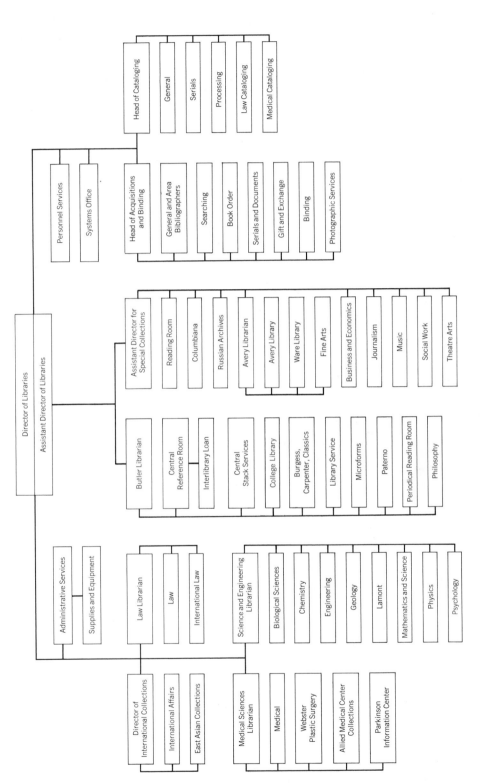

Columbia University Libraries

Director of Libraries

Assistant Director of Libraries

Personnel Services

Systems Office

Head of Cataloging
- General
- Serials
- Processing
- Law Cataloging
- Medical Cataloging

Head of Acquisitions and Binding
- General and Area Bibliographers
- Searching
- Book Order
- Serials and Documents
- Gift and Exchange
- Binding
- Photographic Services

Assistant Director for Special Collections
- Reading Room
- Columbiana
- Russian Archives
- Avery Librarian
  - Avery Library
  - Ware Library
  - Fine Arts
- Business and Economics
- Journalism
- Music
- Social Work
- Theatre Arts

Butler Librarian
- Central Reference Room
  - Interlibrary Loan
- Central Stack Services
- College Library
- Burgess, Carpenter, Classics
- Library Service
- Microforms
- Paterno
- Periodical Reading Room
- Philosophy

Administrative Services
- Supplies and Equipment

Law Librarian
- Law
- International Law

Science and Engineering Librarian
- Biological Sciences
- Chemistry
- Engineering
- Geology
- Lamont
- Mathematics and Science
- Physics
- Psychology

Director of International Collections
- International Affairs
- East Asian Collections

Medical Sciences Librarian
- Medical
- Webster Plastic Surgery
- Allied Medical Center Collections
- Parkinson Information Center

September 1, 1968

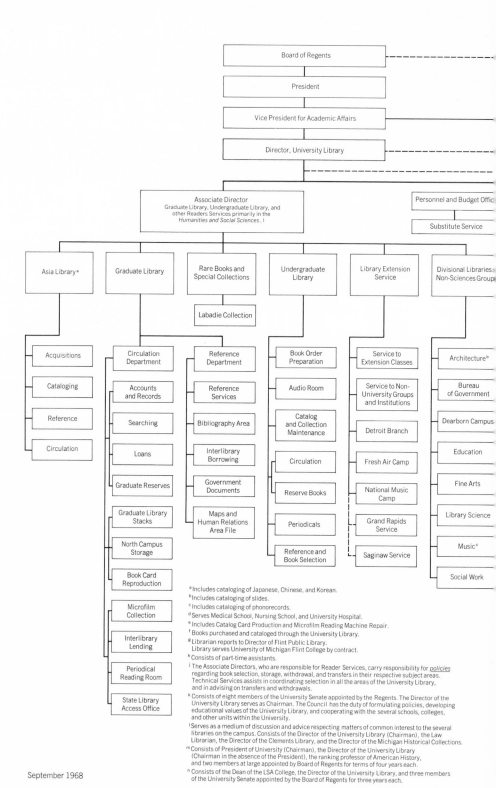

Board of Regents

President

Vice President for Academic Affairs

Director, University Library

Associate Director
Graduate Library, Undergraduate Library, and
other Readers Services primarily in the
Humanities and Social Sciences . ʲ

Personnel and Budget Office

Substitute Service

Asia Library ᵃ

Graduate Library

Rare Books and Special Collections

Undergraduate Library

Library Extension Service

Divisional Libraries: Non-Sciences Group

Labadie Collection

Acquisitions

Cataloging

Reference

Circulation

Circulation Department

Accounts and Records

Searching

Loans

Graduate Reserves

Graduate Library Stacks

North Campus Storage

Book Card Reproduction

Microfilm Collection

Interlibrary Lending

Periodical Reading Room

State Library Access Office

Reference Department

Reference Services

Bibliography Area

Interlibrary Borrowing

Government Documents

Maps and Human Relations Area File

Book Order Preparation

Audio Room

Catalog and Collection Maintenance

Circulation

Reserve Books

Periodicals

Reference and Book Selection

Service to Extension Classes

Service to Non-University Groups and Institutions

Detroit Branch

Fresh Air Camp

National Music Camp

Grand Rapids Service

Saginaw Service

Architecture ᵇ

Bureau of Government

Dearborn Campus

Education

Fine Arts

Library Science

Music ᶜ

Social Work

ᵃ Includes cataloging of Japanese, Chinese, and Korean.
ᵇ Includes cataloging of slides.
ᶜ Includes cataloging of phonorecords.
ᵈ Serves Medical School, Nursing School, and University Hospital.
ᵉ Includes Catalog Card Production and Microfilm Reading Machine Repair.
ᶠ Books purchased and cataloged through the University Library.
ᵍ Librarian reports to Director of Flint Public Library.
  Library serves University of Michigan Flint College by contract.
ʰ Consists of part-time assistants.
ʲ The Associate Directors, who are responsible for Reader Services, carry responsibility for *policies*
  regarding book selection, storage, withdrawal, and transfers in their respective subject areas.
  Technical Services assists in coordinating selection in all the areas of the University Library,
  and in advising on transfers and withdrawals.
ᵏ Consists of eight members of the University Senate appointed by the Regents. The Director of the
  University Library serves as Chairman. The Council has the duty of formulating policies, developing
  educational values of the University Library, and cooperating with the several schools, colleges,
  and other units within the University.
ˡ Serves as a medium of discussion and advice respecting matters of common interest to the several
  libraries on the campus. Consists of the Director of the University Library (Chairman), the Law
  Librarian, the Director of the Clements Library, and the Director of the Michigan Historical Collections.
ᵐ Consists of President of University (Chairman), the Director of the University Library
  (Chairman in the absence of the President), the ranking professor of American History,
  and two members at large appointed by Board of Regents for terms of four years each.
ⁿ Consists of the Dean of the LSA College, the Director of the University Library, and three members
  of the University Senate appointed by the Board of Regents for three years each.

September 1968

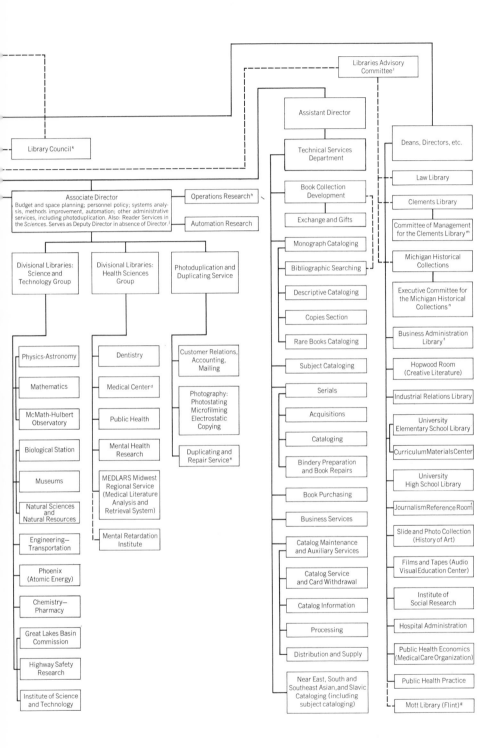

University of Michigan Library

University of Minnesota Libraries

1968

Vice-President—Academic Administration

Senate Library Committee

Affiliated Libraries
Law
Journalism
University High School
Morris Campus
Duluth Campus
Agricultural Schools and Stations

Director of Libraries

University Librarian and Associate Director

Assistant Director for Administration
Assistant to Director
Systems and Automation
Technical Information Service
Copying Service
Shipping and Receiving
Library Office

Assistant Director for Resources
General Acquisitions
Gifts and Bloc Purchases
Special Bibliographers

Assistant Director for Processing
Cataloging
Humanities
Science
Added Copies and Editions
Catalog Maintenance
Serials Records
Social Sciences
Serials

Business Operations
Orders and Receipts
Accounting
Binding Preparation

Reference Services
Reference
Periodicals
Documents
Inter-library Loans
Newspapers
Maps

Circulation Services
Circulation Desk
Reserve
Stacks
Storage

Special Collections
Manuscripts and Archives
University Archives
Immigrant Archives
Social Welfare History Archives
Asian Collections
Ames Library of South Asia
East Asian Library
Middle East Library
Rare Books
Kerlan Collection

St. Paul Campus
Central Library
Biochemistry
Veterinary Medicine
Forestry
Entomology
Plant Pathology

Departmental Libraries
Architecture
Art
Chemistry
College Library
Education
Engineering
Geology
Mathematics
Mines and Metallurgy
Music
Natural History
Pharmacy
Physics
Public Administration

Bio-medical Library

James Ford Bell Library

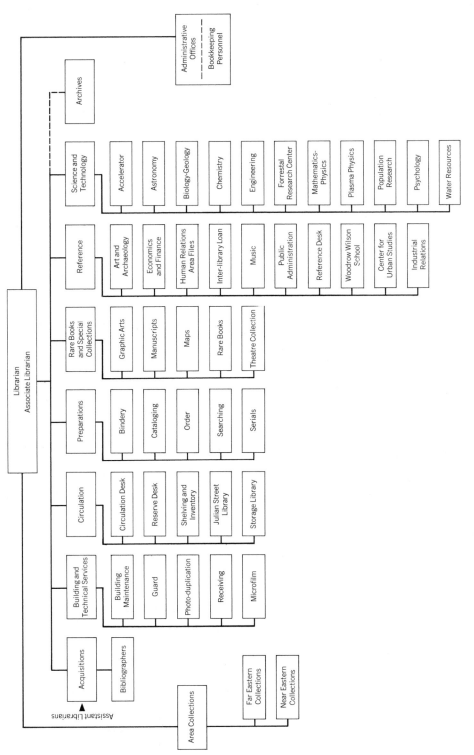

Princeton University Library

1962-1963

Stanford University Libraries

President's University Library Council

Coordinate Libraries:
Hoover Institution
Law
Jackson of Business
Lane Medical
Food Research
Linear Accelerator

Provost

University Archivist

Director of Libraries

Academic Council's Committee on Libraries

Associate Director for Administrative and Central Services
- General Reference Department
  - Current Periodicals Service
  - Central Map Collection
- Central Circulation Department
  - Interlibrary Loan Service
  - Technical Information Service
- Government Document Department
  - Microtext and Newspaper Division
- Special Collections Department
  - Manuscript Division
- Personnel Office
- Financial Office
- Business Services Department
  - Building Services Division
  - Photocopy Division
  - Building Projects Office

Assistant Director for Undergraduate and Branch Services
- Meyer Memorial Library
  - Circulation Division
  - Reference Division
  - Residence Libraries
  - Audio Division
  - Film Rental Service
- Science Department
  - Engineering Library
  - Earth Science Library
  - Chemistry Library
  - Mathematics – Statistics Library
  - Physics Library
  - Biology Library
  - Hopkins Marine Library
  - Computer Science Library
- Art and Architecture Library
- Education Library
- Music Library

Assistant Director for Bibliographic Operations
- Acquisition Department
  - Order Division
  - Gift Division
  - Exchange Division
  - Serial Records Division
  - Binding and Finishing Division
- Catalog Department
  - Monograph Division
  - Serial Division
  - Special Materials Division
  - Special Collections Division
  - Meyer and Overseas Division
  - Catalog Production and Maintenance Division
- Automation Department
  - Analysis/Design Division
  - Data Preparation Division
  - Data Control Division
  - Publications Office

Associate Director for Resources
- Curatorial Offices:
  - Germanic
  - Romance
  - Slavic
  - Latin American
  - East Asian
  - African

Director of Stanford Computation Center

SPIRES-BALLOTS
Programming Manager

1-1-70

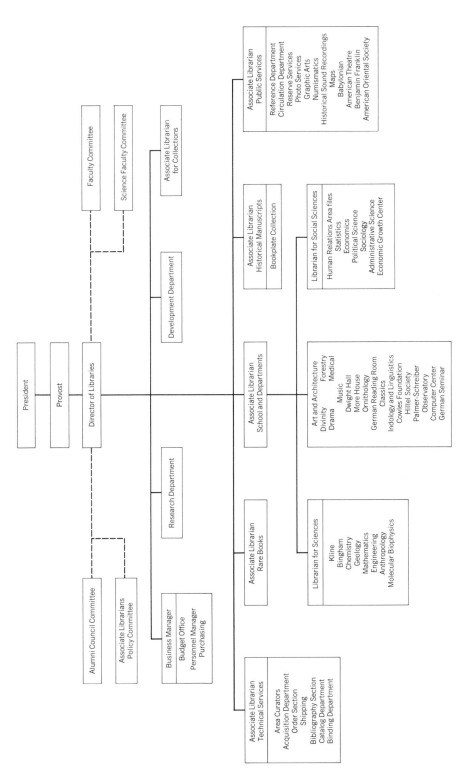

Yale University Library

May, 1969

President

Provost

Director of Libraries

Faculty Committee

Science Faculty Committee

Alumni Council Committee

Associate Librarians Policy Committee

Research Department

Development Department

Associate Librarian for Collections

Business Manager
Budget Office
Personnel Manager
Purchasing

Associate Librarian Technical Services

Area Curators
Acquisition Department
Order Section
Shipping
Bibliography Section
Catalog Department
Binding Department

Associate Librarian Rare Books

Associate Librarian School and Departments

Associate Librarian Historical Manuscripts

Bookplate Collection

Associate Librarian Public Services

Reference Department
Circulation Department
Reserve Services
Photo Services
Graphic Arts
Numismatics
Historical Sound Recordings
Maps
Babylonian
American Theatre
Benjamin Franklin
American Oriental Society

Librarian for Sciences

Kline
Bingham
Chemistry
Geology
Mathematics
Engineering
Anthropology
Molecular Biophysics

Art and Architecture
Divinity   Forestry
Drama   Medical
Music
Dwight Hall
More House
Ornithology
German Reading Room
Classics
Indology and Linguistics
Cowles Foundation
Hillel Society
Palmer-Schreiber
Observatory
Computer Center
German Seminar

Librarian for Social Sciences

Human Relations Area files
Statistics
Economics
Political Science
Sociology
Administrative Science
Economic Growth Center

forces that may affect ultimate patterns. First, the greater variety of acquisitions techniques, the greater emphasis on library rather than faculty responsibility in collection building, the increased number of foreign and, especially, esoteric languages with which university libraries must work, and the increasing variety of formats — all of these factors work toward bigness and complexity, and these, in turn, tend to bring about independent departmentation. On the other side of the picture are the forces growing out of automation that tend to suggest that closer working relationships may overcome some of the complexities and inefficiencies that result from separation. It is a reasonable expectation that the availability of machine-readable cataloging copy and its efficient utilization within an automated system may bring even closer relationships than ever before between acquisition and cataloging; and it may be that the coordinate pattern will become more prevalent, with the whole technical services operation falling into a super-department but with chiefs of the component operations at a level at least equivalent to that which prevails in the independent pattern.

Even without analysis *in extenso* of the growth of departmentation in university libraries, the foregoing suggests certain trends. The pattern tends to be one of more major units subdivided by more subsections of increasing importance. It is to a large extent a consequence of the increasing size of the library staff. But the development coming with growth is heightened by the quantity and diversity of acquisitions referred to earlier. There is no single prescription for injecting order into such potential chaos. The university library administrator must watch the growth of his operation and be prepared to strike some balance between willingness to experiment organizationally and extreme conservatism in changing organizational patterns. In general, there is something to be said for the latter course since frequent reorganization can be confusing to staffs.

The traditional patterns of university library organization are not without logic. Technical processes, branch libraries, and reference or reader services constitute major functions and provide some guidance for further departmentation.

A major department is likely to exhibit a number of characteristics: (a) it constitutes a significant and substantial segment of the total mission to be accomplished (e.g., acquisition and cataloging); (b) it involves a substantial number of people (technical processing) or a more select group of people with highly specialized talents (curators in a collection-building effort) requiring coordination and oversight either within the group or vis-à-vis other major organizational units; (c) it is concerned with important extramural relationships (reference service to industry) or serves a large, important, and demanding segment of the academic community (science departments); furthermore (d) the specialized nature of the work (official documents and rare books) may also dictate departmental status within an academic community where the material handled is in great demand even though the number of staff members is small. A library director should be chary of creating numerous departments and thereby unduly widening his own span of control and increasing the coordinating and communication problem within the total organization.

One should not be too dogmatic about span of control because different administrators have differing capacities for exercising control. Nonetheless, coordination of an operation that involves great diversity, specialization, and complexity (technical processes) is much more demanding than the coordination of a string of similar units (branch science libraries). Six major units might be a fair span of control for a department head in the first instance and twelve in the second.

Competence of personnel will also affect the wisdom of a broad or narrow span of control. A relatively unseasoned supervisor should not be loaded with broad responsibilities. To overburden such a supervisor is almost certain to result in a need for rescue operations by the person or persons at the next higher echelon, morale problems within and between units, and adverse relations with users. A strong and seasoned department head may be able to direct those activities assigned to him and lend a helping hand elsewhere, or even permanently broaden the scope of his responsibilities. An administrative assistant may enable a broader span of control to work effectively.

Although caution has been counseled in creating new departments, times and procedures are changing. New techniques brought about through automation may suggest combining some units (acquisition and cataloging), and an automation division or department may be advisable at an appropriate time. In fact, automation constitutes an interesting case study in departmentation. A logical course might proceed along these lines: as a library begins its approach to automation, an automation committee may be formed, or one member of the staff may be assigned the special responsibility for keeping abreast of automation developments. This may evolve into specialized experimentation with automation (in a book catalog or in circulation), at which point a small cadre might be set up in the director's office. If the automation effort becomes broader and involves basic activities like acquisition and cataloging, a full-fledged department is probably indicated, possibly headed by an assistant director.

It should also be kept in mind as a basic premise that the more one fragments an organization the more the communication problem is enlarged. This is true if the fragmentation is horizontal; the likelihood is multiplied if the number of levels below the director is increased, thereby removing the line employee further and further from the director. Administrative theory at one time held that organizational patterns were right or wrong without respect to individuals and that organization should not be skewed because of the extraordinary weakness or strength of supervisors. But theory has bent somewhat, and any experienced administrator will realize that there are times when he should let his organization follow natural lines of force, perhaps building an acquisitions program or team around a strong person or reassigning divisions from a department with a weak administrator who cannot be removed. The effects of individual librarians on the organizational pattern can be very strong indeed. This tendency is not one to be fought; rather it is a sign of strengths or weaknesses on which to capitalize or against which to build protection.

The extent to which an organization can or should tolerate a weak supervisor will depend upon the position he occupies, his length of service and contribution to the organization, and the deleterious effects of his shortcomings on other staff members and the operation as a whole. While due consideration must be given to humanitarian treatment of such persons, it is suggested that there is great danger in focusing on the welfare of one individual and sometimes being insensible to the devastating effect that such a person can have on a host of other people and on the success of the entire library program.

BRANCH LIBRARIES

Perhaps the most persistent and difficult organizational problem for the director of a university library is the question of the degree to which branch libraries will be allowed to proliferate. Anyone who has worked in a general research library like the New York Public Library or the Library of Congress will appreciate the tremendous advantage of centralized collections. Anyone who has worked at the Harvard University Library sees the disadvantages of decentralization. Even in highly centralized research libraries, the deployment of departments and collections over many acres of floor space and into annexes requires some duplication of materials and service expense. In the decentralized libraries, the frustrations of readers, the number of extra card catalogs to be maintained, the thinness of staff services, and the strains on the budget are severe.

Although centralization is a very meritorious principle, obviously a university has special problems, usually geographic, that call for patterns that do not apply in nonuniversity libraries. Even if a main university library building is somewhere near the center of a campus, it may be very inconvenient for those faculty members whose work is located a quarter or a half mile away. It is folly to hold to the view that there is no justification for departmental libraries; it is equally unwise to honor every request for a new campus library irrespective of the merits of the case.

University librarians are aware of the extraordinary cross-disciplinary use of facilities. Biology and chemistry, mathematics and physics, and education and psychology are classic relationships. But equally worthy of consideration is the need for like materials on the part of economists and business school students, of sociologists and linguists, of industrial engineers and business school students, of classicists and art history majors, and of city planning and architectural students. Recent studies have indicated an incredible amount of cross-disciplinary use in the university community. A new field, a new discipline, and eventually a new academic department springs from the intersection of traditional disciplines (e.g., bionucleonics, astrochemistry). This may be expected to increase as there are more and more interdisciplinary research and teaching. Under such circumstances, the unbridled creation of branch libraries would be a disservice to users unless financial resources were to permit complete duplication of materials and service hours (but the resources never do). It is in the latter respect that many people who plead for branches fail to grasp the cost and significance of the small, as well as of the full-fledged, departmental libraries. To maintain an important collection with unique materials for a limited number of hours may be a real disservice to over half the potential users. This point of view has been very ably articulated by Robert Vosper, University Librarian of the University of California at Los Angeles, in his 1962/63 *Annual Report:*

> I am convinced at this point that the overall needs of the University, as we look to the next decade or more, would be best served if we could somehow develop a single, physically centralized library to serve the engineering and physical sciences. The success of the centralized Biomedical Library is proof enough of the effectiveness of such a divisional unit when the academic departments concerned are reasonably close together, as is the case at UCLA. Two other factors bring me to

this opinion. One is the increasing importance of interdisciplinary research in the sciences, as witness brain research in the biomedical area, as well as the new and expanding program in the space sciences which involves people and publications in all of the engineering and physical sciences plus certain of the biomedical sciences. These great interdisciplinary developments are poorly served by scattered libraries conceived along disciplinary lines. Secondly, the whole new development in the direction of automated library systems, which arises because of the proliferation of scientific literature and the difficulties of controlling it, urges a more centralized library pattern in these fields than we have at present. We are in a far better position in the biomedical field to move forward with new systems than we are in the physical sciences where there are several small and discrete units on which we cannot so effectively focus a major effort.

The director of university libraries, with the assistance of the faculty library committee, should have some control over the estab-

A browsing collection providing a "gentleman's library" within a university library — The Morrison Library, General Library, University of California, Berkeley

lishment of new campus libraries. It is not possible to lay down inviolate rules for approving or disapproving such requests, but various factors should be taken into consideration, including geographical location of the principal users (and their number) in relation to existing resources, the adequacy of existing resources, availability of appropriate space, size of collection, service hours proposed, and financial resources available. At present levels of cost, a full-fledged departmental library can easily require $50,000 annually for books, processing, and staff, plus extraordinary costs for creating basic collections and providing suitable space. Commitments of this magnitude should not be entered into lightly.

The following typical policy statement indicates the basis for controlling the establishment of departmental libraries:

a. The creation of a new departmental library or library branch requires prior approval and provision of continuing funding. Authorization is in part contingent upon the requirements that all books and other materials shall be cataloged, recorded in the Union Catalog, and accessible during adequate hours to the entire University community. Application for creation of a branch of the University Libraries should be made to the Director who will consult the Academic Council Committee on University Libraries before acting upon the application. Applications should be made to the appropriate dean or director for creation of a branch of an autonomous library.

b. When it is proposed to discontinue the library collection of any department, special project, or research program, notice should be sent to the Director of University Libraries. The Director will decide, subject to the terms and conditions under which the library was established and funded, whether it should be continued as an authorized branch library, assimilated into the University Libraries collections, or otherwise disposed of.

c. Professional services of the Acquisition Department and the Catalog Department and assistance with the public services are available only to the departmental and branch libraries which have been established in the authorized manner.

Some collections are more easily decentralized than others from the standpoint of the adverse effect that removal of certain materials from a central collection may have on remaining users. It is safe to say that any such cleavage is not without disadvantages, but legal and music materials probably pose fewer problems than do some others like economics or history.

These are somewhat dangerous generalizations because law schools are tending to expose their students to the whole domain of social science. There may be rather wide-ranging need on the part of lawyers for government documents (because of the rapid growth of substantive administrative law), for medical material (consider modern views on abortion and organ transplants), and material on economics (for corporate and international law, domestic corporations operating abroad, etc.). Conversely, business and engineering students and political scientists need access to legal materials as never before. Music may be a better example because of its distinctive notation system and the need for musical scores in close proximity to classrooms, studios, and practice rooms. However, present-day university librarians, constantly impressed by interdisciplinary needs, find it harder and harder to agree to multiplying service units except when dictated by geographical remoteness.

Decentralization may be dictated by reasons other than subject demand. Undergraduate libraries are a good example. The undergraduate tends to be confused and intimidated by the paraphernalia of a large research collection. He needs to be introduced to such collections, but a gradual approach is preferable. As a concomitant, the undergraduate floundering in a research collection requires a degree of help that becomes quite expensive, and at the same time he may be getting in the way of users requiring the full panoply of collections and services. In a university setting, the undergraduate may tend to become the forgotten man; so the creation of a library facility tailored precisely to his needs can expedite and encourage study if the institution can afford the very considerable cost of such separation. Full-fledged undergraduate libraries (Harvard, Michigan, Texas, South Carolina, and Stanford, among others) require staffs of 35 to 40 people, extensive duplication of materials, and budgets of $300,000-$400,000 annually. Nonetheless, excellent library facilities of this nature permit a quality of education and a degree of academic experimentation not otherwise possible. It is true that a college library within a university library building can fulfill this objective in part, but this solution is likely to result in a much more limited book collection and seating accommodations (both in number and diversity) than a physically separate undergraduate library.

The major university libraries are turning more and more to combining smaller departmental libraries into major complexes situated in the center of a cluster of academic departments that use the collection. Examples include a central Science Library, Social Science Library, Health Sciences Library, and Engineering Library (where the unified Engineering Library serves specialized needs in electrical, civil, mechanical, aeronautical, chemical, and industrial engineering, as well as materials science and engineering-economic systems). This degree of centralization is a response to the limited hours, nonprofessional staffing, and space uncertainties of small branch libraries as well as to the unnecessary duplication of collections and splitting of disciplines that prevail in such smaller units. In the first stage of branch growth, a unit may accommodate up to 6,000 volumes and 10 to 30 readers in 1,500 square feet with a part-time attendant who may be a student. The second stage of branch growth may accommodate up to 15,000 volumes and up to 50 readers in an area as large as 4,000 square feet, probably under the supervision of a full-time clerical assistant. The third stage of branch growth would require a librarian and at least one professional assistant to handle the work. This shift in personnel is an important factor, and the expense must be justified by enough book selection, reference work, staff supervision, and book collection demands to require that size staff. Such a branch may accommodate over 100,000 volumes and as many as 100 readers in up to 15,000 square feet of space. Circulation may run as high as 30,000-40,000 volumes per year.

Small branches pose special problems in regard to future growth and eventual space needs. The extent to which several such units can be combined into a single library will lessen this uncertainty, justify a higher quality of service under more expert direction, lessen unnecessary duplication of materials, and offer longer hours of service. A major centralized library in the sciences may contain hundreds of thousands of volumes, accommodate hundreds of readers in over 100,000 square feet, and be open 100 hours per week.

With the development of state university systems, overseas study centers, and specialized centers remote from the main campus (as, for example, a marine biology station or an astronomical observatory), library directors sometimes find themselves responsible for administering libraries literally at long range. In such cases, it is well to have basic responsibility for such operations centralized in an appropriate office of the main library. If overseas campus libraries are undergraduate in nature, the responsibility may rest with the undergraduate librarian. On the other hand, if the problems of such libraries are primarily of a processing nature, the responsibility may rest with the catalog department. If the remote library is scientific, it may report to the head of all science libraries. In all such cases, there will probably be more than ordinary need to confer with the local director (e.g., of an overseas campus), executive head (of a marine biology station), or the dean of the school within which the facility falls. Library staff at remote locations must be especially reliable, and extraordinary efforts have to be made by all concerned to communicate policies and decisions. A manual of procedures outlining major lines of liaison with the central campus can be very effective in such a situation. The local academic director may take a more direct interest in the library than would a comparable official on the home campus. On the other hand, the library staff is less likely to be adequate and there may be less flexibility in overall staffing to meet emergencies. Recruiting may have to be completely decentralized, and salaries may follow a different pattern because the competitive situation will probably be different from that of the main campus.

AUTONOMOUS UNITS

This brings one to a consideration of variations in the patterns of campus-wide financing and administration of libraries, both of which have some bearing on decentralization. In some universities, like Harvard, there is extensive decentralization (approximately ninety units). Each library is essentially a departmental financial and operational undertaking. The administration of the central library or libraries (as at Harvard) may perform a strong cooordinating role, effecting near uniformity in staff salaries and privileges and contributing to standardization of processing techniques and service hours. Such a system is likely to produce greater numbers of departmental libraries than a highly centralized administrative pattern such as exists in most state universities.

The existence of autonomous units may stem from a lack of cooperation at some earlier point, from the burgeoning growth of a particular unit with which the library system could not or would not cope at some time, from accreditation "requirements," from independent development at another geographical location, or for other reasons of campus politics or finance.

Law libraries are probably the most frequently autonomous libraries, followed by medical libraries and business libraries. Law libraries have achieved this status primarily by virtue of accrediting policies for law schools that imply the desirability of but do not "require" such autonomy. [1] This has been breached at some universities, notably Chicago and Columbia. Medical schools are often at locations remote from the main campus; this has tended to encourage autonomous development of their libraries.

Financial reasons have frequently dictated the creation of autonomous units. A school, institute, or other unit of the university has needed library services which could not be funded adequately. Having access to special financial resources, the school, institute, or other unit, sometimes in pique or disgust, has created its own library which, with the passage of time, has grown to a major unit.

The existence of autonomous libraries may be regarded as both a plague and a blessing. Such units may be stronger in collections, specialized staff, and financial support and closer to their clientele than would have been the case had they been a part of a coordinated system. Conversely, there are likely to be problems of communication and lack of coordination in collection building, cataloging, and public service policy. No one pattern will be "best" for all institutions; no recommendation can be made in the abstract.

One arrangement that could be useful in a decentralized univer-

---

[1] The American Bar Association states: "It is a cardinal requirement of the American Bar Association that each approved law school shall maintain an adequate debt-free, law library, composed of useable up-to-date volumes and owned or controlled by the school with which it is connected." The Association of American Law Schools in its comparable standards states: "Whether the law library is to be under the ultimate control of the law school or is to be operated as a part of a centralized library system is a matter for local decision within the university. Under either type of organization, it is essential that the law library have a sufficient autonomy in matters of administration, including finance, book selection and processing, reader service, and personnel, to assure a high standard of service commensurate with the needs of the law school program."

80

sity, however, is a balanced (centralized-decentralized) federated division of responsibility. This would provide more effective coordination of effort than does complete autonomy; it retains the strengths that derive from autonomy. It might take a form wherein the director of university libraries had the responsibility to provide functions best supplied by one large central administration: a union catalog of university holdings, a central serials record of titles and generalized holdings data, a campus messenger service, a library bulletin for the staff, a central personnel recruitment service and promotion listing, building planning advice, and guidance on service policies and technical processing policies. The director of libraries would also have responsibility for supporting the interests of these schools or institutes with national library association programs, in foundation applications, grants from Federal agencies, and in publicity and other public relations activities. On the other hand, the director of libraries might have the authority to exercise a limited control over functions where he can provide special expertise, where a degree of uniformity is advantageous for the university, or where he can effectively promote improved services or economies: approving budget submissions by the local librarian to his school dean or institute director, passing upon professional appointments above the entering rank, approving building plans for major alterations or additions, serving ex officio as member of a Search Committee to recommend a new librarian of the school or institute, participating ex officio or designating a deputy to serve on the library committee of the school or institute, and exercising authority over major public service policies and technical service policies including their budget expression. The director would not be answerable to the local library committee nor to the dean of the school or director of the institute, but there would be a channel through the provost if there were a dispute in the exercise of authority.

An alternative in a university with a strong tradition of autonomous units would be to form a university-wide library council. Such a group might meet once every one or two months and concern itself with problems where coordination is especially needed — acquisitions policies, staff classification and salaries, fund raising efforts, physical facilities planning, cataloging standards, and other areas where close mutual efforts could be advantageous to the university. No matter how it is achieved, it behooves the university to effect a reasonable coordination of efforts so as to rationalize service to students and faculty, make best use of financial support, coordinate the bibliographic instruments of the university, and improve the quality of administrative decisions.

COMMUNICATIONS WITH STAFF

Successful communication is a keystone of good administration, and yet communication is one of the most difficult of all functions to carry out. The need for improved and increased communication progresses at a much faster rate than staff numbers. Organizational complexity and fragmentation, geographical dispersion, and particularly the number of levels from lowest to highest, intensify the need for communication. It should flow upwards, and horizontally across the organization, just as much as it must flow downwards. Failure of communication produces misunderstanding of objectives, feelings of isolation, and working at cross-purposes, with attendant expense and adverse effect on morale.

The reason that good communication is so hard to achieve is that there is not a single formula other than "eternal vigilance" that applies. Nothing contributes so much to good communication as a library-wide awareness of its importance and a constant thoughtfulness directed toward informing the appropriate people when anything of significance occurs, when a new policy is under consideration or when a decision is reached. Such a general spirit is a condition precedent to success. The means of achievement are varied and must be tailored to the problem at hand.

The mere existence of certain communication machinery will help to achieve the communication objective. The director should set the pattern with a periodic conference with key administrators. The common device is a weekly Administrative Council or Director's Conference. At such a meeting, major problems involving several departments or general policy are discussed; there should also be an opportunity for department chiefs to report on major developments in their respective zones of responsibility. To assure efficient use of time, agenda should be circulated in advance, and, whenever possible, documentation should be provided for study prior to the meeting. Out of such meetings, decisions will flow and an occasional ad hoc committee will be established to wrestle with specific problems.

The results of such meetings should invariably be recorded and copies of minutes distributed; otherwise discussions will have to be repeated all too often after a few months' lapse. This is an axiom that is worth following for any important meeting. As a matter of course, the minutes can be circulated to subordinate staff. If confidential or sensitive issues are discussed that require privileged treatment, an edited version can be released.

The mere fact that the director holds periodic meetings is no assurance that supervisors will be equally concerned about communication within their spheres of responsibility. The director will do well to inquire occasionally into the adequacy of communication at lower levels, realizing that unnecessary meetings are wasteful but that six-month intervals are unlikely to be justified.

Most university libraries will have a bulletin directed to the staff every week or two. This may or may not contain material of wider university interest. The mere existence of such a publication is a constant reminder to supervisors to communicate. If this is not the appropriate vehicle in which to publish information to the faculty — it often will not be — a separate series of quarterly or occasional faculty bulletins may be issued. These can contain substantive decisions or descriptions of important developments such as changes in faculty borrowing regulations, acquisition of major collections, new hours of service, activation or deactivation of branch libraries, and some detail on book selection responsibilities and procedures.

An active staff association can be another channel for communication. Meetings of the association may provide a setting for periodic reports on progress and problems or for a discussion of salaries, tenure, and status. Orientation meetings, described elsewhere, are often conducted in part through staff associations, and, since communication travels up as well as down, the staff association may be the best source through which the director can learn of staff ideas or dissatisfaction. The existence of a staff suggestion box may provide a similar but somewhat more impersonal way of getting the same information.

The director should be seen in all major library units every few months. This may require concerted effort because he can become involved in problems that seem to keep him in his office for weeks at a time. If the director occasionally shows important visitors through the libraries, there will be a natural flow of branch calls. He may want to take extra time when in another part of the campus on other business to drop in at several branches. If he needs to transact business with the head of a departmental library, the director should occasionally go to the department, branch, or school instead of asking the subordinate to come to his office.

It is equally desirable for the director to appear before staff groups periodically. Retirement and Christmas parties are welcome times to mingle with the staff. The staff association may request the director to speak to members at least once a year to review the budget situation, to explain important developments, or to review accomplishments and objectives.

GENERAL COMMUNICATION AND PUBLICITY

The annual report should not be overlooked as a means of reaching staff, faculty, and other university officers. Major issues confronting the library should be identified in the report and major trends forecast. An annual report is not an action document but it can serve to communicate in a very important way. University library annual reports usually cover such subjects as important gifts; outstanding acquisitions; operational improvements; new buildings and services; major personnel changes; highlights in cataloging, acquisition, and circulation; and reference to major problems. Some reports go beyond this and describe especially noteworthy library developments on the national or international scene — like Public Law 480 or the National Program for Acquisitions and Cataloging — or major developments in library automation. The report usually concludes with a series of statistical tables relating to expenditures, acquisition, cataloging, growth of collections, circulation, and staff.

Libraries are usually much more active publishers than they realize, and numerous works can do much to spread information. Staff manuals, while not published in the conventional sense, are an invaluable communication device. Specialized working papers developed for knotty problems in processing, automation, binding, or more prosaic aspects of the operation can often serve a wider educational purpose than that of reaching a decision.

Many libraries post vacancies to give staff members a chance to

84

express interest in transfer or promotion. This is a kind of communication that intimately touches individuals. The existence of such a system may provide a regular channel for announcing staff changes. (See Chapter 2.)

The issuance of a new form with accompanying explanatory matter may herald a new procedure. The creation of the form itself, if properly done, will be an exercise in communication since its preparation should involve many if not all of the affected people. A centralized forms control officer will interject needed consistency in forms development and assure consultation among all interested persons, in addition, hopefully, to eliminating unnecessary and overlapping forms and thus using the budget dollar wisely.

Handbooks for students, subject guides, bibliographical leaflets, staff directories, and published technical studies of library costs or new developments all help to inform users and friends of the university of significant library activities and procedures. Most libraries issue one or more acquisitions bulletins to keep specialized audiences informed of significant new materials being added to the library in certain fields (e.g., engineering, government documents, East Asian publications). Lists of serials currently received in a broad area, like science, may be published and reissued periodically. Major, book-length bibliographies may be prepared that systematize information in an extensive field — German-language serials or statistical documents or census publications — and are immensely useful within and without the university community. Exhibition catalogs are commonly issued and can serve multiple objectives. They have an immediate usefulness in guiding visitors through an exhibit; they make resources known to a wide audience; and they may inspire prospective donors to give collections to the library. Still more of a commitment to communication is evident in a library journal which may be issued quarterly. These journals sometimes have faculty editorial assistance and can be impressive publications as, for example, are those from Texas, Yale, Rutgers, Cornell, and Harvard.

Staff members qualified to write on subjects of general interest should be encouraged to write for publication in professional journals. A reasonable amount of support from the library in the form of typing or related help is justified in cases of this kind that put the institution before a wider audience.

In an administratively decentralized system, there should be periodic meetings with the heads of autonomous libraries and with library committees. The mere bringing together of administratively independent people can be salutary. Where there is substantial overlapping of activities and interests, regular, specialized meetings in areas like acquisition and automation may prove fruitful, buttressed by extensive ad hoc consultation by telephone or in smaller meetings.

No matter how diligent the effort or how many the channels established, communication will be less than perfect. The methods suggested here will not assure perfection in an inherently imperfect art, but they can contribute toward the goal of total communication. Ample and adequate communication is of fundamental importance in any effort to administer successfully at any level in the library organization.

SELECTED REFERENCES

Blanchard, J. R. "Departmental Libraries in Divisional Plan University Libraries," *College and Research Libraries,* 14 (July 1953), 243–8.

Logsdon, R. H. "Changes in Organization at Columbia," *College and Research Libraries,* 15 (April 1954), 158–60.

Lundy, Frank A. "The Divisional Library at Nebraska," *Library Journal,* 80 (June 1, 1955), 1302–3.

McAnally, Arthur M. "Organization of College and University Libraries," *Library Trends,* 1 (July 1952), 20–36.

Metcalf, Keyes D., and Edwin E. Williams. "The Administrative Structure of the Harvard University Library," *Harvard Library Bulletin,* 7 (Winter 1953), 5–18.

Miller, Robert A. "Centralization versus Decentralization," *ALA Bulletin,* 33 (February 1939), 75–9, 134–5.

4. BUDGETING AND FISCAL MANAGEMENT

A university library budget is a formalized statement of all accounts having monies available for a specified period (usually a year) allocated according to categories (books, binding, equipment, travel) or operating units (Catalog Department, Chemistry Library, Administrative Department). Since a substantial part (approximately 60 per cent) of a library budget is for staff, individual staff names and salaries may constitute a sizable segment of the budget information. The source of available funds (e.g., general funds, endowment income, grants) may appear both on individual budget sheets and on a summary tabulation. Income from small endowments, gifts, income from the sale of duplicate books, specialized grants, and funds earned by self-sustaining operations (e.g., photocopy service) may or may not be included in the formal budget but in either case will be administered through separate accounts.

Budget administration or fiscal management is a year-round occupation; and the procedure of preparing, presenting, and negotiating the budget is rapidly becoming a continuum that is likely to begin over a year in advance of the fiscal year to which the budget applies. The budgeting process becomes more protracted as sources of funds multiply, institutions become larger, and the organization proliferates through institutes and a variety of research centers. State universities that operate on a fiscal biennium require the library director to be exceptionally resourceful in forecasting the need for funds. Private universities pressed for sound estimates of financial need may require five- or ten-year projections reinforced with clear forecasts over a year in advance of a fiscal year.

No university library should operate without a set of goals. Even if there are no published goals, the hard realities of budgeting require certain assumptions as to inflow of materials, workloads, service and staffing. For that reason, the library with clear-cut pro-

Volumes being prepared for transfer from conventional open-shelf stacks to more economical high-density shelving — Annex Library, Princeton University

grams is likely to be able to prepare a budget with greater assurance and speed than would otherwise be the case; and if goals have been developed with the participation of the faculty and university administration, much of the defense of the budget is built-in.

THE BUDGET PROCESS

Preparation of a budget in an established institution requires a reference point upon which to build; this is the budget "base" which comprises those general university funds, sometimes including specific library endowment income, appropriated by the governing authority for library purposes. Miscellaneous gifts, grants and anticipated income (e.g., from fines or sale of duplicates) are not usually part of the budget base.

It is often customary to group increases to the base in three categories: maintenance, improvement, and capital funds.

Maintenance funds — or maintenance of effort funds — are the additions that are necessary to maintain the current level of operation with no expansion of program. This category usually includes a percentage cost-of-living increase for salaries of the present staff, a factor to offset increased book costs (assuming no increase in volumes acquired), and a corresponding price-rise increase for supplies and services (postage, telephone, stationery, forms, etc.).

Improvement funds are those that permit an increased level of operation or new services. Money to buy more books than heretofore, increased staff to process the enlarged acquisitions intake, staff to activate a new branch library, and a new position for a full-time personnel officer are all examples of improvement items. It could be argued that a budget item for more staff required to handle a 10 per cent rise in circulation is needed to "maintain" service; however, that budget increase is commonly treated as "improvement."

Capital funds are one-time expenditures to increase the library's real property or tangible goods, and they usually relate to buildings (new construction or major reconstruction), major items of equipment (a sizable bookstack installation or a ten-year purchasing program for catalog cabinets), or a large book collection in a field or facility that represents a new academic effort (a new undergraduate library or an art history program at the doctoral level).

Gift, grant, and contract funds are customarily either unpredictable or of limited duration and are not considered part of the base. Activities carried out with such funds have a terminal date or, as in the case of gift-supported activities, can be expanded or contracted without long-term staff commitments or serious disruption of the basic operations of the library. Universities will vary on how these may be handled. It complicates the budget activity to include transitory funds; on the other hand, inclusion of funding available for at least twelve months, of funding likely to be continued, and of any sum above $10,000 is certain to make the budget document more meaningful because it is more comprehensive, and decisions can be based on the larger picture.

Library endowment funds may be considered such an integral and major part of the support that they are treated as part of the budget base. The activities so financed have continuity and would presumably be carried on from general university funds if library endowment income were not available. Smaller endowments, such as those under $25,000 that support limited book purchasing in a fairly specific field, may be omitted as part of the base even though, in total, they may constitute as much as 5 per cent to 10 per cent of available book funds.

Depending on the university's budgetary process, the call for a firm statement of requirements is likely to come a year or more in advance of the fiscal year for which the budget is being prepared. In anticipation of this, the director should have canvassed all of his senior departmental officers for a statement of their requirements. If, as is usually the case, there are to be constraints on what may be requested, it is better for the director to lay down certain guidelines for requests from supervisors rather than to have them go to great lengths to prepare requests that have no possibility of fulfillment and whose very preparation may inspire unrealizable hopes. Supervisors should be asked to review their operations to determine whether savings can be brought about that can be utilized elsewhere in their departments or can be assigned to other departments. Whereas a general admonition to make such an analysis is advisable, it may be even more effective if the director can ask for a response on specific points. The chiefs of acquisition and cataloging might be asked to study economies that might be realized through combining order searching and pre-cataloging searching. The chief

91

of the binding department might be asked to explore alternative sources of binding that would produce lower unit costs without prolonging the time that books are unavailable or without sacrificing quality. The head of interlibrary lending might analyze the requests for loans to determine if an unreasonable workload is being generated by certain institutions.

In his turn, the director may be on notice from the university administration that only a certain level of support is possible. If the faculty library committee participates in the budgetary process, even if only to the extent of giving it general endorsement and support, the committee may insist on a full statement of needs in order that the dimension of the library problem may be impressed on the president or provost. Either at the staff level or in the final budget request, priorities should be established in order to facilitate intelligent budget making. This is not always simple because items will be interdependent, and what should happen to items x, y, and z may depend on the outcome of a, b, and c. Whether demanded in the initial presentation or not, the director must be prepared, and probably will be required, to set certain priorities. If he cannot or does not, someone else is likely to do a less intelligent job.

If certain standards are built into long-range planning or goals, this, too, can facilitate the budget presentation and justification. Crude standards like "one dollar of processing money for each dollar spent on acquisitions" can be useful. If more careful analyses have been made, it may be shown that for each thousand titles (or volumes) acquired, so much staff is needed — for example, one technical services staff member for each 1,200 volumes, the average salary throughout the processing department being $6,500. Ratios may also be established for binding funds by analogy with other university libraries; experience seems to indicate that binding funds constitute an amount equivalent to at least 17 per cent of the amount spent for books in the better libraries. Finally, certain university-wide standards may obtain, such as average percentages for salary increases for existing professional and clerical staff, or a cost-rise percentage permitted for equipment, or a set allowance per staff member for equipment and per librarian for travel.

State-supported institutions not infrequently apply standard formulae to budgeting — e.g., so many staff positions per 100 FTE (full time equivalent) enrollment or per quarter or semester hour.

Such an approach has the danger of any rule of thumb. Libraries vary greatly, as analysis of their statistics demonstrates. Thus library expenditures in relation to total university expense for instruction and research may reasonably vary from 3.5 per cent to 7.0 per cent, just as expenditures for books and binding may range from 30 per cent to 50 per cent of the total library expense or the library staff may be from 33 per cent to 40 per cent professionals.

Formulae bear resemblances to performance budgeting (for which see pp. 97-8).

BUDGETING PROBLEMS

When a library has access to substantial special funds for acquisitions outside the regular budget, the director may have to go to special lengths to point out the impact of windfalls in book money without commensurate processing funds. A library can work itself into a neat processing arrearage through such good fortune. Moreover, if the character of acquisition is changing, it may have a decided impact on processing ratios. If many more books are acquired by gifts-in-kind or by exchange, a considerable workload may be generated that is not reflected in the book budget. If book dollars are stretched as a result of fortuitous *en bloc* purchases or from foreign purchasing missions, those factors can throw ratios awry. Furthermore, the unit costs of certain foreign materials may be low in comparison with the Anglo-American book trade. A university library that becomes heavily involved in international studies — as most do — discovers that traditional ratios need reexamining.

University budget officers may have to be educated with respect to the rising costs that seem to characterize the book trade. Once this is accepted, a certain percentage of the total acquisitions fund may be recognized as a needed annual increment just to maintain the status quo in purchasing power. Depending on the composition of domestic-foreign purchasing, serial subscriptions, retrospective buying, rare book emphasis, and so forth, this percentage may run 6 per cent to 9 per cent. At this writing, 7 per cent is considered appropriate at Stanford. Harvard currently estimates the need for an annual increment of 10 per cent to compensate for rising prices *and* to maintain relative purchasing scope in a steadily expanding publishing market. Each university must determine what is justifiable in the light of local practices. Prices will vary substantially depending upon area concentrations (e.g., unit prices are lower in Africa and China than in Eastern or Western Europe) and upon acquisitions methods (foreign purchasing missions and *en bloc* purchases may very substantially reduce unit costs). Published book price ratios may be useful as an indication of trends, but these are wholly or preponderantly weighted toward American publishing; and, because of the heavy emphasis on foreign books and on non-book materials in universities, the writers reemphasize the need to analyze local experience as the only really firm basis for estimating the cost of books.

The director may be able to persuade the university to adopt a "program approach" to major problems. There are at least two versions of this approach. One involves large inputs of money over a stated period after which the need is met and the special funding can cease. Clearing of a backlog or a program to fill in retrospective holdings are examples of this approach. The second type projects a new, higher level of operation on a continuing basis. This cannot be achieved in one year, but the budget can be built to the higher level on a planned basis. Doubling the level of current acquisitions, a commensurate doubling of the processing staff, building new book collections to support a new academic department, and raising the binding expenditure from 10 per cent of acquisitions to 20 per cent are good examples of this second kind of programmed attack on major problems.

As a practical matter, it is worth noting that certain ventures of the program type, such as building the basic collection for a new undergraduate library, for a computer science library, or for a departmental library in a recently activated art history department may require several years of lead time. Three or four years may be the minimum time needed in advance of opening a new library to select, acquire, catalog, and mark 50,000 volumes. The magnitude of such an undertaking is not always apparent to general university administrators who may be reluctant to face the budget implications of such a long-range effort. The library administration must explain the operation with sufficient clarity and detail to enable others to understand and accept the soundness of proceeding systematically rather than throwing together an eleventh-hour project that will leave the library staff exhausted and still unprepared on opening day of a new facility.

94

SPECIAL BUDGETING TECHNIQUES

Four other aspects of budgeting merit special attention:
1. Capital liquidating funding
2. Contingency funds
3. Revolving funds
4. Performance and program budgeting

Money is usually not available within the library's budget base to finance major new programs, for example, in international studies, or to make possible a completely new level of acquisition or hours of service in a system of branch libraries. Major gifts, government and foundation grants, or other university funds can sometimes be obtained to launch these ventures. In fact, it is surprising how often these funds can be found within the university if the library director starts exploring with the provost, vice president for finance, or the deans of schools. Such funding, irrespective of source, is likely to be available for a limited time, and the library must find the means to finance the higher-level operation. This can often be done on a capital liquidating basis which, in a sense, is a variation of the program approach. Under the capital liquidating technique, a substantial input of special support is obtained with the understanding that it will be spread over several years and phased out as the library gradually assumes the financial burden. Needless to state, this must be sanctioned by the budgeting authority or someone at the provostial or vice presidential level. Five years is a typical capital liquidating span, but periods of two to ten years are used, depending on the circumstances. Gift, grant, or special funds are used to finance the entire cost of improvement the first year, perhaps 75 per cent the second year, 50 per cent the third year, and 25 per cent the fourth year. The library's budget is gradually built up to assume the balance of the burden: 25 per cent the second year, 50 per cent the third year, etc., until it sustains the full cost in the fifth year. The advantage of this method of operation is that it makes possible the attainment of a higher level of activity much more rapidly than a slow build-up.

Almost any large undertaking requires a contingency fund as part of the financial support. A contingency fund is a general fund not designated for a particular purpose but reserved for unanticipated needs. It is usually small in relation to the total budget, perhaps 1 per cent to 3 per cent for general purposes. The percentage is likely to be smaller — even less than 1 per cent — as the budget gets larger. On the other hand, contingency book funds may be as much as 5 per cent to 10 per cent. Libraries are called upon frequently to lengthen hours in response to demands of schools or departments, to hire supplemental staff because prolonged illness has immobilized several staff members, to undertake searching of very lengthy bibliographies that cannot be handled by the regular staff, to purchase a major item of equipment to replace a device that is unrepairable, to process a large and unexpected gift collection, to undertake a major shift of collections because a book storage area is suddenly preempted for other university purposes, and to make other unanticipated expenditures. If there is sufficient flexibility in regulations governing the use of funds, these emergencies can often be met by shifting money within the budget. But such a practice may distort the balance of the library operation and divert money from worthy purposes. A more orderly approach is to have a contingency fund set up as part of the regular budget.

A third type of specialized financing is the revolving fund. A revolving fund is basically a fund that provides working capital for an activity, but the phrase is also used loosely for income that comes from a source somewhat apart from the main activity of the library but over which the library maintains some control. (This is sometimes called a "zero" or "wash" account because income and expense should theoretically wash each other out to leave a zero balance of available funds.)

A photocopy account is a good example of a revolving fund. Fees received for photocopying services are credited to the account. Photocopying equipment will be purchased or leased from it. Salaries and wages of persons directly connected with the photoduplication service will be charged to the account, as may be supplies and miscellaneous items of equipment such as desks, chairs, safes, cabinets, cash registers, dating machines, adding machines, etc. A publications account may operate in the same way, with income from sales of publications flowing into the account and the costs of printing, binding, editing, advertising, mailing, etc., charged to the account.

A third example of a revolving fund would be an account set up to handle income from a specialized library service to industry. Fees for memberships, and charges for lending of books, for photocopying, for mailing, for answering reference questions and for bibliographic searches could be credited to the account. Staff salaries, cost of forms, postage, rental of a delivery truck, supplies, and furniture would be charged to the account. A certain amount of the income might be set aside for the purchase of books for the collections since service to industry is viable by virtue of the extensive holdings of the university, and more than the direct costs of handling, mailing, or photocopying journal articles or answering reference questions is involved.

As is suggested in Chapter 1, university libraries are large operations, and as a consequence they need to adopt some of the management techniques that are commonplace in business. Cost analysis in technical processing can lead to more rational procedures and may provide very convincing arguments in budget presentations. Establishing the cost of service to faculty, staff, graduate students, and undergraduates, respectively, may have a powerful indirect budget impact if this information can be used to establish a more favorable overhead rate to be charged for indirect costs on government contract work performed by the university. Maintenance of a carefully selected set of statistics is a requisite of sound budgeting and, if well done, will obviate many a special study of costs. The libraries at Michigan, Pennsylvania, and Purdue have found it useful to have a specialist in operations research tackle selected library problems.

"Performance" budgeting and "program" budgeting are rather imprecise terms although in practice they refer to techniques that are widely utilized. Performance budgeting was identified and named by the first Hoover Commission in 1949 and is commonly used in Federal and other public agencies.

Performance and program budgeting begins with a statement of *objectives*. The following are library examples:

1. To catalog 10,000 titles each year from the backlog
2. To acquire and catalog 10,000 additional volumes each year for three years
3. To bind 5,000 additional volumes each year for five years
4. To establish a new branch library in Mathematics

The second step in the process is *programming*, i.e., to state in detail the cost of attaining the objective, drawing on experience. In example 1, above, it may be known that the average cataloger, supported by one clerical assistant, can catalog 1,400 titles per year (descriptive and subject cataloging). These two staff members may require $150 worth of supplies. If the backlog to be cataloged is general in nature, a production of 10,000 titles may require 7 catalogers at an average salary of $8,500 each and 7 assistants at $5,000 each, plus 11 per cent fringe benefits, or a total of $104,895 plus $1,050 in supplies. To get the books marked, plated, and placed on the shelves may require one and a fraction persons for an additional $7,000. The total cost of objective 1 would therefore require an increment of approximately $115,000. If the backlog is in serials, cataloging production may be lower, with a consequent need for more staff and a higher total cost.

A total budget built along these lines permits the budgeting authority to make decisions in terms of objectives with accompanying price tags (sometimes called "cost benefit analysis"). Because this method requires more precise information on the part of the library director, it is also instructive as to the efficiency of his operation, and particularly so if costs can be compared with those of other institutions.

The establishment of a new branch library poses a much more complex problem than an attack on the cataloging backlog and will involve costs of materials, cost of acquisition and processing, physical equipping of a new facility, operational staff costs for a given public service schedule, etc., but even this more complex problem can become intelligible if the components are analyzed and if costs are associated with each element.

Even though a university librarian may not be required to present an entire budget in accordance with performance and program budgeting techniques, he will probably be asked to present his case for some improvements in these terms. With respect to the total budget, it is also possible that budget categories may be allowed to follow traditional lines such as cataloging, acquisition, public service, etc., and that the director will be asked only to summarize the budget in accordance with performance and program concepts. This is done in some Federal budgets like that of the Library of Congress and is not uncommon where conventional budgeting is well entrenched and successful. The summary is a recasting of basic data to reveal cost relationships of particular interest to the reviewing authority.

The budget procedure will naturally not be uniform. The broad categories used in negotiation, the treatment of one-time capital expenditures, the degree of departmental discretion or decentralization in decision, the reliance on formulae or percentage adjustments, the extent to which the incomes of small endowments are incorporated in the operating budget, and timing — all these aspects will vary among universities. States with biennial budgets present additional complexities, partly because forecasts for positions and book funds must be done further in advance. A new position added for the second year of a biennium cannot be converted to a half-time position for two years. Funds appropriated for the library for the second year of a biennium may actually be reduced by the university — or conceivably increased — if special circumstances justify reassignment within the university in the eyes of local budget officers. Changes either upwards or downwards in Federal support for books will not ordinarily result in any compensating readjustment of state funds. Yet a sharp fluctuation in National Defense Education Act funds, in National Science Foundation support, or, indeed, in endowment investment return, can well serve to initiate an internal review of allocations. Salary improvements for existing positions will normally be handled in a biennial budget as under an annual budget, that is, negotiated annually with the local university administration.

NEGOTIATING THE BUDGET

Budget negotiations will require conferences with the person to whom the director reports or to his representative. The officer who manages the endowment portfolio may need to be consulted. The controller or budget officer may assist in some facets such as form of presentation. A series of submissions may be called for, ranging from gross estimates of needs to rather highly refined presentations with priority indications. All of this may take from three to six months before the library's budget is incorporated into a broader university presentation to the board of trustees or other appropriating authority. In general, the library director defends his budget at the level of the president, vice president, or provost. These officers are likely to negotiate with higher and final authority.

In summary, the budgetary process relies to an extraordinary extent on objective information and well-defined and accepted goals. The library director who has developed his goals on a broad base that includes general university administrative agreement, who has taken the trouble to isolate ratios that are widely accepted or that can be honestly demonstrated on analogy with other libraries, whose budget requests are not capricious but will stand close scrutiny, and who operates in his fiscal management as well as in his requests on the principle of openness and integrity is likely to get an even break for the library. In the last analysis, the library should be of a size and nature appropriate to the rest of the university, and the director should emphasize that he is not building his own empire but is strengthening the entire university.

FISCAL ADMINISTRATION

Fiscal administration has already been described as a year-round operation. The director himself will find it advisable to participate extensively in the oversight of funds, even though — in contrast to his efforts in budget negotiation — he will probably have to delegate a good deal of the budget management to other staff members.

A set of budget accounts may include the following as samples:

Library Account Numbers

AA 10 Director's Office	BA 20 Romance Language Office
AA 90 University Archives	BA 30 Germanic Language Office
AB 10 Business Services	BA 40 Latin American Office
AB 12 Mail Room and Messenger	BA 91 (etc.) — special surveys
AB 13 Supply Room	of holdings
AB 14 Building Superintendent's Office	
AB 15 Casual employees, special	BB *Acquisition Department*
AB 20 Supplies and equipment, general	BB 01 Administration
	BB 10 Exchange Section
	BB 20 Gift Division
BA *Resources Development Program*	BB 30 Order Division
	BB 40 Serial Records Division
BA 02 Book selection, general	BB 50 Binding and Finishing
BA 10 Slavic Language Office	Division

100

BC   *Catalog Department*
BC 01   Administration
BC 10   Monograph cataloging
BC 20   Serial cataloging
BC 30   Area cataloging
BC 40   Book catalog cataloging
BC 80   Searching section
BC 85   Filing section
BC 90   Card duplication section
BC 92   Catalog maintenance
          section
BC 95   Theses processing

CA   *Circulation Department*
CA 01   Administration
CA 20   Loan Desk
CA 22   Auxiliary Library Loan
          Desk
CA 30   Service to Business and
          Industry
CA 40   Reserves for courses
CA 50   College Library circulation
CA 55   Browsing collection

CB   *Reference Department*
CB 01   Administration
CB 10   Reference Division
CB 20   Interlibrary Loan Section
CB 30   Government Document
          Department
CB 40   Map Section
CB 50   Newspaper and Microtext
          Section
CB 90   Film Rental Service

CD   *Branch Libraries*
[perhaps divided by Faculty or
into broad subject categories]

DA   *Special Collections*
DA 01   Administration

DA 10   Rare Book Reading Room
DA 20   Manuscript Division
DA 30   Southern History Room
DA 40   Theatre Collection
DA 80   Medical Library branch

F   *Special Accounts*
FA 10   Photocopy services
FA 20   Sales via Interlibrary
          Loans
FA 30   Theses filming/binding
          account
FA 40   Exhibit support
FA 50   Publications
FA 60   Archive of Recorded
          Sound Sales

G   *Preservation*
GA 10   Binding
GA 20   Rebinding
GA 30   Repairs
GA 40   Microfilming — archival
          program
GA 50   Microfilming — replace-
          ment of originals

K-Z   *Book Funds*
K   Book funds, general
[various accounts will exist under
this and the following categories]
L   Discretionary book funds
M   Undergraduate book funds
N   Residence Hall book funds
O   Area Programs, special
R   Faculty of Arts and
          Sciences
S   Faculty of Law
T   Faculty of Business
U   Faculty of Education
V   Faculty of Medicine
W   Faculty of Divinity

Against each of the above may be charged expenses coded for one or several of the classes below. A good system will provide summaries by broad expense category. (Only classes relevant to libraries have been listed.)

Expense Classification Codes

100 — *Personnel*
131 Librarian
133 Editor
135 Analyst/Programmer
139 Other professional
140 Research assistant
156 Other technicians (including Library Technician)
170 Secretarial and Clerical
181 Executive/Director
184 Other administrative (including Business Manager)
199 Hourly payroll (casuals)
200 Benefits, staff

400 — *Capital equipment*
420 Office equipment
426 Books (Library only)
428 Equipment, general

500 — *Travel*
530 Domestic
531 Foreign
535 Moving expense
536 Consultants' travel
539 Local

600 — *Expendable materials and services*
610 Office supplies
612 Publications—including expendable books and periodicals (used for laboratory and administrative office collections only)
613 Postage and freight
619 Laundry
622 Equipment maintenance and repair (including service contracts)
623 Equipment rental
645 Photoreproduction service
646 Printing Plant service
647 Computation Center
648 Physical Plant
649 Health Service
650 Telephone and telegraph
651 Utilities
677 Insurance
683 Depreciation
980 Indirect costs
990 Cost sharing

Salaries will comprise a substantial share of the budget, and it might be erroneously assumed that this part of the budget would automatically take care of itself, but even a computerized university accounting system is no better than the information fed into the system, and an inevitable number of errors are bound to creep into tens of thousands of transactions. Salaried or hourly employees will be improperly coded, and the library may even find its budget being used to pay nonlibrary personnel. Overpayments and underpayments will be made occasionally and must be corrected.

A senior staff member must be charged with a monthly review of expenditures to assure accuracy. Proper controlling starts in the library with the document which initiates action. Its coding must be exact, and each form properly completed. A change of one digit may put a cataloger on the circulation payroll, may charge personnel to an equipment account, or may charge history books to an engineering book fund. The heads of major departments should be supplied regularly with budget and fiscal information on their units. This information may include annual budget sheets; monthly expense statements; monthly statements of personnel, book fund, and other commitments; and departmental summaries of expenditures and uncommitted balances. When mistakes are discovered or when adjustments have to be made, corrective action should be requested in writing, usually on special forms provided by the controller. If the university accounting or data processing office must make corrections, written requests will need to be reviewed the next month or two until adjustments are actually reflected in a subsequent expense statement.

Within the library, authorization to change a budget should also be made in writing by the proper official. This may take one of three forms:

1. a correction in amount or category code within an account
2. a transfer in expense from one account to another to shift the debit
3. an increase in available funds deriving from a major gift, a supplementary appropriation, or a transfer from a different department of the university

The transfer from another department may also include funds which are budgeted commitments but appear as a "reduction of expense" in the annual printed budget since such funds are carried as expenditures in another budget. (For example: foundation funds to a language center which in turn allots a sum for a library salary. That position should appear on the library budget as funded, though the university expense will show in the language center budget. Thus the transfer of funds must be accomplished at some time in a monthly expense statement to cover the budgeted "reduction" in the library budget.) All of these changes occur with sufficient frequency and are so spread throughout the year that accurate records are essential for management just as much as for accounting purposes.

Unless the university has a standard procedure, policies will have

103

to be established by the director with respect to lapsed salaries and wages accruing from vacancies or leaves without pay. It may be decided that the department making a saving may use these monies without further approval. More commonly, however, such savings throughout the operation are regarded as a common pool to be allotted by the director for special contingencies that may develop. Some budgets anticipate such savings, and the actual amount provided would not cover all salaries if all positions were filled throughout the year, something that never happens in a large staff. Such savings may be put to very good use in hiring a replacement to overlap a terminating employee, in executing special projects, or, if

the budget regulations permit, in advance-hiring personnel for positions approved in the next budget year. This application of funds is particularly worthy because it enables the library to recruit desirable employees when available, to work on backlogs, and to enter a new fiscal year with a fully trained staff. In some institutions, salary savings may also be used to give salary increases to deserving staff members, particularly to newer employees, perhaps after the probationary period, as long as the budget base is not distorted.

The principal funds requiring monitoring other than salaries and books fall in the administrative category. Chapter 2 suggests ways of handling travel funds. Equipment and supplies also require advance planning and careful oversight. Very early in the fiscal year, equipment priorities should be reviewed (this may begin two or three months before the fiscal year starts) and a substantial part of the equipment budget committed. There is little virtue and some risk in delaying the purchase of equipment or supplies in a constantly rising market. In both of these categories, however, it is well to conserve at least 25 per cent of the initial budget to meet contingencies. Even so, such reserves should probably be committed by the beginning of the final quarter.

Depending on the institution, different degrees of latitude prevail with respect to the use of funds. In a strict line and item budget often found under civil service or in state institutions, funds may be expended only for the precise purpose indicated in the appropriation and none other. This prevents the use of salary money for books, for example, or vice versa. Very cogent reasons can be offered for this method of operation, but the larger the budget, the more painful do such restrictions become; and private universities are likely to enjoy much greater freedom, some even complete freedom, in the use of funds. Even so, if budgeting has any meaning, there should be some correspondence between what is requested and how it is spent. Needless to state, the funding of regular positions from "soft" money (that is, money generated within a budget or one-shot appropriations or grants) is a hazardous and inadvisable procedure.

In a large library, the management of the budget, if not a full-time job, is at the very least a major assignment in terms of the time involved and the level of responsibility. Foremost among various duties is that of monitoring expenditures to be sure that they are

105

A commodious faculty study providing shelves for personal books or books charged from the library collections for use in the professor's research — O. Meredith Wilson Library, University of Minnesota

charged to an appropriate account, that funds which are restricted as to purpose and may thus be difficult to use are applied whenever feasible, and that funds are not excessively over- or underspent in relation to the time of year and the nature of the account. For example, at the end of the first quarter, it may be entirely appropriate that 75 per cent of the equipment account be expended, and that some endowed book accounts may be exhausted, but the salaries should show a balance approximating 75 per cent of the budget. Furthermore, the financial manager should be alert to the possibility of tapping other sources of university funds for special purposes. This may include a "classroom fund" which could refurbish a library conference or multipurpose room, a "public events" account which could cover a special exhibit expense, or a provost's contingency fund which may be called upon for moving expenses of new librarians.

The financial manager must be party to all decisions on transfers within the budget, and he will make most such decisions himself, although the director may make some. The point is, however, that the manager cannot intelligently discharge his functions if he is not fully apprised of all actions affecting the budget. He will alert the director to surplus or deficit situations, and the two officers will probably consult on remedies for deficits as well as on allocation of surplus monies. There will need to be a great deal of consulting with departmental administrators regarding these same matters and on procedural details. The financial manager will initiate written requests to correct or adjust accounts and to carry forward year-end balances. If such transfer of funds from one year to the next is not permitted, expenditures must be monitored with the greatest care. Insufficient exactitude in monitoring can produce embarrassing deficits, or surpluses that may be lost, despite great needs, because funds revert to the university or to the state. The monitoring of revolving funds and project or grant funds may not be quite as exacting; on the other hand, grants sometimes carry with them special reporting requirements or conditions with respect to expenditures that make them very demanding of close scrutiny.

In a sense, fiscal and budget management is the director's responsibility, but of necessity he will have to delegate a substantial part of the duties, perhaps to an assistant director, to an administrative assistant, to a business officer, or to a combination of individuals. Whatever the extent of delegation, the director must have complete confidence in the person or persons performing the work and must periodically be thoroughly briefed on the status of funds and on activities that relate to budget adjustments and correction of accounts.

BOOK FUND MANAGEMENT

The administration of acquisitions funds may be centered in the library business officer or in an accounting section of the acquisitions department, but the director will wish to keep advised of the flow of funds and of excessive over- or underspending. Book funds are likely to be complicated by restrictions on those derived from private donations or benefactions. It may take concerted effort to spend funds that have extremely restrictive covenants attached to them, e.g., a fund in public speaking. Donors should be encouraged to make unrestricted gifts or to specify very broad fields such as "history" or "literature" in order not to make administration of the funds unduly costly. Of course, there will be times when it is better to accept restrictions rather than forgo the fund. If some donors want periodic reports on the use of their funds, the maintenance of fund files to provide this information is an essential though burdensome task — one, it is hoped, that may be simplified with computer applications.

The speed with which book funds are spent may be very instructive as to needs or as to the performance of staff members doing the selecting. General university accounting systems, even computerized ones, are unequal to the task of providing information on balances that are sufficiently accurate and up to date to be meaningful. Until automation has been fully applied to acquisitions records, a share of the burden of book fund accounting and any analysis of expenditures are likely to fall on the library. In fact, irrespective of the system and its degree of automation, the library does, and probably always will, have a basic responsibility for such monitoring.

Some system of encumbering is in most cases essential in administering book funds. It is meaningless just to be able to tell the balance in each fund after invoices are paid; as books are ordered, some measure of the liability imposed on each fund must be maintained. A simple system is to total the real or estimated costs of the items charged to each fund daily (or weekly) and to subtract this

107

amount from the free balance. A duplicate order slip, marked "encumbrance," is part of the multiple-part form constituting the regular order slip. When an item is received, the price is confirmed or corrected. Adjustment tapes are run daily (or weekly) by fund, and encumbrances are adjusted to bring the free balance into line.

One type of book fund, the departmental allotment, is passing from the scene in most universities. Established at a time when funds were more scarce, such allotments insured a share of meager funds to each department. With greater affluence in book funds and with a more competent library curatorial staff, the *raison d'être* for such funding and the very considerable red tape that accompanied it have vanished. Blanket order arrangements have contributed to the relinquishment of the allotment system also because many books are acquired across the whole range of disciplines. Intense competition in the secondhand market has made it essential for the library to free itself of red tape in order to be able to act with dispatch. A ponderous system that involves a great deal of time between receipt of secondhand catalogs and placement of orders will almost surely result in the failure to get most of the wanted items.

Most large libraries will be well advised to undertake periodic reviews of "status of funds" of all types. A reading fairly early in the fiscal year, perhaps at the end of the first quarter, may give assurance that things generally are in order. As the year progresses, more frequent reviews are advisable and at least monthly periodicity is recommended during the final quarter.

INSURANCE

It is the responsibility of the library director to see that collections under his charge are properly protected by insurance or, if he works in a university that is self-insured, that the appropriate university authority (probably the vice president for business affairs or the business manager) is informed of the value of the library's collections and catalogs. The library director should also be conversant with the methods of establishing loss for insurance purposes, should this become necessary.

One of the basic risks that most libraries are exposed to is that connected with the custodianship of material borrowed for exhibition. Usually the lender, whether personal or institutional, will have a floater policy that covers any loss that may occur when materials are in transit or outside the immediate custodianship of the owner. In such cases there should be a clear understanding, *in writing*, as to the value of borrowed items and the identity of the institution or person carrying the insurance. If the borrower is the insured, it is probably a requirement of the policy that the value of specific items be reported to a central insurance office. Such prior understanding can save endless trouble in the event of loss or damage.

A university that is self-insured has probably built up a reserve fund over many years to cover losses of buildings, equipment, or other property, such as books. Since the holdings of a university library may be worth $10 million to $60 million, the responsible officials must be aware of the extent of the risk.

Where insurance is carried, there is likely to be a deductible feature, which means that the university in effect is self-insured for lesser losses. Very expensive items (very rare books) are sometimes insured by specific identity. The more common practice is a general policy that protects against fire and other hazards (but not mutilation or mysterious disappearance).

In the event of a sizable loss, the library will have to be able to prove the extent of the loss. Some libraries microfilm their shelf-list, official catalog, and even the public catalog to provide (a) documentary evidence of book losses in the event that the catalogs and books are destroyed or (b) a source from which to reconstruct the catalogs or trays therefrom if lost or destroyed.

Insurance companies will usually agree on an average cost per volume lost in the case of extensive losses. If losses are in art books, for example, the library may have to demonstrate that per volume costs in this field are higher than in, for example, American literature. Like department stores, libraries are allowed replacement costs, meaning a realistic per volume cost in the current market plus the cost of acquisition. The cost of replacing records (like catalog cards) may have special aspects. The actual cost of the paper, typing, and photographic techniques required to recreate a catalog or several trays would probably be covered, but the total intellectual effort of cataloging materials from scratch would probably not be covered.

Generalities are somewhat dangerous in writing about insurance. Suffice it to say that it is a complex subject but an important one in which the library director has certain responsibilities for informing himself and others on coverage, risks, and special steps to take prior to loss.

SELECTED REFERENCES

American Library Association. Library Technology Project. "Insuring the Library," in *Protecting the Library and Its Resources: A Guide to Physical Protection and Insurance. Report on a Study by Gage-Babcock and Associates*. Chicago, American Library Association, 1963. pp. 119–206.
    See also Appendices G and H.

Devaney, C. William. "Examples of Program Budgeting for Nonprofit Administrative Decisions . . . ," *Price Waterhouse Review,* 13 (Summer 1968), 45–53.

Frodin, Reuben S. "Finance and the College Library," *Library Quarterly*, 24 (October 1954), 374–81.

Lyle, Guy R. "Business and Financial Affairs," in his *The Administration of the College Library*. 3rd ed. New York, H. W. Wilson, 1961. Chapter XIV.
    See especially the treatment of "departmental book fund allocations," pp. 335-7, and the details in note 6, pp. 347-9.

McGrath, William E., Ralph C. Huntsinger, and Gary R. Barber. "An Allocation Formula Derived from a Factor Analysis of Academic Departments," *College and Research Libraries*, 30 (January 1969), 51–62.

Maybury, Catherine. "Performance Budgeting for the Library," *ALA Bulletin*, 55 (January 1961), 46–53.

Metcalf, Keyes D. "The Finances of the Harvard University Library," *Harvard Library Bulletin*, 7 (Autumn 1953), 333–48.

Mixer, Charles W. "New Developments in Insurance and Protection of Library Contents," *Library Trends*, 11 (April 1963), 427–35.

Richards, James H., Jr. "Academic Budgets and Their Administration," *Library Trends*, 11 (April 1963), 415–26.

Rogers, Rutherford D. "Appraising a Research Collection," *College and Research Libraries*, 13 (January 1952), 24–9.

Young, Helen. "Performance and Program Budgeting," *ALA Bulletin*, 61 (January 1967), 63–7.

5. BOOK COLLECTIONS

A distinguished collection of books is the *sine qua non* of a great research library. Librarians and nonlibrarians alike may forget this because of the current preoccupation with computers, the enormous fiscal problems associated with larger and larger library buildings, and the vexatious bibliographic problems of controlling huge bodies of materials in increasingly diverse formats. However important these other factors may be, we should not forget that they are subsidiary to the root element that gives the library its name — *liber*, the Latin word for book.

It is common practice to use the term *books* generically to cover the vast array of things that make up a research library's collections: monographs, serials, phonorecords, films, manuscripts, microtexts, magnetic tapes, broadsides, photographs, prints, video tapes, etc. These graphic media are all in some way distinctively intellectual and informational. They differ in form and character from three-dimensional materials such as framed paintings, swords, armor, flags, precious stones, furniture, statuary, vases, stuffed animals, and other museum objects. The wise librarian will recognize that his domain is sufficiently diverse and complex if he restricts his collecting to what is obviously library material and leaves museum objects to the custody of other more appropriate agencies.

Of all policy issues confronting a university library, none is more central to the nature of the institution or has a greater single impact on costs than the program for collecting books, journals, and other informational materials. Every increment in annual acquisitions carries with it collateral processing costs and formidable implications for physical facilities. If the increments involve extensions into new languages and subjects, such expansion may carry with it the seeds of new departmental libraries and may require linguistic and subject specialists not heretofore employed.

An additional $40,000 for books generally requires a commensurate increase for processing staff, plus $20,000 in stack space and

113

A special collection in a "period setting" within a department of rare books, providing controlled access for qualified scholars — Henry Charles Lea Library of Medieval History, Charles Patterson Van Pelt Library, University of Pennsylvania

equipment. These relationships will vary, of course, depending on the type of materials purchased: serials, rare books, pamphlets, books in English, books in Arabic, and so on, but the figures given represent valid averages and relationships at this writing. If the higher level of acquisitions is maintained, there is a continuing annual need for additional stack space and an eventual need for stack employees. The $40,000 increase in acquisitions expenditures maintained over a ten-year period can be translated into expenses in excess of $1 million.

While these figures are substantial, they are inherent in the nature of libraries, and acquisitions policy should be determined by institutional needs rather than intimidating statistics. Granted the validity of this viewpoint, the collection building operation is of such significance that it needs to be coordinated at a very responsible level in the director's staff.

THE PROGRAM FOR ASSEMBLING COLLECTIONS

Every university library must have a collecting policy or series of policies whether this is kept in a few minds or is written down. Since collecting policy is so momentous and affects the work of more and more staff members, there is much to be said for a written policy. A word of caution, however, is in order. It is possible for a great many staff members to spend many hours working out acquisitions policy statements, and there is some tendency in such exercises to set laudable and quite unattainable goals. Specialists are likely to be somewhat astigmatic in judging the merits of their own disciplines, and a strong central force must provide balance and reality in the light of general university programs.

A policy statement is likely to be most useful if the views of many specialists are reviewed and leavened by a seasoned central selection officer and then carefully edited by the director to represent the best balance for the university as a whole. The final document will usually describe various levels of collecting intensity such as representative or reference coverage, working coverage, research coverage, advanced research (or comprehensive) coverage, and exhaustive coverage. The statement should constitute an agreement among library, faculty, and administration; and to that extent it

114

may be a very useful exercise. It will not provide an automatic mechanism for precisely judging whether to buy or not to buy. The statement in Appendix II was designed to assist a university library's staff and faculty to ascertain the responsible specialists in various selection areas and to point out those bulk-purchasing arrangements that have especial impact on the need for individual recommendations. (The names of the specialists in the selection areas are omitted.)

Another university has a similar statement, from which a section has been extracted in Appendix III to suggest how specific fields might be dealt with in a large library.

Appendix IV illustrates another method which may be used when various libraries within a university share an interest in a field or region.

If there is a procedure by which the director and designated deputies approve substantial purchases, say those exceeding $100 whether of a single volume or set, policy to a certain extent will evolve in practice. Under any policy, collecting is conditioned by changes from a tight to a plentiful book budget, and this in turn reformulates the policy. Internal allotment of book funds to specific subjects, like music, American history, university press books, exchanges, etc., imposes limitations that should have roots in policy, and emergency requests for funds from any source should be cause for review of how funds are being spent.

The overall book budget will probably be derived from a congeries of individual local needs buttressed by analogies from good libraries in comparable institutions. A pretty strong case can be made in support of increased acquisitions funds if a library ranks fifteenth among the members of the Association of Research Libraries in money spent for books when the parent institution considers itself among the top ten universities in the country, or if a university spends 10 per cent less on books than any of the three or four institutions with which the university administration compares itself.

Cogent though this argument is, budget authorities will welcome individual instances of need. Faculty evaluation of the collections they use can be very persuasive. New professors may demand special library funds before they will agree to accept an appointment to the faculty. Demonstrable inferiority in collections in fields like music, linguistics, or Arabic can be quickly documented if a

115

doctoral program is announced on a clearly inadequate library base. One effective means of proof is to get statistics on the size of specialized collections in universities having programs of some distinction in the area being analyzed. This is likely to show a wide disparity between the local collection and one of established excellence. Another classic proof is to make an extensive bibliographical survey that reveals the paucity of holdings when checked against standard bibliographies. This can be an expensive and time-consuming exercise, but it produces hard facts that are likely to be persuasive.

If collections as a whole are substandard, the director should try to induce the provost or president to accept as a desirable target a level of current acquisitions at least equal to the level of good libraries in universities which are considered to be on a par in faculty distinction, range of academic offerings, and quality of student body. If one's university is moving upward to a new level of excellence, the library comparison should be made with the target level and not the present level. If the university administration will accept goals developed in this way, it may raise to an adequate level the purchasing of current imprints, but there will be a companion problem of building weak collections to strength. The university administration may be persuaded that certain gross amounts should be available each year for this purpose on the theory that the collection deficit is general and represents so many tens or hundreds of thousands of volumes. The advantage of generalized targets of this nature is that they become long-range goals within which to program annual budgets without the very substantial effort that is required to demonstrate need on an area-by-area basis. However, if the latter basis is required by the university administration, the library should make its case as solid as it can using comparative statistics, bibliographic analyses, and faculty support.

Collection deficiencies in a library that is generally strong require more refined justification in the form of faculty testimony and specific bibliographical analysis. If book funds are becoming less and less adequate because of increased book production and spiraling costs, the director must arm himself with publishing statistics, general book-price data, and figures derived from local experience that demonstrate increasing per volume costs. For instance, a selective study of increases in serial prices over the past three years may clearly demonstrate a special need.

MONIES FOR PURCHASING MATERIALS

Most libraries enjoy access to specialized book funds derived from current gifts or from endowments established through gifts or devises. Until well into the 1960's, the Harvard College Library was able to finance all annual book purchases in this way although it can no longer do so. Few universities will even approach such affluence, and yet specialized endowment funds may make the difference between sufficiency and insufficiency in acquisitions.

As is suggested in Chapter 4, specialized funds vary in their nature. The most desirable are unrestricted funds that permit purchase of any book. Restricted book funds impose limits, usually by subject, and if these funds are established by living persons, they may require periodic accounting of titles purchased. Clearly, unrestricted funds are much to be preferred, and the library needs to impress this preference and the reasons therefor on the university fund raisers. The administrative apparatus that needs to be established to assure the expenditure of narrowly restricted gift funds and to provide the information for reporting on them is both cumbersome and expensive. Consider the task of finding in the current trade enough titles to justify a fund producing $3,000 annually for university interests in public speaking and you will have some measure of the difficulty of administering one hundred funds having restrictions. Under such circumstances, the controller or provost who reviews fund balances in the library may jump to the erroneous conclusion that there is really plenty of money for books; but such officials will be misled by fund balances that are composed of hard-to-use funds of the kind described while in reality there may be severe shortages in more general areas.

The establishment of book funds can be made a reasonably attractive idea to potential donors to the university. Many people who cannot afford $500,000-$700,000 to endow a professorship or millions to finance buildings are attracted by this aspect of library support. There is a considerable range of opportunity from very limited gifts to very substantial ones. It is possible, for example, to encourage a great many donors to give small amounts (ten to fifteen dollars) to a memorial fund. If properly organized, these gifts can serve to honor living people on special occasions (birthdays, graduation) or to memorialize a person who has died. There should be attractive bookplates that can be adapted to such cases and that make possible the addition to the plate of the name of the donor and the person being honored or memorialized. The university fund-raising office or the library must be prepared to (1) acknowledge the gift to the donor and (2) inform the person being honored or the family of the person being memorialized of the generous action of the donor. Once a person has contributed, he should receive forms for further donations together with an acknowledgment of his gift. This is an expensive array of paper work that can be simplified with handsomely printed forms. To make such a system at all effective as a money-raising device, donors should be encouraged to give $15 or more for each volume. Such an amount for a single volume can be justified by current book costs plus the costs of processing. In the interest of public relations, it is essential that any gift, even though substantially less than $15, be processed as the gift of one title. A surprisingly wide range of support can be generated by a well-devised program of this kind publicized in the alumni bulletin or other general publication.

The attraction of a more substantial book fund is that it becomes a permanent memorial to the person honored as well as a permanent acknowledgment of the donor's generosity through continuing purchases and through the use of an appropriate bookplate. A distinction needs to be made between an expendable gift and an endowed book fund. Some institutions set a lower limit such as $10,000 for an endowed book fund, taking the view that a smaller amount (producing less income than $500 annually) does not justify the accounting and other overhead; and one university has said it won't sell fame in perpetuity for a lesser sum. This lower limit sometimes inspires a donor to make the minimum commitment with the understanding that funds will be built up to this figure over five or so years.

In general, books purchased with expendable gifts should be plated with an attractive general plate that can have appropriate names typed on it. However, sometimes donors of very substantial amounts, say $50,000, wish the money to be expended rather than established as an endowment. In this case and in the case of all but the smallest endowments, the library should be prepared to have special bookplates designed and printed. Much of the success of a program of book funds may turn on the quality of design, paper,

118

and typography that go into the memorial bookplates; therefore the objective should be overall excellence. Good graphic design talent, whether on or off campus, will be worth the comparatively modest investment that is involved.

THE UNIVERSITY BOOK SELECTION PROCESS

Book selection in the modern university library differs in two important respects from what it was a generation ago: it is much more a library responsibility, and it is infinitely more varied and complex. The two factors are not unrelated. As book selection has become bigger (in terms of number of items) and broader (in terms of number of countries, agencies, learned societies) and more varied (in terms of the methods used to insure adequate coverage), the library has had to establish more elaborate machinery to carry out this basic mission. Other members of the university community, like the faculty, still play an important role, but it tends to be in the form of specialized consultation on major purchases or the recommendation of isolated titles.

One of the distinguishing characteristics of a research library, as opposed to a large public library, for example, is the catholicity of its purchasing. A university library needs to acquire broadly and in some depth. To some scholar at some point in time every publication can be important. Yet a university cannot hope to acquire "everything." So it aims for the more important slice of "everything" and relies upon the Farmington Plan[1] and the National Program for Acquisitions and Cataloging (see Chapter 6, pp. 182-4) to pro-

---

[1] The Farmington Plan is a cooperative program under which various research libraries undertook, beginning in January 1948, to bring into the United States every book and pamphlet of research significance wherever published. Various libraries accepted responsibility for certain subjects or areas and attempted to collect fairly exhaustively therein, to catalog receipts promptly, and to see that they were listed in the National Union Catalog of the Library of Congress. Later in the Plan's history, cooperating libraries sought to alleviate the serial selection problem by having overseas dealers send an initial issue of a serial for evaluation and possible subsequent subscription. The name comes from Farmington, Connecticut, where the plan was discussed for the first time, in the form it eventually assumed, at the home of Wilmarth Lewis on October 9, 1942, at a meeting of the Council of the Librarian of Congress of which Mr. Lewis was chairman. Principal architects of the proposal were Keyes Metcalf (Harvard), Julian Boyd (Princeton), and Archibald MacLeish, Librarian of Congress.

tect its flanks and interlibrary loan to come to the rescue. Yet, as Verner W. Clapp noted,

> there is no substitute for immediacy — for having the wanted book on the shelf. We have recently been reminded by the custodian of our greatest university library that "borrowing by interlibrary loan is a poor substitute for a good book collection." Immediacy is so important to us that we are willing for its sake to make genuine sacrifices — sacrifices such as overcrowded shelves, such as forgoing a little larger slice of "everything," or forgoing better bibliographical control of that portion of "everything" which we now possess, of even forgoing standard bibliographical treatment of the material which we have already in our own collections. These are very genuine alternatives.[2]

And thus the burden falls back on the library to choose which items to acquire from all the world output of five hundred years. The response to this enigma is what sets one library ahead of another. The response is formed of the thousands of decisions on acquisition options that are made each year by the librarians and faculty. Their judgment, their selectivity is the crucial element. As Donald Coney expressed it:

> But what books shall we have in our uncomprehensive single libraries? What books must there be for those who move in the orbit of my library building? How shall we select those books? The dragon of "everything" is not really dead until we have fashioned the lance of selectivity — and used it.[3]

The catholicity of purchasing is matched by a heavy emphasis on foreign publications. This results in the acquisition of more elusive and ephemeral material and in substantial effort to obtain books from countries that are notable for the lack of organization in their book trade and lack of trade bibliography. The sheer number of different titles to be acquired has made title-by-title selection of materials of obvious research value anachronistic not to say prohibitively expensive for the preponderance of accessions.

The confluence of these several forces and factors has led to a multiplicity of selection techniques. These techniques, by and large, result in the receipt of a broader range of materials with a much

[2] *Changing Patterns of Scholarship and the Future of Research Libraries*, pp. 69-70.
[3] *Ibid.*, p. 87.

reduced need for decision making on individual titles. This, in turn, has meant that the library must monitor several major programs of acquisition, and the faculty is called on for expert advice in more highly specialized situations, usually involving heavy expenditures for a collection or even a single title. (Procurement techniques are treated in the next chapter whereas this section covers some of the same aspects as part of the book selection methodology.)

All publications of university presses may be obtained automatically through standing orders. If this arrangement is sufficiently publicized and understood, members of the faculty and of the selection and order-searching staff can assume that one copy of each such title will be received, and they need be concerned only about the requirement for second or added copies.

Blanket orders may be used domestically or in foreign countries. This is an arrangement under which a vendor is authorized to send one copy of each publication of research significance within certain restraints or with certain exceptions. A blanket order may cover all the publications of a country or be limited to a major field like history. General blanket orders may specifically exclude certain subjects or types of material not of interest (e.g., veterinary medicine, textbooks, pamphlets, and serials), and if unwanted items are received, there is usually provision for their return by the library. It is not unusual to provide for receipt of the first issue of a new serial, with decision reserved to the library about its continuance. If it is decided to subscribe, the subscription may be placed through the blanket order dealer or, more probably, through a regular serial vendor.

Under a foreign blanket order contract, the dealer usually agrees to airmail one or more copies of the current issue of the national bibliography, indicating by a check or other symbol the items that have been selected. The library's specialized selection staff can review unchecked items and make additional choices. These supplementary selections are ordered by returning a copy of the checked bibliography to the dealer. Such an arrangement precludes any undue delay in receipt of all desired publications, whether selected by the dealer or the library staff.

It is also advantageous for university libraries to arrange "on approval" programs to cover certain subject fields, usually for domestic imprints. Under such an arrangement, a vendor undertakes to provide a copy of each important work in a field like science before or immediately after publication. Library specialists can review these books with copy in hand. Those that are wanted for the collection are forwarded for cataloging (the dealer having supplied a completed order form to expedite the purchase); rejected items are picked up by the dealer, if local, or shipped back to him at frequent intervals.

National acquisitions programs are also having an impact on the larger university libraries. Under the Public Law 480 program operated by the Library of Congress, LC is authorized by Congress to purchase books with excess soft currencies generated in foreign countries by the sale of surplus agricultural commodities. Such currencies are available only in selected countries which are of widely varying importance as originators of publications of research significance. Among those that are, or have been, the loci of PL 480 operations are Indonesia, India, Pakistan, the United Arab Republic, Israel, and Yugoslavia. The drying up of surplus currencies and political troubles have interfered with some of these operations. However, the program has been of immense significance because, in each area of operation, multiple sets of publications (much like general blanket orders) have been obtained for the Library of Congress and for from twelve to eighteen other research libraries specializing in the areas in question. A recipient library is not obliged to keep every publication sent to it, but it is encouraged to offer unwanted publications to other libraries, and it must undertake to make available on interlibrary loan or otherwise publications obtained under the program, and it may not dispose of unwanted publications by sale.

The great drawback with the PL 480 program has been its fortuitous, haphazard nature from the standpoint of research library interests. Operations have been confined to those countries which happen to have surplus U.S.-owned soft currencies. By and large, Africa, Latin America, and the Far East have been excluded.

Federal financial support of college and university libraries authorized by Title II of the Higher Education Act of 1965 provides special inducements to cooperative undertakings. It may be anticipated that groups of libraries within states and regions may find it advantageous to share resources to an ever-increasing extent. The classic example of such a mechanism, long antedating the 1965 act,

One shipment of PL 480 books, reflecting the types of materials in foreign languages which require specialized staff, often imposing special staff and space burdens due to delays in processing — Yale University

is the Center for Research Libraries (formerly the Midwest Inter-Library Center) in Chicago. Started as a depository library for little-used materials by a group of midwestern universities, the Center has been enlarged to national membership and continues a program initiated early in its history of acquiring on behalf of member libraries certain categories of materials of importance but of such relatively infrequent use that a single copy should serve all members. Foreign college catalogs, foreign government documents, and foreign dissertations are examples of materials so acquired.

It is surely evident that blanket orders and sweeping national programs like PL 480 have an impact on the selection process. By a reverse twist, the problem becomes one of selecting-out publications that arrive automatically. To do this promptly and effectively requires very specialized staff that is more or less continuously available. This fact, together with the general increase in the selection

burden brought about by more ample book budgets, has made it essential to move the prime responsibility from faculty to library staff. Most university (and all other general research) libraries have engaged specialist bibliographers or curators whose training is often at the Ph.D. level and emphasizes linguistic and subject competence rather than librarianship per se. These curatorships have usually been built around language areas (Slavic, Romance, Far Eastern, Germanic, Hispanic) but there is also a rationale for curatorships in areas like the behavioral sciences, medieval studies, Latin America, and Africa. Furthermore, the general level of departmental librarians and reference librarians, increasingly selected for subject specialization, constitutes a subsidiary level of curatorial competence that is most useful in collection-building. As a result, as many as forty librarians and linguistic or subject scholars on the library staff may make varying but substantial contributions to the selection process.

Faculty and students should be encouraged to call the library's attention to needed materials, and faculty should be consulted by curators, particularly on costly purchases like long retrospective serial sets, microtext sets, and expensive individual items. To make this part of the program work, lines of communication need to be established between the phalanx of library selection experts and faculty members. Sometimes it is a natural development for a library-oriented faculty member to provide this liaison. Occasionally a department will designate a liaison representative voluntarily or can be encouraged to do so. Some departmental library committees designate one of their members to undertake such responsibility. However it develops, faculty support and interest should be encouraged and cultivated. A shared responsibility may be organized as follows:

Slavic

The weekly Russian national bibliography *Knizhnaia letopis'* is regularly checked in history by Professors P. and F., in economics by Professors G. and B., in government and law by Professor F., in language by Professor L., in literature by Librarian G. following Professor M.'s pattern of last year, in art by Professor S. and in bibliography by Librarian G. This bibliography is used as a final check on whether the Library is getting the material the faculty feels it should. Librarian G. checks the weekly bibliographical bulletin *Novye knigi* in the above-mentioned fields. Those items published in limited editions are requested on exchange. The Lenin Library and Leningrad Public Library supply many of them.

Out-of-print lists are shown to the faculty members mentioned. In addition, Professor S. checks literature, Librarian G. Armenian history, Professor P. Georgian history, and Professor P. indicates Middle East items which he feels we should have. He would like us to do more in the way of acquiring Russian translations of the literary writers of the various peoples of the U.S.S.R. — Kazakh, Kirghiz, Tatar, etc. — since Russian is the only language in which these people probably will be read in this country. Dr. S. also selects material on the Middle East.

Professor W. does all the checking in the social sciences and humanities in Polish. This includes the weekly national bibliography *Przewodnik bibliograficzny* as well as the weekly pre-publication listing by Ars Polona called *Zapowiedzi wydawnicze.*

Library Assistant K. and Librarian G. check the weekly Czech national bibliography *Česke knihy* in the same fields already mentioned for Russian and Polish. The monthly Slovak national bibliography *Slovenské knihy* is similarly checked in the humanities and social sciences.

Professor L. checks the language section of the monthly Bulgarian national bibliography *Bulgarski knigopis.* Professor W. checks in history. Librarian D. checks literature and Librarian G. bibliography.

The same holds true for the semimonthly Yugoslav national bibliography *Bibliografija Jugoslavije,* except that Library Assistant S. checks Yugoslav literature.

Faculty members are among the most mobile people alive. This is a natural consequence of sabbaticals, foreign area studies, overseas consulting, foreign campuses, and university participation in programs of the Agency for International Development. Graduate students are only slightly less mobile. The library can profit from this fact by enlisting the aid of faculty members and mature students in foreign purchasing. Under the curatorial system, the library will also find it profitable to send some of its own specialists abroad on purchasing missions. Whether or not the overseas emissary is a member of the faculty, a graduate student, or a member of the library staff, careful advance planning is essential to the successful accomplishment of each mission. Want lists can prevent wasteful duplication and convey to foreign dealers the seriousness of the representative's intentions. Adequately prepared representatives can more than save the cost of a journey. In some fields, items cost one half to one tenth of what they would cost through domestic middlemen. On the other hand, a wheeling and dealing purchasing venture without a precise goal or want list can produce rather fantastic duplication by faculty or staff.

It will be desirable to make on-the-spot purchases in some countries. Therefore, representatives will have to carry some funds in the form of traveler's checks or letters of credit. Wherever possible, however, purchases should be made on a contingency basis subject to confirmation and payment from the library in the United States.

Properly instructed representatives may lay the groundwork for productive exchanges and future commercial relationships as well as perform direct purchasing. Such responsibility should be entrusted to senior, well-instructed people to avoid commitments that may prove to be impossible of execution and therefore productive of bad feeling.

It is worthwhile to analyze outgoing interlibrary loan requests to identify particular weaknesses or areas of interest needing attention. This can be a practical and direct device for strengthening collections.

University libraries in this country usually have special access to publications of their own university, a fact which makes exchanges more advantageous than would otherwise be the case. Books of the local university press can usually be obtained at very substantial discounts, and departmental or school journals may be obtained free or at cost.

Deposit is another principal method of obtaining materials, especially government documents. Deposit of Federal or state publications implies certain obligations as to retention, disposal, and service to nonuniversity users (consider PL 480 discussed above). But this is usually an important, easily available channel for obtaining publications. Unfortunately, the publications included in a Federal depository set do not encompass the total output of official documents. There is a surprising array of non-GPO publications (not issued through the Government Printing Office) which agencies themselves generate directly or indirectly. The Library of Congress has, for some years, operated the Documents Expediting Service as

126

Example of generous space with adjacent shelving near a shipping dock to handle incoming and outgoing books, furniture, and other equipment required in a university library — Sterling Memorial Library, Yale University

a central mechanism to track down and obtain such publications for participating libraries. Cost of participation ranges from $175 to $525. Each participating library determines the amount of its contribution. The size of the contribution and precedence in joining the project determine the subscriber's priority rating in the distribution of materials that are in short supply.

Foreign and international documents present special difficulties. Many foreign nations lack the highly centralized control that characterizes much of the official publishing of the United States. Therefore, it is necessary to correspond with each separate ministry to obtain its publications, and such correspondence must be conducted in the principal language of the country if the effort is to succeed. Certain regional associations, for example in Africa, are so inadequately staffed or funded that their publications are virtually unobtainable except through highly personalized and priced arrangements. The ability to establish direct contact through the visit of a library emissary in such situations may make the difference between success and failure.

ENCOURAGEMENT OF GIFTS

Receipt of gifts is the passive way of collecting, in contrast to the active ways described above. Gifts can be a mixed blessing: a good source of publications and of revenue if properly handled, or a nightmare if indiscriminately administered. Gifts of no obvious use or resale value should be diplomatically declined or directed to institutions that can benefit from them. An occasional exception is justified when the library does not wish to alienate or offend a person whose good will is desired. Gifts that may seem ordinary, such as long runs of current news magazines, may prove valuable in replacing worn-out or missing issues. Gift monographs are often a source of replacement or desirable extra copies. Many good but unneeded books can be sold, thereby augmenting unrestricted book funds.

As is the case with memorial gifts (see p. 118), a successful gift program usually involves a great deal of correspondence. Donors should be thanked by the library director for each gift, and suitable expressions may come from the president of the university for large gifts or for those from good friends of the university. Many libraries have found handsomely printed acknowledgment forms a way of simplifying this paper work, at the same time providing the donor with attractive evidence of his generosity.

Gifts of money and of books — whether of individual titles or entire collections — are a classic way for a university library to build extraordinary strengths. The effort expended in relations with collectors can be very rewarding to a library director who enjoys books and understands the enthusiasm of others who do, and the library is sure to benefit from such effort. The amount of time devoted to relations with donors will vary depending on the interests of the director and the array of problems that confront him, but it is safe to state that this effort will occupy a discernible amount of the time of the head of every university library.

A number of university libraries have benefited greatly by organizing a group of Friends or Associates. Several questions should be answered before attempting to proceed with such a group: Who is going to bear the major staff responsibility? Who are the people who can form a nucleus of such a group and assume the burdens of leadership? What is the breadth of membership desired and what dues structure is appropriate? What is the focus of the Friends' effort? What are to be the perquisites of membership? the program?

A successful Friends group will not succeed without a great deal of highly personalized attention of an important official of the library. Two obvious candidates for this role are the director and the chief librarian of the Rare Book or Special Collections Department. Although one may assume the primary responsibility, both of these officials are certain to be deeply involved if the group is to be successful.

In a university, the obvious constituents of a Friends organization are the alumni, but other valuable members may and should be enlisted outside the university community. It is desirable if several enthusiastic people can be persuaded to assist in the formation of the group and in soliciting broader membership. The breadth of the membership, the objectives of the Friends, the dues structure, and the perquisites of membership are interrelated. Few such groups have long remained extremely exclusive with dues in three or four figures. The most successful organizations seem to be those that have had a broad charter from the beginning. Their founders have stressed close personal interest in the library; its general growth and effectiveness; articulation of its needs and problems to others; and not mere "money-getting." This has meant a fairly large and economically diverse membership and a scale of membership dues that may range from $10 to $25 at the minimum for general membership, $50 to $100 for sustaining membership, to $1000 or more for life or contributing membership. The dues are not the principal method of financing major purchases. These are handled, depending on their magnitude, by a wide appeal or by an appeal to those known to have extraordinary means. The more successful groups may regularly contribute $200,000 or more to the university library. Beyond this, the members communicate the needs of the library to nonmembers, explain special problems, and are constantly on the alert for collectors who may be willing to give important single items or collections to the university.

Friends groups are likely to support a newsletter, gazette, or bulletin or receive as a perquisite of membership a more general scholarly periodical published by the library. Free library privileges are also commonly granted members. One or more major functions will be arranged each year for the Friends. These will range from invitations to exhibit openings and speeches of a literary or biblio-philic nature, to dinners with speeches and business meetings. Not uncommonly, several of these events may be combined in a major undertaking.

No matter how broadly based a Friends organization may be in theory, it is likely to concentrate on rare and special collections. Those who join such groups are likely to be bibliophiles and collectors themselves, and their interests are certain to affect the nature of the Friends organization. The challenge to the director is to channel this enthusiasm to areas of major need, thereby building strengths that could otherwise not be achieved, or through such channeling to release general funds that may be used to benefit other, more prosaic and less attractive but nonetheless essential parts of the library's program.

COLLECTING SPECIAL TYPES OF MATERIALS

Government Documents

Much has been said earlier in this chapter about government documents. These are an indispensable source of information which involve modest purchasing expense per item but substantial personnel costs for acquisition, cataloging, and servicing. No university library can forgo access to a substantial number of Federal, state, and municipal documents as well as foreign documents and documents of international organizations and agencies. The extent of the university's commitment to international studies, foreign and international law, monetary policy, comparative political and economic studies, or international education will affect the degree to which foreign and international documents should be collected. Technical reports emanating from government-sponsored research are quasi-government documents which will also be needed in universities with a strong scientific or engineering orientation. It is likely that there will be some difference of opinion as to the importance of technical reports. Many seasoned engineers and scientists believe that the information in such reports, if significant, will find its way into major publications and that great staff effort is not justified in acquiring and servicing them. Nonetheless, a collection of such reports will attract substantial faculty and student use as well as requests from local industry.

130

One means of displaying current issues of periodicals and serials prior to collating, binding, and shelving in the classified collections — Gest Oriental Library, Princeton University

Book Collections

Serials

Serials are likely to form the backbone of the university library's collections. It is not uncommon for large universities to subscribe to 25,000-50,000 serials on a current basis. Six to ten thousand subscriptions may be for scientific publications alone.

With serials, it isn't the original cost but the upkeep that counts. The initial subscription may cost a few dollars (although serials are likely to average substantially more than monographs); but once the subscription has begun, the cost of maintenance is built in from year to year, and the total annual serial bill can easily constitute 20-25 per cent of the total book budget. Serials are expensive to catalog; each issue must be checked in, frequently more than once (in a central serial file and in a departmental file); control of unbound issues is difficult; preparation for binding is, in total, a huge undertaking; binding costs are staggering in the aggregate; and the claiming of issues not received is a burdensome, often unproductive, but essential chore.

Serial selection should be scrupulously reviewed in the light of the foregoing factors. The faculty can perform a real service for the

library in exercising reasonable restraint in demanding subscriptions to new serials and occasionally reviewing the titles in selected fields as a basis for discontinuing subscriptions. It should be remembered that 90 per cent of the citations in *Chemical Abstracts* come from about 1,000 journals and that 10 per cent of the citations come from 9,000 journals. Should a library of moderate means concentrate on the first 1,000 or struggle in a vain attempt to acquire 10,000? The case in other disciplines may not be so clear, but the need to impose some restrictions where funds are not unlimited suggests a careful selection program.

Libraries vary in their methods of subscribing to serials. A few attempt to deal directly with publishers, but this may place a heavy burden on the library. Specialized vendors can be effective in handling subscriptions, in responding to claims, and in offering competitive subscription rates. If subscriptions are placed for from three to five years, special discounts may be granted; such an arrangement also lessens the library's renewal and bill-paying workload. It is almost always possible to convince the financial staff of a private university of these advantages, and many universities supported by public funds have succeeded in establishing this method of operation although it violates certain principles of public financing, especially the requirement that current expenditures should represent current and not future obligations.

Microtexts

Publication of microtexts seems to be of increasing commercial interest, and every library will be faced annually with a series of decisions in regard to acquisitions of this type. Pricing is often irrational, and at times the same publications are available in competing forms at widely different prices. There are many other technical and practical liabilities, as described in Chapter 6, pp. 161-4. The library profession needs a Fair Trade Commission or a Consumers' Report that will analyze these factors on each major microtext project. Until such guidance is available, libraries will all too often support unworthy projects and indirectly lay the foundation for future problems and expense of incalculable magnitude.

Despite shortcomings and caveats, there are meritorious microtext projects. They will require the most careful consideration as to editorial merit, basic importance, technical quality, bibliographic control, and price. Whenever possible the technical quality should be tested before a long-term or major purchase commitment is made. Residual hypo[4] in microfilm or poor resolution in any type of microtext may be a good reason to forgo participation in a project.

Reprints

The unattractiveness of microtexts for many purposes, particularly for heavily used materials, has stimulated a fairly active market for reprints. These may be very limited editions produced by the Xerox Copyflo process or offset editions of greater size if the market warrants. These projects are often developed with the cooperation of libraries and library associations, and they fulfill a real need because of the economies made possible by modern methods of duplication. It is well to inquire whether or not permanent-durable paper is used in these projects since most of the items thus republished are needed because the inferior paper in the original edition has disintegrated in many libraries. Any library with a heavy program of retrospective buying, particularly in serials, may find that it can save thousands of dollars by taking advantage of available reprints rather than searching in the out-of-print market for originals, with the latter sometimes offering poorer quality paper. Some reprint projects are built around subject disciplines; this possibility should be investigated in a general effort to strengthen collections in special fields.

Despite the increase in the availability of microtexts and reprints, the size of the effort in retrospective collecting is so great that a university library will be heavily involved in searches in the o.p. market. It is sometimes possible and profitable to recruit a staff member from the book trade if the volume of this work is large enough. An experienced man can also literally work wonders in turning up o.p. materials with rapidity and at attractive prices. If a library has to place orders for o.p. books with a vendor rather than use its own specialist, it is advisable to pick a firm that specializes in this type of transaction. Vendors that specialize in current trade books will often perform poorly with o.p. orders.

---

[4] Residual hypo is the unstable chemical, ammonium or sodium thiosulfate, which should have been washed out of the film in the process of development but which because of inadequate treatment remains in sufficient quantity to decompose at room temperature and form by-products that destroy silver images.

Book Collections

Rare Books

Libraries will vary considerably in the zeal with which they build rare book collections. Too many libraries have diverted funds from basic but commonplace research materials to have a rare book collection or a few examples of conspicuous consumption. Rare book collections should, as a general rule, be firmly grounded in the academic needs of the institution. Almost any university library of any age will have on its open shelves *bona fide* rarities that should have the care and oversight that all rare books deserve. These rarities may have attained their status through the passage of time. Curators and other selection specialists should be alert to these possibilities and should recommend for transfer to the rare book room items so identified. (A guide to selection is included in Chapter 8, pp. 257-9.)

Any library will need to purchase some books that are by definition rare, not just because they are expensive but because they are in exceedingly short supply. This can easily be true in English literature; it will surely be the case in Renaissance studies. The advice offered here is that most university libraries will do well to use general funds for instances of this kind only if the purchases bear directly on the academic program. This is not to say that a rare book program is out of the question for even the newest or smallest university.

Among the alumni and friends of a university are likely to be many avid collectors or affluent individuals whom the library can interest in supporting specialized collections. The forthright cultivation of these people may produce gifts of books and money that make a special collections or rare book program possible without detriment to the more prosaic research needs of the library. And since excellence attracts excellence, the existence of a strong collection of this kind may attract other gifts, particularly if it can be demonstrated that the collections are suitably housed, cared for, exhibited, and otherwise publicized to the scholarly world. Sometimes gifts of this kind contain provisos that they will be kept together forever and be designated by a certain name. This may or may not be possible or advisable, and a commitment of this kind should not be made without careful consideration. Nothing can so hamstring a library with the passage of time as restrictions to keep collections intact.

134

Book Collections

Manuscripts

Manuscripts have many of the characteristics of rare books or other special collections. An ill-considered program of acquisitions may bring in a great deal of material of minimum educational significance. Manuscripts are expensive to organize, to make available, and to house. Intelligently acquired, they can be a superb supplement to book materials and of very great research potential for undergraduates and graduates. Leads to manuscripts will often come through alumni and friends. The daily newspaper provides a surprising number of references to collections that can be obtained with proper approaches to the owners or custodians. The head of the manuscript department will probably be an ardent acquirer, and hopefully, a good organizer. In many instances, this individual will be expert in local or regional history and can "talk the language" of owners of manuscripts. Hence such a person may be the library's best specialist in acquiring collections. The director or one of his deputies should approve in advance the effort to get any large collection because of the workload and space problems inherent in such an acquisition, and in the case of very important collections the director himself will want to be involved in negotiations.

Both rare books and manuscripts, and especially the latter, should be acquired within a very carefully developed acquisitions policy. In general, a university should concentrate in the several fields of its major academic interest. It may be useful to have a special committee to advise on and solicit materials for such a collection. A well-considered statement of acquisitions policy at Yale follows:

> Although practically every school and departmental library at Yale engages in the acquisition of manuscripts in the area relating to its particular subject matter interest, the two chief manuscript collecting agencies in the Yale Library system are the Beinecke Rare Book and Manuscript Library and the Sterling Memorial Library.
>
> In the Beinecke Library all materials are considered to be a part of what is known as the "General Collection" or of one of the special collections. The so-called General Collection is the direct outgrowth of the former Rare Book collection of the Yale Library. It is to a large extent a vast collection of books and manuscripts relating to British writers covering the whole period from the 17th century to the present. (There is also, however, a large group of medieval manuscripts and rare manuscripts from all over the world in the General Collec-

tion.) A large part of the General Collection is comprised of materials donated by wealthy collectors or purchased from funds made available by benefactors of the library. In recent decades, as a result of large donations or purchases, there has also been established the extensive Yale Collection of American Literature, a Yale Collection of Western Americana and the Yale Collection of German Literature. In general, I think it is fair to say that in its manuscript collecting activities the Beinecke Library has been oriented chiefly in the direction of the needs and interests of the university's English Department and, more recently, with the establishment of the Yale Collection of American Literature, of the Department of American Studies.

The manuscript collections in the Sterling Library are generally called "historical manuscripts" as distinguished from the "literary manuscripts" which predominate in the Beinecke Library. This very loose distinction chiefly means that the materials in the Beinecke Library (with the exception of the Yale Collection of Western Americana) are of greater interest to scholars working in the field of British and American literature than they are to historians. The manuscript collections in the Sterling Library, on the other hand, are used primarily by historians and other scholars in the social sciences. The chief faculty relationship has been with the History Department. The manuscript collections in the Sterling Library until some decades ago were largely collections of colonial, Revolutionary War and Federal period family archives of the Connecticut area. These were later supplemented with large groups of papers of Yale officials, personal papers of important Yale faculty members, and prominent business and professional men holding Yale degrees. In the last few decades Sterling Library has begun making an effort to acquire for its "historical manuscripts" collection the personal papers of any individuals who have played a significant role in contemporary public affairs, and has obtained such important collections as the papers of John W. Davis, Edward T. House and Henry Stimson. The distinction between what is placed in the custody of Beinecke Library and Sterling Library is becoming lost, however, as Sterling Library has in the last few years acquired for its "historical manuscripts" Collections the papers of men like Max Lerner and Walter Lippmann.

As is always the case, acquisition policy has been affected by the particular interests of members of the faculty of the Department of History. For instance, during the 1950's, because of the special interest of a particular faculty member, Sterling Library acquired huge quantities of older business records of businesses in this general area of Connecticut. The History Department no longer has this interest and the emphasis on acquisition of business records has been dropped. Some of the more bulky and less valuable collections of this kind of material are now being given to other libraries.

Generally speaking, unlike the Beinecke Library, the "historical manuscripts" activity in Sterling Library has made no effort to acquire rare individual manuscripts, and it almost never purchases manuscripts. Emphasis is placed on acquisition by donation of large groups of personal papers of individuals, which, as a collective entity, have high research potential. Little importance is attached to rarity in the collector's sense, and the donation of single discrete items is discouraged, unless they are related to other holdings.

Manuscripts are also collected at Yale by the Science Library, and by the libraries of the following departments and schools: Music, Law, Divinity, Medicine, Art and Architecture. Hitherto there has been little or no coordination between the manuscript activities of the school and departmental libraries and those of Beinecke and Sterling Libraries. Discussions looking toward the formation of a policy on this matter will be held shortly. For instance, the interest and participation of the Yale Law School in the Civil Rights movement of the past ten or fifteen years has led it to request that a manuscript collection and activity on that subject be initiated, but the material that is gathered will be deposited in Sterling Library.

Nothing has here been said about the extensive archives of Yale University which are administered by Sterling Library as a part of its manuscripts and archives activity.

Other Materials

Sound recordings of music and the spoken word can play an important role in a university. Musicians find the interpretation of instrumental or vocal selections by the great artists of the early twentieth century invaluable in the study of their field. To hear Theodore Roosevelt, Franklin Delano Roosevelt, Robert Frost, T. S. Eliot, Adolf Hitler, or Benito Mussolini is to experience a dimension of reality that no description can provide. As a result, many university libraries have built collections running into tens of thousands of items on discs, cylinders, and tapes as an important adjunct to the book collection. Very few of these need actually to be purchased. Private collectors abound who have amassed such collections. The problem is to define the limit of the collection to assure some coherence and to avoid rampant duplication. Tapes of speeches and performances of important visitors to campus may be added to such a collection through a relatively modest investment of staff time in setting up recording equipment. In such cases, however, it is essential to obtain a signed release or authorization to make the recording and to use it under controlled conditions (usually precluding further duplication for distribution purposes).

Documentary films may also be a library responsibility. It is possible to fulfill an active need through a well-organized service that borrows or rents such films (at the borrowing department's expense). However, such procedure involves inevitable delays, and if funds permit, it may be decided to build an in-house collection of motion picture films and filmstrips. (This will probably also entail the provision of projection equipment.) Because of the very considerable expense of films, there should be reasonable assurance that one that is purchased will prove useful in the university setting. A film curator with substantial experience may be able to predict this, but in many instances, prepurchase consultation with a faculty member or members may be desirable.

Rather than the common guides and trade bibliographies used in book selection, specialized tools must be used in the selection of films. The *Educational Media Index* is a useful general guide in this field. The *Educators Guide* series (*. . . to Free Films, . . . to Free Filmstrips, . . . to Free Tapes, Scripts, Transcriptions*) provides very useful annual guides to new materials. Among other specialized selection tools used almost daily by a film curator are *Film Evaluation Guide* (and supplements) published by the Educational Film Library Association; Indiana University's *Educational Motion Pictures*; Pennsylvania State University's *Educational Films, Slides, Filmstrips, 1959-62* and supplements; the University of California's *Films 1967-69*; Washington State University's *Films for Teaching*; and Florida State University's *Educational Films*.

A great deal of social science data is now available in machine-readable form, and there is sure to be a substantial demand for this by both faculty and students. Even more than films, such material is expensive and should be selected with great care and after considerable consultation with the faculty. It is unlikely that a university will be able to afford all the desirable material available, and therefore rational selection must be the rule. If there is no central service, individual researchers will flounder around trying to locate tapes reputedly on campus but "lost" for all practical purposes.

138

Again, as in the case of films, census and voting data cannot be used without ancillary equipment, i.e., the computer. But beyond this, the user of social science data in machine-readable form must manipulate the data to produce specialized results. This can only be done through computer programming, and it is exceptional to find a student or faculty member in the social sciences who is capable of devising his own program. Either the library or the computation center must provide such service. This is a worthy (but expensive) library service, and the library may restrict its assistance to selecting, housing, organizing, listing, and lending tapes. This in itself will be invaluable if a complete service, including programming, cannot be offered.

CREATING SPECIAL LIBRARY COLLECTIONS

Undergraduate Libraries

The establishment of a separate, full-fledged undergraduate library presents special problems in collection building. In all probability the collection will largely duplicate materials elsewhere in the library system, usually by as much as 90 per cent. But the problem is to select the relatively few books that are particularly appropriate for undergraduates. Such a collection should be alive, basic, and carefully shaped to the students' needs. An upper limit of 125,000 to 150,000 volumes (meaning 85,000-100,000 titles) is a long-range goal with half that number being a fully acceptable starting point. Copies of shelflists or catalogs of existing undergraduate libraries like Lamont at Harvard, the Undergraduate Library at the University of Michigan, the Meyer Library at Stanford, or the California New Campuses List may provide a valuable basis on which to build. Titles from these sources can be arranged by subjects and submitted to faculty and library specialists for refinement (meaning deletions and additions). The process should be based on detailed policies as to the purpose of the library. (See table, pp. 140-1.)

Will it aim primarily at lower-division students? Will it cover all undergraduate course-related needs including collateral reading, except perhaps in the physical or biological sciences? Will it provide a strong support to general education by providing the "best" scholarly works in all subjects relevant to the undergraduate curriculum, thereby forming a well-balanced and comprehensive collec-

139

tion such as a student would find in a college library had he gone to a good college instead of a university for his undergraduate program? Will part of the needs be left to residence libraries? Will reference works be limited but a few items heavily duplicated? Will there be special dependence on the central research library for microtexts (e.g., the New York *Times*), government documents, foreign language materials, audio and visual materials, and back runs of the major periodicals?

If a collection is to be created more or less from scratch, it may require fully three to five years of effort depending on the collection policies, the material at hand, the effort to be expended in obtaining out-of-print works, and the size of staff to manage the program. Such a separate library can be a boon to the undergraduate student. One must remember, however, that it requires substantial professional staff effort to maintain the quality of collections. A poorly selected or outdated undergraduate library collection is a disservice to education.

Residence Libraries

Library collections in student residences are common in many universities. Harvard's house libraries are outstanding examples in this genre. Each collection there averages 10,000-15,000 volumes, well- (and sometimes superbly) housed under the supervision of a student librarian. Such libraries offer excellent study facilities and extensive enough collections to accommodate a fairly broad range of interests. The Julian Street Library at Princeton is also notable for its quality (a catalog has been compiled by Warren B. Kuhn

	HARVARD		MICHIGAN	
	Per cent	Volumes	Per cent	Volumes
Literature and language	37.5	14,820	31.0	16,430
History	18.2	7,215	17.0	9,010
Social sciences	17.3	6,825	18.0	9,540
Religion, philosophy, and psychology	8.8	3,525	12.0	6,360
Fine arts	6.9	2,730	8.0	4,240
Science	11.3	4,485	8.0	4,240
Miscellaneous (General and Reference)	—	—	6.0	3,180
TOTALS		39,600		53,000

and published by Bowker, 1966). Few universities approach this excellence in residence libraries, although some universities being developed on the residential college plan are attempting similar libraries. These are to be applauded and, where they can be financed, are a mark of quality education. The building of collections of this type rests on the highly selective principle already enunciated for separate undergraduate libraries. If the houses or colleges are built around specialized subject fields, the collections should reflect these interests.

The more common residence library is extremely modest — a few hundred or a thousand volumes. The use of the word *library* is probably a misnomer because such collections are rarely more than a few basic reference works sprinkled with some undergraduate texts, a few popular periodicals, and an abortive collection reflecting the interest of a sometime curator. Such collections are study facilities rather than libraries. If they are the responsibility of the university library, at least a part-time staff member needs to oversee their operation. Emphasis in collection building should be on general reference books plus standard works in fields of undergraduate interest. These can sometimes be assembled from gift duplicates or be gradually developed with a moderate expenditure of book funds.

Branch Libraries

Branch and departmental collections will vary widely in size. Some collections are almost literally working collections consisting of the standard handbooks and the half dozen important journals in a specialized field like micropaleontology, orchids, plasma physics,

CALIFORNIA NEW CAMPUSES LIST		STANFORD	
Per cent	Titles	Per cent	Titles
32.2	17,203	32.5	12,735
18.7	10,006	20.2	7,920
20.8	11,101	19.1	7,470
8.9	4,779	9.4	3,668
7.5	3,977	6.6	2,565
9.5	5,083	10.9	4,253
2.4	1,261	1.3	518
	53,410		39,129

alcohol, econometrics, or hypnotism. A full-fledged departmental library is likely to have a collection of from 25,000 to 125,000 volumes in a field like earth science, biology, music, or education. The head of one of these libraries has to approach, or equal, curatorial quality. He will exercise extensive independent responsibility for selection and will probably have numerous consultations with faculty on book selection. He will supervise the expenditures of restricted book funds and will adjust his rate of spending to spread the funds throughout the year.

The preceding account assumes fully decentralized and delegated authority. Department libraries should function in this way, and most do. There should be some central monitoring of the use of book funds, and the director or the chief of the acquisitions department may have to be consulted if unusually expensive purchases have to be funded. Collections of this type will contain the preponderance of the university library holdings in the special fields represented. Acquisition, especially in science and engineering libraries, will be heavily in the serial field supplemented by standard monographs, handbooks, and other works of reference. Music libraries will include phonodiscs and phonotapes, sheet music, and scores, as well as musicological monographs, serials, and definitive sets of the works of classical composers. The departmental librarian may also serve as the selection specialist in one or several peripheral fields, recommending materials to be acquired for the main library or other parts of the system.

In contrast to the full departmental library, which is commonly a complete research library in its field, the "working library" referred to above is deliberately limited to the handbooks, journals, basic monographs, and current report literature needed to support teaching or research in a narrow field. A laboratory or office library is a working library, and book selection is strictly utilitarian.

In between these two extremes in size and function of branches there is a type of branch which corresponds in scope to the full interests of a department of instruction — not econometrics but economics, not hypnotism but psychology. This branch is also perhaps accurately called a departmental library; but the book selection is different from that of the full-fledged departmental library when the department has its main research collections in the central library. These then are essentially duplicate collections, sometimes very small (perhaps in a field like Classics), sometimes substantial (perhaps for history or English literature). A librarian is almost never directly in charge. The branch may occasionally serve almost as a graduate student lounge and seminar room. Here again the book selection is based on the young scholar's practical need for these duplicates. Such branches sometimes are in a sense rather full working libraries. And they often are supported by gifts and endowed funds since the relative luxury of buying extra copies for this type of branch with funds from general unrestricted monies is an expense hard to justify.

DUPLICATION AND PRUNING OF COLLECTIONS

As explained in Chapter 3, there is an inevitable amount of duplication in any research library. University libraries, because of the dispersal of facilities and the existence of interdisciplinary research and class demand, will require extensive duplication. If this is completely uncontrolled, it can result in a heavy drain on already inadequate funds. The traditional inadequacy of funds imposes its own kind of control. Expensive items should come under scrutiny in the director's office if a system of approval is required for such items. This offers a mechanism for direct control. If the library has a supervisor of science libraries or of departmental libraries, that official should exercise some control over duplication. The practical distinction to be made is between duplication that is justifiable and that which is not.

Duplication for circulation purposes is usually more easily justified, and adequate provision should be made for this requirement. Books of general circulation should be duplicated at the rate of one copy for approximately ten reservations or "notify" requests that readers have placed on that title. Books for course reserve can be duplicated by a formula (see Chapter 7, pp. 216-17).

Unnecessary duplication is most difficult to prevent where there are numerous autonomous libraries with overlapping interests. The solution lies in close working relationships among those involved in collection building, in frequent consultation by telephone, in a tradition of sharing the cost of important and expensive items, in some mechanism for regular meetings such as a monthly acquisitions council, and in written understandings as to division of fields or chronological specialization. That such a program can work has been proved in a number of university libraries. Failure usually can be traced to defective machinery or personality clashes rather than to the inherent impossibility of a viable system.

There is probably no university library director who has not been asked by a university official or trustee why more books cannot be discarded in the hope that an expensive library building can be postponed. Reference to the annual statistics of most university libraries will indicate that there are substantial withdrawals each year. On the average, about 5 per cent as many books are discarded as are acquired. Good housekeeping and the pressures for space are likely to force some weeding of outdated textbooks, agricultural experiment station reports (in a university that engages in no research or teaching requiring such materials), foreign dissertations in a field left to a neighboring institution, old engineering handbooks, newspapers that have been replaced by microfilm, and so forth. As annual acquisitions have burgeoned, rather heroic withdrawals look pitifully small by comparison.

The withdrawal of any material requiring clearing of records involves very heavy costs. A library should probably regard the weeding process as having the same priority as selection, but few can afford the additional staff this would require. Sound weeding requires an exercise of discretion that equals or exceeds that needed for the selection process; in short, it cannot be done by unskilled people. And one person's opinion is insufficient. Faculty opinion should, by rights, be exercised as a cross-check. (It is common experience that it takes one person to select one item for acquisition, but it takes an entire faculty department to discard one item.) Anyone who has followed this lengthy and tortuous course will recall the contradictions it produces and the conflicts of opinion that result. Nonetheless there is sure to be some residue of material that can be discarded.

No formula can be enunciated here for successful weeding other than to follow some of the procedures implied in the foregoing and outlined in Chapter 7 (see p. 241); do some weeding every year; use trained talent for the job; take no single person's opinion but cross-check, preferably with the faculty; recognize the record-clearing problem; and do not expect that weeding can be undertaken without an impact on cataloging production or without additional staff.

Book Collections

SELECTED REFERENCES

Carter, Mary Duncan, and Wallace John Bonk. *Building Library Collections.* New York, Scarecrow Press, 1959.

Clapp, Verner W., *et al.* "The Balance of Conflicting Interests in the Building of Collections: Comprehensiveness versus Selectivity," in *Changing Patterns of Scholarship and the Future of Research Libraries: A Symposium in Celebration of the 200th Anniversary of the Establishment of the University of Pennsylvania Library.* Philadelphia, University of Pennsylvania Press, 1951. pp. 65–89.

Danton, J. Periam. *Book Selection and Collections: A Comparison of German and American University Libraries.* New York, Columbia University Press, 1963.

Danton, J. Periam. "The Selection of Books for College Libraries: An Examination of Certain Factors Which Affect Excellence of Selection," *Library Quarterly,* 5 (October 1935), 419–56.

Fussler, Herman H. "Acquisition Policy: A Symposium. The Larger University Library," *College and Research Libraries,* 14 (October 1953), 363–7.

McKeon, Newton F. "The Nature of the College-Library Book Collection," *Library Quarterly,* 24 (October 1954), 322–35.

Metcalf, Keyes D. "Problems of Acquisition Policy in a University Library," *Harvard Library Bulletin,* 4 (Autumn 1950), 293–303.

Metcalf, Keyes D., and Edwin E. Williams. "Acquisition Policies of the Harvard Library," *Harvard Library Bulletin,* 6 (Winter 1952), 15–26.

Orne, Jerrold, ed. "Current Trends in Collection Development in University Libraries," *Library Trends,* 15 (October 1966), 197–334.

Vosper, Robert. "Acquisition Policy — Fact or Fancy?" *College and Research Libraries,* 14 (October 1953), 367–70.

Wallace, Sarah L., ed. *Friends of the Library: Organization and Activities.* Chicago, American Library Association, 1962.

Wilson, Louis R., ed. *The Practice of Book Selection: Papers Presented Before the Library Institute.* Chicago, University of Chicago Press, 1940.

6. THE TECHNICAL PROCESSING FUNCTION

This chapter deals with those technical processing operations concerned with acquiring and preparing materials for use — acquisitions, cataloging, classification, binding, and the total preservation program — and concentrates on policy matters, standards, interdepartmental relations, staffing, and economic issues.

ACQUISITIONS

A university library is a collection of selected materials to support the institution's instructional and research programs. The acquisitions department's function is to purchase expeditiously and from the most advantageous vendors the materials chosen by the book selection officers, to process materials otherwise procured, and to forward promptly and to the proper places all materials acquired. This large business operation must be performed economically. The economy involves the selection of agents, methods of purchasing, treatment of returns, and sale of discards, although foremost is budget expense control.

Expense Control

The traditional method of apportioning funds is to set up departmental allotments, thus giving each department of instruction control over a certain amount, but the stronger libraries are trying to break away from the allotment system. When it prevails, the faculty library committee usually advises on the allocation. The library generally retains sums for reference works, bibliographic collections, continuing serials, and contingencies. Individual departmental sums may be spent upon authorization of the department chairman, or a committee, or one member assigned full departmental responsibility.

This allocation may be necessary when funds are not ample to

147

An illustration of why technical processing staff needs larger than average work space to accommodate book trucks, shelving, tables, files, etc.: a corner of the Catalog Department, John D. Rockefeller, Jr., Library, Brown University

cover all reasonable requests. It may not be necessary where the faculty have confidence that, even when funds are short, the director is doing the best possible job to use the funds in the most equitable fashion. This confidence will be strengthened if there is suitable publicity about the selections made by the library and reasons are given for denying any faculty requests. It will also be strong to the extent that able curators and other library specialists demonstrate scholarly knowledge and bibliographic judgment.

If funds must be allocated, there should be a deadline — perhaps after three quarters of the fiscal year has elapsed — after which uncommitted funds revert to library control. This will enable the library to take care of departmental requests when allotments are insufficient and to meet other needs seen by the library.

When allocations are not considered necessary, the library has a great responsibility to determine departmental needs, to monitor the relative strengthening of subjects, to fill the important lacunae in a rational order of priority, and to make expenditures with the greatest discrimination. A rough apportionment among broad subject fields may still be desirable for purposes of budgeting. It will be desirable to keep in a contingency account at least 10 per cent of total funds so that the chief selection officer may respond to special departmental suggestions; such funds are also useful when extraordinary opportunities occur.

The other side of fiscal control is the management of fund expenditures. Funds are of three types according to source — endowment income, general fund appropriations, and library-derived income. (Library-derived income may include current gifts, sale of duplicates, lost-book fees, circulation fines, and business-industrial use fees.) For accounting or management reasons, these may need to have budgetary separation. There are also two types of funds according to use — unrestricted as to use and restricted as to use. The library is obliged to follow legal restrictions and donor stipulations, and it uses departmental and internal library allocations to set up administrative restrictions. The word *restricted* is used by accountants to mean "specified as to which 'department' of the university may make commitments," the library in this context being one department; and a university may use the term *designated* to mean restricted as to use by subject, language, field, etc. There may even be restriction as to who may make expenditures.

148

Such restrictions and designations may oblige a university library to manage up to 350 separate accounts. The library will try to reduce the number of these accounts in order to simplify the paper work in the accounting section of the acquisitions department. One such simplification is to place all undesignated funds in a single account. It may also be possible to average the cost of books at a figure like $10 so that an endowment that produces $100 per year would be memorialized with ten bookplates that year; one that produces $1,900 would be memorialized by pasting appropriate bookplates in 190 new acquisitions. Yet under no circumstances may operational efficiency outweigh the administrative necessity of maintaining the restrictions and meeting accounting requirements. This dilemma should encourage the library to acquire endowments having the greatest freedom from specified use. It should also prompt the library to work with the university treasurer or development office in order to have a policy on endowments and restrictions, as discussed in Chapter 4, p. 91. (See also pp. 17 and 20.)

Just as it is occasionally necessary to prepare a brief listing of special or particularly valuable gifts of materials, so it may be desirable once in a while to maintain a file of books purchased with an endowment or gift for current use. Such a donor file enables the library to report with ease on publications acquired. This may enhance donor relations and may lead to further gifts or bequests. If book funds can be assigned to a purchase after its receipt, instead of being committed before the order is placed, as is commonly done, the selection of books to be charged to the fund will be more accurate.

When procedures can omit departmental allotments and purchase commitments, there can be substantial staff economies and a more rapid execution of orders. If the library can omit assigning a fund name and making a commitment, there is a clear saving for purchase orders which are never filled — as is often the case with out-of-print items from dealers' catalogs. Use of the blank check as a system for paying single-title purchases from major currency countries (usually with a limitation of 90 days and $100) is another economy. This procedure provides a signed check not to exceed $100; the vendor enters the precise amount due in the payment line.

The rate of book fund expenditures from the various funds must be closely monitored to assure that general flow of expenditures is

149

of the right magnitude, to check on selected critical accounts, and to determine the need for accelerating or slowing the rate of purchase. This review may be monthly; it must be at least quarterly, with more frequent checks during the last four months of the fiscal year. The use of the contingency fund, or director's discretionary fund, comes into play increasingly in decisions during the latter part of the year. (Chapter 4 gives other information on the financial administration of funds available for buying library materials.)

Book Vendors

The selection of vendors is a decision of such importance that the director of libraries will usually be deeply concerned even though he delegates the major responsibility. One agent who offers an advantageous discount may be slow in locating copies from minor publishers. Another may give excellent service on standing orders for works in parts or other continuations but have unclear or delayed invoices. Faculty members occasionally will urge that the library use one favorite bookseller who is good in some subject fields but poor in others. The library will prefer to use one or a few proven vendors in each country for in-print materials. Service by a dealer is usually best if he knows he has $10,000 or $100,000 of business rather than a very small amount. Furthermore, the fewer the dealers the fewer the invoices to process.

The chief of the acquisitions department will have to determine these relative advantages as best he can. More important, he will be responsible for monitoring the service of each agent, since personnel will change and work that was good may deteriorate rapidly. The director will be concerned with the balance of speed, accuracy, quality of service on difficult procurement, and discounts.

In some instances the university purchasing department may advise on, or need to approve, selection of dealers. The book trade, however, cannot be equated with dealers in equipment and supplies. Each variant printing or new edition of a title has its best dealer somewhere in the world. This is the specialty of the librarian. Consequently, nearly all universities find it expeditious and economical to place with the library full purchase responsibility for book materials.

A few libraries are bound by state regulations to receive open bids on equipment purchases, and books are often defined as "equipment" requiring capital expenditures. Bidding seldom results in better use of state funds. It frequently results in greater personnel expense for paper work and in the loss of some items which go out of print or out of stock during delays. Some of the best dealers refuse to enter into bid arrangements. All in all, the library must work within its legal restraints, and the librarian may join with the university purchasing agent to request deletion of the bid requirement as it applies to library materials.

Although the library may be designated as the purchasing agent for library materials, this authority may be spelled out in a resolution of the board of trustees (see Appendix V). Such authorization is almost certain to place some limitation on the library in executing large purchases or in entering into agreements involving university liability beyond a certain amount.

Book Purchasing

Procurement presents a number of economic issues. There is of course the pressure for speed. This may involve the use of air mail, overseas cables, or catalog galleys from secondhand dealers to permit more rapid placement of orders. Even more important may be the internal efficiency of routing catalogs, obtaining selection decisions, searching in the local files to determine duplication and entry verification, and typing and placing of the order. The director will be concerned that these are well organized. Since selection is such a large segment of the collection-building problem, the university library should have at least a general statement of responsibility for selection and of the areas of interest, with some indication of the degree of interest. Examples drawn from such statements are given in Appendixes II, III, and IV.

From a strictly fiscal point of view, the *method* of purchasing is of greater concern than the assignment of selection responsibility. There are at least the following methods: (1) single orders; (2) grouped orders in which many single orders are mailed under one set of instructions; (3) paired orders in which duplicates needed in various units are combined for economical handling during and after purchase; (4) standing orders in which an agent keeps an open purchase for all parts of a serial or all works by one author or publisher; (5) blanket approval orders in which an entire subject field or all national publications are supplied by an agent under an open-ended contract document, with unwanted items returned for credit; and (6) block orders in which an entire personal library or section of the holdings of a dealer are bought *en bloc* without individual listing of titles. The last two methods may involve legal points which should be cleared with the university's legal counsel; they are certain to raise questions about the return or disposal of titles that turn out to be duplicates or are outside the scope of collecting. In Appendix VI are examples of (1) instructions to a serials vendor for a continuing subscription to a publication; (2) an on-approval agreement in the field of science and technology; (3) a blanket order agreement covering a wide spectrum of materials from several European countries to be obtained through one dealer; and (4) an *en bloc* agreement.

Standing orders should be periodically reviewed, and blanket and block orders must be very carefully monitored. Economic conditions vary with each purchasing method, and each method requires careful evaluation and continuing study.

The handling of unwanted returns is important. They serve to indicate the quality of library searching before ordering, the accuracy of the blanket approval contract in reflecting wanted items and exclusions, and the quality of dealer service. Study of the percentage of returns and the specific causes for the error can suggest necessary management changes. A normal percentage of returns may be from 5 per cent to 10 per cent of blanket approval orders, and should be below 5 per cent for other types. The lack of detail in many bibliographies and catalogs makes it unrealistic to expect complete accuracy. A strong searching section, probably supervised and at least partially staffed by librarians, may be an essential factor in efficient ordering. Many items will progress through processing to cataloging or even to shelflisting before it becomes evident that a copy is already in the collection. There also is the question of disposition. In cases where it may cost two dollars to return an item for credit, it may be economically sound to place it in a book sale or even give it away.

One other common problem concerns the procurement of book materials for nonlibrary university offices, laboratories, and institutes. This purchasing can easily run over $100,000 a year and may include some of the most troublesome of all orders. Problems arise because the book budgets in these units are buried under the rubric of "supplies," the budgets fluctuate greatly in their terminology for books, and the secretaries or other fund managers are not trained in bibliographical citations. Mingling of administrative and library purchasing is likely to lead to confusion in accounts and dealer relations. Because persons in academic departments charged with ordering books lack the proper training, the distinction between serials or monographs in series is not recognized, technical reports or reprints are not so cited, standing orders are placed without understanding of implied obligations, and other problems abound. The university may require such orders to be handled by the library so that the library can process them economically and can be aware where book collections are being formed. If the library does not serve as the purchasing agent for book materials, orders may be handled by a campus bookstore, by a cooperative society, by the university purchasing office, or by the unit itself in direct contact with an outside vendor. Each institution will have to decide which arrangement is best for its set of circumstances.

Serial Records

Management of the records of receipt for serial publications demands thorough experience with serial peculiarities and a talent for excellent housekeeping. University libraries commonly handle from 25,000 to 50,000 serial titles, including dailies, weeklies, monthlies, quarterlies, and annuals, items regularly issued at other frequencies, items irregularly issued in numbered series, items irregularly issued in an unnumbered named series, and works issued in parts and purchased as serials though they conclude in a few years. An efficient manager should keep current the recording of issues and should systematically claim and reclaim issues which were skipped or which are overdue. The use of a limited number of agents can help simplify the claiming and billing. However, the titles will come also with society memberships, by gift and exchange, by transfer from other university units, and by government deposit. Good procedures are second in importance only to a good staff.

One policy question concerns the number of serials that are to be routed to staff members and the staff level eligible for such routing. If routing is not kept under some limitation, current issues will never be on the current periodical shelves. Some libraries resolve the problem by purchasing a limited number of duplicate copies specifically for staff use and routing no others. Others may route only to department heads and above, or route no more than four or six titles to each librarian. A workable policy may authorize the routing of journals to any librarian who initials and dates a routing slip for forwarding within twenty-four hours, dropping the individual from routing if that practice is not followed rather conscientiously and buying duplicate subscriptions if five or more request routing. Where abuse is frequent, the library may discontinue routing and require librarians to check out periodicals overnight only or in conformance with the policy applicable to faculty.

The extent of public information service is another policy question and one which may be affected by the building. If the serial receipt unit can be located convenient to the circulation and reference area, it can accommodate requests for information on holdings. This can generally be handled with no great staff inconvenience; inquiries are likely to be intermittent and can be minimized by catalog references under open-ended serials which say "If volume desired is not on the shelf or charged out, detail of holdings may be checked at the Serial Record Desk" instead of "For record of university holdings, inquire at the Serial Record Desk." Telephone inquiries from branch libraries or from off-campus may be reduced and service improved by the preparation and distribution of lists of currently received serials. This practice is especially useful in the scientific fields and will save much staff time; it is followed at MIT, Michigan, Illinois, and many other universities.

Gift Acceptance

Gift policy is highly important. It is not enough to say the library will accept only those books it would be willing to select from a dealer's catalog. One may often need to accept an entire collection rather than choose only the volumes one wishes. Many gifts come with "strings."

Most of the greatest libraries have built their reputation on the superb private collections that they have been given and with the income from endowments they have received. These gifts stem from cordial relations — the president talking with a recent graduate, a trustee being thoughtful of a business associate, the library ref-

154

One of many ways in which student assistants can help: preparing book spine labels on a Selin device in the finishing department — Main Library, Stanford University

erence librarian going out of his way to help an undergraduate or a townsman. The director of libraries will frequently be called upon to welcome visitors, escort guests touring the university, or speak to alumni groups. Although most friendships are developed over many years, it may be the simple, considerate treatment of the most routine request that indirectly results in a devise to create a $100,000 book fund or the bequest of a major Petrarch collection.

There are substantial legal questions in the acceptance of gifts. Monetary gifts may come with the intention of use made clear, but the wording should have enough latitude so that the university may use the gifts to advantage. No restrictions whatever are preferred. It is not in the donor's interest for gifts to be so restricted with "strings" that they cannot be useful to the university; yet some may say that the interest of the donor must become the interest of the university or else it should not have accepted the gift. This is a question often resolved by requiring all university departments to report to the trustees for formal acceptance all gifts of money or gifts in kind above a certain valuation. There may be a policy against certain types of restrictions, such as nam-

ing a room or keeping a collection intact in perpetuity. Most universities will have some policy guidelines and will then judge each major contribution on its own merits, that is, its value to the institution.

Gift forms for processing books can be useful. They may be of three types: an agreement of legal transmittal, an informal acknowledgment usually signed by the director of libraries, and a calendar for purposes of accession and appraisal. The legal transmittal is used when an executor is disposing of part or all of a large or valuable collection, and it can be a wise safeguard against charges of misappropriation or misuse of books. Such an agreement should indicate the library's freedom as to bookplating, shelf location, circulation, sale, exchange, or other use of the material.

Gifts present a special problem not common to other types of acquisition. Many donors wish to benefit, as they are fully entitled to do, from tax credits appropriate to their gifts. However, the Internal Revenue Service has shown increasing concern about evaluations placed on gifts of books (and of art objects). The recipient is considered a party at interest, and any evaluation made by the receiving library is particularly subject to challenge. It is advisable to confer with the university's legal counsel on this matter. The ideal situation is for the donor to arrange for his own evaluation by a third-party expert. Some libraries pay for such third-party service, but this may be considered objectionable also. Some donors try to shop around for high evaluations with the intention of making a gift from which they will reap the greatest benefit. Needless to say this is unethical and, as a matter of policy, a library should not be party to any evaluation of a gift that is prospective only.

Among other legal problems to which the librarian should be alert are (1) collections which may be given to a rare book department when much of the material should properly go with the general collections, (2) collections designated for a particular building which is unlikely to have a continuing existence, (3) collections containing predominantly materials of which ample copies already exist in the university, and (4) gifts containing a proviso that a specified curator be attached thereto for his or her lifetime. Such questions are frequent; their answers often require agonizing study.

The staff time devoted to checking and sorting of gifts and cata-

156

loging, shelf space, and future maintenance of the gift as a physical entity and the space it occupies may constitute a sizable commitment on the part of the university unless a major endowment accompanies the gift material. The Harvard University Library has publicized this need by calling attention to fund terms that might well serve as a model, specifying that principal and income

> be used for the acquisition of books and other materials for the collections of the Harvard College Library, and for such of the costs of selecting and preserving books and other materials acquired by the Harvard College Library as may be allocated thereto by its Librarian, provided that the amount so allocated shall not exceed 25 per cent of said principal and income.[1]

University lawyers are frequently involved in drawing up or counseling on the terms for gifts.

Gift disposal is another question. It takes a skilled librarian to know when it is best to sell *en bloc* to a dealer, when to use specialist dealers, when to use materials in exchange programs, when to sell individually, and when to give away. Giving material to other institutions may cut personnel handling costs so much as to make the gift economical, to say nothing of the good will gained. In many institutions, if staff time and storage space are limited, the best disposition may be a sale to the university community. Although valuable books will be individually priced at something near or less than the amount a dealer would offer, most may be given a flat price during the first hour with a 20 per cent discount each hour thereafter — and thereby save very considerably on staff effort. A sale open to persons from outside the university community may in several states raise tax questions and is certain to attract book scouts who will siphon off the cream and destroy whatever student-faculty rapport might have been gained by the sale. Donor feelings are another factor to be carefully considered in handling disposal.

It is important that books that have been withdrawn from the collections and subsequently offered for sale be carefully stamped (across the bookplate perhaps) or otherwise marked to indicate

---

[1] *Annual Report for the Year 1959-60*. Cambridge, Harvard University Library, 1960. p. 18.

clearly that the book has been withdrawn and discarded. If this is not done, it will be impossible to tell who the legitimate owner is, and the library may in later years have "lost" books returned by other libraries or individuals on the mistaken assumption that the items have been misappropriated. A great deal of needless searching of records may ensue with the result that time and postage are wasted by third parties and the library staff.

Exchange Programs

It is generally cheaper and faster for a library to buy a publication if this is possible rather than acquire it on exchange, but exchange may be the only way to procure materials from some organizations in soft currency countries, because institutions in such countries may be under currency restrictions or be denied foreign credits for purchase of foreign publications.

Exchange has many hidden costs in staff time spent in packing, mailing, and record keeping. A library should carefully weigh the advantages of exchange in cases that require it to purchase domestic trade books as a basis for obtaining foreign publications. There must be caution if the request is for a government-sponsored technical report which may not be made available without government clearance.

To support exchange programs, the library will need official university publications, library reports and bibliographic studies, selected unwanted gifts, and university press monographs and serials. All but the press materials will generally involve no expense. The press, however, may provide 80 per cent of the necessary exchange materials, and these may be available at something like 50 per cent of retail price. The press has to balance its financial books; so it is reasonable for it to charge actual cost. It is in the interests of the university to acquire foreign research reports, a process which may require the availability of press publications in return. Occasionally a press will turn over stock remainders to the library.

The other aspect of exchange is selectivity on the part of the library. The book selection officers should be just as discriminating with exchange offers as with purchase offers, and a shade more discriminating than with gifts. The publications of an organization will tend to be of a somewhat uniform level of research value, so that decisions by officers need not be made in every instance; the person in immediate charge of exchanges should be able to judge nearly all examples after some months of experience. Serials can be the most useful and the most troublesome exchanges. Periodicals and monograph series are issued less regularly by organizations in the less affluent countries; the exchange staff will need to work closely with the serial records staff in claiming parts before they go out of print.

Libraries in the United States must monitor such exchanges carefully because there is some tendency for foreign exchange partners to flood the American libraries with low priority or unwanted publications, thereby building up a credit which the exchange partner wants satisfied with expensive, specific titles. Whether exchange is priced — that is, the country of origin establishes the price on each piece and expects a *quid pro quo* of equal value — or is on a page-for-page or piece-for-piece basis, the admonition to monitor carefully applies. Balancing of the accounts is a matter of practical efficiency. It appears that all universities, where it is not forbidden, now balance most accounts on a piece-for-piece basis, but a major segment of the foreign exchange group, including most notably Soviet libraries, insist on priced exchanges. Balancing is usually not done on an annual basis; rather it is watched routinely so that it never gets far out of balance.

Format Selection

Choice of format can be a major responsibility of the acquisitions staff. This includes the choice between hardback and paperback editions, the British and American editions, the original and a reprint edition, and the original and a microtext edition. Decisions are based on consideration of purchase price (though greater importance should be given to questions of service to readers), suitability for use, and physical longevity. The hardback edition will outlive the paperback and will usually permit several rebindings, which are not possible with paperbacks. The American edition will commonly have a better binding than the British. A reprint edition may noticeably lose legibility in the process, may not have as ample inner margins as the original may have, and may be in a reduced format which makes the type harder to read. Still, a reprint may be on paper with prospects of a longer life and be given a more durable binding.

159

In selecting among these alternatives, one must be alert to differences in text. Is a different introduction present? Are the notes and references identical? Do both formats have the index, all appendixes, all illustrations? Pagination is the major clue if it is available in trade lists.

Microtext editions present all the problems noted above, as well as others. Careful consideration is necessary to determine when it is economical and wise to choose a microtext over the original publication. The relative costs of buying, binding, and shelving microtexts and the originals involve facts which are frequently overlooked or misstated for advertising purposes. The expense of buying, maintaining, and providing special housing for microtext projectors, and reader acceptance of microtext, should also be remembered in reaching decisions.

In deciding whether to buy or create a microfilm, three arrangements with differing economic factors must be taken into account:

1. If the library itself does the microfilming of the original book, it is clear that the process does not result in a saving within present technology. (Evidence to support this statement is found in the articles listed at the end of this chapter by Pritsker and Sadler and by Clapp and Jordan.)

2. If the library can purchase microfilm or microcards in cooperation with several other libraries, then the economy is a significant one. Such a cooperative action is ordinarily in lieu of purchasing the original and is merely another form of acquisition rather than a substitution for the original. An example is the project that makes available foreign newspapers, administered by the Association of Research Libraries through the Center for Research Libraries.

3. If the library purchases a published *edition* of microtext to replace an original that is already owned, the extent of the economy probably depends upon whether the library has already bound its original copy. There is a saving if the microtext is published in an edition so that the cost of the negative is distributed among many libraries.

   a. If the library purchases microfilm or microcards in lieu of binding journals or books that it already has acquired, or needs to acquire concurrently for immediate use, there might be a slight saving for the first year and each year thereafter depending on the cost of binding and provided the original texts are discarded after the period of current use. Substitution for the original texts is now widely used with newspapers, and can be selectively extended to journals.

b. In replacing a file that has already been bound, the saving does not come until the difference in annual building maintenance charges per unit (book or microtext) have amounted to the cost of buying and processing the film replacement. If the replacement cost is more than the accumulated housing costs for fifty years, an institution has made an investment which will not be paid off, with interest, for a somewhat longer period of time. The saving for a back file placed on microfilm is not reached for something like one hundred years, if one assumes compact housing of the original books. (The New England Deposit Library has heat, light, and other storage costs averaging about $.02 per volume.)

A library should make these distinctions. Furthermore, before a final decision on whether to purchase in microfilm is reached, consideration should be given to several inherent disadvantages of microtexts in comparison with texts in the original format. The disadvantages, outlined below, are of varying degrees of importance. A decision is a matter of balancing the determinable economic advantage of substituting microtexts against these disadvantages, and in any decision it is better to have a microtext than not to have any version of the text.

1. Lack of standardized quality. Standards of film quality for libraries were first established in 1943. Sequential treatment of newspapers was standardized in 1949, and guidelines were extended to books, maps, and other materials in 1954. The first standard for micro-opaques was issued in 1961. Many current microform publications do not conform to these standards.

2. Lack of bibliographical standardization. The descriptive matter of the film and its container — to provide bibliographical indexing of the materials — is in an even more primitive state. Only in 1966 were bibliographic standards included with the technical in *Microfilm Norms*. Many libraries have purchased tens of thousands of pages of microtext without adequate thought to its bibliographic

control. The existence of useful microtexts is unknown to readers in many libraries because of the absence of traditional card catalog controls. Even the catalog cards provided with some series prove to be inconsistent with local cataloging practices and are therefore unfileable. Substitute controls in the form of published indexes are often inadequate, inaccessible, and largely unrealized, one notable exception being the Readex Microprint edition of United States Government documents.

3. Lack of standardized formats. There has been little standardization of format, and therefore microtexts are issued in transparencies and opaque sheets in at least seven sizes. This makes housing and reading equipment both confusing and expensive. It is a considerable expense. There will always be at least three formats to cope with; but, at this early stage of development, the field has been so wide open that many mistakes of judgment have been made and material is sometimes placed in unsuitable formats.

4. Lack of flexibility in use. Scholars are unable to read microtexts except in locations having the piece of equipment appropriate for that form of microtext. Portable reading machines have not been so constantly in use that individuals own them as they do typewriters. Individuals are thus restricted as to the hours and locations for the use of microtexts.

5. Awkwardness in use. While eyestrain during reading of microfilm is a matter of continuing debate, there is a rather widespread aversion to reading film. Many persons believe that reading on a screen is especially tiring, and this feeling is not allayed by the fact that machines are poorly designed and the library microtext reading quarters are commonly inferior.

6. Slowness of library service. A trained library assistant must usually locate the material because of its small and delicate nature; he may mount it on the projector and often instruct the user in how to operate the projector. Items are particularly easy to disarrange, especially the microtext sheets or cards, and cannot be rapidly filed in correct order. These extra service costs have not been considered in published reports on the costs of using film.

7. Loss of color. Only in 1960 were the first journals, such as *Life*, filmed in color. In fields such as medicine and fine arts, this lack has heretofore been a considerable drawback to an increased use of microtexts, although high quality color filmstrips are now

Provision of semiprivate work space in a catalog department with flexibility to meet future changes: staff cubicles — O. Meredith Wilson Library, University of Minnesota

being marketed for authors like William Blake whose works contain important color illustrations. Art books are also accompanied occasionally by 35 mm color slides.

8. Lack of shelf classification. Because of the uniform appearance of microtexts and the necessity of using reading machines even for browsing, it has not been advantageous to arrange microtexts by subject on the shelves. Therefore a scholar does not have the chance of purposive browsing through the collection. In addition, it is a slow task to refer from one book to another, or to refer from title to index to chapter.

9. Difficulty of copying. Although it is simple and quick to make a personal photographic copy of an illustration or textual matter in an original book, to get good copies from transparent microfilm is more expensive, and definition is lost with each succeeding generation of film. The student monopolizes the expensive reader-printer, or he must list pages he wants copied as he utilizes the

more plentiful standard reader and then moves to the other machine for printing enlargements. The possibility of enlarging from micro-opaques has existed only in the last decade, and the quality is still inferior.

10. Textual analysis. For the study of bibliographical points, it is essential to have the material in the original format.

For all of these questions of format selection, the staff must be guided by the aphorism *caveat emptor*.

Staff for Acquisitions

Acquisitions personnel require as much linguistic ability as clerical business competence. The staff may be one third librarians, employed for their knowledge of bibliography, subject and language ability, and organizational and supervisory talent. A diversity of skills can be an asset since materials will be handled in many languages from many countries. The clerical staff will often include wives of graduate students and faculty; but, as with part-time specialists, too heavy a reliance on persons who offer only a few years of potential employment puts a heavy burden on training and supervision. Finding persons with the requisite accuracy and bibliographical skill is not easy. Still, this is a sound assignment in which to start a career. A sample university library chart of staff and production follows:

Typical Acquisitions Staff and Annual Production

Department Chief, Librarian IV
Assistant Department Chief, Librarian III
Secretary

Order Division (36,000 volumes)

2 Librarians II	7 Junior library assistants
3 Senior library assistants	1 Accounting clerk

Gift Division (13,000 serial pieces and 21,000 volumes)

1 Librarian III	1 Student assistant
1 Library assistant	

Exchange Division (14,000 serial pieces and 900 monographs)

1 Supervising assistant	1 Library assistant

Serial Records Division (25,000 current titles, 800 new titles this year, and 5,000 pieces in back sets)

1 Librarian III	1 Student assistant
2 Library assistants	

The Technical Processing Function

In book selection, reference work, and preservation programs, the graduate library school gives students only a limited preparation for university library assignments. Consequently the library must select intelligent individuals with a broad education and provide them with the special on-the-job bibliographic experience needed to deal with the range of materials, languages, and sources that are part of the daily routine in a university. It is fruitful for the institution and the profession if a number of promising students can be hired as part-time assistants, for this is one of the best places to show them the career opportunities in research libraries. Furthermore, library interns, trainees, or other preprofessional help will find acquisitions work one of the better departments from which to gain insight into the profession.

Budgeting

Budgeting for acquisitions staff should stem directly from the collection-building policies. Once book funds have been obtained and policies for use determined, the acquisition, cataloging, and finishing operations should be provided automatically. There can be no question of relative emphasis among these operations. The input to the pipeline determines what must come out the other end. Any backlogs in the pipeline will result in arrearages. So the entire technical processing operation must be seen as a single function, and it must receive the same priority of emphasis as does the collection-building program.

The objective is to attune the level of staffing to the workload. Each process should be as efficient as possible. Ideally, no one department should bear more pressure week by week than another. The director must determine the staffing for the program with a view to the organizational efficiency of this function and the relative pressures it bears. If the proper level of staffing cannot be afforded, the director is left with the alternatives of downgrading policies, tolerating the growth of arrearages, or accepting certain undesirable shortcuts in processing (e.g., excessive use of blanket orders, sale of all gift duplicates to dealers, or relying on an agent for items which could more economically be obtained by exchange).

To help in judging the program load and efficiency, ample statistical evidence of workload is required. As the quality of searching increases, the number of staff may be increased without

165

commensurate increase in work volume. As a general rule, each individual in the searching and ordering process should be able to handle the equivalent of 6,000 volumes (4,000 titles) per year. This will be affected, however, by the effort being placed on such activities as retrospective purchases, procurement of microtext sets, blanket orders, and searching for items from countries lacking an organized book trade. Differences such as these help to explain why one university may have half again as much staff as another university to procure the same number of volumes.

Budget justification must therefore go far beyond the bare quantitative data. Each section needs analysis — its program, its procedures, its ability to keep reasonably up to date, its physical or personnel handicaps, and the particular pressures on the section. It is healthy for any unit to have some pressure of work; it is the comfortably staffed unit which overorganizes its work (i.e., develops extra files and procedures to ensure smooth functioning).

The pressures on a section may stem from service loads, student or faculty demands, and from the director. For example, the director may decide that it would be useful to cooperate in a regional union list of currently received serials on the assumption that the extra work can be fitted in by tightening up regular procedures and exerting more effort. This would have to be decided in the light of the opinions and facts presented by the department head and head of the serial records unit. The department arguments may be persuasive enough so that some student hours or regular part-time temporary help may be provided. Another example would be the amount of retrospective checking which the order department may be able to handle. Faculty members may ask that new authoritative lists of titles essential for graduate programs be checked for local holdings. No one can deny the utility of such checking, though handling several such lists in close succession can swamp the basic operation with impossible pressures. But perhaps sampling or spreading the work over several months will make the pressure reasonable.

In these years of integrated systems and the development of a national shared cataloging program, the efficiency of procurement processing must approach that of cataloging. The provost or dean who challenges the need for more staff must receive a clear explanation of the reason for the process and the problems involved in adjusting this part of the system to keep up with the workload. There should also be periodic studies as to the simplest procedures, the best use of personnel, the most useful multiple forms, the application of machines, and a comparison with similar departments in other universities. This attention to procedures, their effectiveness and economy, is fundamental to the budget process. It should not be left until the weeks just before budget requests are submitted. The director cannot argue persuasively with his budget officer unless he, himself, is convinced and receives clear concise documentation.

Departmental Relations

The interrelationship between cataloging and acquisitions work becomes closer as the years pass. This is most clear in the integrated computer-based system where acquisitions staff captures the data in verified state and cataloging staff imposes a refinement once the book is in hand. In a manual system, it is demonstrated in the dual use of information collected in a single search. The motivation of libraries which establish a technical processing group is, in part, to reduce the waste involved in duplicate searching conducted in both acquisitions and cataloging.

As part of the order process, efforts need to be made to set a standard for bibliographic data that will serve the purchasing operation well and serve also as a base to be supplemented, not repeated, during the cataloging operation. It is a goal not easy of achievement, though it is significantly advanced by the utilization of the increased flow of Library of Congress cards resulting from the National Program for Acquisitions and Cataloging (NPAC) made possible by Title IIC of the Higher Education Act of 1965, as amended (see below, pp. 182-3). Where LC cards or card numbers are not provided, a clear order form, one copy of which goes through processing with the book, can serve.

An equally important aspect of the acquisitions-cataloging relationship is the information flow among the selection officers, acquisitions department, cataloging department, and the book stack. For example, a block purchase in art history may be so large as to require a shift of catalog personnel and may require some moving of collections in the stacks to accommodate the unanticipated extent of growth in one part of the classification. Or the selection officers may know that they must intensify the acquisition of books in Hebrew, Turkish, or biophysics. Such a change may profoundly affect cataloging needs, and communication is essential to enable timely staffing. Large gifts also pose special problems of temporary and permanent storage, sorting, and possibly cataloging manpower. Any large subject purchase, the addition of an especially large set, a shift of book selection emphasis to a new subject field, or reduction in some collecting field should be communicated. Periodic meetings devoted to just such topics are sure to prove useful.

Personnel at nearly all levels should have an understanding of the procedures in the other department; supervisors, administrative assistants, and section heads should keep constantly in mind the needs of the other department. To the extent that the two departments work effectively as a team, the normal bottlenecks, arrearage, and procedural problems can be minimized.

CATALOGING AND CLASSIFICATION

A building filled with books is not a library unless the books have been organized for access and made available for use. The cataloging department's function is to organize the total library resources with suitable bibliographic controls to facilitate access to the resources by students, faculty, and staff. The traditional means for accomplishing this goal are descriptive cataloging, subject cataloging, and classification. This assignment requires effective records prepared with all reasonable economy.

A university may have a million volumes and not deserve its accreditation; students may be unable to gain access to a considerable fraction of the collection through defective bibliographic records such as the following: no entries under joint authors, insufficient title or subject entries, no analysis of monograph series, no open serials listed in the main catalog, and no access provided to the units of microtext sets. Other failures may result from not having catalogs in the most useful places, filing too many entries under a subject without subdivision, using a variety of classifications so that systematic perusal at the shelves is not possible, and a host of other possibilities.

168

The Technical Processing Function

Cataloging Policies

Bibliographic control policies are a responsibility of the director, with the advice of the department head, who must become expert in the alternatives with their comparable effectiveness and economies. The fundamental policy must be to create records appropriate to the university's program and constituents. A university with a particularly active dramatic arts program, for example, must not only acquire specialized materials but also create more analytical cataloging than would the Library of Congress — so that plays, playbills, criticism, works on staging and all subtopics are locatable through the catalog. A universal example is the desirability of displaying in the card catalog the contributions of local faculty members to collections like symposia or festschriften. The overriding policy of local appropriateness creates, of course, the local variations which cost money and raise issues of conflict with national standards.

The principal policies that must be established will be those that are concerned with descriptive cataloging rules, subject cataloging rules, and classification systems. These may not be difficult problems when a university library is started; they will certainly involve complex considerations if an institution is more than a few decades old. Descriptive cataloging rules locally applied must show a high degree of consistency. Yet a library that is thirty or more years old may once have operated under the 1908 ALA cataloging rules, then under the 1949 LC rules, and may now need to apply the 1966 Anglo-American code. Wise administration is required to determine how best to apply a new code. It is not possible to remain with the previous code when entries in the National Union Catalog will begin to reflect the new rules more and more; so it is rather a question of the degree to which the library should change to the new rules. In this event, should all entries created under previous rules be changed, or can cross-references be used to relate the superseded forms to the new? A high degree of logical consistency in the accumulating catalog records is necessary if the catalog is to remain intelligible, irrespective of whether codes change. The consistency must be rather exact; otherwise the varying forms of the name will confuse the reader, lead to snowballing of filing errors and to use of outmoded entries, and result in a filing shambles which can cost a great deal to set right.

Subject cataloging rules can create a similar situation. A local codification may have been followed until a national code forces a different consistency. The precision must come not in the choice of new subject terms but in the format of phrases, their punctuation, and the syndetic structure. Under any code the degree of subject heading specificity should at the lowest (most detailed) level be inclusive of the *full* subject. (Two or three headings will sometimes be required for adequate treatment.) Thus, a change in code creates the same problems of substitution or partial implementation as do changes in descriptive cataloging codes. A change may significantly improve the catalog, but change almost always carries a price tag. Each proposed change will need the most careful study by the department head before a library policy can be adopted.

Each change of code raises the specter of recataloging. If libraries can cope with code changes by gradual or partial implementation, they still face the need for recataloging when, for example, names of nations change, two names used as authors are found to be one individual with a pseudonym, or later editions create the requirement that more detail be added to identify the early edition. Few universities have a policy on recataloging other than to hold it to a minimum. Each library must consider the condition of its catalog as a guide to the extent and type of recataloging that may make sense in terms of service and economy. A considerable expenditure of time on recataloging indicates the inadequacies of earlier cataloging policies or the folly of present policies.

The making of analytics to facilitate access to important subparts of a publication (a periodical article or a contribution to a festschrift) is justified when the analyzed part is unusually significant. There is universal recognition that scholars benefit from the analytics prepared for over half a century by the New York Public Library. Today a university library can rely upon printed indexes for an increasing amount of analysis and it can purchase from the Library of Congress card sets for many monograph series, but it will probably decide to do some further analysis itself. Some series which the Library of Congress does not handle, such as the many microtext sets, require exceedingly laborious use patterns for person after person if analytics are not prepared. Frequently the library will needlessly purchase a title because an analytic does not reveal that the item is already in the collection. The library will need to weigh

170

the cost of analytic work against improved service and judge the effect upon the cataloging workload.

Classification is the third area of standards which requires policy consideration. In an academic institution, a systematic shelf organization offers great benefits for scholars at all levels of sophistication. Browsing is part of the need and the tradition of a liberal education. However, as with cataloging, problems in the application of classification increase with the passage of time. A classification once thought adequate may not be maintained by its creator over the decades. Or, if it is, then the extensions and changes in successive editions create revision problems for the library which has used it. This prompts reclassification in greater or lesser degree. It may, on the other hand, prompt a change of classification. Cornell University has undertaken complete reclassification, as have many small and medium-sized libraries. Harvard has adopted a selective change of classification. Stanford chose a complete change of classification with practically no reclassifying. In determining how classification will be applied, it is necessary to weigh advantages and disadvantages in the light of local circumstances. In general, when a large library adds 100,000 or more volumes a year and when auxiliary collections are becoming common, a university library would not be wise to undertake complete reclassification. Yet what is the wise decision in one university will not necessarily be wise for another.

The varying depth of cataloging is another policy issue. At one extreme, a rare volume may receive far more than the norm of complete descriptive cataloging and may also be listed by date, printer, place, and provenance. At the other, the tenth variant printing of *Hamlet* may be given a brief entry and no other point of access. These variations from maximum to minimum cataloging are common in any university, but there should be guidelines for determining how different classes of material will be treated. For example, libraries which have auxiliary or storage collections may choose to have no subject treatment, a limit of one subject entry, or an extra quantity of entries. Each policy may have its justification — e.g., economy becomes the controlling factor, or service via catalog records is needed to offset the lack of browsing, or only duplicate or variant titles are placed in storage and so can be found even without added entries. Examples of material often treated as excep-

171

tions on the minimum side are government documents, technical reports, pamphlets, and auxiliary collections; and on the maximum side: rare books, special collections, bibliographical works, and sometimes musical recordings and art prints. Each library must determine its policies in the light of special local needs and financial resources.

Book-form catalogs can be used to publicize university library holdings with copies in a variety of branches, to share resources with other institutions in the state or region, and to distribute information widely in a large building or to faculty and other offices. The advantages are clear and the disadvantages are equally clear; they have not changed much since being enumerated by Cutter in 1876 though technology has made it much easier to produce them. Many libraries have issued, or have permitted commercial publishers to issue, catalogs of special collections or of entire holdings. But very few indeed have replaced their card catalogs entirely with book catalogs. The costs are not inconsequential even if some sales can be counted upon to help amortize the investment. The cost of producing supplements and the cost of periodically reissuing the cumulated set must be weighed against the values of multiple copies with the consequent greater accessibility and improved service. Until automation enables a library to put its catalog on-line, the production costs of the book catalog are likely to limit its usefulness to small collections, such as the undergraduate library, or to specialized libraries rather than to the general library.

Staff for Cataloging

Staffing and organization of catalog departments follow a diversity of patterns. Linguistic and subject competence is stressed even more than in acquisitions. The staff may be one half librarians, though this will vary to the extent that original cataloging is replaced by use of Library of Congress and National Union Catalog copy, and to the degree that the most capable library assistants may develop professional skills. Assistants are increasingly used to process pamphlets, literature, material found in the National Union Catalog, and other volumes which do not require subject cataloging and where the assistant can lean on a librarian for classification guidance and main entry revision. Finding persons with a

172

capacity for accuracy, with the ability to follow rules, and with bibliographical skill is not easy. It is a sound assignment in which to start a career and provides excellent background for increased responsibilities in this and other departments.

A sample university library table of staffing and production follows:

Typical Cataloging Staff and Annual Production

Department Chief, Librarian IV or V
Assistant Department Chief, Librarian III
Administrative Assistant, Librarian II
  3 Librarians III
  9 Librarians II
  8 Librarians I
  1 Secretary
  5 Supervising assistants as section heads for searching, transfers,
     added copies, filing, and card duplication
  4 Senior library assistants
12 Library assistants

Cataloged	Titles	Volumes
Books	23,351	26,902
Serials	1,521	1,521
Analytics	1,681	—
Added volumes	—	932
Added copies	—	3,389
Theses	678	695
Overseas branches	2,947	3,498
Microfilms	85	950
Phonorecords	90	97
Recataloging	446	329
Reclassification	3,504	7,417
Replacements and re-enters	165	168
Cancellations and withdrawals	2,788	3,386
Transfers	5,856	6,954

Card duplication	Titles
Sets typed	7,703
Masters Xeroxed	9,278
Masters typed	13,303
Sets Multilithed	34,763

Cards distributed	
Public catalogs	178,448
Shelf lists	36,892
Refiled	24,645
Special files and extra cards	37,398

The exact organization of staff in the catalog department may be based on autonomy between descriptive cataloging and subject cataloging or it may be based on the language or subject of the materials being cataloged. Different universities have organized their departments in different ways, and the largest university libraries tend to use a combination of methods for organization. The illustrated organization of one very large catalog department (see p. 175) indicates some units established by form, others by language, and others by subject. An organization which is highly streamlined for the ultimate in efficiency may not provide the staff with job satisfaction nor may it lead to professional development or career development on the nonprofessional level. These various points will need to be evaluated in any university before the library adopts one or another pattern of organization. The balance in workload from one unit of the department to another is especially difficult when the staff is broken down into minute units. On the other hand, where all materials go through a single assembly line, the quality of the product is bound to suffer since all people will not have equal proficiency in handling subjects or languages.

It is especially desirable to organize a catalog department in a way which will make clear to university budget officials or to library staff the variety of assignments that must be covered. It can be too easily assumed that the catalog librarians all do the same amount of work of uniform difficulty. Why should a budget increase request include yet one more cataloger? A detailed organization can promote processing efficiency and can help to explain what is bound to be the largest and most expensive single operation in the library.

Staff organization also presents a fluid picture. As each catalog librarian is employed or terminated there may need to be some shifts in individual assignments. The department head should evaluate each person's ability in languages, subject fields, and cataloging. With due consideration for the combination of these talents, the department head will plan assignments. Current acquisitions will be given priorities for processing. Arrears will be programmed for processing. As a young cataloger develops proficiency, the assignments increase in difficulty. The training and supervision and careful distribution of work among professional and clerical staff, together with sound policies, are the basis for the economical creation of a bibliographic fabric.

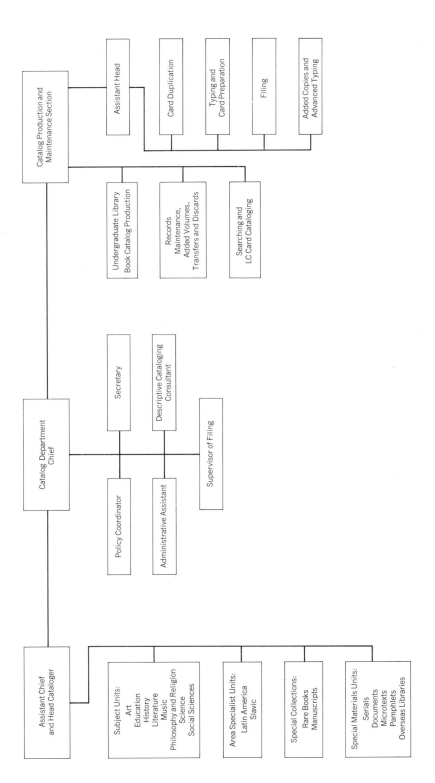

Organization of Catalog Department

Catalog Department Chief

Secretary
Descriptive Cataloging Consultant
Policy Coordinator
Administrative Assistant
Supervisor of Filing

Catalog Production and Maintenance Section

Assistant Head
Card Duplication
Typing and Card Preparation
Filing
Added Copies and Advanced Typing

Undergraduate Library Book Catalog Production
Records Maintenance, Added Volumes, Transfers and Discards
Searching and LC Card Cataloging

Assistant Chief and Head Cataloger

Subject Units:
Art
Education
History
Literature
Music
Philosophy and Religion
Science
Social Sciences

Area Specialist Units:
Latin America
Slavic

Special Collections:
Rare Books
Manuscripts

Special Materials Units:
Serials
Documents
Microtexts
Pamphlets
Overseas Libraries

Budgeting

Budgeting for catalog staff should be of a magnitude to keep processing in relative balance with the rate of acquisitions. To determine the program load and efficiency, there is required ample statistical evidence of acquisitions, current rate of cataloging, and work arrears. As the acquisitions department provides more complete searching and as there can be increased use of LC cards, the precataloging operations can be shortened. As a very general rule for a large university library, the cataloging-classifying production should average 1,300 volumes (this is about the same as 1,000 titles per year) for each full-time staff member. To put it another way and assuming reasonable clerical support, each cataloger should process at least 1,500 titles per year for original cataloging.

For example, a year-long record for 31 full-time catalogers in two major universities shows an average annual production rate of 1,572 titles cataloged — 131 per month including vacations and sick leave. Materials handled included rare books, microtexts, serials, maps, and documents; such diverse fields as music, history, education, literature and science; heavy workloads in Slavic, Latin American, German, and Romance language publications; and descriptive as well as subject cataloging.

Studies indicate that with LC or other cataloging records to serve as work "copy," cataloging should take from 20 per cent to 50 per cent as much time. However, this will be considerably affected by the proportion of retrospective purchases, number of pamphlets and other ephemera, exotic language material, and analytics. Differences such as these help to explain how one university may have half again as much staff as another to process the same number of volumes.

In a library with a rapidly expanding acquisitions program, it is particularly difficult to predict the number of processing staff required. The receipt of a large gift collection may constitute a sizable processing problem. The opportunity to acquire masses of material through the PL 480 program of the Library of Congress likewise introduces a major processing factor. Budget windfalls for books, whether in the form of unanticipated gift or endowment monies, or funds made available for extraordinary *en bloc* purchases, may bring heavy processing workloads without commensurate staffing. These subtleties will not escape the director but

176

may be a mystery to a budget officer in the absence of careful explanations.

Budget justification must therefore go far beyond the bare quantitative data. The library policies discussed above, especially the amount of recataloging and reclassifying and analysis, will need interpretation as to their effect on the production of sections and individuals. Such statistics need to be kept, though the qualitative aspects and training-supervising responsibilities must be given full weight. The result can be compared in gross terms with production in other universities, though valid published statistics for purposes of comparison are still lacking.

The mere fact that an arrearage exists is not automatic justification for a budget increase. Arrears of some small size are desirable. They make for efficient batching of special types of material. They become too large only when they exceed three months of departmental production. When they reach that size, they should prompt a review of production statistics against some norm, a reconsideration of departmental policies, and a study of the balance of budgetary support among departments. (See comments on pp. 92, 94, 97-8.) If cataloging is falling behind and acquisitions is not, some staff redeployment may be reasonable. If processing is struggling and the public services are comfortable, the next budget improvement may concentrate on this weakness. Or some short-term projects may need to be postponed.

Catalog Security and Maintenance

It is worth pondering the value of the card catalog to a library — and the problems deriving from its loss, or even the loss of a single tray of cards. Unfortunately a card file is vulnerable to theft. (This fact is one of the justifications for a book-form catalog.) It therefore behooves a library to achieve a reasonable degree of protection through a microfilm program producing an archival record for storage in a vault outside the building. This should include periodic supplements for cards added since the original filming. Serial records should be refilmed at least every three to five years in order to update the record of exact holdings. Without such a security film, university insurance policies may not in fact cover all labor costs involved in attempting to reconstruct a card file because reasonable due caution had not been exercised in guarding against such loss. Catalog reconstruction methods without a microfilm, such as was reported in the cited reference by Greenwood, can achieve a file of perhaps 95 per cent completeness whereas an insurance microfilm can reach something very close to 100 per cent.

Regular editorial maintenance of card catalog files is frequently delayed under budget pressures. This is like building a wooden house and never painting it again once it is finished. A catalog perforce grows constantly. There are more entries, new names, new subjects, and new rules superseding old ones used in the same file. In most universities, file editing is not the basic continuing staff responsibility it should be. Rather it is put aside under daily pressures and assigned spasmodically to a member of the staff as a fill-in or a summer project. In 1955 Harvard estimated the catalogs in the Widener Library needed $85,000 for updating.

When one reflects on the evolving nature of the library catalog, the need for pruning and selective rebuilding should be evident. Guide cards greatly speed up access; yet a carefully devised system of guides which once spaced them about eighty cards apart will, after some years, find some sections having two or three hundred cards between guides. Subject headings may get so large that they are all but worthless unless chronologically arranged or until subdivided. And the intricacies in cataloging the works of voluminous authors, personal and corporate, are certain to require occasional reconstruction by either a system of conventional titles or hierarchical classes.

Another problem may stem from changes in the records. Typical of these changes are classification changed on the main entry but not on added entries, volume relocated in a different branch but noted only in the shelflist or circulation file, a general reference such as "for pamphlets on this subject see (class no.)" not removed when the pamphlets were divided, or analytics made for the catalog but not noted on main entry so that they were not removed when the book was lost or withdrawn. This deterioration of records also affects the National Union Catalog and regional union catalogs when they are not updated upon loss of books or change in location. The person in charge of catalog editing or maintenance can relieve the difficulty if he is part of the catalog policy committee and in that capacity heads off deterioration of records before it starts. Every long-established university library will, nevertheless, have vestiges of failures to update the catalog. They may stem from nineteenth century manuscript cards, or the short (two-inch-high) cards formerly used, but defects most frequently result from decisions made in all innocence a decade or so ago.

The economics of catalog use are too often forgotten once its form has been established. The costs are inversely related to speed of access and comprehension, which grow out of file organization and rules for cataloging. When file organization is faulty, the access time may easily double and comprehension drop — or, worse still, the credibility of library records deteriorates. An automated system will have built-in controls for file maintenance. The manual system requires this every bit as much.

Branch Libraries

Branch library relationships require special attention in such matters as cataloging policy, choice of classification, proliferation of card files, and decentralization. Here, as in other questions, there must be balance between costs and service, and service must be determined in terms of departmental needs balanced against the needs of the community as a whole. Cataloging policy should start with the assumption that what is good for the main library will be acceptable in branches. Economy obviously supports this view. On the other hand it may be contended that materials in art, music, and special collections, and publications like technical reports, require more descriptive treatment and more points of catalog access. Each instance of proposed divergent treatment should be objectively and sympathetically considered. The nature of the material needs to be understood — the weakness in normal catalog treatment and the cost escalation resulting from proposed changes in routine. Many divergences from the norm are found justifiable in university libraries.

Classification policy is similarly difficult of resolution. Classification schemes are not created once for all time. They require constant updating. This should be kept at the forefront in any decision to adopt a home-made or "orphan" system. Nonetheless there may be fields in which the university has a great deal more literature than can be accommodated by the usual systems. Examples of disparate quantity would be a university archives collection and a research institute in cryogenics. It is less reasonable to decide

179

on a variant scheme for small residence libraries, an undergraduate collection, and for special collections in closed stacks. Every accepted divergent practice is cause for increased costs at one or many points in the library operation. As just one example, consider the problem of a small branch with a different classification which at a later point in time is to be merged with one of the larger library units. The main library collections may be arranged by more than one classification as a result of changes over several decades. But such a situation must not be allowed to serve as an argument for adding still other classification systems; each departure from the present norm must be supported by overpowering justification. A few instances are generally found justifiable in university libraries.

Proliferation of card files tends to result from administrative lassitude. And, as with duplicate copies, some additional files are justifiable and many are not. The task is to discover the existence of such files and to determine which are sufficiently useful to justify their continuation. Every service unit needs a catalog of materials for which it is responsible. Each will need author or main entry listing, and nearly all should have full sets of entries.

A most important point in administering any university library is that a main entry *must* also be in the main library public (or official) catalog making it a local union catalog. This catalog should have a full set for branch books in the humanities or in those other fields for which the major research collection is in the main library.

Most branches will want a file formed of order slips for materials being purchased for their shelves. Questionable proliferation commences, however, when one branch wants a list of what is in another, or when one wants a file of books in its broad subject or in related subjects that are shelved in the main library. Such proliferation can occur when a major departmental library administers a small working collection (e.g., an engineering library and a branch for sanitary engineering) or when a branch is in a field close to main library strength (e.g., a psychology branch or one supporting a Latin American area studies center). The same growth of files is frequently found for serial records. Serial issues will be checked in on central records and again at the service center, though the latter may be in the same building or even on the same floor as the central serial records. Service can be more rapid when detailed records are kept locally. Yet these duplicate records may be an expensive form

180

of self-protection from faculty or student criticism. There is, of course, another side to the question, for the service unit may properly be striving for a high level of accurate and immediate service; it may have found the central serial records slow or unavailable or occasionally inaccurate, and the local records may be maintained by a staff member who otherwise would sit at a circulation desk and read a book. There is here a policy issue which cannot be given a simple answer. But generally, a university library should try to hold duplicate files to a minimum.

The other branch issue concerns decentralization of processing. It is normal for the cataloging — and usually for all of the technical processing — to be decentralized for branches serving law and medicine. It is not normal for branches serving sociology or chemistry or for an undergraduate library. In between these examples there is broad latitude for decision with sizable economic significance. The branch will almost certainly perform full processing if it is administratively independent of the main library system. If the largest branches are centrally administered, they may still handle processing. This is reasonable when the head librarian is highly expert in his subject field, the branch has the requisite bibliographical tools, and the annual processing volume is sufficient to require at least one full-time cataloger. If the faculty is large enough or active enough to make special requests and suggestions which need local attention, the case is strengthened. It is not possible to say with certainty that a library branch of 100,000 volumes adding 3,500 volumes per year has reached a point where decentralization of processing may be justified; but clearly a collection of 50,000 volumes growing by 1,500 volumes per year would constitute a branch too small for economical decentralization. Subject branches requiring specialized cataloging or cataloging in exotic languages may be especially worthy candidates for decentralized cataloging if the volume of growth requires a full time cataloger; examples might be art photographs, musical scores and recordings, or the languages of the Far East, Southeast Asia, or South Asia. Under either a centralized or decentralized condition, cataloging policies need rationalizing in order that the university's libraries function as a coordinated system, and records produced by different administrative units be capable of synthesis in a union catalog. Myriad local factors would enter into each decision, including space

181

and personnel questions. The issue is certainly one having administrative importance and economic significance.

Interlibrary Cooperation

Interlibrary cooperation is a way of investing time or money so that the load may be shared. In collection building, cooperation may involve a division among libraries of the most expensive collecting in seldom-used fields or materials. In the acquisitions process, this may mean sending the Library of Congress a copy of the order form for new publications in countries covered by the National Program for Acquisitions and Cataloging (see below). In cataloging it may include participation in rule codification, sharing of special classifications, and contributions to union catalogs. Rule drafting, codifications, and testing require planning on the national level. Universities should work with the Library of Congress in its effort to maintain the LC classification and subject headings and with the Dewey office at the Library of Congress for that classification. Any specialized classifications devised locally should be shared via the Special Libraries Association pool at the John Crerar Library.

Universities rely increasingly on shared cataloging. Two unique programs are the Public Law 480 Program and the National Program for Acquisitions and Cataloging. The former program was authorized by an amendment to the 1954 Agricultural Trade Development Assistance Act and has been administered by the Library of Congress since funded in 1962. Under this law, as explained in Chapter 5 (see p. 122), foreign currencies owned by the United States in "soft currency" countries can be used to buy selected foreign publications and pay for their cataloging. These publications and their catalog records — from countries such as Indonesia, India, Pakistan, the United Arab Republic, Israel, and Yugoslavia — are deposited in over three hundred research libraries. The plan is especially economical in countries publishing in less common languages and having book trades and national bibliographies that are not well organized. Though there are some minor procedural difficulties, the wide distribution of selected current publications from these important countries is a sound use of public assets, and the shared cataloging is an even more noteworthy achievement.

The Library of Congress also administers the National Program for Acquisitions and Cataloging. Largely through the interest of the Association of Research Libraries, the Higher Education Act of 1965 was amended to include Title IIC, which authorizes the appropriation of money by which the Library of Congress has undertaken a world-wide program for acquiring publications of research significance and for the *prompt* cataloging of such publications. It was this latter consideration which inspired the program because two ARL studies a decade apart indicated that ARL member libraries were able to get help in the form of LC cataloging copy for only 40-50 per cent of their acquisitions. The percentage now may range above 75 per cent. This was a result not merely of limitations on LC's financial capacity to acquire important publications, but of the funding required to catalog promptly such publications upon receipt. As the program is now working, new publications are airmailed to LC for cataloging in order that cataloging copy may be available by the time the publications are received by surface mail in other libraries. Since promptness in cataloging requires additional staff to expedite the work, the funding has taken this into consideration. As of 1968, the program has been implemented to a considerable extent in Western Europe and in selected other locations, and plans exist for complete coverage.

Since university libraries are moving more and more into international studies and are getting increasing numbers of foreign publications, the PL 480 and NPAC programs are invaluable as a source of centralized cataloging copy in languages for which there are national shortages of specialists. They hold forth the promise of truly centralized cataloging and offer such ancillary benefits as enabling libraries to rely increasingly on clerical assistants for cataloging. LC is accepting citations from national bibliographies as a basis for descriptive cataloging, a practice which is likely to have a reciprocal influence. It will almost certainly bring greater bibliographical uniformity internationally. Foreign countries may, under NPAC, as they have under PL 480, get access to cataloging copy for vernacular publications faster than has heretofore been the case from their own domestic sources. When this copy is available for an extensive segment of a nation's publications it can, with little further effort, be converted into national bibliography. Libraries in the United States learn more promptly of the existence of important foreign publications through reviewing of LC cards, and the total LC effort contains within it implications of tremendous significance as libraries move into full-scale automation. Just as the LC card service at the beginning of the twentieth century was soundly grounded on extensive domestic holdings built from copyright deposits, so may the computerized bibliographical record of the future find its basis in the extensive collecting made possible by PL 480 and NPAC.

To support regional union catalogs is an altruistic activity for the larger university libraries and directly beneficial to the smaller. All universities gain by support of the National Union Catalog and its subsidiary elements for master microfilms and newspapers on film. The *Union List of Serials* and other such joint efforts are unquestionably more expensive forms of cooperation since they involve large, or very large, efforts in a brief span of time. Especially troublesome are the projects of small groups or large organizations which may require some dozens of hours on the part of library staff to submit local holdings, ferret out items in manuscript collections, or determine which variants are found through collation so that a microtext project can use the items. The larger libraries can be inundated by such requests. The originators are generally to be faulted for not constructing a realistic budget which would pay researchers for undertaking the work in major libraries. A project like the ULS is of inestimable value to all universities. Other projects have to be weighed against the library's selfish motivations of prospective use or desired publicity, the value to scholarship generally and to its local faculty in particular, and the immediate staff shortage or processing arrears that the library faces. Every union list project, large or small, will require time which cannot be assigned to other library programs.

BINDING AND PRESERVATION

The function of binding and preservation is to provide suitable protection for each item added to the collection and to take action to preserve it for the use of future generations. This includes the entire physical preparation for use: supplying cover strength appropriate to weight and presumed use, stubs for missing parts, pockets for loose parts, bookplates or other marks of ownership, internal marks of identification, and circulation devices; lettering spines; and repairing damaged leaves and binding. It should also involve attention to atmospheric conditions for longevity, use conditions to permit continued service, and shelf conditions that show sensitivity to the needs of the book.

Policies

Binding policies can greatly affect efficient service and economy. When thousands of students handle tens of thousands of books each year, the amount of wear is staggering. There needs to be a policy on duplication and replacement of titles. This should be a major responsibility of the gift librarian and of all book selection and circulation staff members. The policy should support fairly heavy duplication, especially of items published more than a few years ago. Additional gift or purchased copies of heavily circulated titles are necessary. A program of microfilming may be a necessary part of any preservation program.

Another policy should deal with the quality of binding. It should generally be appropriate to weight and anticipated circulation. By this rule, some volumes expected to receive slight use require a minimum of treatment with wire stitching and/or plastic covering; others to receive moderate use may need the stronger LUMSPEC (Lesser-Used Materials Specification) level of treatment; at least 50 per cent of acquisitions which may receive somewhat heavy use will need Class A bindings (a better standard so far than the newer ALA standard); and some which will receive very heavy use (e.g., selected bibliographic works) require extra reinforcement of hinges, headbands, corners, end-leaves, or the attachment of "pulls." The library will need to achieve reasonable binding attractiveness with a sufficiently protective binding to maintain the collection. Although it is tempting to say that no item should be added to the shelves without a stiff cover, some collections such as technical reports would properly be exceptions.

The missing parts problem is a continuing one and needs to receive major attention. Innumerable incomplete serials and mono-graphs-in-parts will lead to increasingly broken files and constant damage to issues waiting for the volume to be completed. This eventuality can be reduced through prompt binding upon receipt of the last part; however, service needs suggest a delay in binding until at least one more recent issue is available to readers. Other points to be considered: a staggered binding schedule for titles duplicated on one campus, a duplicate subscription for current use of the few most heavily used or most often pilfered titles, and a microfilm subscription for research use in lieu of binding issues subscribed to for current use.

A policy on bookplating is required. Plates must represent the fund from which the volume was purchased. And plates bearing the correct names must be used when a volume has to be rebound. There is really no shortcut around the legal requirements. The alumni and development offices will be interested in bookplate design and use. An extra effort on this decorative binding element will be well repaid.

Choice of Binderies

Selection of binderies deserves top-level attention, for the choice may mean good, economic binding, promptly executed, or shoddy workmanship, intolerable delays, and fancy prices. Some universities are required to obtain competitive bidding. Most, however, are in a position to consider whether to use a campus bindery, to use a neighboring commercial firm, or to try several commercial firms. No library would consider establishing an in-house bindery unless no adequate commercial firm was within two hundred miles and inexpensive semiskilled labor was locally available; any library which has a bindery is certain to have recently considered getting out of the business. Binding is a trade best left to experts who have enough volume (over $150,000 worth of business) to pay for the machines necessary for competitive pricing. Few if any universities would require their libraries to use campus binderies despite higher prices, for an edition bindery is a different operation from a hand library bindery in that the equipment and staff talents of the latter cannot be interchanged to achieve greater efficiency in the entire process.

Which commercial firm to select is therefore the typical question. Following are the principal requirements:

Competitive prices are maintained for comparable work.
Turn-around time in the shop is no more than one month.
Special service (e.g., one or two weeks) is given "rush" requests
    for reference works or books for circulation reserve.

186

Size of bindery is sufficient to handle the university's work without fluctuating production volume.

Transportation time from the bindery is one half work day for special recalls, and deadlines are met.

Ability is demonstrated to provide bindings to national specifications and to any desired simplifications thereof.

Ability is demonstrated to save the maximum amount of the margin when sanding the spine for rebinding.

Shipping and billing procedures are good.

Occasional special requests (e.g., leather work, solander cases, and slip cases) can be handled.

Building is fireproof and contents fully insured.

Management personnel are cordial and staff has a history of competence and stability.

It will be useful to send a sample shipment to any firm being considered, including an expendable volume which can be used to test performance or to take apart to see its construction. Workmanship and price can then be inspected before any large change is made; and any shift of a large account should be with advance notice as a courtesy to both firms. Many universities will use two or more firms for regular books, sometimes another firm for paperbacks and rare books, and some overseas agents for binding as part of purchasing; independent branches may use still others. A repair service in the library is essential for torn leaves, damaged pockets, and cracked spines; the repair service staff may develop proficiency with pamphlet covers and inexpensive plastic-type binding substitutes, and it may even have a person expert with rare books.

Budgeting

Budgeting for preservation can include three elements. One may be for staff and supplies to conduct a repair, mending, and special covering program. The amount budgeted may vary depending on local need. A second may be a figure for the microfilming of items selected for preservation from among irreplaceable books with poor paper or with further rebinding not possible. A flat sum may be provided, though it is preferable to allocate a percentage of total book funds (a minimum of 2 per cent, a maximum running to as much as 7 per cent). The third element will be the budget for purchased binding. This item is unfortunately often used to balance the budget request, and nearly all libraries continue to under-budget. The proper figure for a university library should be at least 20 per cent of the anticipated expenditures for all book materials (or at least 17 per cent of the total book, periodical, and binding budget). If the figure is less, there will very likely be a backlog distributed among various library collections, materials will be lost or damaged, and the total personnel and binding cost of correcting this deficiency will exact a premium. In times when more and more periodicals and paperback books are being collected, the desirable percentage will undoubtedly edge up slowly. While the cost of books and salaries of librarians tend to follow a national market, binding is like clerical costs and follows a local market. So libraries in some areas (e.g., the West Coast) will need to increase the percentage.

Binding simplifications may cut unit costs appreciably, and careful attention to each cost factor can result in many more units being bound. This is true for most commercial binderies, which will be pleased to offer discount prices to libraries with a large volume of work proposing simplifications compatible with the production process. The economy should be based on branch library agreement with the main library on most points. The main library may be willing to dispense with spine rub-offs or accept buckram of a single color, contrary to branches with a greater percentage of new materials in reading rooms. On the other hand, the medical library may wish to discard advertisements before binding whereas most others wish all ads retained. Skilled binders receive a high union wage, and any steps which eliminate unnecessary lettering, standardize treatment, and reduce unneeded quality in binding will stretch the binding budget.

One final point concerns binding allotments. As with book funds, binding funds which are inadequate may require that each branch or departmental library state anticipated needs in terms of *units* or *dollars*, receive an administrative allocation, and live within the established maximum. (Using *units* with quality controls is preferable to using *dollars* since the unit system does not permit branch librarians to reduce quality excessively to obtain more units.) Each library will have arrears which should be kept under inventory just as cataloging arrears should be monitored. Such an inventory is needed for budget justification. It also serves as a reserve pool when the normal flow of materials is unseasonally low and some volumes are needed to even out staff workload and shipments. This procedure also obtains for large sets in need of rebinding, such as reference works.

Staff

Staff relations with other departments and branches require that the staff responsible for binding and preservation be clear as to policy, cordial as to relations, and highly organized in a process in which considerable judgment is essential. Typical staffing and production for a binding and finishing department is as follows:

Typical Binding and Preservation Staff and Annual Production

Staff
1 Librarian II
1 Librarian I or Supervising assistant
2 Senior bookbinders for in-house work
2 Bindery preparation clerks
5 Library assistants for finishing tasks (plating, tagging, marking, and pocketing)

Annual production

Volumes sent outside for binding	15,300
Volumes rebound internally	4,000
Volumes repaired	12,800
Volumes finished	85,000

The binding department usually reports to the assistant director for technical services, sometimes to the head of the acquisitions department, and occasionally to the head of cataloging or serials. The variety of possibilities stems from these many relationships of binding and preservation and the long-term service and cost implications of these responsibilities.

Of the many relationships, a few can be mentioned. The connection with the serial records department constitutes an important relationship since a very large proportion of all binding will be of serial publications, and their complexity is legendary. Questions must be answered concerning location of payment data and renewal periods, notation for shelf listing once binding is complete, and place for holding title pages and indexes. The catalog department or the binding department will perform the important function of designating the quality of binding warranted. The special collections department has legitimate concerns over security and special binding treatment for its materials. And branches will carry more responsibility than departments in the main library for collation, handling any inventory of arrears, choosing volumes needing rebinding or mending; larger branches may even ship directly to the bindery. Binding staff may perform all these functions for service units in the main library. A printed form is useful to assure that collation once performed is not repeated; it is certainly unnecessary for the bindery staff to repeat, and charge for, collation already performed by trained library personnel.

Preservation Programs

A preservation program should provide a complete protection service, beginning with systematic cleaning of the collections at suitable intervals. (Cleaning should be done annually in unairconditioned buildings in those areas having much dirt in the atmosphere.) In due course, nearly the entire collection will have to pass through repair, rebinding, replacement, microfilming, or some new stabilization process. This is an awesome thought. Librarians have been among the first to recognize that heavier and heavier student use of books, the increasing air pollution problem, and deteriorating quality in paper and book manufacturing are combining to present universities with a prodigious preservation problem if they are to have the materials essential for scholars of the next century. Libraries will need to appoint a *conservateur* who will be expert in leather preservation, insect control, mold, and foxing, as well as binding and lamination. He should also be an expert in photographic reproduction. He should guard against all chemically unstabilized articles, specify the atmospheric conditions, and protect the books against damaging faults in book trucks, book ends, and book return devices, and against excessive exposure to sunlight. He should know the problems of housing manuscripts, maps, and sheet music. These aspects are just as much the responsibility of librarians in research libraries today as they were of librarians one hundred or more years ago.

All research libraries are faced with a prodigious problem in the preservation of research library materials. The Association of Research Libraries has had a committee devoted to this subject for a decade, and the Council on Library Resources has been imaginative and constructive in supporting research into the causes of paper deterioration. Most of the Council's support has been directed to the W. J. Barrow Research Laboratory of Richmond, Virginia.

It has been said that most modern book papers may reasonably be expected to last only fifty years and that most books published since the last quarter of the nineteenth century carry within them the seeds of their own destruction. Beginning in the 1860's, greatly increased demand for paper led manufacturers to substitute wood pulp for rags as a basic ingredient. For many years this was thought to be the cause of deterioration. However, Mr. Barrow's experiments pointed to hyperacidity as the principal villain, and he developed specifications for book papers using long-staple fibers sized with alkaline-compatible material. Such papers, his tests showed, could be expected to last eight times as long (four hundred years) as ordinary modern papers. These "permanent durable" papers are being used more widely by printers in the United States, although only a fraction of the market can be said to be affected. There appears to be ample evidence, furthermore, that atmosphere polluted with sulphur dioxide or nitrogen dioxide increases the acidity of paper irrespective of its original alkalinity and consequently can contribute substantially to deterioration.

Another element in paper deterioration appears to be temperature. Recent research indicates that it is possible to increase the half-life of paper from two hundred to five hundred years by reducing temperatures from 77° to 68° Fahrenheit. Although not enough is known about the effect of relative humidity on paper deterioration, there is at least theoretical evidence to indicate that an r.h. of 50 per cent is adversely high.

Although some paper manufacturers dispute the findings with respect to acidity and temperature, there seems to be enough substance to them to lead some libraries to design new buildings with stack areas susceptible of being cooled to lower temperatures than heretofore achieved, and the Barrow Laboratory and others have experimented with deacidification baths or sprays that might extend the life of millions of books now in libraries.

Since libraries now spend as much as five dollars for rebinding, twenty dollars for a copy of a small edition reprint, and thirty dollars for an electrostatic replacement, they can afford a fairly expensive alternate method of preserving an important original publication if a technique of proven effectiveness is developed. However, it is probable that only an enormous national program supported by Federal funds and based on cooperation among the major research libraries will be equal to the problem. The program would have to identify and preserve at least one of the "best" surviving copies of each book and provide scholarly access to the text through some method of reproduction — perhaps a photocopy or microtext. The impact of such a program on the prevailing tradition of rapid access is sobering, and yet this alternative may be the only option that assures the preservation of millions of deteriorating publications. If this is, indeed, the shape of the future, it suggests the urgent need for dramatic improvement in our antiquated methods of transmitting text from one point to another.

The entire subject of paper deterioration has been productive of conflicting testimony and inconclusive findings, but it is of such major importance that it will be of critical concern to all library directors.

SELECTED REFERENCES

Acquisitions

Clapp, Verner W., and Robert T. Jordan. "Re-evaluation of Microfilm as a Method of Book Storage," *College and Research Libraries*, 24 (January 1963), 5–15.

Miller, Robert A. "The Improvement of Book Collections for Academic Libraries," in *Library Lectures*. Baton Rouge, Louisiana State University Libraries, 1968. no. 8, pp. 43–54.

Morris, T. D. "Techniques of Appraising the Administrative Strength of an Organization," *College and Research Libraries*, 13 (April 1952), 111–16.

Osborn, Andrew D. *Serial Publications: Their Place and Treatment.* Chicago, American Library Association, 1955.

Pritsker, Alan B., and J. William Sadler. "Evaluation of Microfilm as a Method of Book Storage," *College and Research Libraries*, 18 (July 1957), 290–6.

Randall, William M., ed. *The Acquisition and Cataloging of Books.* Chicago, University of Chicago Press, 1940.

Skipper, James E. "Organizing Serial Records at the Ohio State University Libraries," *College and Research Libraries*, 14 (January 1953), 39–45.

Tauber, Maurice F., *et al. Technical Services in Libraries: Acquisitions, Cataloging, Classification, Binding, Photographic Reproduction, and Circulation Operations.* New York, Columbia University Press, 1954.

Vosper, Robert. "Allocation of the Book Budget: Experience at U.C.L.A.," *College and Research Libraries*, 10 (July 1949), 215–19.

Williams, Edwin E., and Ruth V. Noble. *Conference on International Cultural, Educational, and Scientific Exchanges, Princeton University, November 25-26, 1946: Preliminary Memoranda.* Chicago, American Library Association, 1947.

Wulfekoetter, Gertrude. *Acquisition Work; Processes Involved in Building Library Collections.* Seattle, University of Washington Press, 1962.

Cataloging and Classification

Bentz, Dale M., and Thera P. Cavender. "Reclassification and Recataloging," *Library Trends*, 2 (October 1953), 249–78.

Greenwood, Anne. "Project India," *Library Resources and Technical Services*, 4 (Fall 1960), 318–22.

Haykin, David J. *Subject Headings: A Practical Guide.* Washington, Government Printing Office, 1951.

193

Kingery, Robert E., and Maurice F. Tauber, eds. *Book Catalogs*. New York, Scarecrow Press, 1963.
    See especially the papers by Weber, Tysse, Stevens, and "Preferred Practices in the Publication of Book Catalogs."
Osborn, Andrew D., and Susan M. Haskins. "Catalog Maintenance," *Library Trends*, 2 (October 1953), 279–89.
Reichmann, Felix. "Cornell's Reclassification Program," *College and Research Libraries*, 23 (September 1962), 369–74, 440–50.
Reichmann, Felix. "Costs of Cataloging," *Library Trends*, 2 (October 1953), 290–317.
Shera, Jesse H., and Margaret Egan, eds. *Bibliographic Organization: Papers Presented before the Fifteenth Annual Conference of the [University of Chicago] Graduate Library School July 24-29, 1950*. Chicago, University of Chicago Press, 1951.
Tauber, Maurice F., ed. *The Subject Analysis of Library Materials: Papers Presented at an Institute, June 24-28, 1952, under the Sponsorship of the School of Library Service, Columbia University, and the A.L.A. Division of Cataloging and Classification*. New York, Columbia University School of Library Service, 1953.
Tauber, Maurice F., *et al. Technical Services in Libraries*.
    See above under *Acquisitions*.
Weber, David C. "Book Catalog Trends in 1966," *Library Trends*, 16 (July 1967), 149–64.

Binding and Preservation
Adams, Randolph G. "Librarians as Enemies of Books," *Library Quarterly*, 7 (July 1937), 317–31.
American Library Association. Library Technology Project. *Protecting the Library and Its Resources: A Guide to Physical Protection and Insurance. Report on a Study by Gage-Babcock and Associates*. Chicago, American Library Association, 1963.
Barr, Pelham. "Book Conservation and the University Library Administration," *College and Research Libraries*, 7 (July 1946), 214–19.
Barrow (W. J.) Research Laboratory. *Permanence/Durability of the Book*. Richmond, W. J. Barrow Research Laboratory, 1963–67. Publications I-IV.
Lydenberg, Harry M., and John Archer. *The Care and Repair of Books*. 3rd ed. New York, Bowker, 1945.
Smith, Richard Daniel. "Paper Impermanence as a Consequence of pH and Storage Conditions," *Library Quarterly*, 39 (April 1969), 153–95.

Tauber, Maurice F., ed. "Conservation of Library Materials," *Library Trends*, 4 (January 1956), 213–334.

Virginia State Library. *Permanent/Durable Book Paper: Summary of a Conference Held in Washington, D.C., September 16, 1960*. Richmond, Virginia State Library, 1960.

Weber, David C. "Binding Simplifications," *Library Resources and Technical Services*, 1 (Winter 1957), 9–13.

7. THE READER'S SERVICES FUNCTION

This chapter deals with the library's role in the promotion of and assistance to reading and research. It treats the service operations concerned with facilitating the use of materials — reference assistance, circulation, interlibrary borrowing, photocopying and maintenance of the book stacks. Like the preceding chapter on technical processes, this will concentrate on policy issues, standards, interdepartmental relations, staffing, and economic issues.

THE PROMOTION OF READING

Created as a facility for shared use by the university community, the library exists to provide reading material and other graphic sources to support the purposes of the institution. As the major depository for reading matter, it is in a unique position to promote reading; as a service organization, it must facilitate reading; as part of a pedagogical institution, it should play an active role in making books a significant part of a university education.

The tremendous increase during the 1950's and 1960's in the use of quality paperbacks has had its impact upon the university library. Use of undergraduate reserve books has declined as a result of the fact that so many titles are now available in paperbacks in college bookstores. However, in studies of student reading, the present condition reflects that reported a decade ago by Lester Asheim:

> The overall pattern is very much the same in all of the studies and is invariably discouraging. . . . 8 per cent to 15 per cent of college students withdraw no books from their library in an entire academic year; . . . 35 per cent apparently read one book a month. . . . From 90 per cent to 94 per cent of all student reading is required curricular assignment. The correlation between scholastic standing and library use is

197

low, though students with the higher scholastic rating tend to do more "free" reading. . . . It seems quite clear that the amount of reading can be increased where the course is so designed as to motivate more reading and in those schools where the tradition of wide reading is established.[1]

The teacher can be the prime stimulus to student reading; yet the objectives of the university are broader than the goals of individual courses, and the library will have failed if it does not fulfill part of its proper function by providing extracurricular reading and by stimulating interest in books. Librarians are in a unique position to contribute to such stimulation and should not neglect the opportunity. This collaborative effort may instill in the student an enthusiasm for reading that will produce permanent enjoyment and profit after graduation. As he grows older, the former student may forget the facts he had to learn for class. Likewise, some of the body of knowledge he was taught becomes obsolete unless refreshed; but the adult should retain the enthusiasm instilled by the able teacher, and he should remember the open door to all worldly knowledge which was revealed through his library use. The knowledge of books, discrimination in their selection for reading, manipulation of the bibliographic instruments for their location, and the experience of satisfaction and pleasure in their content should remain a lifelong joy. This major benefit of a higher education derives from the library; some expenditure of library effort and funds should promote this end.

General or unstructured leisure reading may be prompted in significant degree by programs of independent study, directed reading, seminars at even the freshman level, colloquia, and other innovations in educational practice. The habit of general reading may also develop from research for honors papers.

When these newer programs are characterized by individually pursued study under the guidance of an instructor, they serve to bring the student to the library of his own free will. The library may be viewed under such circumstances as an attractive resource for personal satisfaction and achievement rather than as a facility for meeting the chore of required reading for a class deadline — a crucial change in attitude. This development in higher

---

[1] Reported in Jacob M. Price, ed., *Reading for Life*, pp. 16-17.

education could be especially significant in the 1970's, just as were the "concentration and distribution" of courses introduced in the first part of this century and the general education survey courses of the 1950's.

Although the library should facilitate use and encourage general reading, faculty members bear the major burden for the success or failure of the university in promoting reading. If the intellectual atmosphere in the classroom and the nature of class assignments foster the use of a large number of books, the library effort will be rewarded and the student's education will benefit. Robert Vosper has stressed the importance of maintaining on campus the overall climate in which a regard for reading may develop widely. Under ideal circumstances, the distinction between required curriculum reading and general reading should largely disappear. Reading should become at once a means of meeting class requirements and at the same time a pleasurable occupation which will be pursued for its own sake. The library can encourage this general reading so that the enthusiasms of college years are given full range; and the student thus forms the patterns for adult life, bearing witness that no one's education is ever in a literal sense a closed book.

Whereas the promotion of reading underlies all activities dealt with in this book, there are basic student desires and attitudes which must be satisfied in a library program to support reading.

The most significant step the library can take in fostering general education is to provide freedom of access to collections. The ease with which one can reach the collections will affect one's attitudes. This is true of research collections as well as those specifically for undergraduate needs. And it also serves to justify the highly selective collection gathered for purposes of nurturing the "general education" of the undergraduate — such as the collection of from three thousand to ten thousand volumes in the Morrison Library at Berkeley, the Tower Room at Dartmouth, the Alumni Room at Columbia, the Farnsworth Room at Harvard, and others — assembled for those who eschew the gluttony of the research collections in order to savor the gourmet delicacies of titles and editions carefully selected for the palate of the young scholar.

Another significant aid is omission of red tape in the use of the collections. How exasperating are some circulation procedures! What better way to quell enthusiasm for scholarship than by placing obstacles in the path of a youth who seeks on his own to follow the example of the teacher who has stimulated his inquisitiveness. Classic frustrations include the information void that occurs when a book is recorded in the catalog but cannot be found, when a desired journal has been in a professor's office for weeks, or when a volume has departed to spend a month at a bindery. A library staff sensitive to the needs of its clientele must be aware of such failings and do what it can to prevent them.

In promoting general reading it must also be borne in mind that intellectual interests vary markedly and that the library's collection should be correspondingly wide ranging. Students form an increasingly heterogeneous group, and the library should seek to reach those on the fringes just as much as those in the main stream. Diverse home backgrounds, cultures, nationalities — in fact all the socio-economic variables — obtain in student populations today. The library traditionally reaches the common majority of students; only by unorthodox program efforts can the library reach those interested in such causes as the new student movements — the so-called free university, the new left, the pacifist unions, the Third World Liberation Front, or the student power movements. This is true of less extreme instances, be it regions of the world with Peace Corps activity, or concerns with minority treatment, domestic poverty, guerrilla theater, or popular music. Reading is a lonely act; yet the subjects explored usually help the individual relate to a social need. There must be relevance, as students today often point out.

In addition to the foregoing basic inducements, there are a host of specific efforts that may be made and that have proven worthwhile in encouraging the minority of addicted readers to read more widely than they might otherwise. These include student book clubs, book collection prizes, bookstore tie-ins, rental collections with extra copies of popular titles, exhibits, display shelves for new acquisitions, the distribution of lists of significant new acquisitions, publicity via the student paper or radio, series of public lectures or readings related to books or printing, and browsing collections. Each of these can stimulate reading, as can many of the types of publications mentioned on p. 85. Different efforts will inspire different readers. Each activity has its place and should be considered as part of the total library program. Staff talents, space limitations, exhibit facilities, special fund opportunities, student interests and responses, and other factors may shape the specific program.

It is worth dwelling on the browsing collection of limited size. Such a collection, with the books chosen for their broad contemporary interest rather than for curricular relationships, may occupy part of the main library reading room or a special room such as those at Berkeley and elsewhere mentioned above, it may constitute a residence or dormitory library, or it may form the greater part of an undergraduate or collegiate library. Careful selection for current relevance is the key to any browsing collection. Its value in the promotion of reading is based upon the fact that the novice will appreciate the careful selection of the "best" recent books, both fiction and nonfiction, on a subject that interests him. The reader has been saved the effort of selecting the most appealing or most pertinent works among the many. This is one of the prime justifications for a separate undergraduate library. It is one means by which the large university research library can provide one of the best features of certain small liberal arts college libraries — the encouragement of reading through discriminating selection of the best books. Such browsing collections are welcomed by the student who is hard pressed for time yet wishes to broaden his intellectual interests.

The intellectual atmosphere in a university is made up of many conditions and intangible factors. There are the fame of a distinguished scholar, the student residence programs, the admission and curriculum standards, the research projects, public lectures and performances, the publications of the university and its press. Many others might be cited, but one of the most significant is the library. The library's collections are basic to the intellectual life of the university. No less important are the special collections, the display of unique materials, the quarters in which students may study, the service policies, and, above all, the quality of the library staff and its service to the community.

Taken as a whole the library should contribute significantly to the education received by the student in his years at the university. A dynamic program designed to promote the general reading of the students is the best way to assure that the library will be effective. With a well-conceived program to encourage and facilitate

201

reading, the library will engender a warm regard on the part of its patrons and will be known as a home for the scholars of today and tomorrow. Its availability to students is, in fact, one of the striking benefits they may derive from the experience of higher education.

REFERENCE AND INFORMATION ASSISTANCE

The reference department function is to help the library's clientele locate book materials, citations, and information, and to provide other bibliographic advice. The traditional means of providing this guidance is through personal reference assistance from a desk, lectures or group tours, handbooks or guidebooks, and selectively prepared bibliographies. The reference desk assistance may involve interpretation of or direction to library records, direction to or interpretation of bibliographies and other reference works, information on citations and analytic bibliography, and use of any part of the library facilities and collections. The staff are the library's experts on use of the library; their talent and training are available to groups or to individuals as needed.

General Policies of Service

Policies evolve because there are relatively few limitations on the extent of reference help, other than availability of staff time, and an inquiry may lead in any direction. A graduate student who obviously is in critical need of one reference may require and deserve rather extended help. Or a professor who provides considerable book selection assistance may request preparation of a bibliography which would be of help to many students. It is from the mosaic of such actions that guidance is developed on policy issues.

General principles of service need discussion; they frequently are given less attention than they deserve. As a rule, the librarians in reference service should be instructors in the use of libraries and should assist with *all* of the general collections of the library, not merely with the "reference collection." Too many librarians provide the factual answer or conduct the search instead of showing the reader how to do it. And they appear to limit their service to the threshold of the reference room. This latter attitude may be out of a false feeling that books in other departments are regarded as the property of the departmental librarians. But it probably stems in large measure from the method of teaching reference work in library schools. Louis Round Wilson noted that the

> prevailing method which library schools have employed . . . has been to present the special characteristics of a number of reference works in a number of fields and to assign problems. . . . This procedure has depended largely upon memory of facts about specific reference books and the ability to use the reference collection in answering inquiries. It has minimized subject specialization and the ability to use the resources of the library as a whole in aiding inquirers. It has also emphasized the answering of questions by the reference worker rather than familiarizing the inquirer with the materials of the collection and aiding him in learning how to use them effectively.[2]

As a consequence, the university library needs to teach its staff a different set of attitudes and policies. This should be based on the fact that the faculty provide the subject discipline through formal studies but are not always skilled in library use. Students are inquisitive and highly independent to the extent that most will prefer to serve themselves in use of the library. Even as freshmen, students are widely disparate in their ability to use libraries, so that what one needs to learn as a sophomore one January evening, another may not need to learn until an October mid-afternoon when he is a senior.

The reference service, therefore, requires relatively long open hours, needs to facilitate self-help, needs to provide spur-of-the-moment instruction for students from elementary to advanced levels, and must treat each library building as *one* facility (as the student sees it) with the reference collection but a selected portion conveniently shelved separately because of its great use and restricted circulation. Librarians should constantly review the volumes selected for this prominent collection, often deleting and replacing items. They should regularly watch notices of new publications for items to be brought into the library as well as very selectively into the reference collection.

Reader service policies in a university library can be designed to supplement and complement the work of the faculty. The policies

---

[2] In Pierce Butler, ed., *The Reference Function of the Library*, p. vii.

should recognize the growth of the individual from freshman matriculation to graduation, yet they should accommodate the transfer student and the variety of graduate student pursuits, and they must acknowledge that not all high schools in this country and abroad provide the same level of preparation. Service policies then can follow the basic principle that the staff should help readers to learn to use the library but not, in general, answer questions for them. Readers should be given every aid to serve themselves, through signs, simple means to locate materials, and an easily evident and logical pattern of staff service points.

In 1955 Keyes D. Metcalf summed up Harvard's policy with regard to service as follows:

1. The basic principle has been that the staff should help readers to learn to use the Library, not in general, answer questions for them. Free access to books in the stacks has been provided whenever feasible. . . .

2. The number of service points can be reduced, with resultant economies in operation. . . .

3. Charging systems . . . should be as simple as possible.

4. Service . . . is most satisfactory when every effort is made to enable the reader to serve himself.[3]

The "self-help" policy affects all of the library service departments and should be emphasized. Cataloging records, classification, circulation procedures, branch library location, current periodical location, government document use, photocopying — these and other aspects of the library operation must be as clear as possible; otherwise the library will need to bolster its facilities with extra staff to explain or direct or assist. Concise, easily understood, attractive signs can contribute a great deal toward this objective. A handbook or set of guides can also help those too timid to ask questions, provide carefully thought out and expressed answers to such problems as location of a Short Title Catalog film, assemble basic information about all branch libraries that not all librarians would know, list other special library resources within a few dozen miles, and be available at all service points at all hours when the

[3] *Report on the Harvard University Library*. Cambridge, Harvard University Library, 1955, p. 27.

library is open. Adequate self-help may in fact require not only a general handbook, but also one on the undergraduate facility, another on the document collection, and perhaps a set of subject leaflets on basic research tools aimed at upper-class students.

One other very important topic is collaboration with the faculty. The university library is a tool for instruction, and the librarians should work closely with the faculty to this end. Basic use of the library must be taught in one of several ways. It should be coordinated with particular undergraduate needs — e.g., the first library problem, the first bibliographic essay, the first major research paper, and the first independent study project. This should result in lectures by librarians during the required freshman English course; a few film, filmstrip, or slide programs specifically related to topics being studied by the class; or a set of short tours announced in class. Librarians should make every effort to offer these services to professors responsible for key courses, both undergraduate and graduate. Audio-visual techniques can be used effectively since the number of students reached at different times is sufficient to justify a substantial expenditure of funds, particularly if the result is a more effective presentation which will be useful for several years. Collaboration with the faculty may also serve to stimulate their use of the "library method" of teaching. This method is eloquently upheld by professors; and yet, even in the finest universities, there are too few men who use the library as a teaching laboratory. Discussion of the library potential with faculty members should serve to suggest to them ways they can use it to better advantage in their courses.

Another instructional possibility is for the library to offer a half-year elective course in use of the library. This serves a different purpose from the orientation described above by providing for more detailed teaching. Such a course may concentrate on modern bibliographic method and be aimed at lower division undergraduates, using as a text a book like Jean Key Gates' *Guide to the Use of Books and Libraries* (McGraw Hill, 1962) or R. B. Downs' *How to Do Library Research* (University of Illinois Press, 1966). Or it may concentrate on English literary bibliography from Elizabethan through Victorian times and be aimed at upper-division undergraduates and graduate students, using as texts books such as Ronald B. McKerrow's *An Introduction to Bibliography for*

Literary Students (Oxford, 1928), Fredson T. Bowers' *Principles of Bibliographical Description* (Princeton, 1949), and Arundell J. K. Esdaile's *Manual of Bibliography* (Rev. ed. by Roy Stokes. Allen & Unwin, 1967). The former course would be attractive to historically minded research students in the humanities. The latter is of special use to students in history and literature, and must, of course, have a skilled instructor of unimpeachable scholarship and must also receive support of the appropriate departments of instruction. Beyond these possibilities, a library may offer a variety of undergraduate seminars under such names as History of the Book, Use of Manuscripts, Transmission of Recorded Knowledge, and Censorship and Freedom of Speech. A colloquium series in which are reviewed seriatim the bibliographic instruments of particular fields is still another possibility — e.g., two-hour sessions in the late afternoon in successive fields such as engineering, political science, and economics. These possibilities all depend on the competence of the librarians and the receptivity of the faculty and academic officers.

Service to Particular Groups

The extent of service will vary. The university library will provide different help to such groups as undergraduates, graduate and post-doctoral students, faculty and research associates, university staff, the families of the foregoing, and persons outside the university community. The undergraduates require propaedeutics, or introductory level instruction. This is frequently done in class sessions and through use of a special undergraduate collection which simplifies the transition from limited high school libraries to the sophistication of research libraries. Each undergraduate should be given all possible help commensurate with the needs of the entire group. Pedantry and condescension are intolerable; cordiality and every evidence of a wish to be of professional service are essential.

Graduate students require a far more specialized level of instruction, and their needs are best served not by mass treatment but by small sessions with seminar classes. Students using the very small departmental libraries may receive little or no expert assistance, since each of them is staffed with a single nonprofessional assistant, whereas those using the larger ones may receive more expert assistance than students using the main library since the branch librarian may be a specialist in the literature of the field in question. This assistance may include a high degree of subject expertise, but it will *not* ordinarily include the type of "special library" service common to industry, which covers literature surveys, abstracting, translating, and critical bibliographic studies. The discrepancy may well serve to explain the view of librarians held by some scientists; they received brief guidance when they were undergraduates and they receive mediocre help now they are professors, yet their colleagues who work for business and commercial firms receive superior support from "information scientists" or documentalists paid to perform these extended services. Some departmental libraries do offer specialized services, such as annotated lists of selected current acquisitions. Yet costs prevent the university library from extending this dimension of service as much as faculty and librarians might wish.

Faculty members increasingly have funds for research associates and employ graduate students part time as research assistants. These groups now constitute a large number of users who may need considerable assistance, some of whom may deserve studies or carrels for their work. This becomes a special problem when the graduate student is working actually for an off-campus profit-making firm. Universities attract research firms which use professors as consultants and expect them to use the library in their consultant work. The question is discussed later in this chapter under circulation service (see pp. 219 and 223).

Each group has its needs, and reference personnel can help each group in somewhat different ways. Typical of a good policy statement is the following from the University of Illinois *Staff Manual*:

Reference Desk Service

The amount of assistance given is commensurate with the apparent need of the inquirer. Extended search is often made for the faculty member or graduate student engaged in research and for undergraduates when the purpose and subject matter justify the expenditure of time.

Questions on overlapping subjects may involve material in several departments. After consultation of general reference works, the reader is advised what procedure to follow. Readers are referred directly to departmental libraries when the subject matter falls definitely within a subject department and cannot be satisfactorily answered by general reference material.

The Reference Department is glad to cooperate with other departments in searching for information and to assist members of other departments by offering suggestions and advice when the usual sources have failed.

A large amount of work is done with undergraduate students in answering inquiries of all types, whether the inquiry originates from the student's personal interests and reading or in the preparation of themes, class reports, and term papers. The instructional phase of reference assistance is emphasized by explaining the proper use of reference books, card catalog, and other library tools, and by making suggestions as to methods and materials suited to the student's needs.

Service to readers often involves help at the general catalog during hours when the Information Desk is unattended.

Assistants on duty at the Reference Desk are responsible for completing the search for questions received. They are, however, free to call upon anyone in the Department for aid and frequently several members cooperate. As far as possible, questions are completed at the time of inquiry. When more extended search is necessary, material is held at the desk for the reader's use later.

Telephone inquiries are answered directly if possible. If interpretation of information is involved, as is often the case with statistics, the inquirer is urged to come to the Library to make personal use of the material.

No extended help is given in genealogical work. Inquirers are shown the usual reference books and indexes and advised how to obtain material from the general catalog.

Information Desk Service

An Information Desk near the general catalog, attended by a reference assistant during busy hours of the day and evening, serves primarily as a clearing house for library information. Its function is to give help in the use of the catalog and in choice of material from it, to give advice about material available in the Reference Room and in other library departments, to interpret library rules, regulations, and procedures, and to give directory information about the Library, campus, and community.

As libraries grow in size and complexity, as the bibliographic apparatus becomes too extensive for any man to cope with alone, all groups of users will need more assistance. Even the professor is seldom the master of the bibliography of his field. A cadre of subject specialists will need to be formed to help users, whether the library collections are decentralized more or less. The more they are decentralized, the easier it will be for someone working in the departmental or branch library for his field. Yet the majority of readers in a university will not be in any one of those specialized centers; thus personal assistance must be provided in the use of the university library.

Staffing

Service standards are increasingly difficult because the library school degree by itself does not insure sufficient subject background. Librarians with a subject master's degree, or at least a very strong undergraduate major, are essential. This is a development of the past thirty years, during which the previous function of "referring" persons to a card file or book to supplement the conventional bibliographic apparatus was joined by the newer "information" function, wherein persons are provided facts and theories they are seeking. The staff now must provide help to the student who wants a certain sixteenth century recipe as well as the one who needs a reference to "PBB" deciphered.[4] The librarian may answer as many as sixty questions an hour. With thousands of students, the librarian must be a generalist as well as a specialist. He must be knowledgeable in matters of footnote references and form of citations, in analytical or critical as well as enumerative or systematic bibliography, and perhaps even in paleography and the more esoteric aspects of linguistics. Special background will be required in major branch libraries just as it is needed in the main library or undergraduate library, except that in the latter instances four to eight reference librarians can each offer a specialty and thus contribute to a greater subject competence for the whole department.

The development of reference books in this century is striking; each year there are dozens of new directories, union lists, bibliographies, library catalogs, etc. No student or professor can hope to keep up except in a narrow field. The library staff can provide this

[4] "Paul und Braune's Beiträge," entered in the catalog as *Beiträge zur Geschichte der deutschen Sprache und Literatur.*

information, but it doesn't always require a librarian to provide clear instruction in the use of most of these. A bright subprofessional assistant can serve to handle the majority of directional and interpretive questions; or a preprofessional assistant, intern, or trainee may be used. A key attribute of a good staff member is to know when one needs to refer the problem to someone else or to another library department.

A typical university library table of organization, qualifications, and responsibilities follows:

Typical Reference Staff and Annual Production
in a Main Library Department

Department Chief, Librarian IV
Assistant Department Chief, Librarian III
3 Librarian II
1 Librarian I
1 Secretary
1 Library assistant in charge of circulation, graduate reserves,
    and current periodicals
3 Senior library assistants for newspapers, maps, and microtexts
3 Library assistants

Informational and directional inquiries	16,700
Reference questions	21,700
Research questions	813
Problem questions	130
Bibliographies compiled	4
Graduate reserve circulation	25,000
Microtext sheets filed	97,130
Microfilm reels shelved	3,580
Sheet maps filed and listed	1,300

The use of reference librarians for book selection is increasingly possible and desirable as they offer subject specialties and have developed closer ties with academic departments. The book selection team may need experts in areas where full-time curators cannot be afforded and where a faculty member does not carry the responsibility. Fields such as theater arts, oriental art, Afrikaans literature, and western Americana are indicative of subjects for which a few hours a week of selection work may be provided by a reference librarian.

210

Computer-printed monthly list of thousands of serials, being used by students with the assistance of reference librarian — University Library, University of California, San Diego

Finally, the staff of the reference department has special responsibilities for some acquisitions and processing operations, for example, those having to do with playbills, auction catalogs, sheet maps, loose-leaf services, and faculty reprints. Reference librarians in the main library building and librarians providing book selection and reference service as departmental librarians regularly check book-reviewing journals, publishers' announcements, new book lists, second-hand catalogs, and subject bibliographies to supplement the purchase of material recommended by faculty members and to build and maintain quality collections. There is also a considerable amount of processing of library materials carried on by the public service units, including the maintenance of serial and catalog records of various kinds, and in some instances limited classification and cataloging for maps, pamphlet files, microtexts, newspapers, slide collections, curriculum guides, tests, and other specialized materials.

Budgeting

Standards for financial support do not exist in reference services. Since the reference department usually also has responsibility for current periodicals, newspapers, the map collection, interlibrary

loan, and the microtext reading room, there is a sizable staff. Each section will need analysis to determine reasonable work load and the effect upon service if staffing is increased or decreased. Schedules may need scrutiny. Service points should be combined as much as possible, although the building design may frustrate these attempts.

A library may radically reduce its strength in reference service or increase it, without significant reaction from its clientele. One expert librarian may handle several hundred inquiries each day; a second could collaborate to provide evening and weekend service. But, if four or six additional librarians are budgeted, can the increased help be quantified and justified? Herein lies the difference between the institution which must educate very large enrollments at a good quality level and the institution which handles smaller enrollments and strives for a slightly better quality level. It is the extra endeavor in, for example, book selection, the catalog instruments, the special collections, and reference assistance which brings to some university libraries a reputation *par excellence*. And the extra staff does actually result in a better service. Questions can be answered more fully. More time can be spent in tracking down citations needed by students and faculty. A second or third person on the service desk may encourage a timid student to ask a question, as he would not if he saw a single very busy attendant. It may be a vicious circle; since the best professors will attract the best students, both will require better collections, and this in turn will require better overall library services and facilities. The quality of the university library cannot be divorced from that of the institution.

The extra reference work is something of an obligation to libraries which are part of the unofficial national research library facility. Federal support increasingly recognizes its existence. Interlibrary lending, photocopy services, checking of the *Weekly List of Unlocated Research Materials* from the National Union Catalog, and sending cards to the NUC are the best known evidence of membership. The answering of reference inquiries by mail and the accommodation of visiting scholars are equally important. Even in universities with the largest libraries, the faculty and graduate students constantly profit from this national research cooperative.

These factors make it difficult to evaluate budget needs in this area. Careful insight is required. In very general terms, the public services should be staffed as tautly as are the technical processing operations. At least as much pressure here as elsewhere is needed to see that every university dollar is used wisely.

Relations with Other Library Departments

Departmental relations are an important responsibility of the reference department. In the discussion of collection building, mention was made of the reference librarians being called upon for selection. This responsibility extends to other activities: seeing items that should be selectively acquired when readers ask for help in finding a book not in the library, watching interlibrary loan requests for key items the library should have, and, most importantly, watching all sources systematically for bibliographic and other reference volumes that will be useful acquisitions. In the area of cataloging, there should be collaboration between departments to assure that records are reasonably clear for self-help, e.g., pointing out monograph sets especially deserving of analysis, mentioning use of a newly published index to save individual listing of holdings, or suggesting that a subject heading has grown to a point where it needs editorial attention. If interlibrary loan responsibility is assigned to the circulation department, there is obviously a close relationship to reference.

Among other relationships, the most important may be with special collections, government documents, the undergraduate library, and the autonomous branches. In the first two departments there are special card files or printed lists and a great many elusive items not separately cataloged; hence especially close working relations are needed. In the case of the undergraduate library, the burden is on the reference staff in that facility to know the limitations of the collection, to know the type of resources available in the main library or special libraries, and, when occasions arise, to introduce the student to a reference librarian in another library which may have the resources he needs. Temporary rotation of reference staff between the main library and other major units may be mutually profitable, and it also may be useful in working out summer schedules to accommodate vacations.

It is especially important that the reference staff in the main library know the staff and collection strengths in autonomous

213

branches. Periodic visits are needed so that librarians of the central reference department know of these resources; "business" as a subject is, for example, too broad a term to use in referring students to the business school library, whose collections may include special strengths in transportation, early economic history, or the manuscripts of a publishing or chemical firm. The other hazard is that the reference librarian in the branch may try to answer a question that should properly have been addressed to another unit. The student cannot always be expected to know in which library the problem may best be solved; therefore, reference staff must be alert to the need for a cordial referral. Even in a university with completely centralized administration, the tendency to parochialism must be countered.

CIRCULATION AND PHOTOCOPYING SERVICES

The circulation department's function is to lend material, borrow material for use if it is not already in the collections, and provide photocopying as a substitute for borrowing or transcribing. In different institutions these functions may be assigned to one, two, or three departments. The bookstack management is generally combined with circulation service, yet it is here separated for treatment merely to distinguish the lending operation from the custodial responsibility. The lending operation is performed by all service units under somewhat varying policies. Since it presents most of the concerns found in other circulation units, the major circulation service in the main library will receive primary attention. The mechanism for circulation is a system which is designed to maximize the availability of books to all users, allowing each the greatest practicable use without causing others excessive delay. The system should be easy for the patron to use, with accurate and highly current records, rapid in canceling records and returning books to shelves, reasonably flexible for clerical staff operation, and inexpensive. Each institution must select the system best suited to its needs.

There will be some variation of policies within any one institution; there must be consideration in each service unit of the local needs of faculty and students; and policies will be affected by the size of the clientele, the peculiarities of materials, and building conditions. Variations in borrowing privileges, loan periods, renewal practices, and fines for abuses are a major annoyance to students and professors and should be kept to a minimum. Nevertheless, there is an obvious difference between the problems of administering a general research collection of one million volumes and the problems in a small branch with a limited clientele well known to the staff; and variations may be necessary with special classes of materials such as atlases or corporate reports, or because of a very small staff or inferior building conditions, or because of the requirements of a departmental faculty library committee with strong views. To cite a few examples: a graduate department in geology may have only fifty students and insist on no fines whatsoever; a business school may have a program for large-scale corporate financial support and may include library privileges as one of the benefits; a chemistry department may have such good library quarters next to the laboratories that it wishes to circulate nothing outside the building; or a school of education may have a teaching credentials program for which it wants loans of curricular materials to be for one month instead of the typical two-week period.

Some variation in policies is certain to occur. The library handbook should summarize the most important differences. A faculty and staff administrative guide should outline all generally useful services. (See Appendix VII for a typical statement on facilities and services.) The main library circulation or loan department should be the central point of information about these policies. The director must satisfy himself and his faculty library committee that variations are based on significantly different local conditions and take into consideration the needs of university groups other than those constituting the primary users for the unit.

Lending to Students

Student use presents two issues of special concern: the treatment of books placed on reserve for a course of instruction and privileges accorded the student once he has graduated. Books become "reserved" when an instructor asks the library to place them on shelves not open to students and to lend them for an hour or two at a time. There are many ways of arranging and servicing such collections. For many students the reserved book room constitutes practically the entire college library inasmuch as the great preponderance of undergraduate borrowing is from this collection. Many students are antipathetic to the library because assigned reading represents to them a required chore done under time pressure in unattractive quarters. The reserve book arrangement was designed to increase the mobility of a few copies of a book in which each student must read a prescribed portion. It is mass consumption, like cattle feeding at a trough. Neither librarians nor students like the arrangement; so it behooves the library to find ways of changing the conditions of use. On their part, some faculty members will retain the textbook method of instruction, others will turn to a syllabus or to mimeographed data, and still others will find a group of inexpensive paperbacks from which assignments can be made in order that students may purchase copies rather than cope with the library system. In fact, the use of paperback titles is a great boon to the library. Many institutions found that the circulation of reserved books decreased during the mid-1960s and ascribed it to this development. The practice serves to reduce a library function, encourages the students' collecting of books, and promotes bookstore-library cooperation.

The librarian may, on his part, make various improvements in service of course reserves. This effort is necessary since there is no indication that required reading will be completely handled in other ways. There is the possibility of procuring more and more copies of reserved books until the pressure of access to a copy is removed and the book can return to open shelves. The budget implications are great, and no university has found the means to provide all students with a personal copy of all books essential to his courses. Nevertheless, a liberal number of copies should be made available. A very general rule of thumb is one copy for each ten students, although copies for very large classes or for lengthy readings may be scaled down to a substantially lower ratio. A working policy might be roughly as follows: For books to be charged out for *two hours*, one copy is needed for the first ten students and one additional for the next ten students. For larger enrollments: four copies would usually be sufficient for fifty students, five to seven copies for one hundred students and ten copies for three hundred students. For books charged for *one day*, one copy may serve twenty-five students and three copies may be adequate for one hundred students. The number of copies needs to be

216

modified according to the difficulty of the text (mathematical versus literary, for example), the length of time that may be required by the reading schedule for the course, use of the same title in two or more courses, and past experience with a given course or instructor. Faculty members will usually want more copies on reserve than experience shows are needed.

Alternatively, books may be charged from reserve for the time limitation and used outside the room as a student wishes. Adjacent rooms then become, in effect, the reserve book room. Photocopy equipment is only a minor palliative and makes no fundamental correction.

A fundamental change comes about when the reserves are merged completely or in considerable degree with a carefully selected college collection, or "browsing collection" as described earlier in this chapter. Therein is the major promise and justification of separate college or undergraduate libraries, whether they have quarters within the main library or in another building. This supports the tentative conclusion drawn thirty years ago to explain a common problem with reserves:

> Instructors who place from one to two hundred books on reserve . . . do not really expect all these books to be used heavily. Why then do they put them there? Inquiry points to the conclusion that they are trying to get them out of the stacks with the thought that individual books are more or less buried when left in the stacks, and that the greater accessibility secured may result in some of the titles being used which otherwise would have remained untouched. Faculty members have quite generally fallen into the habit of placing on reserve all the books pertaining to a course given, irrespective of whether or not they will be in heavy demand. Instructors and librarians in other words are working at cross purposes in the reserved book room to a considerable extent. The former are endeavoring, rather vaguely, to make of it a more easily accessible college library; the latter merely to increase the circulation of books under heavy demand.[5]

Many undergraduate libraries have been established since 1949, each trying to make the reserve book system more palatable and to create "a more easily accessible college library." Thus Harvard,

[5] Harvie Branscomb, *Teaching with Books*, pp. 120-1.

Michigan, South Carolina, Texas, Cornell, Stanford, California at Berkeley, Illinois, the University of Washington, and other universities find this a solution to the space problem, to the pedagogical problem of providing required readings, and to the dual problem of relieving the undergraduate of the complexities of a research library and relieving serious research workers of the impediments frequently posed by the uninitiated who flounder around in a library not designed for their needs.

When the greatest university libraries were built up during the first half of this century, the intimate advantages of the nineteenth century were lost. Here then is a partial return to the advantages of the seminar library without its disadvantages. Yet the undergraduate library typically does not place in one alcove or set of shelves all materials related to one course; such a system has usually been felt to be a wasteful duplication or an expensive arrangement if done for all courses. Libraries need, however, to move as far as financially possible toward the provision of educationally useful library facilities.

Lending to Faculty Members

Faculty use involves other important issues. One is the consideration of circulation abuses. It must be remembered that the first university libraries existed almost exclusively for the professors, who selected the books and monopolized their use as far as they wished. The professor is still at least as important to the institution as is the student. The professor expects the library to provide promptly and completely the materials he needs for his research and his course preparation and the materials his students need for course assignments, research papers, and dissertations. The library should expect the professor to appreciate the need for accurate circulation records for books removed from their regular shelf positions, to be considerate of the need of others when he is requested to return a book, and to be prompt and understanding of library routines in his preparation and submission of reserve book lists. Similarly, it should expect him to remember to notify the library when he changes or adds assignments in the midst of a course, to recognize or consult with the staff about library limitations when he suggests student research topics, to cite his reference fully when requesting that a book be procured, to work within library staff and budget limitations when he requests the purchase of entire collections or the checking of a great many out-of-print purchase suggestions, and to be cognizant of student needs for bibliographic instruction and reference service. The professor who is willing regularly and systematically to check current trade lists or national bibliographies and suggest acquisitions in his subject should be rewarded with special gratitude and all reasonable library assistance in return.

Any professor will understandably be puzzled by one or another library procedure or condition. He should receive a full and candid explanation in every instance; and since his question will probably reflect the puzzlement of others as well, its implications should be considered. For instance, he may ask why books he wants are neither on the shelf nor charged out, why a classification has been moved in the stack, or why he needs to return or report each year on a book not requested by another reader. Good relations with the faculty are essential, and they are formed in part by courteous explanations. Many a library process has been improved as a direct result of a professor's identifying a problem, sometimes merely by asking why a certain condition cannot be improved.

In any faculty there will be a few who are thoughtless, egotistical, rude, or impatient. It is to be expected that among professors as among other professional men, there will be some who combine brilliance with idiosyncrasies. The chief of the circulation department and other members of the library staff must be tolerant and must know when to question a library policy or relax a rule and when to refer the professor or report the problem to the director. An example of a complex issue is the professor who, in his capacity as consultant to a commercial firm, has assigned a major library project to a graduate student who serves as a research assistant and desires to have full use of one of the limited number of carrels, or the professor who, on the side, has set up a commercial bibliographic service for industry and wants library privileges for his staff.

A wise attitude toward the faculty is expressed in the following statement:

> Each one has his hobby or his pet grievance. Many are worn by the demands of a throng of students who must be guided or coerced into acquiring a modicum of knowledge. The librarian must be quick to

recognize periods of stress and strain and be ready to soothe tired nerves. He must respond quickly to requests for assistance even though the pressure of his own work is great. He must listen attentively to tales of better days and to suggestions for improving the service. All these things help him to a surer grasp of the situation, if not to improved methods of administration. If the librarian can project himself into the attitude of mind of his interrogator, he will acquire a perspective which will relieve his consideration for others of its perfunctory character and give him a sympathetic understanding of the individual which will be of inestimable value in meeting the problem of his position.[6]

It is a real scholar who wants to assess the library collections in his field before accepting a job at a university or who requires a prior commitment of book money for him to spend. These will be the constantly heavy users of the library. The circulation department should do all it can to assist these scholars.

Sooner or later, every university library is faced with the problem of what to do with a few hard-core faculty members who consistently fail to respond to recall notices when books charged to them are needed by other readers or for reserve. The overwhelming majority of faculty members are not delinquents nor do they have any sympathy for those who are. A few universities charge fines to faculty members and to staff members who fail to return books. In even more libraries "lost" books must likewise be paid for, and there is a surcharge for processing. The most common way of dealing with faculty delinquents is for the library director to refer cases to the executive head of the delinquent's academic department, to the dean of his school or to the provost or other key university official, usually in the sequence named. Appropriate action is very frequently taken at the lower levels, although heads of academic departments themselves are often delinquent.

Lending Outside the University Community

Extramural loans are conditioned by many local factors, the greatest being the degree of surrounding urbanization, the pres-

---

[6] William M. Randall and Francis L. D. Goodrich, *Principles of College Library Administration*, 2nd ed. Chicago, American Library Association and University of Chicago Press, 1941, pp. 159-60.

Example of small spaces providing security for a graduate student's notes and personal materials: bookstack area — Harvey S. Firestone Memorial Library, Princeton University

ence in the community of research-oriented industry, and the strength of other institutions of higher education. They are also strongly affected by the amount of public tax support.

In an urban locale, a university library will attract use by school students even when the high school or public library provides adequate facilities. Some such use of university facilities results from the need to find books not otherwise available, while other use stems from the desire to associate with a collegiate group. The girls hopefully are asked for a date, and the high school boys follow the girls. Public school teachers constitute another type of load on the university library. They may wish to complete work for an advanced degree at another university and need material for a research paper. Or they may have curricular needs which their school library has not satisfied. If they are taking a university extension course, they are given special library privileges. Each person can be assigned to one or another category which receives a degree of access to the shelves, a privilege to borrow up to a certain amount, and admission to one or several university library units. The set of privileges may last for a day or for longer

periods. It may require a prior written request from the school librarian specifying titles or explaining the reasons for special needs. And it may involve a fee for extended time, perhaps for use for more than one week. University relations with the community are affected; so discussions with the school and public librarians are essential preliminaries to the formulation of policies. Furthermore, the university dean, the director of public relations, and even the trustees may wish to pass upon proposed limitations and fees.

Another distinct group comes from other colleges or universities. One must remember that students and faculty *go* from even the largest universities to use special collections and other resources in collegiate libraries — sometimes merely because they live close to them, are visiting nearby, or like the reading conditions. Most university libraries will assume reciprocity toward institutions at a distance or with a comparable neighboring school. The problem can be severe, however, if neighboring institutions have inadequate library facilities, whether in books or buildings.

State universities may need to control library access by undergraduates from other institutions so that their own students can use their facilities. Particularly strong privately supported institutions may need to limit access severely. See, for example, the following statement of reasons for the development of the new Columbia University fee system outlined in a printed brochure released September 25, 1956:

> Ideally, a collection of books belongs to all those who have the desire and the ability to use it. On this principle in times past, the Libraries of Columbia University were open without restriction to all qualified scholars, whether graduates of Columbia or other institutions.
>
> With the rapid and still accelerating increase in population, in book publishing, and in the costs of maintenance and administration, this "free for all" policy grew more and more taxing to keep in force, and finally became impossible. Within one recent year, for example, even with some restrictions in force, the University Libraries received requests from more than 5,000 graduates and visitors for the right to read or to borrow its books. In that same year, the Libraries had to serve a student body and University staff of more than 30,000. With a limited budget and staff, and a limited number of books, it was then clear that demand was outstripping supply. It was no longer possible

222

to postpone the setting up of priorities, however reluctant the officers of the University felt about doing this, and however inhospitable this might seem to our graduates and friends.

After trying and testing a number of plans through the years, the classification of persons and privileges has been arrived at as being probably the fairest to all concerned. It compares favorably with the rules in force at other institutions that face the same problem, and it permits the widest use of our books compatible with discharging our primary obligations, which is to the students in residence and the scholars who teach them.

Individual circumstances lead to a variety of policies. The policy of the Harvard College Library indicates what was found necessary in the urban center in which it is located (see Appendix VIII).

Commercial and industrial firms constitute a discrete group because of their profit-making status. Some universities or their communities have proved to be magnets for research firms. Many of the firms are enterprises on the frontiers of research and cannot afford comprehensive research libraries. When it may be in the interest of the university to develop the local economy and especially to foster basic research, the personnel are generally given access to the university library. Where the volume of such use is great, access may be directed through the library staff in an industrial service center or technical information service. In such circumstances an annual fee or unit transaction charge is commonly required by some privately supported universities. Yet branch libraries serving professional schools may operate under a different financial arrangement because of the type of school relationship with such practitioners as lawyers, physicians, and businessmen. Individual local circumstances lead to a variety of policies.

The alumnus is given a special status. He should always be welcomed for brief periods of time. In some instances he may request loans by mail, as well as reference and bibliographical service. In urban universities the alumnus who makes extensive and continuous use of the main library may have to apply for privileges as any outsider. In such cases, it is common practice to charge the alumnus half the normal fee charged to nonuniversity people. If primary use is made of a branch library, every assistance is commonly given, and no charge is made to the graduate pursuing his personal studies. Whenever an alumnus uses the library as a businessman,

223

he should be treated as a staff member of a commercial firm. In many instances a person will qualify under several different categories of borrower. A typical case is the alumnus working for a neighboring college on a government-supported research project. The circulation staff must then find the dominant relationship by which to apply policies of library privileges. Generosity in handling such matters is the wise approach.

Miscellaneous groups do not often constitute large numbers, yet some may pose problems. There may be lawyers, writers of fiction, journalists and free-lance writers, professors who have retired from other institutions, reprint publishers, and nonprofit research institutes. Typical of the statistics on outsiders who use a large university library are the following recent figures (representing only the central research libraries in the universities named):

	Harvard	*Stanford*
From outside the metropolitan area		
Instructors from other institutions	389	46
Students in other institutions	128	59
Miscellaneous, including foundation fellows	99	36
Total	616	141

	Harvard	*Stanford*
From within the metropolitan area		
Instructors from other institutions	121	70
Students from other institutions	134	227
Persons connected with research or business firms	50	1,100 (est.)
Graduates of the university	158	179
Persons indirectly connected with the university	92	23
Miscellaneous, including employees of the Federal Government	104	107
Total	659	1,706

Reprint publishers pose special problems. It is not right for libraries to lower the portcullis on legitimate business firms which produce the reprints libraries need. Their efforts can, however, do irreparable damage to bindings or diminish the size of leaves for rebinding. If a microtext edition is to be produced, there is concern for the treatment of the book during filming and the scholarly and bibliographic integrity of the product. It should also be noted that reprint publishers are almost invariably profit-making institutions. They need as their principal "capital" the unusual books that some

224

universities have acquired and preserved, often at great expense and for many decades. Neither a commercial enterprise nor another library through such an enterprise has the right to expect to benefit from such "capital" without paying fully the direct costs and overhead of the lending library that makes such material available. It is not improper for the lending library to add some modest fee in recognition of the expense it has defrayed in original acquisition and preservation. As a consequence, a number of large research libraries have adopted a policy like the following:

Policy Regarding Use of Library Materials by Reprint Publishers

The following statement of policy applies to the loan of materials by the libraries for reprinting purposes either in microfilm or original size format.

If a title wanted by a reprint publisher is judged to be one that can be made available for reprinting or editorial review, the volume or volumes may be loaned under the following conditions:

(1) Priority of service to the University community must be assured.

(2) The volume or volumes loaned by the library must be physically safeguarded.

(3) All direct and indirect costs to the library must be recovered, and a reasonable compensation paid by the borrower.

Procedure to be followed:

Before any materials are loaned, the borrower who requests the loan must agree in writing to the following conditions:

(1) A service charge of $5.00 will be made for every volume borrowed by a publisher, whether for reprinting purposes or for editorial review.

(2) An additional reprint privilege fee of $25.00 will be charged for (a) each monograph volume reprinted and (b) each numbered volume of a serial which is reprinted.

(3) The borrower will pay all charges incurred in the shipping of borrowed items, including insurance costs without limitation.

(4) One copy of each reprint will be sent to the University library without charge if requested, as soon as the reprint volumes are available.

(5) The borrower will be responsible for obtaining necessary per-

mits, rights, and copyright clearances in connection with the reprinting or reproduction of the materials borrowed. The borrower agrees to indemnify, defend, and hold harmless the University, its trustees, officers, agents and employees, of and from any and all claims, suits, or proceedings asserted or instituted by reason of the reprinting of any title borrowed from the University. In regard to theses and other manuscripts, the borrower must obtain the author's permission for publication and supply the University with a copy of this permission.

(6) The entire original text of the borrowed volumes, including half title, title, verso of title, tail piece, and other such publication data, will be reprinted without any deletions, so that the bibliographical identity of the original will be readily recognizable. Local markings such as bookplates, call numbers, and local stamps are not to be deleted from Library copies; however, the reprint publisher may delete these marks as desired from the reprint edition.

(7) Additions to the original text (indexes, commentary, addenda, or another text reprint) may not come at any point within the full consecutive printed pagination of the original, and any additions must be clearly labeled as to origin.

(8) The reprint must show that it is reproduced from an original copy in the University library.

(9) Permission to reprint applies only to the edition for which such permission is being requested, and does not apply to any prior or subsequent edition.

(10) Bindings on volumes borrowed from the library will not be removed or damaged without prior written permission from the library unit loaning the work.

(11) The borrower agrees to return all materials borrowed within three months of the date they are received by the borrower.

The undersigned hereby accepts and agrees to comply with the above conditions:

....
Name of the firm

By ....

Title ....

Address ....

....

Date ....

One of the twelve-volume sets of the book catalog of library holdings, located in ten subject-related reference alcoves — J. Henry Meyer Memorial Library, Stanford University

The Reader's Services Function

The university library bears an obligation to promote the use of books. The issues that have been discussed are some of the more difficult ones. Each institution should have a set of policies; these should be documented and may be supplemented by a gloss to explain their nuances for the staff who administer them and to interpret them in a variety of examples. In any institution the policies will need to be constantly evaluated and frequently modified.

Interlibrary Borrowing

The network of interlibrary use is unquestionably one of the best examples of library cooperation. Even in the days of extremely fast airplane transportation, it is a great convenience for a graduate student or professor to have books borrowed for him from several libraries. Every university library can operate under the theory that, given time and a reasonably complete citation, it can hope to provide for its readers a copy of every item which has ever been printed anywhere in the world in the past five hundred years. The benefit to all institutions is reduced most strikingly by the thought-

lessness of a few which do not adequately check references, fail to provide complete citations before initiating a request, or consistently overburden a few of the largest libraries. Not only should the ALA Interlibrary Loan Code be followed, but an institution should *assure* itself that the requests it sends out and the way it treats borrowed volumes are beyond reproach.

Requests for photocopies in lieu of borrowing are increasing. This is a boon to the lending library in that the original is thereby kept available for local circulation. It also means that the "borrower" has paid for the service. Although it is not universally done, postage on interlibrary borrowing of books should be paid by the library, not by the individual for whom it was borrowed, since the loan is to correct a deficiency in the local collection for which the borrower is not to blame. In the case of photocopies, however, there may be quite a difference in cost between a copy of archival quality and bibliographical completeness which the library would be willing to add to its collections and an expendable copy which serves one scholar's purposes. The latter copy may provide only the chapter or single journal article which is needed; and it may be an image which is not completely stabilized. The scholar may properly be required to pay the cost.

If the initiating library can decide at the time of requesting the photocopy that it wishes to add the text to its collection, it then pays to obtain archival quality, a complete bibliographic unit, and a binding margin, if the photocopy is full size, or the standard bibliographic and technical "targets" on the film, if a microtext. This coordination between book selection and the interlibrary borrowing unit, though generally lacking, can prove a valuable means of testing the adequacy of recent selection and determining lacunae that retard local research.

The borrowing of microfilm is increasing as its bibliographic control has improved. There is as yet no code for interlibrary borrowing of film, and the practice varies. Those libraries that have established a master microfilm collection generally require purchase of a print in lieu of a loan of their use copy. Such a purchase may include a surcharge to cover part of the cost of the master. This is entirely reasonable, but it may result in the purchasing library's recording its copy in a union catalog and thereafter bearing the interlibrary loan traffic. As the use of microtexts grows, such relatively minor problems will be rationalized and an acceptable code of ethics will evolve.

Photocopy Service

Photocopying has become an indispensable part of the university library. The reproduction of documents is increasingly resorted to as a method of preserving a copy of a book having deteriorating paper, as an interlibrary loan alternative, as a means of procuring materials not available or too expensive to buy in the original format (provided they are not under copyright), and as a service to readers who are thereby saved hand transcription of text. A large library may now have over 25,000 reels of microfilm and over 300,000 sheets of micro-opaques or transparencies, and it may process well over 1,000 purchase orders for microfilm and produce 1,000,000 electrostatic sheets for customers near and far.

Because a university library may easily have several hundred thousand items in microtext form, it is one of the very largest consumers of microtexts. And since the university library is one of the largest repositories for the originals being filmed, it must be concerned with their reproduction so that the end product is satisfactory for its purposes. This is a fact that too few library schools have understood. And too few university libraries have paid adequate attention to the necessary standards, financial questions, and tax and copyright problems.

Standards are of three types. There are technical standards which are rather well established. There are bibliographic standards — an area in which chaos exists. And there are local service standards nearly all of which have, to date, contributed to the scholar's aversion to using microtexts. In each of these there is a sharp distinction between the expendable copy made for one scholar's personal use and the permanent library copy; the former can be no more than a legible copy — any process is excellent which is conveniently available, quick, inexpensive, and reasonably clean. Electrostatic copiers have filled the great need for this type, and every university library will have several. The machines may be operated under library control or administered by another department of the university. In either case, the machines near browsing, duplicate, or undergraduate collections should be available at all hours during which the library is open, possibly as a self-service facility, whereas machines near the research collections should be staffed in order to protect the books from the present inadequacies of equipment.

For the permanent library copy, however, the technical standard must be archival. The bibliographic standard must be at least equal to good book publishing practice — in fact it should include what was once called prenatal cataloging so that the receiving library, and any libraries later making a copy of the copy, need not duplicate the cataloging. Every university library should fulfill its campus responsibility for achieving the highest bibliographic standards for permanent photographic copies of library materials. Machines for producing such material may be managed by the library, another university department, or a commercial firm. Although local conditions will govern the best arrangements, the proper handling and safeguarding of library materials must be assured.

Service standards should encompass all areas, including adequate card catalog or other bibliographic control for individual microtexts, simple interlibrary photocopy request procedures at all major library service units, comprehensive and easily available information at each service unit on local photocopying facilities and costs, convenient quick-copy service in or near each major unit, reference staff who know the microtext collections well enough to provide competent assistance, and microtext projectors and quarters which are conducive to their use. Universities should provide the very best reading facilities specially designed for microtexts. Microtexts may be expected to become increasingly important in scholarly work; if today's graduate students are given greatly improved services, they will be more sympathetic to the use of library resources when they are professors.

The director of libraries should obtain the highest possible level of microform service within budget limitations because microtexts are somewhat inconvenient under even the best of circumstances. He will also bear responsibility for seeing that bibliographic and technical standards are met; that national cooperative projects are carefully considered for local participation; that filming of manuscripts and other irreplaceable local materials is given priority so they will not be irreparably damaged through use; that a microfilming program is budgeted for the preservation of deteriorating

230

books; that master microfilms are listed nationally and stored to specification; that owner or copyright restrictions on reproduction of materials or of microfilm is observed; and that the price of photocopies is as low as possible for the students.

The financial questions include points mentioned earlier under book selection, preservation, and interlibrary loan. There is the need to have text copies for the library's administrative purposes. There are the costs of film editing, splicing, and cleaning which are necessary for acquisition and preservation. And there is the need for equitable pricing of copies made for students, library staff, faculty, other university personnel, and outsiders. If a library is held to strict accounting with each group of individuals paying its full costs, the bookkeeping can be done only with fairly elaborate records. Most libraries will find it more economical to have one set of accounts for the photographic section, using income from all sources to pay for supplies, equipment, and the personnel directly operating the service. A modest amount of administrative copying may be performed without interdepartmental invoicing, but regular billing should be done for such volume jobs as card duplication, reserve book duplication, and overdue notices. The use of a machine solely for administrative purposes simplifies proper accounting. Back of all decisions should be the desire to keep the cost of copies for students as low as possible and still ensure the reasonable protection of the collections.

Tax and copyright issues are concerns of the university legal counsel, not merely of the librarians. If there is a state sales tax, it may have to be collected on each sale, including those covered by interdepartmental billing to a government-supported research project on campus but not those billed to university administrative and business offices. The institution may even have to pay income tax on profit from sales outside of the institution; the law is being tightened on activities which are not central to the purposes of a tax-exempt institution and therefore counsel is needed to assure that photocopying is handled within the law.

Since present copyright law includes no provision on the specifics of educational fair use, the university legal counsel should advise on suitable local regulations to govern the duplication of copyrighted articles for course reserve or for university offices, indicating when it is necessary to obtain written permission to sell a copy of a major portion of a work under copyright or to control the reproduction of unpublished material. The fact that there are two "rights" — (1) the ownership of the physical manuscript and (2) the literary property right — complicates life in the administration of any manuscript or archive collection. In circumstances in which legal counsel is not available, the library might do well to follow the 1961 recommendation of the Joint Libraries Committee on Fair Use in Photocopying: ". . . that it be library policy to fill an order for a single photocopy of any published work or any part thereof." A prudent corollary would be a rule never to fill an order for multiple copies of any published work under copyright without written permission, especially if the work is in print. Such policy should most certainly be followed for copies needed by the library itself. (It is to be hoped that the new copyright law when passed by the Congress will provide clear guidance and reasonable recognition of the need to permit single-copy reproduction for educational and scholarly purposes.)

Staffing

Circulation, interlibrary borrowing, and photocopy services all present staffing problems. And the issues in university libraries are full of educational ramifications which relate to faculty teaching methods, graduate and postdoctoral research programs, the pace and pressures of undergraduate life, the complications of several dozen branch service units, and increasing mechanization. The problems are not made easier by the fact that these services have a very high proportion of clerical operations so that the responsible librarians are few in number, sometimes only two or three in the main circulation department. This type of work does not serve to train a large number on the job. Each individual tends to become a specialist within the total circulation services.

A heavy load is placed on the group of library assistants, among whom may be some of the most talented and experienced within the entire library staff. The staff must have a high degree of adaptability and the ability to meet and get along with people, as well as calmness, tact, accuracy, and an understanding of bibliography. The public relations aspect of this work appeals to many individuals. The department head needs to have these qualities and be particularly adroit in promoting smooth staff operations and in

232

coping with the infinite variety of problems that service to students and faculty in a university can create. He will need to work with a dean on a student disciplinary case, with delinquent faculty members, with the registrar to determine persons eligible to receive library privileges, with the business office on design details for a machine-readable student card, and perhaps with the graduate school dean on filming of doctoral dissertations. There is a major challenge to provide management of an efficient service organization.

A typical university library table of the staffing and production for circulation, interlibrary borrowing, and photocopy service in a main library follows:

Table of Typical Circulation Staff and Annual Production
in a Main Library Department

Department Chief, Librarian IV
Assistant Department Chief, Librarian III
Secretary

Loan Division
  1 Librarian I
  2 Library assistants in charge of the loan counter
    and stack collection
  4 Senior library assistants
  12 Library assistants

Interlibrary Loan Division
  1 Librarian II
  2 Librarians I
  2 Library assistants

Photocopy Service Division
  1 Senior photocopy operator
  3 Photocopy operators
  1 Messenger

General circulation	207,300
Intralibrary loans	38,400
Outgoing interlibrary loans	9,360
Incoming interlibrary loans	3,950
Photocopy sheets (electrostatic)	1,420,000
Microfilm orders searched and forwarded for processing	200

Circulation staff in branches need the same qualities as those in the main library. Subject and bibliographic competence may, in addition, be of considerable importance, since there may be no separate reference staff. Even a library circulation assistant in the physics or psychology library may be asked an elementary question in regard to the interpretation of library records or the location of an unfound reference. It is to be expected that a user cannot identify at a glance who is a librarian and who is an assistant. For this reason, name and title signs which can be placed on desks are useful in setting professional standards. The situation also accentuates the need for library handbooks at each service point.

Budgeting

Determining the needed financial support for circulation services can be a relatively simple process. It calls for less judgment of quality factors than does the evaluation of cataloging or reference. There can be straight statistical evidence of service deterioration, for example if there is an increase in the percentage of requests not found charged out or on the shelf, or if the proportion of overdue books increases. Other indications can come from student and faculty complaints.

Generally a library will try to provide circulation service at a minimum cost. It may encourage readers to page their own requests. It may permit a longer loan period to reduce the processing of overdues. These actions may, however, result in severe criticism by the library clientele. Borrowers will commend a rapid circulation process in which they are passive, rather than one which requires them to fill out a detailed charge form. The faster the paging of a book from a stack, the more help must be on hand at periods of peak load. The department head must weigh the factors and propose the best combination of efficiency with good service.

Service budgets must reflect growth in the student body, increases in faculty research programs, and creation of institutes. Increase in the size of enrollment is likely to generate accelerated activity in an undergraduate library. Yet there may be subtler changes in many library units as, for example, when an urban research center is created. Service budgets will reflect a good job done in binding and finishing of books for the shelf, an effective job of promoting reading and research, and a capable job of stack design in a new building and competent stack management.

Mutilation, Misconduct, and Fines

Rule infractions are among the unpleasant aspects of library work. Beginning with the selfishness of one who does not return a book needed by another, misconduct ranges from deliberate shelf misplacement to the use of false names, to unrecorded borrowing; and from underlining to cutting out entire journal articles, and even theft by student recalcitrants or professional book thieves. Libraries have used two ways to curb misconduct: fines and university disciplinary action (generally probation and threatened expulsion). Fines in university libraries date back at least to 1848 and may now total over $30,000 a year from sums as small as 5 cents per day or 50 cents per hour for reserved books. Yet fines are not always an effective deterrent and are a real penalty only to the poorer student — or to his parents. Withdrawal of home borrowing privileges is not commonly threatened though it would be a more equitable treatment. So the fine system persists, disliked by librarians, controller, and students.

The library must do all it can to gain the cooperation of the student in abiding by circulation regulations. Students who have not conformed should always be handled as misinformed persons rather than as culprits. When rules appear to have been broken, the library must gather clear evidence before confronting the individual. No action should be taken on an infraction if there is any doubt as to the facts. The more flagrant cases are generally turned over to a dean or to a student judicial group for treatment. No matter how irresponsible and obstreperous a student may be during college, the institution — and its library — acts on the hope that all its efforts will bear fruit upon graduation as an admirable citizen commences to apply his education.

Nothing can be more ingenious and even hilarious than some collegiate pranks. Every library has its share, be it a full-dress Elizabethan sword fight back and forth in the middle of a monumental reading room or the surreptitious adding to the collections (with proper catalog cards, classification, circulation pocket, and even bookplate) of a privately printed pamphlet purporting to be a lecture on morals by the university president. These harmless activities enliven everyone's days and ease the strain of studies. But the person who takes books needed by others, or damages them, must be dealt with promptly and yet with consideration. Such behavior may be an act of mere thoughtlessness, or a sign of impending mental illness, or the result of an undeveloped sense of ethical and social values. Fortunately, these persons, though disturbing, are a small fraction of the university community.

A National Network for Research Resources

A formal network, or set of networks, to extend circulation services to the total national research resources is becoming an essential means to counter the mounting cost of library service to the university research community. A de facto network is very gradually evolving. Major elements of the network are the National Union Catalog, interlibrary borrowing and lending, interlibrary photocopy service, a National Preservation Program, an economical and rapid facsimile transmission device for sending shorter materials by telephone line, and a professional code of standard practice. Only the last three of the six elements are yet to come.

The need for this extension of the circulation services seems evident. University enrollment will have increased greatly by the end of this century. Colleges are educating an increasingly large proportion of youth for advanced graduate study. The literature in most fields is now so vast that all the national libraries together are not able to keep up with the esoterica and ephemera which research projects may require. University library needs are not adequately being met with the funds available.

A carefully drawn code of practice will be necessary because of the economic magnitude of creating and maintaining the network's largest single pool of resources, a National Preservation Library. In due course such a system may be tied in with a computer-based system for rapid automatic access to the nation's research resources. How to share the cost of this national network cooperative will be difficult to determine. But the eventual advantages to higher education and research are likely to justify the effort and expense entailed.

Since 1950 many individuals and government agencies have developed proposals for national information systems. This in itself is indicative of their quest for solutions to problems encountered or foreseen. The achievements of the Farmington Plan and the program growth of the Center for Research Libraries seem to presage national enterprises for the sharing of research resources. The National Library of Medicine and the British National Lending Library for Science and Technology may serve as prototypes. Development of a truly national system must be based not upon courtesy arrangements but upon a detailed assignment of responsibility, accompanied by Federal funds to enable the assignments to be executed.

BOOKSTACK MANAGEMENT

The function of bookstack management is essentially custodial — maintaining the stock of book materials in an accurate arrangement so that various user groups may have efficient use of the collections. This is a major responsibility when the stack may house two or three million volumes and be open to several thousand readers. The stack superintendent usually reports to the head of the circulation department and may be the library expert on preservation. The staff of salaried employees must be conscientious, orderly, and not allergic to dust. Casual or hourly employees are used to supplement the regular staff at peak hours and to carry out large moving or cleaning projects.

The staff may page and reshelve materials that are requested, anticipate additions by shifting books from a full section or particularly crowded range of sections, clean books and select those needing repair or rebinding, remark when shelf numbers are illegible, assign study carrels, and prepare for and conduct shifts to ease crowded conditions or utilize new shelf areas. The staff may conduct an inventory with the help of the catalog department if the library considers one necessary; this is usually done only when shelf conditions are out of control or the accuracy of the count of holdings is in real question.

Access Policies

The treatment due each class of readers is generally detailed in codes of borrowing privileges. There may be a special policy on the assignment of carrels and faculty studies. Special attention must be given to the circuitous routes or culs-de-sac prevalent in old buildings and their additions; and full use should be made of directional signs and classification guides.

One of the major problems is, regrettably, that of improper conduct. Any large bookstack will attract women and especially men who find it a place conducive to misbehavior of one kind or another. The style of self-ventilating stack built during the first third of this century encourages Peeping Toms. Any large stack will have an almost constant series of incidents ranging from personal harassment to writing on walls; and the offenders may be students, faculty, library staff, or outsiders with stack permits. For young women who are students or staff this can be considerably more than a nuisance. Every library must seek ways to design stacks and arrange carrels so as to discourage these problems, e.g., modesty panels on carrels, glass walls in typing or graduate study rooms, a minimum of hidden corners and remotely isolated reading quarters, and indestructible surfaces of a texture or pattern to discourage defacing.

Open-shelf collections in libraries have promoted education and reduced one type of library expense. The proper management of a major stack can, however, be expensive and requires expert attention. It seems hard to conceive of any radically different way of shelving university collections to make them more attractive, easier for students to use, more economical of space, simpler to maintain as inventory, and quicker for book reshelving. Eliminating the stack is a solution for undergraduate collections. However, a better arrangement of a major university library stack is yet to be achieved.

Auxiliary Storage Areas

Storage is increasingly necessary as collections grow, building costs rise, and competition for land close to the center of the university campus becomes acute. Since any university will have some collections which are seldom used, the library should take auxiliary storage into account in planning future space needs. Some regional cooperatives will serve, but many local facilities will be felt necessary as at Princeton, Harvard, Yale, and Berkeley. These areas will be a major, almost universal, factor in future university library service.

Attention must be given to the difficulties of managing collections in auxiliary storage. Among these are the difficulty of selecting for these collections, the catalog record changing required, the impossibility of browsing if the collection has closed shelves or is not classified, the time required for paging, the transportation devices, and the costs. Faculty and students can well be irked if there has been selection and storage without consultation with the faculty members concerned; if there is no location indication on the catalog cards of books sent to storage; if a closed-stack collection is stored or shelved by size, rather than by classification, thus preventing browsing and useful examination of books on the shelves; or if there is a twenty-four-hour wait before books are available for use at the main library, at a branch convenient for the patron, or at the auxiliary facility itself.

It should be obvious that selection of materials for auxiliary storage is of prime importance. Clearly, entire classes are the quickest and cheapest to move if faculty approval can be gained. Selection of individual items based on an estimate of scholarly value should be a secondary approach because it is expensive for staff processing, proves agonizing for the individual who must obtain faculty approval, and leaves a split collection which is extremely frustrating to scholars. Selection on the basis of circulation statistics is even less satisfactory since it results in a collection of broken bindings, pamphlets, and other unattractive items, and is based on no logic except the idiosyncrasies of past readers. Categories which may be scrutinized for relocation to an auxiliary collection may include the following though it should be emphasized that local curricula, research programs, and personal interests of the faculty must enter into any decision:

Superseded editions
Translations from English into another language or from one
    foreign language into another
Vanity press publications
Variant printings, especially of collective works and encyclo-
    pedias
Pseudo-scientific publications
School publications of only historical interest
Textbooks
College catalogs (retrospective files)
City directories, except for a small current selection

Publicity releases

All but the most important booksellers' catalogs, excluding auction catalogs

Advertising material, except significant and comprehensive monographs

Ephemeral materials, such as handbills and pamphlets designed for publicity or solicitation in support of movements

Fiction of definitely minor authors

Government documents of the popular information type, including all but a selection of state and local documents

Juvenilia, except for classics

Books and journals issued by small minority groups and of only limited historical and nonlocal interest

Publications of business houses, such as corporation reports and trade union releases, unless important and accurate statistical or organizational material is included

Nonbook materials of merely historical or curious interest

Bulk manuscripts of potential scholarly value but not of immediate use and not of outstanding quality

Works on sports, games, and hobbies, except for outstanding or recent works

In any case, the collections should have a high degree of classification, if not complete notation, since it is not comforting to conceive of a university with hundreds of thousands of locally available volumes in an unbrowsable condition. Besides, the formidable magnitude of classification costs and the expense of space needed for intercalation of added volumes is illusory. The major saving in storage stacks can be the land value, and the type of building can prove a close second. Most books will have been in the active collections so they have class numbers, and any change is an additional expense. And good management can result in auxiliary stacks used to within 98 per cent of absolute capacity.

This line of development suggests that the auxiliary area have some study carrels, photocopy machines, and a small collection of reference books. It may become the focus of advanced study in certain fields in which retrospective research is relatively slight but the collections are large — e.g., textbook collections, educational history, juvenile literature, popular low-quality fiction, state documents, military history and diaries, and archives of the records management type. If scientific laboratories sprawl toward the campus periphery, it may house all the older collections in the physical sciences and even serve as the main research library for all sciences, technology, and mathematically oriented social sciences.

The exact shape of auxiliary collections will be conditioned by local circumstances. The experiments at Yale, Harvard, Chicago, Wisconsin, Michigan, and California-Berkeley vary, with differing results. Many similar undertakings will be attempted before a pattern emerges to show the most effective and economical way of coping with research collections which exceed the needs of immediate heavy use.

Planning of Major Shifts

Stack shifts are one of the special concerns of the head of the circulation department and the director of the library. It is a simple matter in collections of a few hundred thousand volumes. It can be complex in collections of a million or more. It is a real challenge when the stack configuration is irregular, when there is an uneven distribution of carrels, when books are in two classifications, and when shelf continuity is interrupted by a caged area or two. Collection arrangement is determined from balancing such considerations as the following:

Place the more heavily used classes near the circulation desk to reduce the time for paging

Keep all books of each major class on one floor

Shelve special periodical and bibliographic classes where there are desks so that they may be used nearby

Select small, seldom-used classes for placement at the end of floors on which the major collections may first need expansion

Try to shelve closely related classes (e.g., U.S. history and economics, or art and classics and archeology) on adjacent floors so that students can use them conveniently

Place in cages the minimum of material (e.g., "sensitive" books notoriously subject to theft or mutilation, miniatures, portfolios, books on severely deteriorated paper)

This last point needs emphasis. It is easy to isolate collections and

241

believe one has eliminated a point of trouble. But education is not furthered by secreting books in which the university has invested funds. Books on closed shelves are so many physical objects to be stored and kept in order; displayed to possible readers, the collection becomes alive with suggestion and allure. To remove even the "sensitive" books from sight is a step to be deplored on educational and moral grounds though experience demonstrates the necessity of controlling such materials.

The collection arrangement should be planned to last as many years as possible. This saves both staff effort and user confusion. There are real economic and disciplinary issues which need study in preparation for any major shift and for designing a new stack construction. Staffing for a poorly arranged collection may need to be double that for one that is well arranged.

Preservation and Selective Isolation

In order to preserve the collection for future generations, reasonable care must be exercised in handling books, in cleaning them, in pulling those which need rebinding or which now give evidence of

such fragile paper that they must be segregated in a cage (or other area with controlled access), and in finding those which once were considered ordinary but now are deserving of the considerate treatment provided in a rare book or special collections department. The last function is particularly the responsibility of the book selection staff, catalogers, and reference librarians who have occasion to search for materials and who may come upon the local copy of a book that is now priced dearly or has gained special significance. All the staff should, however, be attentive to materials needing care. It is a special burden of a research library.

243

Instruction in the use of bibliographic sources: reference librarian helping student at the service desk — Reference Room, Research Library, University of California, Los Angeles

SELECTED REFERENCES

The Promotion of Reading

Branscomb, Harvie. *Teaching with Books: A Study of College Libraries.* Chicago, Association of American Colleges and American Library Association, 1940.

Downs, Robert B., ed. *The First Freedom: Liberty and Justice in the World of Books and Reading.* Chicago, American Library Association, 1960.

Knapp, Patricia B. "The Reading of College Students," *Library Quarterly,* 38 (October 1968), 301–8.

Phipps, Barbara H. "Library Instruction for the Undergraduate," *College and Research Libraries,* 29 (September 1968), 411–23.

Price, Jacob M., ed. *Reading for Life: Developing the College Student's Lifetime Reading Interest.* Ann Arbor, University of Michigan Press, 1959.
See especially the paper by Ellsworth, pp. 224-40, the two papers by Asheim, pp. 3-26 and 251-67, and chapters 8 and 12.

Tidmarsh, Mavis N. "Instruction in the Use of Academic Libraries," in W. L. Saunders, ed., *University and Research Library Studies: Some Contributions from the University of Sheffield Postgraduate School of Librarianship and Information Science.* New York, Pergamon Press, 1968. pp. 39–83.

Wecter, Dixon. "General Reading in a University Library," in *The Place of the Library in a University: Conference Held 30–31 March, 1949.* Cambridge, Harvard University Library, 1950. p. 3–13.
Also in *Harvard Library Bulletin,* 4 (Winter 1950), 5-15.

Reference and Information Assistance

Butler, Pierce, ed. *The Reference Function of the Library: Papers Presented before the Library Institute at the University of Chicago, June 29 to July 10, 1942.* Chicago, University of Chicago Press, 1943.
See especially the paper by Halvorson, "The Reference Function in the University Research Library," pp. 103-23.

Hurt, Peyton. "The Need of College and University Instruction in the Use of the Library," *Library Quarterly,* 4 (July 1934), 436–48.

Hurt, Peyton. *The University Library and Undergraduate Instruction,* Berkeley, University of California Press, 1937.

King, Henry H. "Assistance to the Faculty in Library Research: Report from Cornell University," *College and Research Libraries,* 9 (July 1948), 227–30.

Palmer, Foster M. "The Reference Section in the Harvard College Library," *Harvard Library Bulletin,* 7 (Winter 1953), 55–72.

244

Rice, Warner W. Remarks on paper by H. M. Lydenberg, in *Changing Patterns of Scholarship and the Future of Research Libraries: A Symposium in Celebration of the 200th Anniversary of the Establishment of the University of Pennsylvania Library.* Philadelphia, University of Pennsylvania Press, 1951. pp. 103–7.

Rothstein, Samuel. *The Development of Reference Services through Academic Traditions, Public Library Practice and Special Librarianship.* (ACRL Monograph No. 14) Chicago, American Library Association, 1955.

Wilson, Louis R. "The Service of Libraries in Promoting Scholarship and Research," *Library Quarterly,* 3 (April 1933), 127–45.

Circulation and Photocopying Services

Fussler, Herman H. *Photographic Reproduction for Libraries: A Study of Administrative Problems.* Chicago, University of Chicago Press, 1942.

Hawken, William R. *Copying Methods Manual.* Chicago, American Library Association [1966].

"Interlibrary Loans: A Symposium," *College and Research Libraries,* 13 (October 1952), 327–58.

Includes "General Interlibrary Loan Code 1952," pp. 350-8, and related articles by Hodgson, Wright, Kidder, Melinat, and Lucy, pp. 327-49.

Nicholson, Natalie N. "Service to Industry and Research Parks by College and University Libraries," *Library Trends,* 14 (January 1966), 262–72.

Weber, David C. "Off-Campus Library Service by Private Universities," in *Minutes* of the Association of Research Libraries, 62nd meeting (July 13, 1963). pp. 25–38.

Yenawine, Wayne S., ed. "Current Trends in Circulation Services," *Library Trends,* 6 (July 1957), 1–100.

Bookstack Management

Ash, Lee. *Yale's Selective Book Retirement Program: Report of a Three Year Project Directed by John H. Ottemiller.* Hamden, Conn., Archon Books, 1963.

Cooper, Marianne. "Criteria for Weeding of Collections," *Library Resources & Technical Services,* 12 (Summer 1968), 339–51.

Fussler, Herman H., and Julian L. Simon. *Patterns in the Use of Books in Large Research Libraries.* Chicago, University of Chicago Library, 1961.

Jesse, William H. *Shelf Work in Libraries,* Chicago, American Library Association, 1952.

Walsh, James E. "Experiment in the Selection of Library Books for Storage," *Harvard Library Bulletin,* 8 (Autumn 1954), 378–81.

8. SPECIAL TYPES OF MATERIALS

The regular book and serial collections of a university occupy proportionately a very large share of the space devoted to library materials. They constitute practically all of the collections that are circulated. These collections are classified, are usually available for open-shelf access to students, are listed in the general public catalogs, and are also listed in national bibliographies and trade catalogs. However, there are large collections that do not fall in the foregoing categories. As was stated in Chapter 3, a research library is increasingly a collection not only of books but of intellectual and graphic data preserved in a variety of noncodex forms, almost all of which involve special shelving, cabinets or containers and are unorthodox in that they require (1) special access control and circulation rules, (2) special equipment for their use, or (3) unusual bibliographic controls requiring specialized staff to devise or interpret them.

In the first group are archives, manuscripts, portfolios, and fine prints, as well as codexes that are assigned to this category by reason of their size (miniatures), rarity, the inclusion of fine plates, or the inclusion of textual or illustrative material that makes the item unusually susceptible to mutilation or theft.

In the second group are microtexts, sound recordings, motion pictures, slides, punched cards, stereopticon prints, and computer or video tapes.

In the third group requiring special bibliographic controls are a variety of items that may fall into this category by virtue of policies on physical storage or bibliographic treatment in each particular library. The items in this group may be protected in full bindings and fully cataloged as if they were substantial monographs; however, because of the extra expense in such treatment or other complications in their listing and use, it is common practice for many of these to be given a special bibliographic treatment. These materials may be photographs, prints, vertical file materials, offprints, technical reports, sheet music, sheet maps, auction catalogs, govern-

247

Glass partitions provide acoustical isolation but permit supervision of the use of manuscripts in scholars' studies — Department of Rare Books and Special Collections, Harvey S. Firestone Memorial Library, Princeton University

ment documents, and a variety of ephemera or fugitive pieces such as a collection of book jackets, Christmas cards, costume and stage designs, bookplates, broadsides, and other such materials.

To some extent the quantity involved will play a major part in how this third category is treated since, if there are very few such items, they could easily be given full bibliographic coverage in the normal fashion. On the other hand, if one is dealing with 10,000 or more reports, pieces of sheet music, or other materials, they may be rather efficiently organized for use with an expenditure of $5,000 to $10,000 instead of a normal full cataloging expense which would approach $100,000 for such a body of materials. Some materials have both special use controls and special bibliographic controls (e.g., manuscripts, phonorecords, and fine prints).

The three broad types of "special" materials just described may occupy 10 per cent to 12 per cent of the total square footage for library materials (it could be 15 per cent to 17 per cent if the entire government document collection required special treatment). These materials generally require larger reading spaces per reading station, and they are especially demanding in terms of the staff effort to acquire, to provide bibliographic controls, and to provide service. On a unit basis they constitute the most expensive portion of the library. They therefore deserve particularly careful evaluation of their place in the library program.

This chapter cannot deal exhaustively with all of the individual types of material. It will concentrate on general principles for selecting, organizing, and making these materials available for use. Some reference will occasionally be made to technical processing but this will be incidental, and the reader's attention is also invited to Chapter 6 in this regard. Before each of the three categories is treated individually, there are several general points that are worth making.

GENERAL POLICIES

For the reasons already given (expense of acquiring and handling), it will probably be advisable to develop statements of collecting and processing policy for specialized materials. This will often be true of rare books, manuscripts, archives, and government publications, and it may be desirable for technical reports, computer tapes, sound recordings, and sheet maps. For other materials, the text would be acquired as a natural extension of general selection policies — irrespective of whether the item is issued by a government, is published in microfilm, or needs restricted access. In other words, if the library collects a certain author or makes an in-depth effort in a particular subject, a wanted item will often be acquired with relatively little regard for its format.

Because of the expense involved in building collections of special types of materials, the library will want to be fairly certain that there is faculty and student need for them. This requires that the library be scrupulously careful in judging the value of offers of gifts. Such gifts may inadvertently commit the library to major expenditures of staff time and space and equipment required to care for the materials.

A major effort in the collecting of offprints, historical recordings, or sheet maps can be expensive; and a committee composed of faculty from interested departments is often a good mechanism through which to obtain continuing assistance in judging areas of need and in soliciting individual collections through faculty efforts. Such a faculty committee interested in the economic development of the local region may provide useful advice on manuscript sources and can promote the use of these archival materials through graduate study and post-doctoral research. A similar committee concerned with oral history may devise the program that generates the list of people to be interviewed and find sources of funds to finance these activities. The committee members or the departments they represent may likewise stimulate the use of these resources in their own or their students' research.

Such committees may also co-opt nonfaculty and nonstaff collectors as members. Such co-opted members may be resource experts and may donate important materials to the library's collection. These committees may meet only once or twice a year, yet serve a very useful purpose in counseling the library on acquisitions and the use of materials.

However, a word of caution is in order. Enthusiastic collectors, faculty or nonfaculty, may have bizarre interests which they wish to transfer to the library, where better physical facilities or greater acquisitions leverage may be exercised than in their homes — not to mention the personal considerations involved if a collection or room is named for the donor. Unless a collection has substantial scholarly utility, immediate or prospective, a library director should not allow the opportunity to get "free" collections or advice obscure the fact that he may be making a commitment that will prove to be impossibly expensive in space and staff time (including his own) in relation to the merit of the gift. Not many libraries can justify postage stamp, picture postcard or glass negative collections. Even some rare book collections, although inherently valuable, may represent such a degree of duplication and carry so many strings for prime space and curatorial staff that they might better be declined.

The extent of staff effort committed to a special collection will vary depending on the collecting, cataloging, and service efforts. Staff organization and service policies may be handled in various ways. A program in oral history may be organized as an Office whereas a manuscript program may constitute a Division and government documents or rare books may be formed into a Department within the library's organization. The choice will depend upon the size of the staff and the collection, although the extent of use and the character of funding and physical location may also be determinants. If a unit has to be housed outside the library there may be more need to give it an enhanced organizational status than if it is within the same building and within the same room as another major function under whose umbrella it can be assigned. If the program is created with annual funding by a donor to the library or by a foundation grant, it might not receive the status in the organization that it would have if it were assured continuance through a commitment of general university funds. On the other hand, even a one-man program may be of major importance to a particular part of the academic effort, and the physical location and funding should not be considered as controlling its importance. A new program for computer tapes of data archives may be so important to several large academic departments that it deserves a major standing in its own right with a proportionate share of university funds committed to its continuance.

Quite typically the department of special collections will be assigned responsibility for manuscripts and perhaps for the university archives. The circulation department may be assigned responsibility for technical reports, government documents, microtexts, and even sound recordings and films. The reference department may be assigned responsibility for vertical file material, photographs,

250

Elaborate equipment behind service desk: remote delivery of audio selections to student positions and tape drive or turntable for local control at most listening positions — Audio Library, J. Henry Meyer Memorial Library, Stanford University

prints, slides, offprints, sheet maps, and playbills. And perhaps the acquisitions department may have responsibility for auction records. There is no universal logic in placing one type of special material in one department or another; rather, each university will have to determine which is the most logical place given the work load in the various departments, the overall administrative talent, the availability of a competent and interested staff member who has time to supervise the material, the question of space for physical location, the desired degree of centralization, and perhaps even the matter of related subject or service interest (such as slide collections for architecture and biology, or one map collection for oceanography and geology and another for historical studies).

For a great number of these items there are special bibliographic control problems. The catalog department usually designates one person to handle sheet maps or recordings or rare books, or it may set up a separate unit of several persons. Such staff may, as an exception, be located at a distance — perhaps in the music library — in order to take advantage of the sound reproduction equipment that is located in that branch or of the special bibliographical tools that are needed for cataloging.

Some of these materials will often be handled in short-cut fashion to simplify processing. Checklists, calendars, or printed sheet catalogs may be chosen, and occasionally it may be merely a systematic shelf organization with a single card reference in the catalog (for instance an extensive collection of early comic books or pulp magazines).

Special materials should be given adequate attention in the overall cataloging policies of the university library. The director of libraries should be concerned with the priority assigned to them, and he must be assured that none of them is ignored to the point where a major backlog is created requiring an extraordinary commitment of time. This fact must be kept in mind when deciding to build up collections or to accept gifts of specialized types of materials. A case in point might be newspaper clippings of theatrical reviews, an effort which might have very considerable interest to two or three individuals concerned with dramatic history but is so specialized that the library can seldom afford to maintain the index without special endowment, and the records as they exist when the collection is donated rapidly become outdated and lose their value for scholarship.

Related to the collecting and special bibliographic control efforts is the need to find a competent person to manage a program in one of these specialized fields. This should be relatively easy in the case of rare books or government documents, areas in which graduate library schools offer courses and train students with a beginning competence and interest in these areas. It is much more difficult when one gets into a field such as a map collection or sound recordings. In these cases one may have to turn to an institution which has made a specialty of such a program (such as audio-visual work at Indiana University or San Jose State College) or give attention to special short-term training institutes. The recruiting of talented help for an area such as data archives on computer tapes is still more difficult. In many instances the library will have to develop competence within its own staff or try to locate a person locally, perhaps a faculty wife, who can start with an avocation and gradually become an expert in a special type of material by working in the university library. Special consideration in job classification and a premium rate of pay can easily be justified for one who is truly proficient in a highly specialized area of importance to the library. The job market for rare specializations is slim and the specialized position on the library staff may not be full time when started. Consequently, the recruiting of persons to handle some of these types of special materials may require a good deal of effort, and continuity of program may at times be difficult to achieve. Yet these can be exceptionally appealing jobs and can be performed with special enthusiasm and energy when the right person is found.

Special physical quarters and equipment for a good many of these items are essential. In the case of materials requiring a high degree of access control for security purposes, there may be the need for heavy wire cages or sheet metal partitions to secure the materials. In other cases the requirement may be for special security devices such as smoke or fire detectors, door alarms or electric eye or laser beam devices to signal unauthorized entrances, and, in rare instances, even a uniformed security guard. In other cases the materials may require rooms with special temperature control and light modulation, such as those for reading microtexts or working at computer terminals with visual screens. And in other cases only vertical files may be needed, or special containers to be placed on regular book shelving. The library's officer in charge of purchasing will need to look into these physical requirements, giving attention to the particular needs for each kind of material and seeking the advice of the staff specialist. For some special types of materials there are periodicals or published reports which can be helpful in describing organizational treatment and physical housing.

After as much preparation as possible before traveling, visiting selected libraries and talking with recognized specialists in order to find the best practice can be well worth the expense. One may visit the Lilly Library (Indiana), the Houghton Library (Harvard), or the Beinecke Library (Yale), to observe good practices in handling rare books; one may need to visit the Bancroft Library (Berkeley), the Clark Library (UCLA), the Library of Congress, or the Huntington Library (San Marino, California) to determine the best treatment for manuscripts; or one may decide to visit UCLA or Harvard for their map collections, MIT or the California Institute of Technology for technical reports, the New York Public Library or Princeton University for photographs and prints. The regional reputation of university libraries with respect to a special type of material can easily be determined; the library will do well to send its responsible staff member to visit a few of these when developing any considerable new program of special materials. The visitor should read extensively in the literature and discuss the issues with persons in his home library before arranging a visit.

A final general policy issue is the degree of physical centralization to be achieved. In administering some of the special types of materials, such as vertical files, offprints, and even sheet maps, there is little need to centralize. The need for a staff specialist to care for and to service the material under controlled conditions presents a good argument for centralization of other types of materials, such as rare books, manuscripts, and archives. Furthermore, special physical facilities such as air conditioning may be necessary for their preservation. There is, of course, the possibility that one may establish satellite collections of rarities in branch libraries. This is often justified when there are special "language" problems, e.g., oriental or music manuscripts. These may be under the curatorial responsibility of the chief of a Department of Special Collections but under the service control of the branch librarian. Under such an arrangement, the books would be in locked cases or in a locked room used solely for this purpose. In other cases a locked cage section of the stack may serve the same purpose.

Decentralization has the advantage of permitting a faculty member or graduate student who is working in the branch library to find related material close at hand. The argument for distributing rare books in the branch libraries is that distribution encourages their use in conjunction with related materials and also minimizes the museum aspect of a centralized treasure room. The contrary argument for centralization follows the line that early books will be used most often in conjunction with other materials from that particular press, or by that binder, or from some other bibliographic point of view, or with materials of that decade or period. Centralized rarities are available for easy bibliographic comparison across all disciplines and furthermore are supported by a corpus of bibliographic works describing rarities, can be given the required degree of security, and can be used for exhibition purposes and as illustrative matter when classes are brought to the rare book room. There is no one pattern of centralization which is certain to be the best in all circumstances although the common pattern in university libraries is for rare book and manuscript collections to be decentral-

254

Quick visual detection of variations between two copies of the same edition: the Hinman Collator, permitting establishment of bibliographic points — Spencer Library, University of Kansas

ized only to the large branches — such as the law library, medical library, business school library, and perhaps the music library, in addition to the central rare book department in the main library.

A different question arises when materials require special equipment for their use. It is obvious that computer tapes and punched cards must be near input terminals or tape drives; in most cases this requires centralization. Another case in point would be microtexts, for which the argument in favor of decentralization is based entirely on the convenience of students and faculty who may wish to find their materials in the branch library. Since some journal and periodical runs may be subscribed to in the original format and then replaced with microfilm for past volumes, it is obviously a great inconvenience if the older material is in a different physical location. And microfilm machines are relatively inexpensive and can be used under almost any reading room or office conditions. On the other hand, the argument for a centralized microtext collection is based

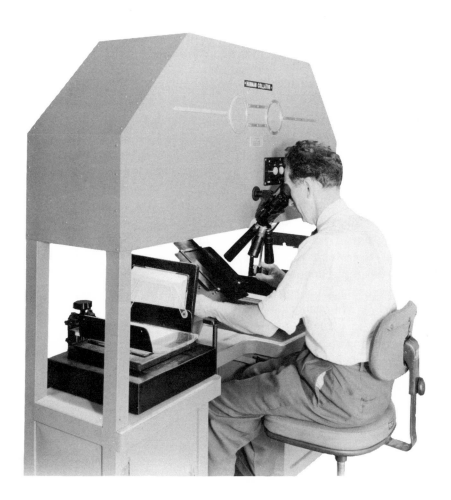

on economy of staffing, efficiency in services, and greater protection for the materials. Considering the service aspect, it is obviously more economical to have the machines in one location where a student can find one that is available rather than to require him to go from one branch to another to find one that is available and that suits his form of microtext. Since some machines are designed to handle microfiche, others microprint, others microfilm on reels, and since still others have enlargement printing capability, there is substantial logic in creating a major centralized microtext reading room — perhaps with a few extra machines scattered elsewhere to meet particular branch needs. Acoustical isolation, more subdued lighting which improves working conditions, and more economical layout of equipment can also be achieved centrally.

There is also economy when a staff member may be given specialized instruction in protective maintenance of equipment, can be expert in the special bibliography of microtexts, and can sometimes be assigned a related service function, such as servicing a newspaper reading room and collection. Finally, there are advantages in air conditioning and air filtering systems, which are highly desirable for protection of the film as well as for maintenance of the reading equipment. Unless the entire library is air conditioned, this requires centralizing the materials in a space so treated.

It may well be that in a few decades university libraries will have sufficient microtexts covering current publications so that there will need to be as much campus dispersal of microtexts as there now is of books. When all library staff is reasonably well trained in the bibliography and equipment and when buildings are suitable to protect the materials, this could well be done. Under such a pattern, there would be a library technician (or a company under service contract) to provide periodic inspection and maintenance of all pieces of equipment and perhaps even a film cleaning service. Until that day of microtextual maturity, each university will have to decide the desirable degree of centralization, given its own set of circumstances of staffing, equipment, building conditions, and campus geography. The same advice must be given for other special materials.

The succeeding sections endeavor to provide more specific guidance on the three principal groups of materials referred to at the beginning of this chapter.

256

Special Types of Materials

Rare books and manuscripts are classic examples of materials requiring access controls. For this reason these two types of materials are often administered through a single department. Likewise certain other materials requiring limited access or supervised use are sometimes included in what is denominated a Special Collections Department. Such ancillary materials may include miniature books, books with fine plates, portfolios of loose plates, erotica, and university archives.

Any university with nineteenth century or earlier antecedents has accumulated some rarities on its open shelves. These may even run into the thousands, and their segregation may form the basis for a rare book collection. The following excerpt from a Memorandum to the Staff on Rare Books issued by Lawrence Clark Powell when he was Librarian of UCLA is instructive as to the types of materials that might be administered through a rare book or special collection department.

Rare Book Code
University of California
Memorandum to the Staff on Rare Books

The Library has a twofold purpose; to serve people, to conserve books. We are judged by the present on how well we serve from day to day. The future will judge us by how wisely we have conserved the research treasure which we inherited, increased, and willed to our successors.

An evidence of a Library's cultural maturity is the care given to its scarce and irreplaceable materials. Its workers must be able to recognize such books at any point on the belt line of acquiring, cataloging, and shelving.

I am asking that every member of the staff share this responsibility of seeing that valuable books be given special handling. Normally the Acquisitions department screens them out of purchases, gifts, and exchanges for review, but the volume handled there is increasingly heavy, and fugitive items will sometimes escape through the finest mesh. Then it is up to the catalogers, and finally the loan and shelf people, to sequester these items which cannot be entrusted to the perils of the stack.

No rules-of-thumb can be devised which will take the place of personal knowledge, intelligence, and discrimination. Attached however is a list of preliminary criteria for recognizing possible rarities which is used by the Acquisitions department. All staff members are asked to study and be guided by it.

LAWRENCE CLARK POWELL

Rare Books

Books and periodicals in the following categories may be considered for inclusion in the Rare Book collection and will be held in Acquisitions for review before accessioning. Inclusion in one of the classes is not tantamount to rarity, and the list is not necessarily definitive. The possibility of rarities outside these criteria must always be recognized. Books finally accepted as Rare will be so designated and given special handling (i.e., the legend will be pencilled lightly along the inner margin of the page following the title page; all ink stamping, perforating, etc., will be omitted; the call number, preceded by a triangle, will be pencilled inside the front cover and inked on a small label pasted to the lower right corner of the back cover; special care will be taken in plating, so that, for example, original bookplates are not removed or pasted over). Current Rare periodical issues will not be date-stamped, will be carefully marked with a pencilled triangle, and shelved with the Rare Books. All Rare materials will be given special care in binding, after consultation with the Head of Special Collections. Hand-binding or the use of boxes will be considered; covers, advertisements, etc., must be preserved intact.

This code applies also to Branch Libraries, for it is recognized that specialized Rare Book Collections exist and will develop in Branch Libraries, as in the history of chemistry and medicine. Branch Libraries will consult the Head of Special Collections on matters of housing, care, etc.

1. Books of value due to early imprint date.
   a. All books printed before 1600.
   b. American books printed before 1820.
      In states west of the Appalachians, according to date printing started (California books printed before 1870; Los Angeles books printed before 1900).
2. Books whose irreplaceability or uniqueness make them rare.
   a. Limited editions (300 copies or less).
   b. Association and autographed copies, when by important or local authors.
   c. First editions of significance.
3. Books of esthetic importance (fine printing, illustration, or binding).

4. Books which cost the library more than $100, or which have a similar auction record.
5. Items of local or archival value or interest, including local fine press books.
6. Erotica, excluding sex hygiene, scientific works on sex, etc.
7. Other books subject to loss or damage.
   a. Volumes or portfolios of fine or loose plates.
   b. Books whose illustrations make them subject to mutilation.
   c. Books of fragile physical make-up.
8. Special collections, i.e., unit acquisitions containing both rare and non-rare material, which need to be kept together.
9. Books with significant manuscript or other materials laid or tipped in.

Other university libraries use a refinement based on dates established for the American Imprints Inventory.

All points in the United States .. 1820
(The 1820 date limit applies to all the Atlantic seaboard and New England states, New York City, Philadelphia, etc.)

Later dates as follows:
New York State outside of New York City 1850
(but Hudson river towns such as Poughkeepsie, Newburgh, Hudson, Troy, Albany, etc., through 1830 only)

Pennsylvania outside of Philadelphia 1830
Ohio 1840
West Virginia 1830
Mississippi 1840
Alabama 1840
Florida 1860
Kentucky 1830
Tennessee 1840
Michigan 1850
Indiana 1850

Illinois (*but* Chicago 1871) 1850
Missouri 1850
Wisconsin 1850
Iowa 1860
Minnesota 1865
Kansas 1875
Nebraska 1875
South Dakota 1890
North Dakota 1890
Colorado 1876
Wyoming 1890
Utah 1890
Montana 1890
Idaho 1890
Nevada 1890
New Mexico 1875
Arizona 1890
Texas 1860
Oklahoma 1870
Arkansas 1870
California 1875
Oregon 1875
Washington 1875
Hawaii 1860

A typical arrangement for the use of rare or special collections may include the following provisions:

1. Facilities include one or more reading rooms with a staff mem-

ber in constant attendance. Books in adjoining stacks are paged by another staff member in order to ensure constant surveillance of readers.

2. Readers are asked to identify themselves and to sign a register.

3. The use of ink is forbidden.

4. Enclosed study facilities or typing rooms have glass doors to permit full surveillance.

5. Readers are not admitted to the stacks.

6. Before exiting, a reader must return all books, and any briefcases or bags are subject to inspection.

7. If a reader needs simultaneously to consult books in the Special Collections Department and in the regular collections, provision is made for prompt delivery of the latter books for use in the Special Collections reading room.

8. The use of reader-owned photocopy equipment is probably prohibited. Any reproduction is made under controlled conditions by specially trained university personnel. Delivery of items to the photographic laboratory is carefully controlled. If books must remain in the laboratory overnight, a safe or safe file is available for security.

From time to time reprint publishers (whether microform or conventional format) may ask to borrow materials for republication. Such materials may have been acquired by the library at considerable cost and preserved (often in a unique copy) for decades. They should be made available, if at all, under rigid controls that ensure the safety of the volume and proper compensation to the lending institution. Many of the larger university libraries have formulated guidelines based on this principle under which such publications may be made available. A typical document of this kind is reproduced in Chapter 7, pp. 225-6.

Despite the difference in format between rare books and manuscripts, the latter present most of the control problems of the former plus additional considerations. Under the United States copyright law at present (1970) manuscripts are not under statutory copyright. (This would be changed under the proposed revision of the copyright law.) But even though not covered by statutory copyright, manuscripts are protected by common law copyright. It is presumably safe to make a single photocopy of a manuscript for the private use of a research worker. *Publication* of a manuscript should not be undertaken without clearance from the author or his literary heirs or from the library if it has been formally assigned the literary rights.

There are two "rights" involved in manuscripts: (1) ownership of the physical property and (2) literary rights. The library usually possesses the first, and the author or his literary heirs the second. A person given access to a manuscript collection may be asked to sign a statement that if he wishes to publish a manuscript he will obtain permission from the library as the owner of the physical property to do so and will be responsible for obtaining permission from the author or literary heirs.

There is at least one important additional factor that library staff members should be aware of in the case of letters. The *writer* of a letter retains the right to authorize publication, not the recipient. Obtaining permission to publish should be the responsibility of the user.

Manuscript materials, unlike books, are occasionally given to a library under restrictive covenants that provide (1) that access is to be permitted only with the permission of the donor or his designee; (2) that no publication right will be granted for x years; or (3) that all access is to be denied to the manuscripts for ten, twenty, or even fifty years. The willingness of a library to accept such restrictions may be governed by the importance of the gift or the sensible nature of the restriction. In many cases, only the board of trustees is authorized to accept a restricted gift of this kind.

Some libraries take the position that members of their own university community should have first chance to undertake research on a new manuscript acquisition. If the work has been acquired at considerable cost, a restriction of this kind for a reasonable period (two years) is probably defensible. Some restrictions may be imposed upon the number of people who may simultaneously attempt to exploit a given body of material. Both of these restrictions will be offensive to some users and, if adopted, must be administered with great care. University libraries will need to adopt a clear policy on use of manuscripts and it may well include at least the essence of the 1951 statement by the Association of Research Libraries reproduced in Appendix IX.

Manuscripts are particularly vulnerable to theft, and for that reason the identification of borrowers and the close monitoring of users are justified. Accountability may be established by a piece-by-piece count of a very important collection at the time it is handed over to or returned by a borrower. In very special cases only photocopies of some collections may be made available.

University archives partake of many of the features of manuscript collections and may be administered under the same department. Board of trustees' minutes, presidential papers, financial records, and other documents may be considered privileged communications for a specified number of years — a restriction which will delay access by would-be users.

Many of the points made in this discussion of manuscripts and archives are illustrated in the document from the Harvard University Library reproduced in Appendix X.

MATERIALS REQUIRING EQUIPMENT FOR THEIR USE

Microtexts, phonorecords, phonotapes, computer tapes, punched cards, and video tapes are prime examples of materials requiring equipment for their use.

The reader is referred to earlier sections of this chapter for factors that may influence centralization versus decentralization in the use of microtexts. A central microtext facility may most profitably be discussed for our purposes. One of the major recurring and increasingly vexatious problems of access to microtexts is that of acquainting prospective users with the availability of specific items. This subject is discussed in the next section. Here, consideration will be directed to service problems.

Despite years of development and promises, fully satisfactory reading machines are not available. Staff must be carefully trained in handling and projector-mounting techniques for microfilm and other types of microtext. Inexperienced readers left to thread film into a machine may break leaders and scratch film. Therefore, principle number one is that this type of service would benefit from better machines. Number two is that a substantial amount of staff time is involved in service.

Persons wanting hard-copy prints of microtexts need access to special projectors that are expensive. Fees will probably have to be collected for such service, but it is unlikely that the fees will truly reflect the specialized equipment, supplies, and staff time involved. This is not too serious if viewed in the light of the availability of extraordinary materials.

Microtext equipment is reasonably expensive, but first-class audio equipment is far more so. It may range from a simple phonograph playback device to elaborate, multi-station, remote-control equipment costing more than $100,000. Electronic equipment of this sophistication and extent may involve a maintenance service contract costing several thousand dollars annually.

Audio library facilities may be used by class-size groups or by individuals. Classes can best be accommodated as a group in acoustically equipped rooms with "speakers." The audio program may be transmitted to the speaker from a central control room, or a disc/type playback facility may be provided in the room for instructor operation.

Most individual listening will be done via earphone headsets. These may cost as much as fifty dollars per pair, and if not attached firmly to the playback equipment, they should be charged out to students from the control desk. It may be well to take students' identification cards to guard against fictitious names and subsequent loss of headsets.

Students and faculty members (even members of the music faculty) may be inexpert in handling phonodiscs, and much damage can result from individual mounting, playing, and replaying of discs. Tapes are more resistant to mishandling, but they, too, can be damaged. It may be advisable to have most of the discs and tapes mounted at central control stations and the sound picked up at audio stations throughout the room.

Nonuniversity users may be excluded from an audio library because of the incidence of use and the expense of the equipment. Curricular use will have first call on group listening rooms and individual listening stations. But noncurricular use, facilities permitting, should be encouraged. For a student to be able to hear Franklin Delano Roosevelt speak, to hear Robert Frost read his own poems, or to hear the Juilliard String Quartet interpret a Beethoven quartet adds a significant dimension to his understanding, cultural sense, and education whether or not it is required by class assignment.

Extensive audio facilities may enable a library to "pipe" programs

263

to individual reading stations outside the audio library. A weekly mimeographed listing of the programs available at given hours will encourage this type of listening.

A full-fledged audio library can benefit from faculty and student awareness of its facilities and capabilities. This awareness can be promoted by leaflets such as that issued by the J. Henry Meyer Memorial Library at Stanford (see Appendix XI).

An archive of recorded sound attempts to preserve historically significant musical and spoken word recordings. The field is so vast that some effort should be made to correlate any collections of this kind with the academic program. The full range of recordings, from Edison cylinders to Mylar tape, will be involved as well as an extensive range of playback devices. Many historical phonodiscs will be copied onto tape for service purposes, and special attention must be given to the proper housing and handling of these materials. Principles that apply to rarities are generally applicable to new discs and tapes.

The most helpful study on the preservation and storage of sound recordings is that undertaken by A. G. Pickett and M. M. Lemcoe of the Southwest Research Institute in San Antonio, Texas, for the Library of Congress. Excerpts from the study appear in Appendix XII. Similar guides to the storage of microtexts exist in the literature.

Computer tapes, like tapes that capture sound, operate on the magnetic principle; therefore, the proper storage (including especially the avoidance of magnetic fields induced by major electrical lines, control boxes, etc.) should follow the recommended practices for phonotapes.

From a service standpoint, computer tapes present highly specialized features. Not only is very expensive equipment required, but also expert programming to manipulate raw data on the tape may be essential to the project in which the student or faculty member is engaged. An ideal arrangement would provide for the library to acquire, house, catalog, and make computer tapes available for use. In its fullest sense "make available for use" would include the provision of expert programming assistance to the student or faculty user.

Social science data (in the form of voting and population statistics) are rapidly growing and in great demand. The librarian with

Collections of microtexts permit student access to materials, including enlargement prints, the originals of which are not in university collections: microfilm reader-printer vision will see this as intellectual material in a specialized form that is an appropriate library concern. Most of the large university libraries have already experienced pressure to play a central role in this field.

MATERIALS REQUIRING SPECIAL BIBLIOGRAPHIC CONTROLS OR ORGANIZATION

Included in this category are those materials requiring the creation of specialized bibliographical controls or the development of shelving sequences that facilitate reader access. It will be seen that certain types of material (e.g., microforms) are treated here as well as in preceding categories. Pamphlets are given more lengthy discussion than other types because of the large quantities handled in, and the problems they present to, any large research library.

Sheet music may be kept in vertical files, alphabetically by title, or alphabetically by title within an overriding chronological or national arrangement: U.S. sheet music, 1920-29, 1930-39, etc. Such an arrangement may preclude the necessity for special bibliographical controls.

Sheet maps and fine prints are usually kept in metal plan files that come in units of five drawers each, each drawer being approx-

imately 52 inches wide, 38 inches from front to back, and 2 inches deep. Arrangement of maps by geographical area or subdivision may prove adequate in a collection of a few thousand items. The multimillion-item collections of the Library of Congress are kept essentially in this way. To facilitate access, maps should be titled in a position that is consistent (usually on a verso corner) where the identity of the map can be readily determined as one or two hundred maps lie flat in a plan file drawer. Frequently consulted road maps (folded) and city maps (folded) may be kept in a vertical file under a rough geographical arrangement (e.g., by states or by major foreign countries).

Some libraries will want to prepare catalog controls for very important map collections or even for single sheet maps. The extent of this kind of treatment will have to be determined in the light of the importance of maps in the academic program, the size of the collection, and the availability of staff to assist readers in finding maps.

Fine prints may be arranged by type (lithograph, etching, silk screen, etc.) but the basic arrangement is likely to be by artist. Since early printmakers often reproduced the work of famous painters, the basic arrangement might be by the name of the painter rather than the etcher. Further complexity is introduced when the painting being presented in print form is of a noted historical figure, in which case access by subject may also be desirable. It can be seen, therefore, that the bibliographical controls for fine prints may vary from zero (i.e., reliance on shelf arrangement) to specialized indexing to provide access by other artists involved, by subject — whether personal, geographical, or historical — and by print medium.

Photographs present the same complexity although they may more easily be duplicated to permit filing under several subjects. Photographs are often mounted on boards of uniform size or several standard sizes. They can then be filed in vertical files or open bins. To the expert photograph curator, single photographs present multiple areas of interest. A photograph of Theodore Roosevelt with three of his cabinet members on a hunting trip may be of interest because of each of the persons photographed, as well as for the background against which they are photographed (if a particular building is in view) or for the outfits they are wearing. A reproduction of an Egyptian tomb painting may demonstrate clothing, household articles, and even the nature of certain diseases (a shriveled leg or hand indicating the possible prevalence of infantile paralysis).

Microfilms of newspaper runs or microprints of United States government documents may be filed in boxes on regular library shelving although the more heavily used films are often best housed in metal cabinets with long shallow drawers permitting the housing of spool films in sequence in individual cardboard boxes, uniformly labeled to display inclusive dates of the issues contained on a particular reel. This is so straightforward that, except for specialized cartons or cabinets, bibliographical controls are simple and correspond almost exactly to those that would be provided for conventional files.

More difficult is the problem of providing access to many microtext series like the *Short Title Catalog* books which are filmed in more or less random order. Other than cataloging each item filmed, the best access is through an annotated copy of the *STC* that shows the specific reel numbers of those items that have been filmed. Indexes provided by the film publisher are cumbersome to use and highly unsatisfactory, and catalog cards sold with the series have been found unusable in many libraries because of differences in cataloging policies.

Technical reports are publications produced as a result of research, often government-sponsored. They are usually hastily issued, and they later get into the regular journal literature if they are lasting contributions. Therefore such reports are often given simplified bibliographic controls and are centrally shelved by issuing organization and then by report number or by date; the collections as a whole are regularly purged. In fact a list of new acquisitions may be issued to alert the faculty and research staff and to request them to indicate any which they feel should be added to the report collection; most others are then discarded. Reports are arranged on regular shelving, commonly as part of the Engineering or Mathematics Library, and weeding follows after five to eight years.

Not only will materials in this category require special housing, but also most of them will require special facilities for their use. Maps can best be consulted on large tables, flat or canted, with only one or two reading stations at a four-by-eight-foot table. Fine prints may be used on flat, canted, or pyramidal tables. As for maps,

267

reader space must be generous to provide room for inspecting and setting to one side large, matted materials.

Pamphlets and other vertical file materials can be a major problem in a university library; a research library, however, attains distinction not merely by acquiring traditional publications but by collecting the unusual and ephemeral item that may shed great light on an issue. Such items often constitute one of the most useful research elements, and yet they do not lend themselves to the normal treatment given monographs. Their value is based on their being passionate statements of political, religious, or sociological issues, or on their treating a specific technical problem which is timely and may at some later date be treated in a chapter of a monograph. Cases in point might be pamphlets, leaflets, and broadsides from dissident student groups; the publications of the New Left; and revolutionary materials from the black community or governments in exile. Many a social institution, *ad hoc* committee, or other group which has no affiliation with a major organization and may be quite transitory in its life history may be a prolific producer of pamphlet and broadside literature. These materials are often fugitive in that they do not occur in the normal book trade and are seldom covered in national bibliographies.

The treatment of such materials in libraries is complicated by the fact that it is exceedingly expensive to give pamphlets the same degree of catalog detail as is received by larger works, it takes as much staff time to process small pamphlets for binding as it does a large monograph, and the bibliographic data of authorship and other title page information is exceedingly meager or nonexistent in many a pamphlet. It consequently behooves a university library to give special policy consideration to its pamphlet and vertical file materials. To what extent should the library be active in soliciting pamphlets by gift, exchange, or purchase? And to what extent should it set up a network of librarians and friends of the library to solicit materials?

Some libraries may set up an open box in which a group of pamphlets may be placed under a broad heading in the book classification, with such a box being given a single subject entry in the card catalog. As alternatives, the pamphlets may be collected unbound for a period of time in file cabinets, or in open boxes in the general bookstack classification, or perhaps on special shelves as an adjunct to the current periodical room. Such a "way station" permits the library to assemble a large number of pamphlets from any one organization or on any one specific topic.

Where libraries decide to collect any appreciable amount of these materials, there will need to be a detailed program as to their bibliographic control. It should be remembered that the more elusive and unconventional the item, the greater the need for such controls. If the library has personnel time available, these pamphlet collections when bound into a tract volume may be given a typed table of contents to indicate the sequence of pamphlets by a brief title notation.

Other questions will be concerned with the catalog listing. Should a pamphlet receive full individual treatment, or should it receive main entry, title entry if it is a very memorable title, and name-subjects or a listing by broad subject category? Some shortcuts are bound to be required. The decision is likely to be based on the degree of emphasis that the university wishes to place on these materials, the extent of cataloging backlogs, and the extent to which the collecting is focused on a few organizations or a few issues, as distinguished from a broad acquisitions program. In most cases the library will decide that these items are approached either from the author point of view or from a broad subject approach, and thus the main entry in the catalog becomes essential. The subject treatment in the catalog will vary, depending on the method chosen for arrangement before binding and the arrangement after binding.

To preserve these collections of pamphlets, they should be sorted for binding into those which are wire-stitched and those which are sewn by thread in order that the binding process may be simplified. The pamphlets should also be sorted into size groupings by height and depth in order that when they are bound together they are of a sufficiently uniform size to enable the binding to hold its shape over years of use. It may therefore be necessary to collect as many as ten to twenty inches of pamphlets on any one subject before they can be divided into relatively uniform groups, measuring from one inch to two and a half inches, which are appropriate for binding.

One of the critical tasks in a library is to assign staff responsibility for watching these pre-binding accumulations of pamphlets, whether they be in vertical files or open pamphlet boxes. The person chosen must keep control over them so that they do not become unfindable as a result of mislocation. Binding should not be delayed so many years that the pamphlets become torn or dog-eared or are lost. On the other hand, they should be accumulated a sufficient length of time so that the processing and binding can be efficiently and economically performed. The handling of pamphlet collections must be carefully supervised in order that the final binding and shelving in the classification not be put off so long that the job presents a monstrous backlog problem which requires special budgeting and staff to cope with the arrears. The ideal would be to set up a system with a competent clerical assistant to work at the task a few hours each week, year in and year out, under the oversight of a responsible librarian.

This prebinding accumulation is sometimes the responsibility of the reference department, sometimes the circulation department, or it may be assigned to the current periodical room, government documents library, or newspaper and microtext reading room. The justification for the reference department's having this responsibility is that a reference librarian needs to know the topics of current interest and will use these materials currently, though items in the file may not be cataloged until they are bound and placed on the shelves. The argument for the circulation division's keeping this responsibility is that if the pamphlets are in open boxes on the shelf, the circulation division should have responsibility for attending to their binding and permanent preservation just as it has responsibility for the shelf location and preservation of the general book and journal collections. Policy decisions on acquisitions programs and interim shelving, as well as physical and personnel conditions, will lead to a program appropriate for each institution.

The whole question of pamphlets, broadsides, and similar fugitive material is one which deserves the attention of the director of libraries. The process should be set up as a simple routine. The materials should be recognized as of research importance, and yet library policies must not give them such complete treatment that they are as expensive to process as a major treatise.

SELECTED REFERENCES

Manuscripts and Archives

Berner, Richard C. "The Arrangement and Description of Manuscripts," *American Archivist*, 23 (October 1960), 395–406.

Bordin, Ruth B., and Robert M. Warner. *The Modern Manuscript Library*. New York, Scarecrow Press, 1966.

Finch, Jean L. "Some Fundamentals in Arranging Archives and Manuscript Collections," *Library Resources and Technical Services*, 8 (Winter 1964), 26–34.

Kane, Lucile M. "A Guide to the Care and Administration of Manuscripts," *Bulletins of the American Association for State and Local History*, 2 (September 1960), [327]–88.

Radoff, Morris L. "A Guide to Practical Calendaring," *American Archivist*, 11 (April, July 1948), 123–40, 203–22.

Schellenberg, T. R. *Management of Archives*. New York, Columbia University Press, 1965.

Vail, R. W. G., ed. "Manuscripts and Archives," *Library Trends*, 5 (January 1957), 309–416.
Especially useful are the articles by Minoque, Dunkin, Peckham, and Lovett.

Wasson, W. W. "Organizing and Administering University Archives," *College and Research Libraries*, 29 (March 1968), 109–16.

Maps

Hill, J. Douglas. "Map and Atlas Cases," *Library Trends*, 13 (April 1965), 481–7.

LeGear, C. E. *Maps: Their Care, Repair and Preservation in Libraries*. Washington, Library of Congress, 1956.

Ristow, Walter W. "What About Maps?" *Library Trends*, 4 (October 1955), 123–39.

Music (see also Sound Recordings)

Duckles, Vincent, ed. "Music Libraries and Librarianship," *Library Trends*, 8 (April 1960), 493–617.
Especially useful are the articles by Colby, and Smith and Watanabe.

McColvin, Lionel Roy, and Harold Reeves. *Music Libraries.* . . . Completely rewritten, revised and extended by Jack Dove. London, A. Deutsch, 1965.

Music Library Association. *Manual of Music Librarianship*, Carol June Bradley, ed. Ann Arbor, Music Library Association [1966].
Includes 13 chapters written by specialists.

Oral History

Columbia University. Oral History Research Office. *Oral History in the United States*. New York [1965?].

Oral History Association. *Goals and Guidelines for Oral History* [mimeographed]. Los Angeles, Oral History Association, 1967.

Schippers, Donald J., and Adelaide G. Tusler. *Bibliography of Oral History*. Los Angeles, Oral History Association, 1967.

Swain, Donald C. "Problems for Practitioners of Oral History," *American Archivist*, 28 (January 1965), 63–9.

Pamphlets

Condit, Lester. *A Pamphlet about Pamphlets*. Chicago, University of Chicago Press, 1939.

Wyllie, John Cook. "Pamphlets, Broadsides, Clippings and Posters," *Library Trends*, 4 (October 1955), 195–202.
    This issue also contains useful articles about newspapers, prints, photographs, musical scores, films, etc.

Photocopies

Boone, S. M. *Current Administrative Practices in Library Photographic Services*. (ACRL Microcard Series, 151) Rochester, N.Y., University of Rochester Press for the Association of College and Research Libraries [1965?].

Cummings, Laurence A. "Pitfalls of Photocopy Research." *Bulletin of the New York Public Library*, 65 (February 1961), 97–101.

Fussler, Herman H. *Photographic Reproduction for Libraries: A Study of Administrative Problems*. Chicago, University of Chicago, 1942.

Hawken, William R. *Copying Methods Manual*. Chicago, American Library Association [1966].

Skipper, James E., ed. "Photoduplication in Libraries," *Library Trends*, 8 (January 1960), 343–492.
    Especially useful are the articles by Bechanan and Muller.

Rare Books

Archer, H. R., ed. *Rare Book Collections: Some Theoretical and Practical Suggestions for Use by Librarians and Students*. Chicago, American Library Association, 1965.
    Especially useful are the chapters by Baughman, Haugh, and French.

Jackson, William A. "The Importance of Rare Books and Manuscripts in a University Library," in *The Place of the Library in a Univer-*

sity: Conference Held 30-31 March, 1949. Cambridge, Harvard University Library, 1950. pp. 26–37.

    Also in *Harvard Library Bulletin,* 3 (Autumn 1949), 315–26.

Peckham, Howard H., ed. "Rare Book Libraries and Collections," *Library Trends,* 5 (April 1957), 417–94.

    Especially useful are the articles by Byrd, Goff, and Haugh.

Powell, Lawrence Clark. "Rare Book Code," *College and Research Libraries,* 10 (July 1949), 307–8.

    Also issued as part of a separate, *Rare Books in the University Library.* Chicago, Association of College and Reference Libraries [1949].

Sound Recordings

Association of College and Research Libraries. *Guidelines for Audio-Visual Services in Academic Libraries.* Chicago, Association of College and Research Libraries, 1968.

Conference on the Use of Printed and Audio-Visual Materials for Instructional Purposes: First Report, prepared by M. F. Tauber and I. R. Stephens. New York, Columbia University School of Library Service, 1966.

International Association of Music Libraries. *Phonograph Record Libraries: Their Organisation and Practise,* Henry F. J. Currall, ed. Hamden, Conn., Archon Books, 1963.

Pickett, A. G., and M. M. Lemcoe. *Preservation and Storage of Sound Recordings. . . .* Washington, Library of Congress, 1959.

Technical Reports

Fry, Bernard M. *Library Organization and Management of Technical Reports Literature.* Washington, Catholic University of America Press, 1953.

Hall, J. "Technical Report Literature," in *Handbook of Special Librarianship and Information Work,* Wilfred Ashworth, ed. 3rd ed. London, Aslib, 1967. pp. 287–308.

9. MEASUREMENT AND EVALUATION

Library use of statistics for management purposes is in a primitive state. Expenditure figures are closer to complete accuracy than are figures on materials acquired or cataloged, whereas circulation and reference figures are ridiculous as absolute measures of use and are faulty even as relative comparisons from one year to the next. It is however, necessary to use statistics as shorthand to convey rapidly to university administrators and others the library's growth, its plans for the future, its problems, and its service to the community.

Measurement is also one of the techniques used in surveys, time and motion studies, simulation, operations research, the critical path method, most qualitative studies, standards of support and use, and cost accounting; and it is an important aspect of accreditation methodology. These management techniques can be of assistance to the library administration. They provide objective data which can serve as hard, definitive evidence of need, efficiency, or accomplishment.

It must be realized that measurement devices only help in the solution of a problem; they do not provide the solution. An academic intellectual operation like a university library cannot be weighed on a scale or price-marked in dollars and cents in any truly meaningful fashion. Therefore standards and accreditation practices now strive to evaluate the intangible, immeasurable human elements as the very best indication of importance, growth, or progress.

Early in this century, efficiency in university libraries was often thought of in terms of the arrangement of furniture, the preparation of a form, the compiling of figures on the size of the collection and books added to the collection. Methods of scientific management were occasionally applied. In the period since World War II, however, university libraries have grown to a point where they can no longer work efficiently and convey their needs to the university administration through such simple practices. The result is that the

275

Variety in the arrangement of tables, carrels, and bookshelving breaking up large library spaces into human proportions: corner of the general reading collection — Reading Room, J. Willard Marriott Library, University of Utah

larger libraries are now being impelled to devote highly specialized attention to their fiscal management and their operations. This requires the use of the most effective techniques of modern management. The medium-sized university libraries will find that in another generation they, too, will need the more sophisticated approach. Furthermore, systems analysis and cost accounting are essential techniques whenever a library embarks in a serious fashion on a large-scale automation program.

Fremont Rider once said that "the finest service that every library gives is the very one that can never be measured." He was of course referring to the human relations between the librarian with a deep knowledge of books and bibliography and the student or scholar who benefits by coming into contact with such a librarian-scholar. This is still the case; but the fact will not in all circumstances convince the president or provost that one more librarian is needed or that one more book or microtext must be purchased. The modern university library will have to rely on statistics, hard facts, and faculty support as well as words of persuasion and selected examples to substantiate the case for library development.

STATISTICS

Statistics are the most common means of measurement. They present a picture of the library which could not be adequately or succinctly stated in any other fashion. Thus, nearly all university library annual reports will give statistics for expenditures, size of staff, size of collection in various formats, number of volumes added in the past fiscal year, and volumes circulated. In some cases, reporting libraries add to these general rubrics in order to cover reference work, photocopies produced, serial titles currently received, ancillary cataloging data such as transfers, and so forth.

Each library will need to assemble those statistics required for national reporting and to use definitions which conform as closely as possible to the national reporting standard. Sometimes adjustments will need to be made with judgment, and consequently each university library will need its own gloss on the national program of library statistics. For example, if the university's accounting system includes or excludes personnel benefits, includes or excludes building operation charges, includes or excludes grant or contract money assigned to library purposes, includes or excludes "contributed" services, or lumps university students employed on an hourly basis with persons outside of the university who are paid on an hourly basis, the statistical figures will have to be footnoted in order to make figures reasonably comparable with those of other universities. An important point to be made is that any deviation from national standards must be explained with the relevant table each year, and any significant change in the method of collecting statistics within the library from one year to the next must also be explained. Thus, if a library has inventoried its collection and the resulting count has increased or decreased markedly, this must be noted. If the fiscal year changes, if the definition of "professional staff" is altered, if the definition of serial titles currently received is changed, if technical reports or government documents were previously not counted but are now — any such significant change must be recorded so that it is self-evident.

A library will find that some statistics need to be collected regularly and published annually. Any statistic which is not essential to the operation each year should not be continuously collected if it could be obtained later either by a one-shot analysis or a retrospective collection of data. A continuous sampling may be a useful alternative. It may be necessary one year to have records of the number of individuals using a library facility during certain evening hours, or to determine the minimum and maximum and median number of accesses to the order file per day, or to figure the net assignable square footage in library facilities throughout the university, or to calculate the local TSCOR (technical services cost ratio). These statistics can be obtained more efficiently through sampling or a one-time study than as part of the complete continuous reporting system for statistics assembled each year.

Many variations can be considered for their usefulness. A number of statistics will need to be collected solely for internal purposes. An example of this kind might be the scatter chart for personnel salaries, or the categorized total of cataloging arrears on an annual or semiannual basis. In some cases it may be beneficial to provide five-year comparisons of expenditure, growth, or use figures. In other cases it may be desirable regularly to calculate percentage increases. Whenever a new manual process is to be installed or a mechanized process is contemplated, the number of statistical

studies will increase markedly. It may be useful in planning a circulation review, for example, to know the frequency of searching for
missing books, the percentage of volumes found in each search
period, the type of books found in each search, and the fluctuations
by time of year or even by the category of users who have requested
the books not available.

It has been mentioned that percentages may be useful. As one
example, it may be desirable to find the percentage distribution in
library expenditures as among salaries, books and binding, and
miscellaneous charges. (The budget typically will be 62 per cent
for personnel, 32 per cent for books and other materials, and 6 per
cent for supplies, equipment, travel, etc.) If the percentage of total
library expenditures for books, periodicals and binding is 20 per
cent to 30 per cent, there may be special reasons why the personnel
costs are so high or it may be that the book collections are not
receiving adequate attention. Similarly, if the expenditure for books,
periodicals, and binding is between 38 per cent and 50 per cent,
there must be some special reasons why it is so high: local clerical
personnel costs may be part of it, staff salaries would affect it
strongly, the amount of decentralization which requires additional
service staff might be another explanation, and so on.

It may also be useful to break down the books and binding total
into books and binding to permit comparison with other university
libraries. Books are going to cost about the same whether they are
purchased in one region of the country or another. Binding costs,
however, vary among regions as do clerical personnel costs and costs
of purchased services. As noted on pp. 187-8, binding costs may run
from 15 per cent to 20 per cent of the books and binding total,
depending upon local circumstances, but the percentage determination is certainly one indication of whether in a quantitative sense
the university is doing enough or too little in the preservation of its
collections.

Occasionally it may be useful to have an in-depth statistical
study performed on one or another aspect of the library operation.
This may be done by a person on the library staff, or sometimes by
a person in the controller's office or systems office, or it may be
justifiable to use an outside consulting firm. It may, for example,
be politic to employ an outside firm to do a cost analysis study of
the university library system as a basis for negotiating the library

component of the overhead formula in government contracts. A cost analysis may give a sound basis for determining the ratio of total cost and per capita cost for graduate students, faculty, and staff groups to costs for the undergraduate student group. For example, the result may show that 15 per cent of the dollar effort is in support of the undergraduate students, 44 per cent in support of graduate students, 36 per cent in support of faculty and research staff, and 5 per cent miscellaneous groups. This in turn can establish a weighting or ratio of per capita costs of 1.0 representing undergraduates to 3.1 representing the combined graduate student and faculty effort.

The aggregation of statistics from a wide spectrum of academic libraries may permit generalizations. Such data, when carefully prepared and discriminatingly interpreted, permit each university to measure itself in relation to this pragmatic norm.

MEASUREMENT TECHNIQUES

Advanced measurement techniques utilizing statistics have infrequently been applied to libraries. Where statistics fail or where they give an incomplete picture, libraries must turn to other means to find the facts. Graphs, for example, use statistics as raw materials from which to plot trends; Purdue University has done this with research library statistics. Purdue's report provides as realistic a comparison with other university libraries as is possible given the faulty local collecting of raw data due to the lack of firm standards of definition.

But more advanced techniques are now available for consideration. Cost accounting, cost-effectiveness studies, the cost-benefit technique, and the PPBS (Planning-Programming-Budgeting System) are financial planning/measurement/control techniques that are applicable to large libraries. (These are commented upon in Chapter 4.) Process or operation planning/measurement/control techniques include time and motion studies, space utilization studies, linear programming, systems analysis, and operations research. These are treated here. Central in these sophisticated techniques is the dynamic element — a fact which makes them useful in library situations. A complex library system involves phenomena that change with time; a steady-state condition does not exist in a university library in the latter half of this century.

Some planning techniques are simple to apply. Time and motion studies are a standard form of using minimum/maximum/mean time intervals for each individual task to determine bottlenecks, find more rapid techniques, and thereby cut costs. Space utilization studies analyze personnel-equipment-operation-traffic requirements at normal and peak times to determine justifications of assignment, slack use of space which can be reassigned, and possible phased use of the same space — with operational efficiency and space conservation the goals. (For illustration see the Cook study of seating in an undergraduate library.[1])

Several planning and scheduling techniques use linear programming: Gantt charts (bar charts describing the relationships of components and time), milestone charts (plotting time targets for component completion), line of balance techniques (actual component production is bar charted in comparison with production objectives and a line of balance is created to reveal revised requirements needed to meet objectives), CPM and PERT, the last two

---

[1] In Barton R. Burkhalter, ed., *Case Studies in Systems Analysis in a University Library.* pp. 142–70.

Gantt Chart

	January	February	March	April	May	June	July	August	September	October	November	December
Gantt Chart												
Systems design	I—	—	—	I								
Software design			I—	—	—	—	—	—	—	I		
Equipment procurement					I—	—	—	—	I			
System testing								I—	—	—	I	
System implementation										I—	—	—

being most advanced in handling time tolerances and the dynamics of interdependencies. The critical path method (CPM), developed in 1956, uses a graphic flow chart to find the longest path to a destination. This is found by determining which operations are most demanding of time and which are prerequisite to one or several subsequent operations. More effort on those subtasks which are on the critical path will then improve the flow of the system, and the resulting economy often considerably outbalances the extra costs. Bottlenecks can be constantly checked and controlled. Slack time or personnel in any task may be determined. Extra personnel can sometimes be taken from uncritical tasks which will then take a little longer. The work load in each department and the system load in all departments become more in balance. PERT (program evaluation and review technique) is milestone- or event-oriented whereas CPM is entirely activity- or operation-oriented. They are now commonly combined and used with varying degrees of sophistication, some systems using earliest-expected and latest-allowable time to provide slack determination and frequent recalculation as changes occur in one or another facet. Both CPM and PERT can best be used in evaluating nonrepetitive programs involving large degrees of uncertainty as well as interdependencies which need to reflect the dynamic nature of changing plans. Thus they are useful

Milestone Chart

Milestone Chart	January	February	March	April	May	June	July	August	September	October	November	December
Begin systems design	△											
Begin software design				△								
Place equipment orders					△							
Place equipment on line									△			
Commence implementation											△	

for complex research and development programs, not for production scheduling and control. The essence of the critical path or PERT network flow chart, however, can be of universal applicability. Simplified presentations of linear programming illustrated in this chapter indicate types of application.

Systems analysis uses detailed analyses as do the preceding techniques, but its essential elements are highly formalized:

1. An objective or objectives to be accomplished
2. Alternative techniques or systems by which to achieve the objective
3. An input of resources required by each system — men, equipment, space, time, money, processes, etc.
4. Models or logical frameworks showing the interdependence of the objectives, techniques, resources, and environment
5. A criterion, relating objectives and resources or expenses, for choosing the best or optimal path among the alternatives
6. A chosen model or solution, generally expressed as a flow chart

The technique is most widely applied as the pre-design phase in sophisticated mechanization or automation programs. (It is commented upon in Chapter 10, p. 303.)

Operations research is a highly sophisticated merging of tech-

Line of Balance

Line of Balance		January	February	March	Ap
Units Processed		January	February	March	Ap
1 Acquired		4,200	4,600	4,700	4,8
2 Descriptive cataloging		4,100	4,400	4,700	4,8
3 Subject cataloging		4,100	4,300	4,600	4,8
4 Book finishing		4,100	4,300	4,700	4,3
5 Card sets filed		4,100	4,700	4,400	4,8

niques. Its application is justified where the prediction of dynamic behavior is difficult but essential; and mathematical models, simulation, and research utilizing computation aids can help. Academic departments have been established in many universities solely to teach this systematized scientific method of logically analyzing complex situations. The function of operations research is to determine the best mix of people, equipment, space, and processes to achieve a fixed goal. The process begins with an enumeration of assumptions, then the defining of acceptable parameters of actions and the use of model-building in which input and output phenomena bring dynamic responses. The range of conceivable actions of people is analyzed, as well as activities outside the situation which conceivably interact with the situation. Then comes validation, refining controls over the action, further testing, and further exploration of the hypotheses as a feedback to regenerate the next cycle of adjusted input/output action/reaction. The specific techniques used include Boolean algebra, set theory, games theory, probability, matrix theory, queuing theory, linear programming, and simulation. It has been applied in libraries to such problems as book storage-access conditions.

Techniques used in operations research require advanced training for their understanding and application. Consequently the library can make use of the technique only if there is sufficient work to justify employing a staff specialist, such as in an Operations

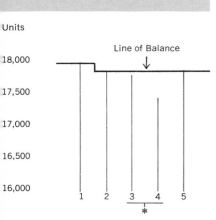

*These two processes lag behind and require improvement while the rate of the first process is creating arrears and adjustment here is also required.

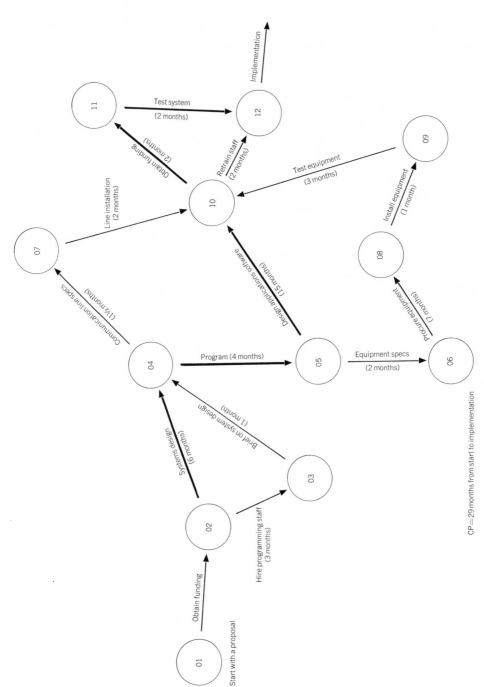

Critical Path Method

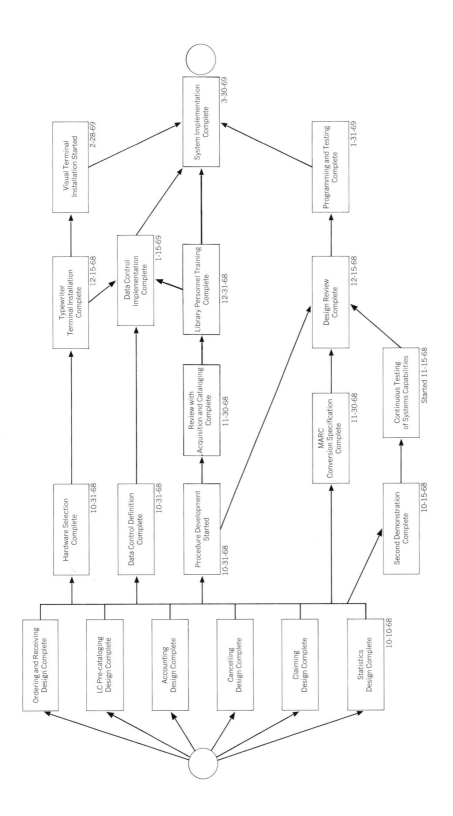

PERT Network

Planning Office (as at the University of Pennsylvania Library), or if a fractional effort can be justified. Fractional effort may be arranged by contract with a management consulting firm, through use of a grant or appropriation to hire a consultant, through sharing use of a university systems or operations office, or through persuading a faculty member to interest a graduate student in using the library as the experimental model for his thesis. Use of such techniques as these will be increasingly common and indeed mandatory as library budgets grow and the system becomes more and more complex.

All measurement techniques use analysis and a systematic, logical approach to evaluation. Intuition is the only reasonable alternative to the use of these techniques; trial and error cannot be tolerated on any scale. Intuition can be remarkable. The "sense" or "feeling" of which route to take may be more correct than the product of the most detailed mathematical model. A sophisticated measurement technique is not an alternative for judgment or intuition based on experience. Rather the two can in tandem lead to a better program. The use of such techniques — together with sound judgment — is becoming essential in the increasingly complex life of a research library.

Measurement and Evaluation

SURVEYS

Surveys are a well established measurement technique though the methodology varies greatly. They are a systematic in-depth attempt to obtain an objective view of a facility and match it against certain standards of efficiency, service, or rate of improvement. The study may be of the entire range of responsibilities of the library or of one specific element in the program such as its collections, its building, its technical processes, or its personnel.

There are two important considerations to be determined with respect to a formal survey. One is to be certain that the survey is needed, that it is the best way to accomplish a stated objective, and that it will be undertaken with adequate financial investment to assure the desired degree of comprehensiveness. The other consideration is whether to do it "in house" or to employ an outside individual or firm. The choice of the individual or group of persons is undoubtedly the most crucial element. The individual must in the first instance be acceptable to the university, including its director of libraries. Second, he must have engaged in enough surveys of similar types of library to be able to bring to bear a strong background of experience. Third, he must be able to devote adequate time to the survey. Fourth, he must be able to call upon assistants in the library that is being surveyed or be able to bring with him one or more individuals to do detailed studies of particular elements of the library program — such as cataloging efficiency, quality of book selection, or merit of building plans. Fifth, he should have enough experience to assure that the study will be conducted within a reasonable time span and be sufficiently convincing to support his recommendations. Sixth, and most important, he must be a person who can be convincing both in his written report and in oral communication with the university administration.

The political influence of a survey is commonly its *raison d'être.* Unless it is effective with the university administration, the trustees, and perhaps the faculty, it will have failed no matter how comprehensive and well stated it is. Consequently the survey director's personal stature in his field and among educators must be impressive if the report is to have the influence that is desired. In the past, too many library surveys have been an application of the "objective" social science statistical techniques of the 1930's; the statis-

287

Provision of reference desks in the entrance gallery, to assist with easy access to collections and services, supplemented with directories, student handbooks, and other instructional approaches — John M. Olin Library, Cornell University

tics mount up but the result is not necessarily a clear or practical recommendation for action.

The value of a survey is in its improvement of the library. In some instances an outside surveyor can produce the best result. Lowell A. Martin points out that there are

> . . . several proper roles for the surveyor. He may have specialized knowledge neither possessed nor expected to be possessed by the administering librarian or the local staff. Examples are the building expert, when a new structure is in prospect, or the cataloging expert, when a change in a classification system is under consideration. Or the surveyor may be called in as a friend of the court to help make the case for a line of action that the librarian wants and may already have proposed. Thus, the campaign of the chief librarian for a more competitive salary scale or for faculty status for the professional staff of a university library may need outside support. The surveyor brings his prestige to the cause or his power of convincing, or both. The expert as a witness for the prosecution has his place, so long as this downright function is clearly recognized as such, but I question this type of survey when the so-called expert is used essentially as a rubber stamp.
>
> The survey and the surveyor seem to me most useful when they are called upon to analyze a genuinely complex situation, with disparate factors and hard alternatives ahead. The most challenging of such situations often involve more than one library: the public or university libraries throughout a state, all libraries in a metropolitan region, or the several libraries serving students in a community.[2]

Since the purpose of an outside survey is to perform a function which could not be achieved by inside study, to smooth over personal conflicts or prejudices that could not be resolved, or to speak to the university administration in words which are more convincing than those previously used by the director of libraries, the choice of the man is more important than the content of the survey. There have been many instances in which a man chosen to conduct a survey has produced a report of from fifty to one hundred and fifty pages full of statistics and tables and words — without the report and its recommendations having the desired effect. In contrast, the right man may be able to spend one day instead of one week visiting the institution, may write a report of five or ten pages

[2] "Personnel in Library Surveys," in Maurice F. Tauber and Irlene Roemer Stephens, eds., *Library Surveys.* pp. 124–5.

instead of a hundred pages, and may in informal conversation with the president of the university be able to have a far greater impact on the future of its library system.

Timing is another factor which is critical since a university which is not in the financial position to give the library a higher priority than faculty salaries, a classroom complex, or student scholarship funds must simply be realistic and ask the library to wait for a more propitious time to mount a campaign. A survey undertaken under those circumstances cannot be successful. A survey undertaken at a more favorable time, however, is likely to be greeted with encouragement and will probably be acted upon expeditiously.

The content of surveys may vary markedly. Those which are directed only to a physical building problem differ in organization and character from those dealing with the photographic laboratory, staffing and personnel policies, or the strength of the collections of a library; and these in turn would be quite different from those dealing with such broad policy matters as whether to encourage the growth of a departmental library system, whether to construct a separate undergraduate library, whether to combine institutes and autonomous elements into a single library system, or whether to set up branches in distant campus locations.

A report of a survey may proceed from a summary of recommendations to the historical setting and general academic program of the university, the administrative organization of and financial support for the library, staff employment and promotion practices as well as salary and status questions, the physical facilities of the library, book selection policies and procurement efforts, technical processing, public services, and special collections and departmental libraries. The survey may also cover interlibrary cooperation and formal contractual arrangements, student or faculty opinion on library services and collections, measurements against a variety of recent lists or bibliographies of acknowledged repute, and perhaps library automation efforts. The coverage of the survey depends on the needs of the institution.

STANDARDS

Standards as a measure of adequacy are among the most nebulous aspects of librarianship and especially of university librarianship.

The standards for a university library should be those appropriate for the university which it serves. As universities vary markedly in character so should their libraries, and any deviation in the library from the character of the specific university it serves may suggest a real inadequacy. The library should be neither too weak nor a great deal too strong in relation to the varying strength of the disciplines offered. This is not to say the library should not anticipate developments in one or another academic department. Indeed, one of the real problems in administering a university library is to get authoritative word sufficiently in advance of the inception of a doctoral program to permit the building of library collections to support that program.

The measurement of library adequacy as compared to the overall university program cannot be obtained in any simple fashion. A pragmatic approximation of adequacy might be reached by interviewing all students and faculty to determine whether reasonable requirements for library service are met. This is a common part of the survey technique. Yet there is a question whether students or professors know what they want if it is not provided. How reasonable are their wants and how effective is their use of what is available?

In view of this dilemma, national library standards are useful. No national standard yet exists, however, for judging the quality of a university library. Some insight into what may constitute a minimum level of adequacy can be gained from "Standards for College Libraries," issued in 1959 by the Association of College and Research Libraries.[3] These standards apply to bachelor's as well as master's programs and they cover faculty needs. The treatment of the book collection is typical of the approach: the collections "should meet" the full curricular needs of students, "should provide properly" for graduate students, and "should contain a generous selection" for the faculty. Similarly, general comments about various types of materials lead finally to a statement that an analysis of college library statistics suggests that a total of 50,000 volumes should be the minimum for any college. Here is an empirical standard, based on the judgment of a few able and experienced college librarians who feel that in some way a smaller

[3] *College and Research Libraries*, 20 (July 1959), 274–80.

collection does not have enough to meet most reasonable needs whereas a larger collection stands a good chance of meeting most reasonable needs.

Verner W. Clapp and Robert T. Jordan in 1964 developed a formula for setting the optimal size of a library for any particular university.[4] It was based on volume needs per individual and per field of undergraduate or graduate concentration. This is similarly empirical but has the advantage of bringing into play the elements which make universities diverse in nature. What this approach does not do is to reckon with the difference in book needs between, say, history and engineering; rather, it assumes a universe of subjects will be covered by the academic community and thus the differences among subjects even out as do the differences in use of the library by individuals. Work on a standard for university libraries is in progress.

The complexity with regard to setting standards for collections is matched by the complexity of standards attempting to set levels of financial support, staff size, space for readers and staff, and so forth. The most important point to be kept in mind is that within a broad range of possible library adequacy, a strong *rate* of growth and the presence of an able, alert library staff are certain to be the most significant evidence in judging any library. This point is recognized tacitly at the conclusion of the college library standards: "These standards should be interpreted . . . in a spirit that will enable the . . . libraries . . . not only to maintain but to strengthen their position in the face of this new . . . era of momentous change." The rate of growth also is recognized as particularly important by the "maintenance of effort" conditions in library resource grants from the United States Office of Education under Title IIA of the Higher Education Act of 1965, designed so that libraries approaching the adequacy threshold would be eligible for assistance.

The philosophy behind the standard chosen for evaluation of the library is of more fundamental importance than any of the quantitative elements. For example, the six square feet sometimes used as a "standard" for table space per reader will be grossly in-

[4] "Quantitative Criteria for Adequacy of Academic Library Collections," *College and Research Libraries*, 26 (September 1965), 371–80.

adequate even for undergraduates if they are doing honors work, working with microtexts or manuscripts, or studying in fields such as art history or archaeology. Such a standard is obviously so low as to be potentially detrimental if used by a business or fiscal officer whose responsibility is to save space or to reduce costs. An average of eight square feet of working surface is more realistic. Another "standard" often quoted is the requirement that at least one third of the student body have seating in the library. Here again no account is taken of major factors such as the strength in engineering as compared to law, the residential or commuting nature of the institution, or the commodiousness of the collegiate residences. Indeed, developments in remote access to audio-visual-digitalized documentation could serve to justify a sharply reduced amount of seating in an institution with a highly developed campus information network. Even the "standard" requiring that 5 per cent of the university's total instruction-research budget go for library support is questionable when a relatively young institution has a full-blown curriculum but an immature library collection, when extraordinary research expenses distort the picture, or when an expensive specialized library component exists, such as a separate and major rare book library, a major archive program, or a substantial extension program in a public university.

The extent of interlibrary cooperative arrangements can have an impact on finances and book collections required for adequate service. Such arrangements cannot, of course, be a substitute for the basic program of the library; but they may provide an alternative whereby 1 per cent to 2 per cent of the library budget could be devoted to local as opposed to regional or national efforts. Evaluation must take into consideration whether a cooperative arrangement will achieve the greater return on investment.

Consequently, methods of judging a library must be based on discriminating subjective evaluation. A specific approach to this difficult process, with particular application in accreditation studies, was prepared by the Stanford Library in 1965 for the Association of College and Research Libraries. This document, entitled "Guide to Methods of Library Evaluation," enumerates the primary evidence of books, reading spaces, and professional staff which are the major essential ingredients of a vital library program. It outlines means of evaluating each of these elements within the context

292

of nationally adopted standards and with the emphasis that the most important condition is a strong *rate* of improvement; the mere fact of meeting minimum quantitative standards is of far less importance. The document continues with secondary evidence such as budget and planning documents, statistics of use, and other evidence which indirectly reflect the quality and vitality of the library program. This secondary evidence may suggest which are the strong or weak points of the library by offering insight into aspects of its work; however, such evidence must be used only as a clue to help further evaluation of the primary evidence. It is particularly useful in evaluating the momentum of the large well-established academic libraries which obviously exceed minimum national standards but may be failing to maintain quality or sensitivity to service needs in one or another facet of their programs.

Finally, favorable consideration may be given to achievements which do not directly alter the fundamental effectiveness of the library but which suggest something about student feeling concerning the library, faculty regard for it, and interest in the library on the part of the general public. These special achievements and activities include the student book club, a lecture series, exhibitions, published guides, handbooks, or bibliographies, and so forth. The result may be a subsurface esteem for the library and a wide public knowledge of its collections and services which augur well for its future support and usefulness. Yet again it is emphasized that these are subtle points and should usually be given slight weight in an evaluation of the adequacy and quality of the library.

ACCREDITATION

Accreditation is the means by which an association formally decides which institutions are qualified for membership in it or are approved by it. The accreditation process serves as a judgment of the institution; at the same time, the process is designed to be of direct service to the institution. Accreditation assists the institution in defining its goals, identifying its problems, and achieving a good rate of progress.

For universities, the National Commission on Accrediting coordinates the six regional accrediting associations and twenty-one professional associations. The newer Commission on Institutions of Higher Education may develop a similar national stance on accrediting. Each association has its own policies and practices for determining whether an institution seeking accreditation is successful in carrying out its own stated purposes. Library standards of these associations vary from the general statement of the American Chemical Society and the Middle States Association of Colleges and Secondary Schools (which has issued excellent "Suggestions on the Evaluation of Libraries . . .") to the explicit specifications of the Southern Association of Colleges and Secondary Schools and of the Association of American Law Schools.

These accreditation standards, even the more general ones, are of value to weak institutions and to those with threshold or minimum qualifications. Presidents and directors of libraries may find them useful measures of standing and progress. Above those levels, goals must be sought by comparing the institution with a selection of those institutions of similar size and condition which are thought to offer a similar academic program. Nationally collected statistics or special compilations may be used to determine norms, a median, or practical goals in lieu of measurement against a minimum national standard.

The accreditation procedure of most associations calls for the institution to prepare a formal report on progress since the last visit of experts (the interval is usually five years or less). During a two-day visit, a team of outside experts then talks with university staff and students in all parts of the institution, including the director of libraries. Members of the visiting committee clarify points in the formal report, determine to what extent the institution's current program meets its own stated goals and relevant national standards, and discuss these points with the institution's representatives. The experts look for and comment to staff members on strengths as well as possible weaknesses as they have observed them to obtain their reaction to the findings. Each team member must ascertain facts to back up any general impressions that he may be forming. He must also keep in mind that self-evaluation by the institution may be more worthwhile than the on-site stimulus of the visiting committee and its eventual report. The report itself normally reviews action on the recommendations of the previous team, commends the institution, where appropriate, on its strengths and progress, points out weaknesses or apparent

294

deficiencies in the program, and makes objective recommendations for action or for further study by the institution. In a very real sense members of the visiting committee are on the campus as consultants as well as educational colleagues. They gain in stimulus just as does the institution. Library directors and other senior library officers benefit their institutions as well as the standing of librarianship to the extent that they participate in the work of visiting teams. In the accreditation process it is abundantly clear that there is no one way to develop effective programs in higher education and that the wide variation in capabilities, interests, needs, and circumstances in the young people of this nation require equally wide variations in the institutions that further their formal education.

The library survey, as discussed above, can be an exceedingly detailed and penetrating document. It is an in-depth study designed to help reshape and enrich the library's activities. The accreditation process is a brief survey, using some quantitative standards and using many qualitative judgments, and it considers the library as an element integral in the university as a whole. As such, the accreditation effort is the most complex form of library measurement and evaluation.

SELECTED REFERENCES

American Library Association. Statistics Coordinating Project. *Library Statistics: A Handbook of Concepts, Definitions, and Terminology*. Chicago, American Library Association, 1966.

Association of College and Research Libraries. Standards Committee. "Standards for College Libraries," *College and Research Libraries*, 20 (July 1959), 274–80.

Blanchard, J. Richard. Planning the Conversion of a College to a University Library," *College and Research Libraries*, 29 (July 1968), 297–302.

Brutcher, Constance, Glen Gessford, and Emmet Rixford. "Cost Accounting for the Library," *Library Resources and Technical Services*, 8 (Fall 1964), 413–31.

Burkhalter, Barton R., ed. *Case Studies in Systems Analysis in a University Library*. Metuchen, N.J., Scarecrow Press, 1968.

Clapp, Verner W., and Robert T. Jordan. "Quantitative Criteria for Adequacy of Academic Library Collections," *College and Research Libraries*, 26 (September 1965), 371–80.

Densmore, Glen, and Charles Bourne. *A Cost Analysis and Utilization Study of the Stanford University Library System*. Stanford, Calif., Stanford University Libraries, 1965.

Dougherty, Richard M., and Fred J. Heinritz. *Scientific Management of Library Operations*. Metuchen, N.J., Scarecrow Press, 1966.

Dunn, O. C., W. F. Seibert, and Janice A. Scheuneman. *The Past and Likely Future of 58 Research Libraries, 1951-1980: A Statistical Study of Growth and Change*. 3rd issue. Lafayette, Ind., Purdue University Libraries and Audio Visual Center, 1967.

Ellsworth, Ralph E. *The Economics of Book Storage in College and University Libraries*. Metuchen, N.J., Association of Research Libraries and Scarecrow Press, Inc., 1969.

Harrer, G. A. "Library Expenditures: An Examination of Their Distribution," *College and Research Libraries*, 18 (May 1957), 210–12.

Locke, William N. "Computer Costs for Large Libraries," *Datamation*, 16 (February 1970), 69-74.

Logsdon, Richard. "Time and Motion Studies in Libraries," *Library Trends*, 2 (January 1954), 401–9.

Morris, T. D. "The Management Consultant in the Library," *College and Research Libraries*, 15 (April 1954), 196–201.

Oboler, Eli M., Ruth Walling, and David C. Weber, comps. *College and University Library Accreditation Standards — 1957*. Chicago, Association of College and Research Libraries, 1958.

Raffel, Jeffrey A., and Robert Shishko. *Systematic Analysis of University Libraries: An Application of Cost-Benefit Analysis to the MIT Libraries*. Cambridge, Mass., MIT Press, 1969.

Rogers, Rutherford D. "Measurement and Evaluation," *Library Trends*, 3 (October 1954), 177-87.

Tauber, Maurice F., and Irlene Roemer Stephens, eds. *Library Surveys*. New York, Columbia University Press, 1967.

Attention is invited to the work in progress (1970) under the direction of a joint committee of the Association of Research Libraries and the American Council on Education, financed by the Council on Library Resources, to improve decision-making processes in libraries through the use of advanced management techniques. No general public distribution of this research is available at this time, but it is expected that significant findings will eventually be published.

10. AUTOMATION

The life of almost everyone who lives in a modern industrial society is affected in some way, often quite visibly, by computers. Department store, telephone, and utility bills, not to mention income tax records, are commonly prepared by computers. Industrial uses range from inventory monitoring through automated machine control to sales forecasting. Space exploration is meticulously controlled by computers and, in fact, would be impossible without computers.

The preceding applications utilize the computer primarily as an arithmetical instrument. But computers are beginning to be used in the storage and manipulation of huge amounts of alphabetic data and text. It is this newer phase that holds great promise for the humanistic world of which libraries are a significant part.

Too many people, including scientists, have not fully grasped the distinction between the use of this technology in libraries and its use in more purely "computing" applications; and many wildly unrealistic claims have been made that have misled university administrators and trustees, as well as many other laymen, into thinking that all the problems of libraries could be solved simply by installing computers. A sobering trend has set in which is closer to reality. The storage of the contents of a large research library is clearly beyond the capacity of the present third-generation computers. The intellectual problem of adapting computers to storing, keeping in order, and updating prodigious files of alphabetic data, and producing a desired selection from such a store, is now regarded in more realistic terms. Considering the magnitude and complexity of this field, sound progress is being made toward solution of basic problems. The principal factor to keep in mind is the time scale of this effort: there is assurance that many technical problems can be solved if we think in years, not months. And we must not lose sight of the practical necessity of keeping technical moves within what is economically feasible.

299

Punched cards used as the input format for updating records on magnetic tape or disc drums of a computerized serials system: checking in a new issue — University Library, University of California, San Diego

Automation

In the last decade computers have become a significant factor in library programs and budgets. A milestone was reached in 1963 when the National Library of Medicine under Dr. Frank B. Rogers demonstrated that bibliographic data could be efficiently processed and printed at electronic speed in upper- and lowercase fonts. Since then a large number of libraries have embarked on automation programs; yet it will be the latter part of the 1970's before a great many university libraries have substantial computer-based systems. The expense of designing systems, of programming, and of operations is currently so great that any library should be very cautious about moving into this activity.

It is clear that the storage capacity of computers is increasing sharply, that the cost of computer storage and of central processing time is being reduced, that terminal devices will become better suited to library needs, that buffer stores and direct-access devices are permitting greater flexibility in systems, and that time-sharing will eventually bring computer applications to every library unit where communication line costs can be justified.[1]

Given this rapid progress in the technology, there are principles and procedures which should be taken into account when computer application is being studied. The same considerations obtain for any complex and expensive system, whether it be sequential card camera applications or facsimile transmission. There is a wide range of data processing equipment about which to be informed. (Bourne's volume or the work by Becker and Hayes, together with the *Annual Review of Information Science and Technology*, cited in the Selected References at the end of this chapter, provides a comprehensive overview.) Computers are here singled out for primary attention because of their exceptional cost, complexity, and flexibility; furthermore, in contrast to other mechanical informa-

[1] A few definitions may be helpful to readers of this chapter. In the broadest and simplest terms, a "terminal" or "console" is a device through which data, instructions, and questions are transmitted to (or "input into") and received from a computer over a telephone-type line. This method of operation is referred to as "on-line" operation. If the line is long (for example, from one building to another), the console or terminal is referred to as "remote." Some terminals are designed to "read" punched cards or other data-bearing media directly into the computer. The console usually has a typewriter keyboard for inputting data and may have a typewriter platen and carriage containing paper (as in a standard typewriter) on which information may be printed out of the computer. Alternatively, the console may have a cathode ray tube (CRT) "scope" on which one can see the message being input into, or being

300

tion handling systems, they can be on-line from any point on campus as a public utility service.

Since manual systems can be exceedingly economical and efficient, and since any computer application is certain to cost extra money before there is any possibility of its saving money, a library must be very discriminating in deciding whether or not to commence computer-based operations. The university's budget officers will know how expensive computer time is and may have established a policy position on university applications. One university may have a faculty which requires a large-scale system to support its research. Another may not be in a position to afford so large a system or may have a large investment in tabulating equipment. Still another may have recently invested in a good second-generation system which is being amortized over several more years.

In other situations, a university may permit a number of computer centers of limited size. Or it may centralize research and instructional activities in a computation center and administrative data processing activities (including those of the library, registrar, controller, purchasing unit, personnel department, etc.) in a business office or controller's computer system. Or there may be a hierarchy of computers, all tied together with communication lines, so that many small-scale computers can be backed up by a few medium-sized systems when extra computing power and storage capacity are needed, and these in turn can rely upon one large-scale computer when the jobs so require.

The library should work within the university organization of computational support. It will have to state its storage volume

---

output from, the computer. The big advantage of the CRT device is that the data appear on the screen (similar to television) at a much faster rate than a typewriter can print the data.

The alternative to on-line operation described above is called "off-line." The common method is to accumulate instructions and data on a magnetic tape using a separate ("peripheral") machine. The computer can then "read" the magnetic tape at very high speed. Similarly, the computer may output data onto a magnetic tape which, also through a peripheral device, can print the results onto paper. This method of operation is called "batch processing." In many areas of application, it can be performed at much lower cost than on-line processing.

load, input and output needs and their user interaction requirements, access time to different files, and other characteristics so that experts in the university may help determine the appropriate system for use, a reasonable priority for regular service, and a priority for design work and implementation. The library may have to wait its turn while budget control procedures are improved or while purchasing systems are designed and implemented. Even with grants or contracts to support library automation, the library is not working in a vacuum. Many officers of the university will participate in determining the time when, and rate at which, the library may embark on major computer applications.

When a library engages in a large-scale automation effort involving other parts of the university, one of the major problems is of a political or public relations nature. This may be explained in several ways. First, specialists in administrative data processing or staff members of the campus computation center may have only a limited knowledge of libraries and a dangerously superficial, oversimplified knowledge of the library's computational needs. Second, the orientation of a computation center is almost always toward scientific research. Such research often involves a relatively limited store of data and a great deal of processing time. Much research of this nature can be in a batch processing mode. The library's needs are almost diametrically the reverse. Library automation involves huge bodies of data, complex file organization problems, relatively limited amounts of central processing time, and often quite urgent time priorities. If the computation facility is operating on a time-shared basis, there are inevitable conflicts between the library's need for priority service, core storage, and software and the other needs of the computation center. These conflicts can be minimized only by endless effort on the part of the library to explain its specialized problems and needs and to negotiate reasonable priorities of service. It is difficulties in this general area that lead many of those people who are active in library automation to see decided merit in obtaining separate, unshared computer hardware to handle the library's work. It should be emphasized that separate hardware can and probably should be under the operational control of the central computation facility. For the foreseeable future, a completely independent library computer operation for any large-scale project is probably inadvisable because of the need for cost-effectiveness which is aided by shared use of a large facility, for system backup from the computation center, and for common software to provide terminal access to bibliographic data from branches as well as from faculty offices and laboratories.

ANALYSIS OF
NEED AND JUSTIFICATION

Before any new application or conversion is undertaken, there must be an exacting functional analysis of present processes and a clear statement of goals and their justification. Analysis should include each functional part of the process, should distinguish among all needed activities and outline them, should compare the best alternative methods of achievement — both machine and nonmachine alternatives — and should determine reasonably accurate costs for conversion, for starting the application, and for normal annual operation. Some of these analyses may not seem essential; nevertheless there will be political and economic reasons for them. They almost certainly will sooner or later answer questions raised by the faculty library committee, a dean, the provost, or some other officer. This is directly or indirectly part of the process of budget justification. It is instructive for the institution and its staff. It is certain to be useful in staff communications. It is advantageous to take this step seriously. (See also comments on p. 282.)

Some of the technical or financial aspects of these analyses may require competence not available on the library staff. This is especially so when a set of conditions not reported in the literature is being considered. For example, a new fascsimile transmitter with a variety of lease-purchase options may require careful financial analysis, or several computer visual terminals with a variety of capacities may need detailed technical analysis in relation to a particular library application. The success of an integrated system rests on informed choices among the many different components that may be available. Yet the design stems from bibliographic requirements of document analysis and collection listing. So the design requires a team of experts: librarians, financial experts, system analysts, systems programmers, and communication link experts, as well as hardware experts.

University experts are usually available for assistance, given suitable advance notice. Such help may be paid for by the departments concerned (e.g., the controller or a systems office) as part of their normal function. Occasionally a problem is of national significance, and funds for a study and report may be available from a foundation or an agency of the Federal Government. Such a study may be concerned with feasibility, costs, systems development, or creation of a prototype.

The justification of a new operation may be in economic terms. In many instances, however, there will be a combination of complex factors, some more vague than others. The picture of relative value may change if one projects conditions three or five years into the future. The benefit to students, to the faculty, to those working in branch libraries, or to the university administration may outweigh costs, space problems, and staff inconvenience. Or a new process may help economize on clerical staff or ease the work of librarians and thereby justify itself. In one instance, a computer-produced book catalog for an undergraduate library was justified economically only by projecting its cost over a six-year period as compared with the costs of three full card catalogs (one on each floor of the building as against four book catalogs on each floor) and by relying upon expected increasing personnel costs and decreasing computer costs to prove that the total expense of the multiple computer-produced copies would be not significantly higher than the cost of maintaining the three card catalogs.

Repetitive processes are the basis for a mechanized system. If the operation is repetitive, it can usually be routinized for clerical processing. If it can be routinized, some machine can handle it. If the machine is already designed and available for purchase, there is a good chance that the economies of the application may favor the machine over manual methods. This is certain to be the case as the workload increases.

The prime challenge is to identify those operations which can be routinized and which have a high enough volume to warrant machine applications. Among operations which hold promise for mechanization are the following: filing, book purchasing, serial check-in and claiming, invoice processing, card duplication, file consultation, storage and consultation of bibliographic citations, book charging and discharging, payrolls, and supply control. Where data used once can be reused elsewhere in a system without any

304

human intervention, the costs decrease sharply. Where volume is sufficient and where speed can be increased, there may be additional potential for automation. Today, the speed of response under manual systems or existing elementary machine systems is so poor for readers and for staff — in file consultation for book selection, purchasing, the establishment of entries, choice of subject headings and classification, and reference access to catalogs — that rapid, high-volume access to data in national libraries and other research libraries could drastically change the economy of operation in all universities. The MARC (machine-readable cataloging project) record from the Library of Congress is a notable start. The challenge to create such national system economies is great. Their justification in service and in dollars should be constantly tested.

In analysis and justification, one will need to determine the broad approach that a library administration should take to a program in library automation. It is entirely possible to put off any action on the grounds that major data processing systems are prohibitively expensive and those which are attempting on-line systems are still in the research and development stage. This approach may well be taken by the university that does not have the computer capacity on campus to support major bibliographical projects or sufficient library staff capability for a major program, or by the university whose library needs to pay all possible attention to such basic operations as building up its book collections, controlling cataloging arrears, and improving services and physical facilities.

In another university it may be reasonable to adopt an evolutionary approach to library automation. This approach recognizes the fact that it is desirable to gain a fairly wide degree of staff familiarity with machine processes and to demonstrate the advantages and minimize the disadvantages of moving into an automated mode. Such a university may well select some relatively simple projects of limited scope which can result in useful products and at the same time give experience to the library staff. The final selection of a project will depend upon local circumstances; yet one might give consideration to circulation control, lists of reserve books, a list of currently received serial titles, or catalog systems for small specialized collections. The university taking this approach will be able to minimize the budgetary impact of its actions, will not need to suffer adverse staff reaction if there are some failures in such relatively small-scale projects, and will certainly benefit from staff members' becoming familiar with the possibilities of automation to the point where they may be eager to take more revolutionary steps toward it.

A third possible approach is to embark upon a major total system change. Even here, because of the state of the art, it will be a somewhat evolutionary program, and it may be debated whether it is better to start with a batch process or move directly into an on-line system. It may also be debated whether it is better to start with the circulation function, or the cataloging function, or the book purchasing operation. The logic of beginning work on an integrated system with the development of a book purchasing subsystem is rather compelling, yet is not accepted by all universities. Some institutions have such massive circulation problems that they have been forced to start with this operation. Another library may feel that it should base its primary effort on the Library of Congress MARC record since it provides permanent catalog data formated to national and international standards, which data may be supplemented locally. Those who start with the book purchasing system argue that such a system should be based on the use of MARC records and that the cataloging operation is merely an "edit" (editorial-type) process which might make minor modifications in what already has been captured at the earliest possible time in the processing sequence. It actually may not make a great deal of difference whether a beginning is made in acquisitions or in cataloging, since the university should base its efforts on the MARC record in either event and will have to do preliminary design work on both acquisitions and cataloging before doing detailed system design on either one.

However a library may start, it must embark upon a program with the recognition that it will take many many months — even years — of staff effort, that there are substantial space implications, and that the budget implications are undoubtedly larger than will be estimated even with the best of advice. It is wise to spend considerable effort in perfecting the manual system so that it is efficient and effective before any thought is entertained of converting to an automated mode. Furthermore, it is essential to develop an in-house staff capability in design work and, to the

306

An early installation of computer equipment in a library to provide on-line as well as batch support of circulation records: a portion of the space in the basement — Fondren Library, Rice University

extent possible, to shy away from outside consultants from any commercial firms which are basically vendors of equipment or software. This is not a point to be taken lightly since salesmen (who may bear the title of systems engineer or the like) will be free of charge but not free of motivation. In addition, as will be emphasized below in considering personnel implications, utilization of such volunteer help does not pave the way within the library staff for acceptance of a radically new program and does not develop staff competence in system design and implementation.

Another point to be considered seriously is the need to take a very hard look to determine which processes, if any, must be online and which can be effectively batched, and which operations must have a visual terminal (a cathode ray tube display) and which processes can be reasonably handled with a typewriter terminal. There are major cost implications in these decisions; the library might well consider adoption of the less sophisticated processes or devices on the theory that it might otherwise have to sacrifice book or staff funds. Finally, it is essential that any design work take into consideration the need for a certain degree of parallel operation until the new system has been proved to be reasonably

free of errors and failures. It is expensive of course to keep two systems going at the same time. On the other hand, service to the university community must be continuous and effective; and therefore it is essential in budgeting for any automated system that while the system is being debugged and changed over, there be funds for a period of time which may extend to several months, or years, especially if the hardware or operating system changes.

PHASES OF SYSTEM DESIGN

In designing any application, whether in isolation or in an integrated system, there are ten phases, some or all of which will need to be executed, depending on the complexity of the system.

1. Data collections. This includes careful quantitative sampling of existing operations and preparation of detailed flow charts.

2. System planning. This phase details system objectives, functions to be achieved, the technical and economic feasibility of the achievement, and the organization and assignment of responsibilities for the phases to follow.

3. Preliminary design. Here are included specific system requirements, operations to be performed to achieve each function, preliminary file configurations, and schematic flow charts for the proposed design.

4. Design evaluation. This phase serves to analyze the preliminary design, reconcile necessary subsystem operations, and test against system objectives and economic feasibility.

5. Systems engineering. This produces detailed specification of requirements for file organization, communication lines, storage devices, terminals, peripheral equipment, all processes, and operational manpower. Technical specifications and internal compatibility of all system elements should result from systems engineering.

6. Programming. During this phase are written all operating computer programs and utility programs, and full documentation on the system is begun. Programs for a sophisticated system will be linked, in phases, and indexed on a direct-access device; they will number well over one hundred.

7. Equipment and communication installation. Simultaneous with the preceding phase, equipment orders must be placed, communication lines and devices obtained, and the site prepared with

electricity, air conditioning, etc. Adequate time must be allowed for factory alterations and for delivery, setup, and checkout of each component.

8. Data conversion. Here is included the conversion to machine-readable form, digital or photographic, of all information desired for the initial operation. Conversion runs concurrently with the last two, if not the last four, phases and continues during the remaining phases.

9. Program testing. This serves to run each computer program on the new equipment with a sufficient body of data to prove each operation. Debugging may require many repeat tests per program and may continue for a year or two.

10. Implementation. This phase provides the first pilot operations, in most instances run concurrently with the previous system. There follows conversion to full system operation as soon as experimental checkout runs smoothly, with program backup constantly present.

Any sophisticated system design will require constant maintenance. A library embarking upon a program of automation must provide *a sizable permanent staff* to correct and improve the operational computer programs and meet changing requirements. This work may be made necessary by some change in output, in accounting demands, or in a complex bibliographical entry that was not anticipated, or by some change in the manufacturer's software or hardware. It is universal experience that modifications and changes will be continuous.

TIME AND COSTS

Time and costs are two aspects of an automation program that are almost always underestimated. It is difficult to offer suggestions for estimating time since the amount and competence of manpower that can be concentrated on a project will affect the time, as will available hardware and other existing conditions, and costs will be affected by a similar number of interrelated factors. Three kinds of projects are mentioned to give some general idea of what may be involved.

The first of these is a list of currently received journals, produced by tabulating equipment. In such a project serials librarians and branch librarians may take twelve months to accumulate the information in a reasonably complete file and to edit it for consistency. The data conversion process may take anywhere from a week to two months, depending upon personnel availability and key-punch access. The costs involved may be only a few hundred dollars, depending upon the size of the file, the number of copies produced by photo-offset, and the method of binding. This is a simple type of project and many universities have chosen it as a useful beginning and one that provides a very practical tool for library service.

A project of larger magnitude would be the production of a book catalog for an undergraduate library. Again, the variables are many; however, it would not be unreasonable to expect to spend as much as a year on the system design and programming, and another six months on testing and debugging the programs. Any preliminary work required to justify such a catalog and to finance the project adds months if not years to the time requirement, and the assembly of cataloging records must also be accounted for. The actual production may be a matter of one to three months, depending upon the speed in the photo-offset operation and the binding process. Thus, a total project may require anywhere from one to three years, depending upon how much the library can base its work on other systems and the extent of the delays it experiences locally. If the undergraduate library has some sixty thousand titles and the catalog is reproduced in some fifty copies, the total costs involved can be well over $50,000 at today's prices. This would include administrative and general overhead expenses, as well as direct charges for system design, program writing, computer time, reproduction, and binding. Annual on-going production costs may range from $15,000 to $25,000.

A project of still greater magnitude would be a program for on-line computer control of purchasing, cataloging, and circulation using a central computer with time-sharing capability. In this case, the library may devote from six months to a year to preliminary data collection and the establishment of rough system design parameters. There may be another period of six months to a year to arrange for the funding of a major project. A year may be required to complete the preliminary design of a total library system, design the individual file structure and organization of the data bank, and embark upon the installation of terminals and communications. Software design to drive visual terminals may require six to twelve months. The applications programs based on the systems engineering may take up to two years for a reasonably complete set of operational programs. This kind of project, rather than being conducted by one person (as in the smallest project described above) or by two to three persons (as in the medium-sized project), may require an effort on the part of ten to twelve individuals combining the talents of systems analysts, systems librarians, systems programmers, and applications programmers, with clerical assistants and with the advice and help of communication experts and persons competent in graphic displays and computer hardware. The costs involved may range from $500,000 to $1.5 million at today's prices for the design and prototype implementation stage. Annual on-going production costs may range from $300,000 to $600,000. (Conversion of each catalog record to machine-readable format would, in 1970, cost from $1.00 to $2.50, depending on the amount of editing required; it costs 60 cents to store a typical bibliographic citation for one year.)

These figures represent a great deal of money. Yet, if one investigates the experience at Chicago, MIT, and Stanford, where major efforts have been under way for a few years, these costs will seem reasonable. Small computers now rent for $2,000 to $12,000 per month, a large one for over $25,000 per month, to which must be added the cost of systems staff. (In 1970, the annual cost to support each systems programmer is estimated at $35,000 — about one half for salary and half for the computer test time he uses.) There is considerable latitude in project costs depending upon the percentage that is in batch mode, the percentage that must be handled on visual terminals, or the availability of time-sharing from a central facility in contrast to the need for a separate in-house library computer. Costs are also affected by the extent of photographic text storage systems required and by the extent to which hardware elements can be assembled from off-the-shelf products as distinguished from new components which must be designed and fabricated as custom items. In a large project, hardware costs may constitute 40 per cent of the total cost of the system, personnel and software costs 60 per cent.

Sample Schedule for a Major Project

FIRST YEAR

Establish management control system for the project that will set schedule and evaluate and review progress (e.g., PERT, Critical Path Method). Such a system is likely to need frequent modification unless staff has substantial prior experience.

Revise existing documentation standards for systems programming and computer operations to include on-line systems. Schedule and write any additional standards and procedures that are needed.

Complete preliminary design of total library system and conduct management critique before proceeding.

Begin detailed design of procurement system, including receipt of monographs and fund accounting.

Design file structure and organization of central data bank.

Review terminal requirements; evaluate and order terminal hardware plus associated computer teleprocessing gear.

Plan and install communications network.

Begin development of software for terminals.

Start accumulation of Library of Congress MARC data for use in catalog system.

Start programming procurement system.

Begin detailed design of catalog system.

SECOND YEAR

Finish development and debugging of software for terminals.

Finish detail design of procurement system.

Finish programming and testing of procurement system.

Start pilot implementation of procurement system.

Modify procurement system as necessary and expand implementation beyond pilot stage.

Finish detail design of catalog system.

Program and test catalog system.

Begin pilot implementation of catalog system.

Start detailed design of continuation (serials) system.

Maintain implemented systems.

THIRD YEAR

Modify acquisition and catalog systems as necessary and expand implementation beyond pilot stage.

Finish detailed design of continuation systems.

Program and test continuation system.

Begin pilot implementation of continuation system.

Begin detailed design of circulation system.

Review terminal requirements for circulation system, evaluate and order terminal hardware.

Maintain implemented systems.

FOURTH YEAR

Modify procurement, catalog, and continuation systems as necessary and expand continuation implementation.

Finish detailed design of circulation system.

Program and test circulation system.

Implement circulation system on pilot basis.

Maintain implemented systems.

STAFF IMPLICATIONS

The design of any computer system or system based on other sophisticated equipment requires a team of experts. This may include a statistician and/or financial expert, a systems analyst, a systems programmer or systems engineer, a computer programmer, and a librarian. There may be several persons of each type. Except for the librarians, few if any of the experts may be on the library payroll, although in a very large project all may be financed by the project. A few universities have librarians who have received training in systems analysis or in programming; yet these computer-related professions are demanding in themselves, and especially so when the language changes with each generation of computers. It is therefore usual for the librarian to work with experts located in a systems office, an administrative data processing center, or a computation center. A typical staff organization chart is illustrated on p. 314.

If the librarian is to work effectively with these experts he must become more than superficially familiar with the equipment and with the software which instructs the equipment. The librarian who carries the responsibility for major mechanized data processing programs will usually be an assistant director of libraries or chief of a library department. He will probably have taken at least

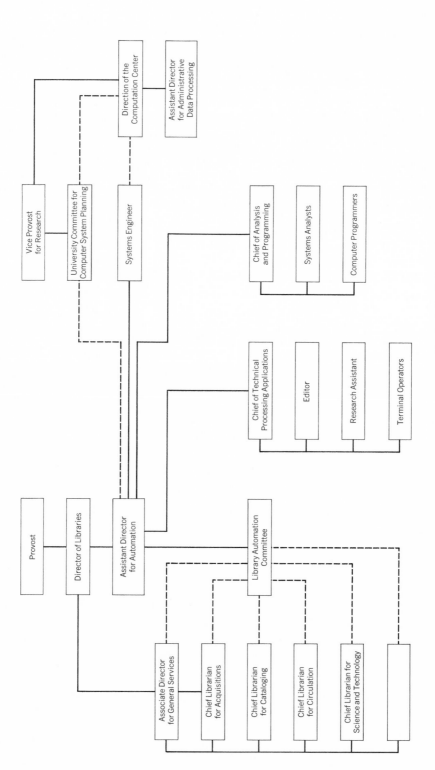

Typical Staff Organization for a Large Automation Program

half a dozen courses in various aspects of data processing in order to be able to state reasonable requirements, to comprehend economic and technical limitations, to be able to discuss file organization problems with the systems programmer, and to be sufficiently informed to explain the new system to the library staff that will operate or make use of it.

This type of specialized training will also be necessary for other staff members who will work with different parts of the system. A number of librarians will need to take several short courses selected for their level of participation. Various clerical personnel will need briefing sessions, and it will be necessary to train some typists to serve as skilled terminal operators. Computer-based systems are far more likely to upgrade librarianship than to make it obsolete. They will enhance the profession by eliminating its routine drudgery, and thus more sharply identifying its really professional nature. Don R. Swanson has commented on this point:

> Those librarians who have some kind of irrational antipathy toward mechanization *per se* (not just toward some engineers who have inappropriately oversold mechanization) I regard with some suspicion, because I think they do not have sufficient respect for their profession. They may be afraid that librarianship is going to be exposed as being intellectually vacuous, which I don't think is so. Even in a completely mechanized library there would still be need for skilled reference librarians, bibliographers, catalogers, acquisitions specialists, administrators, and others. Those librarians in the future who regard mechanization, not with suspicion, but as a subject to be mastered will be those who will plan our future libraries and who will plan the things that machines are going to do. There will be no doubt of their professional status.[2]

Staff members who have inhibitions about machine-based systems will not be effective members of the group. Others who are receptive to the change will benefit by having their job horizons enlarged and their prospects for improved salary and personnel classification enhanced; they will also share in the enthusiasm inspired by a bold new enterprise.

This is not to say that all staff members will enjoy the exacting refinements of a machine system. It is not suited to everyone, and

[2] In Barbara Evans Markuson, ed., *Libraries and Automation.* p. 21.

therefore the nature and purpose of the system must be clearly explained or demonstrated to individuals interested in such an assignment lest they accept it and then become disenchanted with the work.

The importance of telling the staff what is being done in regard to automation, and why, cannot be overstated. Disquieting rumors will abound in the absence of full and frank communication. Monthly or quarterly staff meetings should be held at which progress is reviewed and the next steps are outlined. The staff bulletin should publish summaries of the program and reports on its current status. This information can also be useful for faculty and staff outside the library. It must not be forgotten that the card catalog, the manual circulation system, and common order forms are familiar to all students and faculty. Students will have seen these in their high school or public libraries. Few will have seen a highly sophisticated machine system, and they will often be skeptical about its efficiency; and faculty members may well wonder whether it is worth the cost. The effort to explain one's program concisely but clearly to the library staff, students, faculty, and other university staff can be highly rewarding in understanding, and in moral and financial support.

It is essential to utilize librarians to the utmost in the development of library automation or in any sophisticated data processing system. It has been proved many times that the best library automation efforts result from in-house development, with librarians directing the work of system analysts, programmers, and information scientists. This most definitely does not mean that the librarians should try to do it all themselves; that would be sheer folly and would reveal a lamentable incomprehension of the highly complex skills and knowledge of the other professions working in the information sciences.

A qualified and enthusiastic staff with strong backing from the library administration is the most important single element in a library's automation efforts. This requires that the library administration have a grasp of the intricacies, although the director probably will not himself fully understand all the details involved in the system design. It also requires an understanding of the desire for advancement of those in related professions and the different characteristics of their career patterns, job market, and salary potentials. For at least another decade it is likely that the expert analyst and programmer will receive as high a salary as a division head or assistant department chief, and a qualified systems engineer may well earn more than any department chief and perhaps as much as the assistant director of libraries. The scale is not irrational; it merely recognizes the scarcity of talent in these disciplines and their unquestionable importance to major library automation programs.

The staff devoted to such a program should be formed into a single division or department within the library. The staff of a major project should have a departmental status equal to that of acquisition or cataloging; in some instances these latter two may be combined with an automation division under an assistant or associate director for technical processing. However, it is a rare individual who can give adequate attention both to the complexities of a major traditional library function and to the direction of a major research and development program. Thus the initial organizational pattern may be one of separate but equal status, and at some point in the future the units may be combined under one administrator. In the medium-scale program, as mentioned above, such combination may be possible after a year of operation, or, indeed, the continuing production may be transferred to a traditional department and the systems office left free for further experimentation and development work. In a large project striving toward an integrated system for all of the technical processes and public services, the transfer of production responsibilities to traditional departments may come in no less than three years and perhaps as many as five years. An automation department or systems office would remain to take care of the refinements, maintenance, and development of further applications which are so demanding because of the open-ended nature of a major automation program.

BUILDING IMPLICATIONS

The need for building alterations will become evident as automation programs develop. Simple operations will have no effect upon the building whatsoever. When a major ongoing program is conducted, however, coaxial cable will have to be installed if visual terminals at various places within the building are to be supported, and buffering equipment will probably have to be located within the library if the major computer is located in another building. Such equipment would require air conditioning.

A major problem arises, however, when the library needs to have an in-house computer. At the present time a general-purpose computer can be satisfactorily shared from a campus facility, the arrangement producing an advantage in investment of capital and sharing of qualified staff, space requirements, and costs. When the library's requirements for file maintenance and accesses become very large, as in a total integrated system, a large-scale special-purpose computer can be justified and such a subdivision of campus computing power actually improves the economics. The next generation of equipment will probably provide increased economies and thus large university libraries might purchase in-house computers. Communication costs would then be reduced and the library's requirements would probably support disc drives, a photo-digital store for the less frequently searched information, and off-line printing capabilities. Production scheduling might then improve, too, as well as personal and electronic communication. However, there is a formidable problem of adapting software when a change is made from a special-purpose computer to a major general-purpose computer.

Plans for any new library addition or major new construction should include conduits to all points where computer terminals might be needed. An in-floor duct system may be justified in areas where there is a heavy concentration of staff, such as in the technical processes and circulation areas. The air-conditioning cooling load is not greater than is required for good research library conditions, yet humidity must be kept in the range of 40 per cent to 60 per cent, and the amount of air movement must be sufficient to prevent any hot spots from developing in the computer area. Acoustical work usually involves corrections after equipment is installed, but normal live floor loads are sufficient for computer purposes. Floor-to-ceiling heights must be at least 8 feet in order that a false floor may be installed when necessary to provide cable space of 9 inches to 15 inches. Some hardware experts recommend 18 inches for the larger installations.

From 2,000 to 3,000 square feet of space would be needed for a relatively small but complete library computer facility, including the staff operations and the peripheral hardware. An operations staff of about ten could cover two shifts. The computer itself will require 1,000 square feet; offices may amount to 500 square feet; storage from 400 to 600 square feet; and general work space for proofreading, meetings, keyboarding, etc., from 300 to 900 square feet. Additional space is needed for the systems staff, who will work best in quiet offices. A medium to large computer installation would require 4,000 to 6,000 square feet.

Judging the full extent of terminal availability in a library building in the future is difficult. It is clear, however, that there will be computer applications in virtually all academic libraries within the next two decades, and consequently any building program must make special provisions to meet these physical requirements, thereby adding at least one dollar per square foot over what would, until now, have been termed normal construction costs. In planning a building program, it is essential that relevant current literature be consulted, and visits to libraries that have computer installations can be most instructive.

DOCUMENTATION AND STATISTICS

The documentation of any new system is of importance. This is a function easily neglected under the pressure to work more directly on automation problems. Without documentation, however, one may be in the position of a scientist who has to conduct a detailed experiment because he cannot find his colleague's solution in the literature. There is an oral tradition in most libraries; the technique of filing or searching is passed on by the supervisor, although libraries use staff manuals to formalize some of the techniques. In a system where absolute exactitude is demanded and where costs of system development are high, the necessity of methodically recording the principles and procedures is obvious. This also applies to statistics and financial data.

Statistics will be of two sorts — gross and unit. Figures of volumes processed, personnel effort, machine time, and total time involved must be compiled for the gross production per category. Figures for units of production can be computed, and these can be compared between systems and among libraries. The computer can compile and compute most of the desired statistics. It can also be instructed to compile on a sampling basis; sampling can sometimes be entirely adequate, and it must be remembered that each computer operation (or human operation) costs the university money.

Statistical forms should be worked out as part of the system design. They must be uniformly and continuously kept; otherwise one may attempt to trace a process over several months and find lapses or a terminated series of figures which makes the entire effort almost worthless.

The same processes apply to financial data and cost studies. As Herman Fussler maintained at the INTREX conference, there are at least two major reasons for enlisting an imaginative economist in work on library automation: "First, the adoption of various technical paths and systems designs will be critically dependent upon sound, economic analysis. Secondly, the application of sound techniques of economic measurement in the kinds of changes that are ahead in the library information field need to be better understood than is currently the case."[3] Cost studies must be comprehensive and detailed, since otherwise it will not be possible fully to justify a program or make any comparison with other university libraries. Most programs are justified primarily on an economic basis. Yet cost-effectiveness and cost-benefit studies will be needed during justification of major programs of library automation. Furthermore, economic comparisons among university libraries are one of the common ways to determine whether a process in a library is economically suspect and therefore should be subjected to review. Universities should require competent economic studies as being basic to any program in library automation.

The detail in financial data is especially important because design and development costs will be so much higher than regular operating costs. If the financial analysis is to be of benefit to one's own university as well as others, the phases of system design must be distinguished as to cost. The problem is complicated by the fact that the design phases may overlap, and different parts of the program may be tackled in a staggered fashion. As a result, it is common practice to have all personnel working on a large project keep time-process cards as to phase and operation. These card records

[3] In Carl F. J. Overhage and R. Joyce Harman, eds., *INTREX*. p. 164.

320

may be generalized when an operation continues without any change. Expense coding of jobs can also be used, e.g.:

>   account 001 — Administration and general
>   account 010 — Acquisition subsystem
>   account 020 — Cataloging subsystem
>   account 030 — Circulation subsystem
>   account 040 — Serial-continuation subsystem

Yet tasks frequently mingle to the point where it seems preferable to have a very simple budget expense code and to keep time-process cards for the necessary financial or statistical records. The job particulars and local university practices will naturally affect the particular determination.

SELECTED REFERENCES

American Library Association. Information Sciences and Automation Division. *Proceedings of the Preconference on the State-of-the-Art, 1967*. Chicago, American Library Association, 1968.

Annual Review of Information Science and Technology, Carlo A. Cuadra, ed. New York, Interscience Publishers, 1966-   .

Becker, Joseph, and Robert M. Hayes, *Information Storage and Retrieval: Tools, Elements, Theories*. New York, Wiley, 1963.

Bourne, Charles P. *Methods of Information Handling*. New York, Wiley, 1963.

Caffrey, John, and Charles J. Mosmann. *Computers on Campus: A Report to the President on Their Use and Management*. Washington, American Council on Education, 1967.

Cox, N. S. M., J. D. Dews, and J. L. Dolby. *The Computer and the Library: The Role of the Computer in the Organization and Handling of Information in Libraries*. Newcastle-upon-Tyne, University Library, 1966; Hamden, Conn., Archon Books, 1967.

De Gennaro, Richard. "The Development and Administration of Automated Systems in Academic Libraries," *Journal of Library Automation*, 1 (March 1968), 75–91.

Hayes, Robert M., and Joseph Becker. *Handbook of Data Processing for Libraries*. New York, Wiley, 1970.

King, Gilbert W. [and others]. *Automation and the Library of Congress* [a survey sponsored by the Council on Library Resources]. Washington, Library of Congress, 1963.

Markuson, Barbara Evans, ed. *Libraries and Automation: Proceedings of the Conference on Libraries and Automation Held at Airlie Foundation, Warrenton, Virginia, May 26-30, 1963*. Washington, Library of Congress, 1964.

Mather, Dan. "Data Processing in an Academic Library: Some Conclusions and Observations," *PNLA Quarterly*, 32 (Summer 1968), 4–21.

Overhage, Carl F. J., and R. Joyce Harman, ed. *INTREX: Report of a Planning Conference on Information Transfer Experiments*. Cambridge, M.I.T. Press, 1965.

Stanford Conference on Collaborative Library Systems Development. *Proceedings of a Conference Held at Stanford University Libraries, October 4-5, 1968*, Allen B. Veaner and Paul J. Fasana, eds. Stanford, Calif., Stanford University Libraries, 1969.

System Development Corporation. *Technology and Libraries* [a report to the National Advisory Commission on Libraries]. Santa Monica, Calif., System Development Corporation, 1967.

U.S. National Library of Medicine. *The MEDLARS Story at the National Library of Medicine.* Washington, Government Printing Office, 1963.

Warheit, I. A. "File Organization of Library Records," *Journal of Library Automation,* 2 (March 1969), 20–30.

11. BUILDING PLANNING

Library buildings are a warehouse for books, a workshop for the readers, and a business-home for the staff. Each function must be well served, else the structure has failed. Since library buildings generally have a useful life of seventy to one hundred years, their design is exceedingly important. A mistake in location of a function, a wall, or a window will last to frustrate generations of staff members. Some universities have formal programs to modernize old buildings through replacement of antiquated elevators, out-of-style lights, and carpeting, as well as by repainting. Yet universities do not make a practice of correcting inconvenient flaws in a new building; the staff lives with the condition unless it constitutes a substantial frustration and can be corrected without heavy expense. A wall that is slightly out of place or a stair that is lacking — well, the library "makes do."

It therefore behooves the staff to plan carefully, to devote a generous amount of time to the consideration of space problems, to understand the planning-construction process, to form the best possible team to plan the building, and to prepare a comprehensive written building program which outlines all the requirements in as much detail as possible. Before a building program is written, at least two questions must be resolved. One concerns timing and the other concerns alternatives.

TIME REQUIREMENTS AND TIMING

How far in advance of the date of need should planning commence? How much time will be required to raise funds? For how many years of growth should the building be designed?

Depending on the magnitude of the need, an institution may have to commence planning a new building from two years to ten years in advance. Four years is a normal period for buildings of 100,000 to 300,000 square feet gross: a minimum of one year is

325

Excavations and footings followed by structural forms in the lengthy process of erecting a building — John D. Rockefeller, Jr., Library, Brown University

needed to write a detailed program and gain approval from university officers; eighteen months for full drawings, specifications, approvals, and bids; and eighteen months for construction and occupancy. This period may easily be extended. Some common reasons for the extension of time requirements are the need to scale the program upward (or, more frequently, downward), delays in approval resulting from summer vacations or a variety of administrative concerns, prolonged fund raising and a minimum of an extra month for approval of Federal cost-sharing, construction delays deriving from change orders or strikes or late deliveries when materials are short, and problems of moving an operating library in the middle of a semester.

The current economic condition of the United States and of the university will have a dominant impact on timing. Very few university libraries were built from 1941 to 1946, few from 1928 to 1940, and a relatively small number from 1912 to 1918. Consequently it is no wonder that new library construction was undertaken at nearly every university during the period 1947-1957. At Stanford University, conditions were such that the Main Library received only an underground bookstack addition between 1919 and 1966, when an undergraduate library was opened next door. Libraries such as those of Notre Dame, the University of Chicago, or New York University may have facilities so inadequate in size, to say nothing of quality, that an extraordinarily large investment may be necessary to bring them to strength by current standards. Such a notable deficit can in the long run be to the advantage of the library; it has been seen many times that a moderately inferior physical condition will receive a minor correction whereas a very serious condition will receive a major correction with a better total result. Untoward delays may actually bring about better plans since there will be extra time for the final plans to be perfected. Operational problems during the interim may well be agonizing to students and staff. Careful planning and full support from an informed administration are imperative.

It is impossible to give a simple answer to the question "For how many years of growth should the building be designed?" One cannot simply reply "For as many years as possible" since funds may be better spent on books or faculty. Unless governmental regulations restrict the number of years for which one may plan, it is wise to plan for a minimum of fifteen years and a maximum of thirty. If four or five years are consumed in planning and construction, the minimum would accommodate ten years' growth after occupancy — or only five years before building planning for the next period of years must start. The maximum term would provide for twenty-five years of growth after occupancy — twenty years before starting the next building program. It is too difficult to predict more than thirty years with reasonable certainty, though it is wise to set aside land for one or two building increments to come in another thirty to sixty years, and it is desirable for the architect to design in a fashion to make additions feasible.

The choice between these extremes should be based on (1) realistic fund-raising possibilities, (2) the relative position of library needs within the total university needs, (3) the interchangeability of capital funds with operating funds, (4) the rate and nature of curriculum growth, (5) the degree of enrollment predictability, and (6) the presumed impact of computers, microtexts, and cooperative programs. The first three of these will be affected by decisions of high-ranking university officers, although these decisions can be influenced by the library director, by faculty, and sometimes by students. These are, perhaps, the political decisions, in contrast to the last three factors, which are more subject to quantitative analysis. There are, however, imponderables in the last three. If the nature of the curriculum is shifting significantly, a shorter span for planning purposes would be wise. Similarly, if the nature of the student body is shifting, a more limited plan may be wise. If the university president is expected to retire within five years, the possible impact of a new man on curriculum, enrollment, or building designs should be considered in deciding upon the approach to building problems and in selecting the period of years for which to plan.

Analysis of these factors in the local situation may suggest an approximate length of time between fifteen and thirty years, but the final decision is still subject to the estimated effects of institutional development and library changes such as those that may be caused by computers, microtexts, and cooperative programs. This issue is complex; yet the answer for almost all university libraries is that the impact of these programs will be minimal. Libraries must operate throughout this century with materials in the book-

327

journal format; other formats will be supplementary. Microtexts and cooperative programs are increasingly important and expensive, but they serve only to add the 5 to 10 per cent of resources which enrich an already good research library. They cannot, in themselves, create a good library for thousands of students. Computers will play an increasingly important role in libraries. They are management instruments capable of indexing resources but they can store economically only a minor fraction of data; it is unlikely that they will have much impact on the size of library buildings in the next generation.

Overall, it would seem wise to err by overestimating rather than underestimating space requirements. Enrollment figures grow. More good books are published each year on more subjects from more countries of importance to university activities. It seems certain that no new library building will long seem too large. The building may be in need of internal changes in a few years; nevertheless, it is more likely than not to be found too small well before the time of projected full occupancy.

ALTERNATIVES TO A NEW BUILDING

The question of alternatives concerns two types of problems. One is whether to remove certain book collections, staff functions, or special rooms from the present building or to make better use of existing space. The other problem is whether to remodel or build an addition or build a completely new structure.

Since new construction presently costs twenty dollars to fifty dollars for each gross square foot, ways should be found to prolong the life of a good building. This may be by weeding the collection, either selectively, in blocks, or by removing subject fields. If this action will delay the need for construction, it may be well worth the time and expense. The educational effect of such weeding may seem at the time worse than it really is. One may deplore removing part of the collections; nevertheless, it can be healthful to determine what marginally useful materials are in the collections. And this exercise can be the most eloquent demonstration to faculty and administration that new construction is essential.

Another possibility is to increase book capacity and make better use of space for staff and readers. The Yale University Divinity

School Library was able substantially to increase capacity by turning some of the book stack ranges at right angles and thereby narrowing the aisles without disturbing the overhead light fixtures. Short of such an extreme change, one may consider adding book shelving in wide corridors running along walls, at the ends of aisles terminating at walls, above sorting counters or atlas cases, and even in lieu of stack carrels. The various types of compact shelving may be considered for substitution. They have, however, not proved economical except in urban universities with exceedingly high land and construction costs, and in no university will they be satisfactory for any collection to which students are given access.

The same attention should be given to space for staff and readers. An office may be cut in two, a sorting table may be made smaller or eliminated, book trucks used for shelving may be replaced with full-height sections of shelves, and a horizontal display of catalog trays may be made more vertical. Yet, short of going to two shifts, staff cannot be crowded much without losing efficiency. Reader spaces provide one good possibility for improved utilization because tables seating four or more will generally be used by fewer than capacity. Since very few students wish to occupy the last chairs at an open table, partially enclosed carrels may be used.

Beyond these palliatives, one must look to new construction. It may be desirable to have an architect draw up a master plan before designing the building, even if there seems an obvious place for adding to or replacing the old structure. Such a master plan, looking as many as sixty years into the future, will try to foresee the entire campus development and the initial needs for library space, determine the usefulness of the present structure during the next one or two stages of development, investigate the feasibility of remodeling, and detail the scope and cost of the first one or two stages. Master planning is of major importance in a new or young university; it is essential in an institution with a mature campus and a large library.

Master planning around a monumental main library is especially important if the end result is to function as an efficient entity. Most of the monumental buildings of the first third of this century can produce extra usable square footage through careful remodeling. Light courts, reading rooms with high ceilings, and wide grand staircases offer space to be captured. The question of

329

whether to remodel, build an addition, or build a completely new library can be answered only by an architect working with the planning team.

THE PLANNING TEAM

The librarian and an architect may work together — the former describing his needs and the latter expressing them in a design. This is a minimum team. The other extreme is a planning team composed of the librarian, a library staff committee, a faculty building committee, a committee of students, the provost or academic dean, the university planner or architect, the university business manager, the construction manager, the director of physical plant, the purchasing agent, the design architect and project architect representing the selected architectural firm, and any number of consultants. In some cases a building construction contractor may also be a team member.

Such a large team is common in large universities. Each member contributes his part in the planning process; each may be represented by an associate. One person, generally the university planner, serves as chairman and secretary to assure that each does his share, that no misunderstandings exist, that deadlines are met, that budgets are not exceeded, and that the librarian receives a building as close to his functional needs as is feasible. In a building with a tight schedule, the librarian may spend as much as half his time on the building, from early programming until six months after occupancy. The detailed study of several excellent academic libraries, including space relationships, traffic routes, and vertical elements, can be instructive. (See, for example, the floor plans of the Washington University library and the Cornell University library in Appendix XIII.)

The librarian should play a major role in choosing the architect and in proposing consultants though the final action is taken by the president and the trustees upon recommendation of the university director of planning. In the choice of an architect for a major structure, the following criteria should be kept in mind:

1. The firm should be of sufficient size to have a variety of talent and design ability, yet not so large or so exceedingly busy that this commission would receive less than top-echelon attention.

2. The firm should not necessarily be a local organization though for ease of communication it should definitely have an office in the region — or be willing to establish one as a condition of receiving the commission.

3. The chief designer should himself be the architect, at least through preliminaries (also called design development); and the firm should be selected as much for the project chief as for the principal in the firm.

4. The design architect should have proven competency — be a man of demonstrated stature in his profession.

5. The architect should be a craftsman, in that he is attentive to aesthetics, to planning details, to the economics of construction, and to the niceties of the operational result.

6. The architect should be imaginative — creative in design but not flashy or monument creating — and his work should not be stereotyped.

7. The architect need not have designed a library although academic commissions would be a useful background.

8. The architect *must* be interested in the needs of the owner (rather than be a strong-willed innovator) and willing to create a result exciting chiefly for its brilliance of functional expression and purity of form.

9. There should be no requirement that a firm traditionally used by the institution be used even if it fails to meet the criteria.

For departmental and branch libraries, or for remodeling, some criteria, such as the first, may be relaxed. The strictest of criteria are desirable in the academic center of an institution and in the largest commissions, whether it is for a new building or for the enlargement of an existing structure. The selection process may start with a list of fifteen or twenty firms compiled from various suggestions. Such a list may be reduced to a smaller number, all of which are then asked to state their interest in the job and their present work load and to supply copies of their brochures. After this step, architects representing three to five firms may be interviewed so that they may provide further information and so that university officials may meet the proposed project staffs. A visit to the architect's office is useful before the university arrives at a final selection.

The architect should participate in the selection of consultants. Consultants may be retained by the university or by the architect; their fees may be paid out of or in addition to the architectural fees. Some aspects on which consultants may be considered are the following:

1. Program planning and/or master planning	Use may be occasionally made of a respected outside librarian to consider the broad scope of library development.
2. Program writing 3. Schematic or diagrammatic drawings 4. Preliminary or design development drawings 5. Working drawings 6. Specifications	Unless the university has a librarian with considerable building experience, an experienced librarian should be retained to give advice and criticism on most if not all of these aspects.
7. Acoustics 8. Audio facilities 9. Interior and furnishings	An expert is frequently used to design these elements.
10. Heating and ventilating 11. Lighting	A special expert is infrequently used since the engineering provided or purchased by the architect is usually considered sufficient.
12. Special areas (e.g., rare books and electronic data processing)	An expert may be used if local circumstances require one.

It is worth emphasizing that unless the university's library director or a responsible associate has had experience with all building phases of at least two substantial building projects, it is wise to retain a librarian-consultant to counsel through all phases of the planning.

THE PROGRAM

The program is a thorough, specific statement of qualitative, quantitative, and relational needs expressed in as precise terms as possible.

Building Planning

Buildings have been designed with no written program available to the architect (e.g., Harvard's Lamont Library). However, under such circumstances, there must be stability in the planning team and great mutual respect and understanding among its members as the design evolves. It is advisable in *all* instances to write a program, no matter how brief. A program is desirable when the project is for master planning, and it is essential in work on a particular structure. Under both circumstances, the content of the program can be essentially the same. The director or his associate should write the program.

A typical program will cover the following points in detail, although some may be generalized and detailed only in later memoranda:

Title page

Table of contents

Program justification (often in the form of a separate document written by the director and approved by the provost and the trustees)

Academic plan or function of the building (an articulate exposition)

Location of site and orientation (usually determined by the director, the provost, and the trustees)

Architectural compatibility (usually determined by the planning office, the president, and the trustees)

General building configuration and access (determined by the director)

Functional relationships (includes the juxtaposition of major bibliographic instruments and primary departments — as illustrated on p. 334 — a description of processing work flow and book circulation flow, a detailed statement or chart of typical reader traffic, and any special implications of developments such as microphotography or remote storage or computers)

General restraints on spaces and mechanical equipment (includes ceiling heights, fenestration, module determination, wall insulation and mobility, electric power, lighting, sound control, and ventilation and air conditioning)

Memorial name requirements (specified by the director)

333

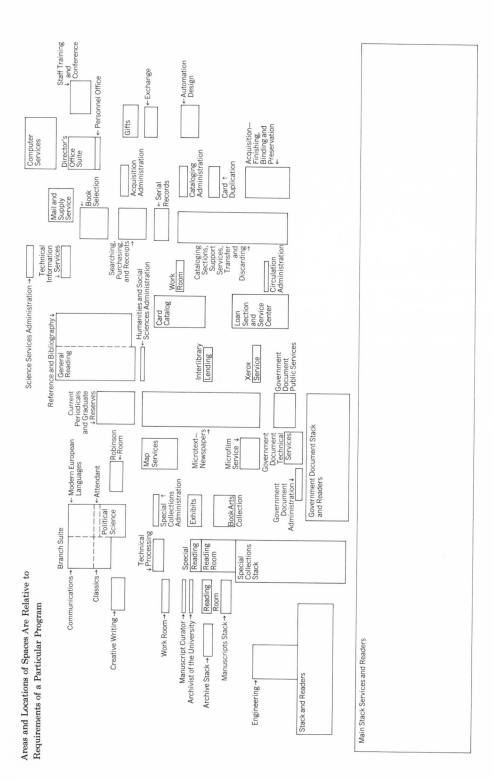

Areas and Locations of Spaces Are Relative to
Requirements of a Particular Program

Main Library Preferred Area Relationships

Building Planning

Architect's scope of work (usually specified by the planning or
business office)

Code references and procedures during design and construction
(written by the business office)

Synopsis of space requirements

Detail of space requirements (each administrative unit to be
described in terms of individual spaces and each space to have
a statement of (1) desired net assignable square footage; (2)
location in relation to other spaces, when important, and special
character; (3) built-in or attached equipment, e.g., shelving,
counter, book conveyor, or washbowl; (4) movable furnishings)

Certain special problems in planning and programming will be
discussed below. Other points are well covered in the works listed
in the selected references at the end of this chapter.

Site Selection

As was indicated under Alternatives to a New Building, a master
plan study is essential whether it be for a new campus or for the
further development of a mature campus. The siting of a main
library is dependent on projections of dormitory and classroom
usage and of pedestrian traffic patterns. The library should be conveniently close to classrooms so that students may use reserved
books and other collections during free hours. The building should
be reasonably convenient to dormitories to encourage evening use.
If it is also convenient to the student union, problems of coffee
breaks can be averted and conversational disturbances minimized.
If the library can be located next to the bookstore, each will support the other. If commuters form a sizable part of the enrollment,
proximity to public transportation or parking lots is important. A
public road is necessary for delivery trucks and public safety vehi-
cles; and some parking is useful for library delivery trucks and for
cars which transport distinguished visitors, elderly faculty, and
physically handicapped readers. These and other factors will have
to be weighed.

A university campus is generally so large that no site is ideal.
Since the research collections in the arts and humanities cannot
serve students satisfactorily if they are scattered, the main library
must accommodate all or nearly all of these collections and be con-

venient to faculty offices and classrooms used by these disciplines. In contrast to the situation in the arts and humanities, the science laboratories are often so large and geographically dispersed that it would be nearly impossible to serve researchers effectively from either a central science library or one main library. As a result, the main library is located with this bias in mind, and branches (as discussed on pp. 341-3) support the needs of the more scattered departments of instruction.

The final choice should include consideration of all available sites, the cost of site clearance, problems of utility lines and other existing underground obstructions, and the suitability of the site for a building of the height and especially the size required for the future.

Expansibility

In these years of burgeoning enrollments and publishing, it is hardly conceivable that any library building will be too large. The probability is that expansion space will soon be needed, and care should be given to making this possible. It may be feasible temporarily to house certain nonlibrary functions within the building: e.g., presi-

dent's office, editorial offices, campus housing office, registrar's office, or office of financial aids. This must be done with care so that functions do not interfere with one another. Yet such an arrangement has been successfully achieved in a number of libraries, and the advantage of having this future expansion space can be considerable.

Another possibility is to build the library as a wing of another building into which it may expand as pressures require. A common and sometimes entirely acceptable plan is to create adjacent or sub-basement space into which bookstacks may expand. Every library building should be planned with such eventualities in mind.

Determining Magnitudes for Planning Purposes

The quantitative determination is especially important for seats, books, nonbook materials, staff, and calculation of the gross. Specialized books treat of these, and only brief discussion is given here.

Total seating should be determined on the basis of estimates such as the following:

Percentage of Undergraduates	Percentage of Graduate and Post-Doctoral Students
50 per cent plus	60 per cent of FTE (full time equivalent) students in the arts, law, humanities, and history
25 per cent plus	35 per cent of FTE students in the social or behavioral sciences and the earth, life, and mathematical sciences
15 per cent plus	20 per cent of FTE students in the physical sciences and engineering

These figures are approximate, being based on experienced judgment rather than research. They will be slightly high for universities with a quality residence program or a strong experimental-creative emphasis in the curriculum (e.g., music performance or creative writing rather than musicology or literary history). Each university must give weight to these factors as its local situation suggests. Branch libraries and the main library work together as a total system, but seating capacity must be somewhat greater if the system is extremely decentralized. Metcalf suggests 35 to 40 per cent of all students for a superior residential university, 25 to 30 per cent for a typical residential university, and 20 to 25 per cent for a typical commuting university.

337

Building to house the major humanities and social science research collections, as well as centralized processing of new acquisitions and administrative offices for a system of libraries — John M. Olin Library, Cornell University

Building Planning

Books and journals can be figured on the following basis:

Collection	Volumes per square foot	Sections per range acceptable	Range aisle width acceptable (in inches)
Specialized open-shelf collections (such as reference collections, reserve collections, and browsing collections)	10	4-6	36-42
Collegiate collections	12	6-10	34-36
Compactly designed research stacks	14-16	10-16	30-32
Auxiliary or storage collections	18-20	16-25	28

These figures are inclusive of main aisles and side or range aisles, but not stack stairs and elevators.

At least one per cent of the sections should be actually counted, physical piece by physical piece, to determine the exact content per 3-foot shelf, or per section with 18 feet of linear shelving. This is essential since volume densities vary markedly by subject and by complexion of collection. The determination gives the basis for calculating shelf needs — after x years of growth at an average growth of y volumes per year and leaving empty, on the average, 20 per cent of each shelf (required in order to obviate constant shifting of classified collections as more publications are acquired for some classes and certain sections than for others). Figures for *full* sections will actually vary from 105 to 250 volumes, depending on the number of pamphlets, technical reports, etc. That figure divided by 18 (the typical length in linear feet per section), divided into the total size of the collection to be housed, and increased by 25 per cent to leave one fifth of each shelf empty, gives the number of linear feet to be provided; the number of linear feet divided by 18 gives the number of sections required. Since statistics of holdings are always suspect, one should also rely on the actual total linear footage in the entire collection as a further check of needs, for doubling of the present footage is generally a minimum to be achieved.

Nonbook materials may occupy from 2 per cent to 6 per cent of the space occupied by books and journals. In specialized branch libraries the percentage may be much higher. (The California State College Library standards allow 25 per cent.) This group includes current periodicals, manuscripts, tape and disc recordings, prints

338

and photographs, sheet music, sheet maps, and microtexts. The space required for each of these materials should be individually calculated and careful provisions made for expansibility because it is especially difficult to project growth rates.

Staff growth will probably be at least commensurate with the growth rate of the book collections until computer applications can be widely used. One can compare the technical processing staff of an institution whose acquisitions program parallels that of one's own library but whose rate of acquisition has already reached the level that one's own library should attain at the end of the planning period. The size of public service and processing staff can be extrapolated. The end result will probably look too large and actually be too small. A figure of 160 square feet per salaried person in technical processing and 135 square feet in public services will allow for card files, shelves for materials in process, sorting areas, counters, file cabinets, book trucks, and other equipment and furniture associated with the staff.

The gross square footage is figured by adding up all required assignable space (the net total) and adding a single factor to cover such areas as corridors, vertical transportation, toilets, electrical and janitors' closets, and heating-ventilating and other machine space. In classroom buildings and dormitories this factor may be 50 per cent, giving a 66 per cent use efficiency. However, in university libraries, the bookstack figures may constitute 50 per cent of the total building. Therefore, depending on whether the main corridors, stairs, and elevators in the stack are included in the net, the net stack figure may be increased by a 10 per cent factor, with 50 per cent added on all other areas in the building to determine gross. The University of Chicago has calculated the gross by adding the net requirements plus 33 per cent on general reading and staff spaces and 11 per cent on stack space, and to the total of these gross figures adding another 12 per cent for mechanical space. In a large library, the overall efficiency should be at least 66 per cent and may reach 75 per cent. In the Library of Congress Madison Memorial Building, an efficiency of 80.6 per cent is planned.

Aesthetics

Too little attention is usually paid to matters of taste. It adds exceedingly little to the building cost to make the arrangements aesthetically pleasing, and it might actually be less expensive if one could translate into dollars the irritation, frustration, or discouragement that students derive from unpleasing surroundings. In former days the most common shortcomings were dim lighting, dismal interiors, bad ventilation, and poorly designed furniture. Nowadays they are obtrusive lighting, garishly distracting interiors, noisy hardware, and crudely designed carrels. Here is a need for the talents of an interior designer, an illumination designer, and an architect attentive to details. Directional and information signs require taste in graphics. The physical orientation of the reader requires consideration, and the environment needs sensitive treatment. The height of the taller furniture needs attention (e.g., counters and divider bookcases). Art forms including sculpture, painting, mosaics, and fountains can also contribute to the total environment. The university may be well advised to reserve 1 per cent of the construction budget for the architect to use on pure aesthetics. The austerity of a library devoid of such beautifications is misplaced economy.

Special Areas

Extra attention is necessary in programming and designing quarters for music and art collections, sheet maps, manuscripts and rare books, microtexts, and electronic data processing facilities. Special problems exist in each of these. A small area for some of these specialized functions may require a major part of the effort in planning, detailing requirements, working on specifications, and ensuring proper contract execution of the details. The best advice is to visit several sizable installations before designing one's own and to consider using an experienced consultant. A charge of $150 to $250 plus expenses for one day of expert consultation can be a bargain expenditure when designing a specialized area.

The problems in music derive from elaborate tape and disc sound-reproducing equipment; and similar but different problems obtain in language laboratories and general speech facilities for students in English or drama. For art and sheet maps, the problems derive from storing, transporting, and using folio and portfolio volumes. For manuscripts and rare books, the requirements are supervised use and the best in physical care. Microtexts present problems growing out of the several formats, the physical care needed in using the material, the awkwardness of the reading equipment, and the atmospheric conditions required. And electronic data processing presents problems of communication cables, dust and temperature controls for certain devices, sound abatement, and flexibility in locations.

BRANCH LIBRARY PROBLEMS

Libraries other than the main library complex will be of four types: major professional libraries, often autonomously administered (e.g., law or medicine); modest-sized research branches with professional staff (e.g., music, art, or engineering); small browsing collections with clerical staff (e.g., a science laboratory collection or a duplicate collection for history or English graduate students); and minor collections with little if any staff which support specialized research projects and institutes. The last of these will not be discussed though they are common on any university campus and can create some administrative problems for the director of libraries.

The major professional libraries may occupy a separate building, but typically they fill part of a larger structure. They can be planned much like a main library except for the need for integration into a larger structure, e.g., priority of floor location, relation to faculty studies, shared staff room, shared elevator controls or a separate library elevator, joint use of lobby, delivery and shipping facilities, and access problems.

The research branches and branches with browsing collections present obstacles in building planning stemming from the frequent confusion of administrative lines and the special difficulty of predicting growth. In most universities the branches will be under the central library administration. They occupy quarters in a building dominated by a department of instruction which will have the primary role in planning its new structure. The best arrangement is for the director of libraries to sit on a university planning committee through which go all building proposals. The provost or his planning assistant can assure communication and enable the library to play its role effectively. The branch librarian should be a primary consultant in the preparation of satisfactory plans.

The director and branch librarian should be alert to anticipate building needs. Inaction may result in the determination of library

341

size and location by the department and of furniture arrangement by the branch librarian or attendant. This is an unsatisfactory beginning since it leaves the central library administration in the position of being negative, of asking for extra time to prepare a program, and in all likelihood of proposing larger or differently located quarters. These and other difficulties can perhaps be averted if the branch attendant can learn that a new building is being planned and inform the library administration as programming commences.

Administrative problems can also occur during design stages and construction. The university should require that all communications to the architect go from a planning office rather than from the chairman of the department of instruction. The result should be that the library sees all stages of the plans, participates in all critiques, contributes to the specifications, is present at bid opening and contract selection, advises on use of contingency accounts, sees all library-related change orders, and carries its responsibility for preparing the "punch list" of final omissions and necessary corrections.

The other major difficulty in designing research branches and branches with browsing collections is predicting the space needed for growth. Growth is dependent on the departmental enrollment, on the rate of development on the frontiers of the field, and especially on the needs of individual professors. When a department attracts a man who is a thorough bibliographer, or is concerned with historical antecedents, or is working on the interrelationships between fields, he and his graduate students may create a major shift in the collection size and complexion. Since predicting the growth of departmental libraries is thus not easy, it is difficult to plan a branch library.

In planning a pattern of branch libraries, it is useful to develop a master plan, especially in the sciences, where branches may be numerous. With each new library, the plan will have to be revised. As a first stage of branch growth, the library may be a reading room with 1,000 to 6,000 volumes. It may have 10 to 30 seats. There may be a student attendant. It would require not over 1,500 square feet.

The second stage of branch growth would require a full-time clerical attendant to handle the work. The collection may contain 2,000 to 15,000 volumes. There may be 20 to 50 seats. Some graduate reserves may be handled. Circulation could run from 2,000 to 10,000 per year. The library would require from 1,000 to 4,000 square feet.

The third stage of branch growth would require a librarian and at least one clerical attendant to handle the work. This shift in personnel is the important factor; and the expense must be justified by enough book selection, reference work, staff supervision, and book collection demands to require the higher level of personnel. A branch of this size may have from 10,000 to 100,000 volumes. The seating capacity may be from 40 to 100. The library would probably handle graduate reserves. It might have a photocopy machine. Circulation would run from 6,000 to 40,000 per year. The library would require from 2,000 to 15,000 square feet and preferably no less than 5,000.

The change from the second to the third stage is significant in operational efficiency. Because of this, branches should be planned which can be of the largest second stage variety or of the third stage variety. It may be possible to establish a third stage branch to serve all the physical sciences and the mathematical sciences. When the collection and student use outgrow one facility, second stage branches may be set up; or it may be possible to move at once to two third stage branches. Eventually there may be third stage branches serving chemistry, computer science, engineering, mathematics, and physics, as well as a few second stage satellite libraries.

There is also the possibility of a fourth stage branch, one which may serve as the headquarters for a group of smaller branches. Thus the engineering library may develop into an especially large library. It could serve as the headquarters for a science department of the libraries. It might house an information and lending service for business and industry. It could provide shelf space for books weeded from the second and third stage science collections.

The determination of a pattern of branches must take into consideration faculty and student convenience, the divisions of academic disciplines, geographic conditions, and library operating economy. There is also the need to plan units large enough to serve usefully and economically for many years. With careful planning, money spent on branch libraries can be as well invested as that spent on a main library building.

Building Planning

Raising funds to construct and equip a building is a difficult job. The vice president for financial affairs, the development office, the office of alumni relations, and the president of the university will spend much of their time on this activity. The cost of a building includes not only the contract price for construction and equipment purchases, but also the sums required to move persons from buildings to be demolished, to clear the site, to pay architectural and engineering fees, to move utility lines, to move into the completed building, and to change signs and names and directories in a host of locations. Furthermore, a new building leads to larger annual operating costs for electricity, heat, and janitorial services.

Federal funds for library buildings may now support up to 50 per cent of construction costs. The Higher Education Facilities Act of 1963 includes three titles to provide this aid. Title I provides grants for undergraduate academic facilities, administered by state commissions. Title II provides grants for graduate academic facilities, administered by the United States Office of Education. And Title III provides loans for academic facilities with a later interest subsidy plan based on local lending agencies. In an application under HEFA substantial time and effort are required to complete the forms in the prescribed manner. The funds obtained are of course desirable; yet a year can easily be required for lead time that covers application preparation before deadlines, processing, and eventual notification. And the grant does impose certain constraints on the project such as the method of taking bids and the degree of changes later permitted in the plans.

The problem of raising funds must be kept in mind. Since the main library is among the largest buildings on a campus, few individuals can afford to donate the full expense. Very few would wish to finance an addition on someone else's memorial. It is, indeed, understandable when a major donor may specify certain wishes as to the form of name, a plaque, a special room, and publicity, yet hopefully such wishes will not extend to building site, choice of architect, academic program, or related elements. The director of libraries may need to spend many hours with prospective donors and with various university officers who work to raise the gifts and bequests necessary to supplement such governmental funds as may

344

be available. Many memorial possibilities exist in library buildings; consideration may be given to rooms, alcoves, carrels, and outdoor plazas, yet it is generally wise to restrict memorials to gifts of substantial size.

The physical growth of requirements for library capacity does not occur at a constant rate of expansion. Growth may be expressed in a generalized illustration which deals only with book storage (see p. 346).

It is possible that a university library over the long run may need to spend annually from 7 per cent to 10 per cent above its operating budget for physical plant additions. Harvard University may be used as a specific example. One may generalize by stating that an amount roughly equal to 10 per cent of the Harvard Library expenditures for current operation (including building service and maintenance charges) seems to be what has been spent annually in recent years for library buildings. It was undoubtedly much more than this in earlier years (perhaps even 20 per cent, as it now may run in young institutions). However, it should be possible to reduce the expenditure for additions to about 7 per cent to 8 per cent of the current operating budget if care is taken to form somewhat larger units of service in departmental libraries, to store or discard a significant number of volumes, and to exploit all available space in existing buildings. It should be theoretically possible to reduce the expenditure to 4 per cent, assuming completely and perpetually adequate space for people and the placement in storage of the full equivalent of volumes now acquired annually.

Any percentage figure, however, tends to imply that long-range planning can become automatic and is statistically accurate. Use of such a figure is in fact unsound. The advancement of theoretical knowledge and the changing nature of publishing throughout the world have their indirect effects on any university library. The appointment of one brilliant man may open up a whole new field and attract new students, create a new research institute, promote a major development in a book-collecting field, and stimulate new publications, thereby throwing off the best of calculations.

To control unnecessary growth, those departments or graduate schools in a mature institution which have achieved reasonable facilities and which do not plan to change radically in the years ahead should meet the normal growth of book collections through

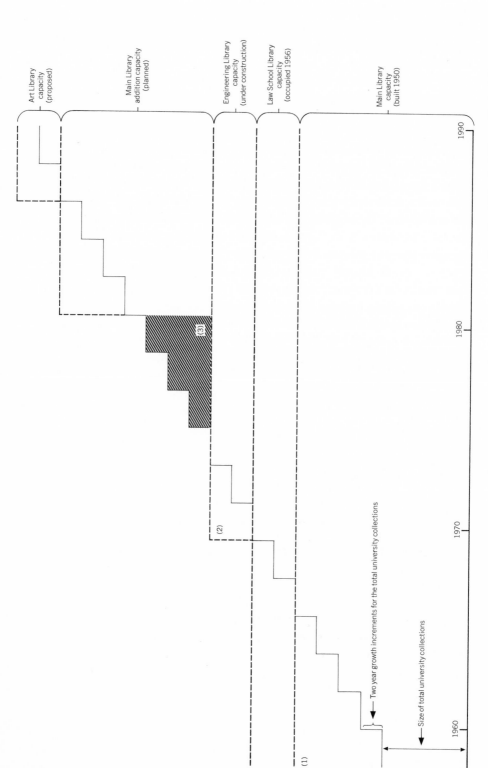

Art Library
capacity
(proposed)

Main Library
addition capacity
(planned)

Engineering Library
capacity
(under construction)

Law School Library
capacity
(occupied 1956)

Main Library
capacity
(built 1950)

(1)

(2)

(3)

Two year growth increments for the total university collections

Size of total university collections

1960

1970

1980

1990

Growth of Physical Plant: Book Collections

transfer of seldom-used books to a storage library facility. Such compact housing arrangements for the auxiliary collection will become standard practice for university libraries in the latter years of this century. Therefore, while some construction in the decades ahead will surely be of the quality which would today cost $25 to $50 per square foot, an increasing proportion of space expansion should deliberately take the form of compact book storage facilities at a construction cost which today might be $15 to $20 per square foot.

Since extraordinary events may change the program of a university, typical patterns of expenditure may not be determined for libraries in this century until the building programs of a fair number of institutions have been compiled and analyzed. Extraordinary events affecting a building program may be the grandness of a donor's conception (e.g., Yale's Beinecke Library), peculiar architectural situations (the tunnels and bridge to the Harvard International Legal Studies library building), or a sharp drop in the activity of construction trades, which can result in bids low enough to permit enlargement of a building even as it begins construction.

Finally, library growth surely takes the form of a delayed reaction to the emergence of national developments — the physical expansion of a country, its being thrust into international responsibilities, its population growth, the sharp growth or collapse of its economy, major new philanthropic programs, severe challenges to the national educational structure such as were created by recent Russian scientific achievements, or emerging governmental policy such as the one that creates vastly increased demands on medical centers. It should be possible for educational historians to find the germ of institu-

Stages of Growth

(1) The Main Library is still shelved somewhat loosely, with capacity for a minimum of eleven years' growth remaining, depending on the proportion shelved in the Law Library.

(2) The Engineering Library may in 1970 receive few or many books from the Main Library to relieve crowding in the latter.

(3) This phase represents the period of congestion and extra staff time and expense needed to operate an overcrowded building; some or all of the excess may have to be stored elsewhere temporarily until the addition is completed.

tional response to these challenges. One member of the faculty may shift his research in a new direction; the creation of a seminar or a noncredit course will follow, and some time later the chain reaction will affect the library. No forecast can be absolutely reliable unless educational and social patterns remain constant. And such constancy is neither normal nor desirable.

Since library buildings are expensive and must serve for many decades, it behooves the university to get the most for its money. This means that the best architects and engineers should be used. Consultants can be well worth their fees. Extra time taken to refine plans can be worth the effort even with construction costs rising sharply each year. The careful determination of bay size and planning module must be based on requirements of bookstack spacing, common sizes of reading areas, and office sizes. (Metcalf's dictum is that in a large library each inch wasted in the spacing of bookstacks may cost $100,000.) The handling of bidding is important (the best bids are sometimes received from December to April as contractors plan during the winter to keep their building trades laborers at work the rest of the year). And a good university construction manager who will assure that specifications are met will be worth his salary.

In the building of most libraries there is almost inevitably some waste of funds. Major points on which to be careful include anything monumental (e.g., stairs or reading rooms), false fronts, mezzanines which cover less than 60 per cent of a main floor area, luminaires which necessitate a light intensity of more than one hundred footcandles, cork floors (universities simply cannot maintain them as necessary), extensive skylights, an excess of stairs and corridors, a multitude of interior bearing walls, interior wells without sound isolation, a basic configuration considerably more vertical than horizontal, split levels or similar lack of floor level consistency, irregular walls, elaborate roof overhangs, structural spans over thirty feet, and basements which are smaller than the main floor.

When a building is occupied there is generally an activation account to pay for moving in, for minor furniture items and signs, and for any small overlooked construction detail which must be given priority (e.g., a safety railing, an aesthetic grille, or an extra light fixture or electric outlet). The dedication ceremony may also be paid for from that or from a separate account. Funds left when

348

the basic construction account is closed out may be added to activation. There is also the question of maintenance costs. Some institutions follow the business philosophy of depreciating a building which will be obsolete in forty or fifty years because of changing educational methods. Most institutions will, however, attempt to maintain their investment in original condition, and some set up a maintenance reserve account for each building (annually supported by a budgeted percentage of the heat, light, power, and caretaking charges) which is always available for any necessary repairs.

EQUIPMENT AND SUPPLIES

The university setting is advantageous in that it provides the library with a support force of controllers, personnel officers, investment specialists, physical plant and protection personnel, and purchasing agents. Purchasing agents perform at least three useful functions. They have a comprehensive file of catalogs in which to find almost anything that is marketed. They are experts in bid documents and "hard-nosed" negotiation. And they can keep the ubiquitous salesman from obfuscating the purchase goals. These are all valuable services.

Their weakness lies in the fact that they sometimes tend to look to the traditional library supply houses for nearly all library items. One sees the danger in this if one realizes that school libraries and public libraries constitute a vast market in comparison with university libraries. All libraries want good value for dollars invested; however, what sets a university apart is the diversity of materials in the collection and the intensity of scholarly activity. The diverse materials require a variety of specialized equipment and supplies. The intensity of use requires larger working surfaces. Thus library furniture design and supplies have been too limited in variety and size, and universities consequently must turn to a great variety of suppliers to meet their needs. Except for metal shelving, wooden catalog cabinets, and booktrucks, the largest universities rarely use the traditional library supply houses.

Custom design may double the expense of an item. However, custom designs can sometimes be kept reasonably competitive if they are prepared by an interior designer who will assure that components conform to manufacturing norms and if the director has the advice of a purchasing agent who will obtain competitive bidding. Any item that is designed so that only one supplier can provide it will be obtained at a premium price.

Some general principles may offer useful guidance: Keep built-in furniture (which will be part of the construction contract) to an absolute minimum. Buy quality in nearly all instances, since libraries are heavily used; a high standard will serve to permeate the system and improve public reaction. Standardize to a reasonable extent; urge all branch libraries to use the same make of desks, but do not require all booktrucks to be the same width or length. Plan purchases systematically; e.g., justified purchase proposals may be requested once a year from all departmental librarians so that library-wide priorities can be set and purchase of identical items can be grouped. Purchase far enough in advance, for it can be catastrophic if catalog cards run out, and stock items of metal and wood sometimes require as much as six months for delivery.

During any library building project, it is desirable to specify as part of the written program what articles of furniture in the existing library are to be used in the new building. As construction is begun, it is necessary to detail what furniture is to be purchased and what is to be transferred from the existing library and reused. Some of this reused furniture may need to be refurbished, or should be, to match a new decor.

Three items require exceptional care because of quantity and expense: the basic reading chairs, the reading tables, and the bookshelving. The basic chair or chairs should be selected with the participation of several members of the staff, the faculty, and the student body. What is comfortable for one person may be uncomfortable for others. Depending on whether it is a table chair or lounge chair, points to watch for are distance from floor to front of seat, width of seat, depth of seat, sculpture of the seat (or structural support of upholstered seat), incline of the seat, width of arm, flatness of arm, length of arm, height of arm on an armchair (to be sure that the table or carrel at which it is to be used will easily clear it), incline of the back (does it hold one up to the table?), "boniness" of the back, ability to glide, and ability to tip on its back legs — as well as rigidity of fabrication, attractiveness of design, durability of finish, ease of maintenance, and cost. A good purchasing agent can be of great assistance in such matters.

350

One of the earlier undergraduate libraries, featuring a top floor devoted to an extensive special collection of modern literary rare books and manuscripts — Academic Center Library, University of Texas

Reading tables can take the shape of individual carrels with full or partial dividers and individual desks with or without railings. In turn these may be nested in a variety of ways. Carrels may be constructed in banks of two to eight. Individual reading stations may also be at tables for four, six, or eight persons, and these tables may have 8-inch or 15-inch dividers or 22-inch dividers with shelves. Desks and carrels may have lockers in which to keep personal notes, books, and even typewriters. The reading position may be wired for use of a microtext machine, tape recorder, slide projector, or typewriter, and may have a bulletin board and a light fixture. Since students have a wide diversity of attitudes and feelings, a variety of reading accommodations should be provided.

Tables should also vary in size. For simple note taking, a surface providing six square feet is normal. For use in consulting government documents, manuscripts, conductor's scores, and similar materials, a surface of eight to ten square feet is needed, and this is the minimum desirable for assignment to students undertaking research papers or theses. For use in consulting art books, atlases, other folios or portfolios, and most microtext reading equipment, a sur-

face of twelve to fifteen square feet is needed. Just as a microtext carrel should have space for the machine *plus* six square feet for books and papers, so should tape and disc positions provide such space in addition to the equipment.

Bookshelving can be either of the case or bracket type. Most wooden shelving is of the former type, but metal cases are used in many rare book departments and reference collections for which extra dust protection or appearance justifies the extra expense. Bracket-type metal shelving is the norm for libraries. A dozen companies provide products of superior quality which vary in minor details and accessories. These accessories, however, may considerably enhance usefulness or attractiveness. For example, good hook-on bookends will cost three times as much as the typical poorly designed wire brackets. Range end panels may be of metal or wood in a variety of designs affecting appearance and cost but not stability. Periodical display shelves are useful though many are of inferior design. Classification label holders on the ends of ranges can be used to detail the range contents yet are seldom of the desirable double-paneled size with each compartment 6 inches by 4 inches or 8 inches by 5 inches. Sway braces are often proposed, though bracing to the ceiling, cross-hat channels, or floor anchors are far preferable, as they permit shelving deep volumes back an inch or so between the shelves of a double-faced shelving without striking a brace.

Metal shelving can be provided in almost any dimensions. Columns can be of any height, and a clear useful height of 7 feet 6 inches is usually minimum. Shelf lengths can be from 6 inches to 48 inches; however, 36 inches has proved to be a good norm for structural reasons, for a favorable capacity-to-cost ratio, for accommodation within building bays, and for the length of space that an eye can easily scan when one stands in one location. For shelf interchangeability, stacks should be laid out so that in an entire installation no more than two different shelf lengths are used. Colors may vary among floors or sections, but again interchangeability should be kept in mind. Shelf depths may vary with the collection; 9-inch shelves will accommodate 97 per cent of the usual university collection. (This shelf depth is actually 8 inches, but there is a theoretical inch of clearance from the back edge of each shelf to the center line of the supporting columns). Some shelves, however, will be needed for quartos and a few for folios and portfolios. Folios and portfolios may be placed on roller shelves (which are especially expensive), on bracket-type shelves 20 inches deep or 10 inches deep with the volumes shelved through the double face, or on 20-inch cantilevered underbracketed shelves so that volumes may be shelved across the space where two shelves meet side by side and thus save space. Each arrangement has advantages, and each library must carefully calculate its needs. Shelving is expensive; hence it is worth spending considerable time on all details of planning.

BUILDING MAINTENANCE

It takes an appreciable sum annually to keep a library building in working condition. A building which is not maintained will rapidly deteriorate physically — whether the problem is a gutter drain or the marring of floor surfaces — and it will then cost much more than normal annual maintenance to restore the building to good condition. The reaction of the students, faculty, and alumni to a building well maintained can foster educational enthusiasm and financial support.

Most of the decisions regarding the building will be made by the director of physical plant or superintendent of buildings and grounds. The library can contribute to the program by reporting conditions that have worsened or are unsafe. If stair treads become worn, a handrail is loose, a pipe is leaking, a door lock is difficult to operate, or a new fire hazard has been brought into the building, the appropriate university officer should be notified. Caretaking will be performed by a special university staff or through outside contract (although cleaning of the books is usually more carefully and economically performed by students employed under library staff supervision). Particular attention should be paid to fire hazards, insects, and locks.

The library staff is not alone in coping with fire. The local fire department will be responsible for putting out fires, county and state building codes are designed to reduce fire risk, and insurance underwriters will inspect the building and require reasonable standards. It is the responsibility of the library staff to understand fire hazards and the part they can play in prevention. This can take two forms.

One act of prevention is to impose special requirements when maintenance or repair men are in the building. A large proportion of all fires and water damage in universities stems from the carelessness of metal workers, plumbers, and other mechanics who are repairing or altering a building. Workmen should not be in the building before it opens or it closes. The fire officers should frequently inspect the performance of every mechanical job. And the library staff should be alert to this special danger.

The second act of prevention is to establish certain publicized regulations for staff and readers. For example, smoking should be allowed only in specified marked areas having excellent automatic fire protection and must never be tolerated in the bookstack; none but the most senior staff should ever be in the building on a day or evening when the building is closed to readers; any flammable substance should be stored in locked airtight metal containers; cardboard boxes should never be used as wastebaskets; and all senior staff should be informed of action to be taken in such emergencies as fire, flood, earthquake, or power failure. Fire inspectors are primarily concerned with human safety and buildings. Only the librarian and his faculty realize the full value of the books; so the librarian must be alert to any condition which endangers them.

Student disruptions pose a real threat to university property and personal safety as demonstrated by vandalism, breakage, or arson at times experienced by libraries in many universities. The best advice for coping with such disruptions is for all senior staff to review adequately in advance the vulnerable physical areas, protection priorities, degrees of reader and staff safety, university notification procedures, limits of staff authority and action, and conditions under which night vigils or other extraordinary measures are justified. Above all, the library must achieve confidence-inspiring working arrangements and effective communication with university security officers who have special responsibilities in such matters.

Insects are a serious threat to a library once they get inside the building, since they then are exceedingly difficult to eliminate completely. Silverfish are the most common pest; and since they thrive on darkness and dampness, unopened boxes and crates and piles of books should never be left for weeks on floors. Nearly any type of insect is hazardous, especially in the warmer climates, and a contract with an extermination company calling for periodic inspections can be a useful expenditure.

Locks and keys are among the most important elements in building maintenance and equipment protection. It is obvious that security is only as good as the weakest link. It is unfortunate that libraries in a university need tight security, but theft and other malicious acts are common. Keys should be issued only to those with a demonstrable need. Signature receipt cards need to be maintained so that records are clear as management staff changes. Key return should be a routine part of any personnel termination. Keys to special areas should be even more restrictively issued, and it may be required that they should always be carried by the person and never left even in a locked desk. And keys to the outside doors should be most restricted. It is essential to have one strong metal keybox or cabinet to which only a small handful of persons have access and in which is placed one tagged copy of each library key with a marked building plan to designate which keys can be used to open a particular door.

University caretaking, engineer, and protection staff will usually need copies of most of these keys. Possession of keys can be minimized, however, if the library can tolerate the performance of caretaking operations completely during library hours of service. Only with the greatest reluctance should the library give faculty members keys to the building (it is not uncommon for branch libraries to receive such pressure), and it is distinctly preferable to pay to have a guard admit them on Sunday mornings or at other times when a major library building is closed. Even if library collections were easily replaceable, changing all of the locks in a large building after the loss of keys would involve an expense of several thousand dollars; therefore, security regulations governing keys should be carefully designed and diligently enforced.

CONCLUSION

Although the discussion of library buildings has been put at the end of this book, this should not be interpreted as slighting the importance of the subject. Books are great consumers of space, a fact that is borne in on us daily as the flood comes in from all over the world. They are also extremely sensitive to light, temperature, dust, humidity, insects, and pollution. Larger and larger staffs are needed to order, process, and assist in the use of books. In operations in which much of the work is repetitive, intense, and fatiguing, attention to good working conditions can have a favorable effect on staff retention and productivity. Students and faculty members have heightened expectations with respect to pleasant surroundings, ample light without glare, colors that are pleasing, ventilation that is adequate, temperatures that are comfortable, acoustics that protect the reader from undue distraction, and seating and work surfaces that facilitate long and often intense concentration. An effective working environment for staff and readers can be a vital element in transforming a great collection of books into a great working library. It is this consideration that has animated the rather extensive attention to buildings in this general book on university library administration.

SELECTED REFERENCES

American Library Association. Association of College and Reference [later: Research] Libraries. Building Plans Institutes. *Proceedings.* Chicago, American Library Association, 1952- .
See especially Robert H. Muller, "Evaluation of Compact Book Storage Systems," in Third Library Building Plans Institute (ACRL Monographs, No. 11), 1954. pp. 77–93.
American Library Association. Library Technology Project. *Protecting the Library and Its Resources: A Guide to Physical Protection and Insurance. Report on a Study by Gage-Babcock and Associates.* Chicago, American Library Association, 1963.
Committee for New College. *Student Reactions to Study Facilities, with Implications for Architects and College Administrators.* Amherst, Mass., Committee for New College, 1960.
Educational Facilities Laboratories. *The Impact of Technology on the Library Building.* New York, Educational Facilities Laboratories [1967].
Ellsworth, Ralph E. *Planning the College and University Library Building: A Book for Campus Planners and Architects.* 2nd ed. Boulder, Colo., Pruett Press, 1968.
Metcalf, Keyes D. *Planning Academic and Research Library Buildings.* New York, McGraw-Hill, 1965.
National Education Association. Department of Audio-Visual Instruction. *Audio-Visual Centers in Colleges and Universities* (Planning Schools for Use of Audio-Visual Materials, No. 4). Washington, National Education Association, 1955.
National Fire Protection Association. *Tentative Recommended Practice for the Protection of Library Collections from Fire.* Boston, National Fire Protection Association, 1968.
National Research Council. Building Research Institute. *Noise Control in Buildings.* Washington, National Research Council, 1959.
Rohlf, Robert H. "Building-Planning Implications of Automation," in Stephen R. Salmon, ed., *Library Automation: A State of the Art Review.* Chicago, American Library Association, 1969.
Spyers-Duran, Peter. *Moving Library Materials.* Milwaukee, University of Wisconsin Library Associates, 1964.
Weber, David C. "Design for a Microtext Reading Room," *Unesco Bulletin for Libraries,* 20 (November-December 1966), 303–8.
Weber, David C., ed., "University Library Buildings," *Library Trends,* 18 (October 1969), 107–270.

APPENDIX I
PERSONNEL EVALUATION FORMS

EFFICIENCY REPORT

NAME: LAST .... FIRST .... PERIOD COVERED .... DIVISION ....

Library Assistant .... Title of Employee .... Salary Requisition ....
                    Grade

Type of work done by employee ....

....

OUTSTANDING	VERY GOOD	GOOD	ADEQUATE	INADEQUATE	NOT APPLICABLE	NO CHANCE TO OBSERVE	
							Care and fairness to the employee and the Library should be exercised in completing this rating. Base your judgment on the entire period covered and not on isolated incidents.

Job Performance

.... ACCURACY
.... ADJUSTMENT TO A LARGE VARIETY OF TASKS
.... ALERTNESS
.... CONSISTENCY IN CHECKING FOR AND CORRECTING ERRORS
.... EASE OF LEARNING TECHNIQUES AND PROCEDURES
.... INDUSTRY
.... INITIATIVE
.... NEATNESS AND ORDERLINESS OF WORK
.... QUANTITY OF WORK OUTPUT
.... SELF-CONTROL AND COURTESY IN DEALING WITH THE PUBLIC
.... THOROUGHNESS

Performance under Supervision

.... ABILITY TO WORK WITHOUT CLOSE SUPERVISION
.... ACCEPTANCE AND USE OF CRITICISM
.... DEPENDABILITY IN CARRYING OUT INSTRUCTIONS
.... JUDGMENT AND ABILITY TO MAKE DECISIONS
.... WILLINGNESS TO DO WORK ASSIGNED

Personal Qualities

.... CONSIDERATION IN REQUESTING CHANGES IN SCHEDULES
.... DRESS AND PERSONAL APPEARANCE
.... LOYALTY
.... PHYSICAL VIGOR: ENERGY AND ENDURANCE
.... PUNCTUALITY
.... QUALITY AS A TEAM WORKER
.... SELF-CONTROL AND COURTESY IN DEALING WITH LIBRARY STAFF
.... SENSE OF RESPONSIBILITY
.... SEPARATION OF PERSONAL LIFE FROM JOB
.... WILLINGNESS TO MEET NECESSARY CHANGES IN SCHEDULE

Overall rating (complete on basis of your itemized report above):

☐ An outstanding employee.
☐ A very good employee.
☐ A good (satisfactory) employee.
☐ An adequate employee (sometimes fails to perform in a satisfactory manner).
☐ An inadequate employee (definitely unsuited for the type of work that he is doing).
☐ Summary statement on reverse.

Appendix I

EFFICIENCY REPORT (CONTINUED)

SUMMARY STATEMENT:

Supervisor's Comments:

....
Department   Date   Signature of Immediate Supervisor

                                                                                                   Title ....

                                                                       ....
                                                                       Date   Signature of Employee

Information should be recorded below when this form is used as a terminal rating.

Positions held:

Dates of employment:

Termination date:

Reason for termination:

                                                                       ....
                                                                       Date   Signature of Division Chief

DIRECTOR'S   Action recommended: Comment:
OFFICE   Promotion
ACTION   Salary increase
                                                                                                   ....
                                                                                                   Signature of Reviewing Officer

                                                                                                   Date ....

360

Appendix I

Librarian's Achievement Evaluation Report
(to be completed at 6, 12, 18 months and annually thereafter)

Name (last name first): _____ Period Covered: _____

Classification: _____ Position title (if any): _____

DIVISION CHIEF'S EVALUATION AND REMARKS

Performance:

	Outstanding	Very Good	Satisfactory	Fair	Unsatisfactory	No Chance to Observe	Not Applicable
Industry							
Quality of work							
Judgment							
Organization of work							
Sense of responsibility							

Comments:

Personal qualities:

	Outstanding	Very Good	Satisfactory	Fair	Unsatisfactory	No Chance to Observe	Not Applicable
Sense of responsibility							
Capacity for independent thought and planning							
Imaginative contributions							
Initiative							
Staff relationships							
Faculty relationships (when applicable)							
Student relationships (when applicable)							
Ability to direct or manage							
Supervisory ability							

Comments:

General evaluation for salary review of over-all performance on his present job:

( ) Outstanding: Check only when he is definitely outstanding and far superior in the performance of his duties. Use with discretion.

( ) Very good: Use to indicate higher than average performance.

( ) Satisfactory: Use to indicate adequate performance.

( ) Fair: Check when his work is not quite satisfactory, when he needs more than usual supervision, direction or training.

( ) Unsatisfactory: Use to indicate inadequate or substandard performance and cases in which the possibility of release should be kept in mind.

Special remarks or recommendations, incl. changes in assignments:

_____ _____
Date   Signature of Division Chief

To be discussed with Librarian; and given to him in duplicate for him to complete verso.
Librarian is then to send original to the Director's Office.

LIBRARIAN'S ACHIEVEMENT EVALUATION REPORT (CONTINUED)

Comment, if any, of librarian and statement of relevant outside activities (association or club activities, research, professional visits, etc.)

Date   Signature of Librarian

Summary information when this form is used as a terminal report:

Assignments held in the Stanford Libraries—

Dates of employment—

Leaves—

Termination date (including terminal vacation)—

Reason for termination—

General evaluation for reference purposes—

Director's Office review:

Comment—

Promoted to _____

Salary increase to _____

Effective date _____

Date   Reviewing Officer

362

APPENDIX II
ACQUISITIONS PROGRAMS IN THE UNIVERSITY LIBRARIES

(A SAMPLE STATEMENT FROM ONE UNIVERSITY)

One of the most striking features of the University library picture in recent years has been the assumption of greater responsibility by the Library staff for book selection. The abolition of departmental book allotments and the substantial increase in book funds have made possible the development of procedures for systematic coverage of current scholarly publications throughout the world. Following is a report on how the University Libraries acquire these publications, including new reprints of older books. Retrospective purchases and journal subscriptions are still largely selected by faculty and staff members from dealers' catalogs, publishers' announcements, or other bibliographic sources with an increasing emphasis on the role of the library. A major factor in this trend toward increasing staff initiative in book selection has been the growth of the system of curators and subject-specialist librarians to whom selection responsibilities are assigned.

Generally speaking, the aims of the University Libraries with respect to their acquisition activities have been the following:

1. To achieve the widest possible coverage of the current scholarly press throughout the world on a regular basis, emphasizing subjects and areas which are of most interest and use to faculty and students.
2. To develop routine methods of selection and procurement to eliminate repetitious and time-consuming clerical work and to insure prompt receipt and rapid processing of newly-published books.
3. To establish close and continuous faculty and student contacts so that the interests of library users may be properly served.
4. To coordinate acquisition work in all the libraries so that unnecessary duplication on the one hand, and disastrous lacunae in the collections on the other, may be avoided.

The following specific arrangements are in force for routine acquisition of new imprints from various areas and of various types. There are in addition many special arrangements — gift agreements, Public Law 480 receipts, purchases made by traveling faculty or staff, for example — which cannot be detailed here. Individual requests or recommendations from faculty or students receive special attention.

363

Appendix II

University Presses: Publications of major university and other scholarly presses and a few trade publishers specializing in scholarly books have been received automatically since 1964. See attached list [pp. 366-8].

Current Social and Behavioral Science Imprints from Trade Publishers: These are shipped on approval and screened by librarians.

Publishers' Weekly: Weekly listing checked for selection each week since January 1967 by library specialists in the following subjects:

American and English Literature	Geography
Anthropology	History
Art and Architecture	Linguistics
City Planning	Philosophy
Classics	Political Science
Communications: Radio, Film, TV	Psychology
	Sociology
Economics	Theater
General Reference	Theology

Science Books: Automatically shipped on approval and checked weekly since 1965 by specialist librarians in the following subjects:

Biology	Geology
Chemistry	Mathematics-Statistics
Computer Science	Physics
Engineering	

CURRENT BRITISH IMPRINTS

Humanities and Social Sciences: Beginning in January 1967, checked weekly in *British National Bibliography* by the specialists listed under *Publishers' Weekly* (CURRENT AMERICAN IMPRINTS).

Sciences: Selected by the science librarians listed above from special bibliographical aids.

CURRENT FRENCH AND ITALIAN IMPRINTS

Beginning in 1963, belles-lettres and historical publications of Presses Universitaires de France shipped automatically upon publication. Screened by the Curator for Romance Languages.
Sciences: As for British imprints.

CURRENT SPANISH IMPRINTS

Beginning in 1968, the Departamento de Estudios Bibliográficos of Seville will each year issue catalog cards representing 1600 currently published Spanish books of special importance, with consignments at frequent intervals to insure prompt notification. These cards will be received by the Curator for Romance Language Materials in the Main Library and will be used for regular selection of significant research publications.

364

Appendix II

Humanities and Social Sciences: Beginning in 1968, selected and shipped on approval by the _____ Company on publication: checked in weekly or bi-weekly national bibliographies for review by Curator and subject Librarians; the books are screened by the Curator and examined by the [branch] Curator, for possible duplication or transfer to [the branch].
Sciences: As for British imprints.

CURRENT LATIN AMERICAN IMPRINTS

Humanities and Social Sciences: Selected and shipped by the _____ Company and Centro Interamericano de Libros Académicos upon publication; screened by the Curator, and all unwanted items returned. The [branch] participates in the screening process.
Sciences: As for British imprints.

CURRENT SLAVIC IMPRINTS

Selected and ordered by the Curator from special bibliographical sources. Selection is in consultation with interested faculty members in all subjects.
The Curator also manages exchanges with Slavic countries.
This work is coordinated with that of the [branch] Curator.

CURRENT AFRICAN IMPRINTS

Selection and ordering are coordinated with the [branch], which concentrates on the period from 1870 to the present in the fields of history, politics, government, and economics.
The Curator of African Collections serves the [branch] as well as all libraries. Publications not included in blanket or other general coverages are individually selected by his staff.

CURRENT EAST ASIAN IMPRINTS

Selection and ordering are coordinated with the East Asian Library which purchases non-Western language titles and the East Asian Curator recommends Western language titles to the Main Library. Art books in Oriental languages are purchased and cataloged by the East Asia staff for the Art Library.

EXCHANGES

In addition to these methods of selection and acquisition, the Exchange Department of the University Libraries maintains an extensive program of exchanges with institutions (universities, museums, academies, etc.) throughout the world. The language and area curators cooperate in establishing these relationships.

GOVERNMENT DOCUMENTS

Acquisition and cataloging, as well as reference and bibliographical services, are centered in the Government Document Division of the University Libraries. Specialist librarians are in charge of each of the following categories of materials:

Federal Documents: The University Libraries have been a full depository since 1924. Publications listed in the *Monthly Catalog* are received on deposit, and non-depository materials in microprint by subscription. Materials issued by agencies are obtained by subscription or mailing list. The Division also orders documents for other campus libraries. All AEC unclassified publications are received on deposit, mostly in microfiche.

Foreign Documents: The Division obtains these by subscription or special order, or on mailing list. Of principal interest are statistical documents of all types from all countries, and the humanities and social sciences generally, with emphasis on economics, government, sociology, education, and related topics such as planning and agriculture. The Division has a very strong collection of British, British Empire and Commonwealth documents.

International Organization Documents: The Library is a depository for United Nations documents, and obtains by subscription or gift the publications of associated agencies such FAO, WHO, ILO, UNESCO, etc. International organizations such as OAS, OECD, and all other important associations of governments are obtained as extensively as possible.

State Documents: These are obtained on a selective basis, corresponding to the needs of faculty members and students. The Division is a full depository for_____state publications and collects extensively from other states, with special attention to constitutional materials, statistics, the social sciences, with emphasis on government and finance, economics, education, sociology, and related topics, and agriculture, for which publications of ten states are actively collected.

For most governmental units the Law Library has the basic collection of statute law and legal codes; Soviet law is in the [branch]. The Law Library also collects in the field of Roman law; the Main Library acquires materials in Greek and earlier law, in medieval law, and aboriginal or tribal law.

PUBLISHERS INCLUDED IN BLANKET ORDER
AND APPROVAL/PURCHASE PROGRAMS

University Presses	Cornell	Illinois
	Duke	Indiana
Alabama	Duquesne	Iowa State
Arizona	Florida	Johns Hopkins
Boston	Fordham	Kansas
British Columbia	Georgia	Kentucky
Brown	Ghana (from Oxford)	Laval
Buffalo	Harvard	Louisiana State
California	Hawaii	Loyola (Chicago)
Cambridge	Hong Kong (from	McGill
Catholic	Oxford)	Marquette
Chicago	Ibadan (from North-	Massachusetts
Columbia	western)	MIT

Miami (Florida)
Michigan
Michigan State
Minnesota
Missouri
Nebraska
New Mexico
New York State University (SUNY)
New York University
North Carolina
Northwestern
Notre Dame
Ohio
Ohio State
Oklahoma
Oxford
Pennsylvania
Pennsylvania State
Pittsburgh
Princeton
Purdue
Rutgers
St. Johns
Seton Hall
South Carolina
Southern Illinois
Southern Methodist
Stanford
Syracuse
Tennessee
Texas
Toronto

United States Naval Institute (Annapolis)
Utah
Vanderbilt
Virginia
Washington (Seattle)
Wayne State
Wesleyan
Western Reserve
Wisconsin
Yale

Trade Publishers
Abrams
Bruckmann (art)
Clark, Arthur
Free Press
Grove (poetry only)
Monographic Press
New Directions (poetry)
New York Graphic Society
Olschki (art publications)
Phaidon Books
Public Affairs
Regnery
Scarecrow
Scholar's Facsimiles and Reprints
Skira (exclude Taste of Our Times series)

Wittenborn (art and architecture)

Institutional Publishers
American Council on Education
Bishop Museum
Bollingen Foundation
Book Club of California
Brookings Institution
California (Institute of Governmental Studies)
Cleveland Museum of Art
East-West Center (received since 1967)
Huntington Library
Jewish Publication Society
Metropolitan Museum of Art
New York Graphic Society
New York Museum of Modern Art
New York Museum of Primitive Art
Smithsonian Institution
Twentieth Century Foundation
Wisconsin State Historical Society

UNIVERSITIES FROM WHICH THE UNIVERSITY RECEIVES ALL OR MOST PUBLICATIONS ON EXCHANGE

1. University of Adelaide
   Adelaide, Australia
   (most publications)
2. University of Western Australia
   Nedlands, Australia
   (most publications)
3. University of Liège
   Liège, Belgium
4. University of Havana
   Havana, Cuba
5. J. A. Komenskeho University
   Bratislava, Czechoslovakia
6. University Karlova
   Prague, Czechoslovakia
7. National and University Library
   Prague University
   Prague, Czechoslovakia

8. University of Birmingham
   Birmingham, England
   (most publications)
9. University of Leeds
   Leeds, England
   (most publications)
10. University of Leicester
    Leicester, England
11. Bodleian Library
    Oxford, England
    (most publications)
12. Haile Selassie I University
    Addis Ababa, Ethiopia
13. University of Helsinki
    Helsinki, Finland
    (most publications)

367

Appendix II

14. Justus-Liebig Universität
Giessen/Lahn, Germany
(most publications)
15. University of Halle
Halle (Saale), Germany
(most publications)
16. Friedrich-Schiller Universität
Jena, Germany
(most publications)
17. Christian-Albrechts Universität
Kiel, Germany
(most publications)
18. Karl Marx Universität
Leipzig, Germany
19. Universität Rostock
Rostock, Germany
20. Freie Universität
Berlin, Germany
(most publications)
21. Humboldt Universität
Berlin, Germany
(most publications)
22. Egyetemi Könyvtar (University
Library)
Debrecen, Hungary
23. University of Baghdad
Baghdad, Iraq
24. Jewish National and University
Library
Jerusalem, Israel
25. Universita Cattolica del Sacro
Cuore
Milan, Italy
26. University of the West Indies
Mona (Kingston), Jamaica
(most publications)

27. Kyushu University
Fukuoka, Japan
(most publications)
28. Bibliothèque Universitaire
Tananarive, Madagascar
29. University of Malaya
Kuala Lumpur, Malaya
30. University of Ibadan
Ibadan, Nigeria
31. Uniwersytetu im A. Mickiewicza
Poznan, Poland
32. University of Poland
Warsaw, Poland
(most publications)
33. Centrala Universitatea
Bucharest, Rumania
34. Centrala Universitatea
"Babes-Bolyai"
Cluj, Rumania
(most publications)
35. Edinburgh University
Edinburgh, Scotland
36. University of the Witwatersrand
Johannesburg, South Africa
37. University of Salamanca
Salamanca, Spain
(most publications)
38. Goteborgs Universitet
Gothenburg, Sweden
39. Lund University
Lund, Sweden
40. University of Stockholm
Stockholm, Sweden
41. University of Uppsala
Uppsala, Sweden
42. University of Ljubljana
Ljubljana, Yugoslavia

APPENDIX III
ACQUISITIONS POLICY IN A
SPECIFIC FIELD

RELIGION (HARVARD UNIVERSITY LIBRARY)

Church History: Widener is attempting to cover very thoroughly the fields of Church History: Pre-Reformation, Non-Protestant Church History and Protestant Church History, the latter with some exceptions. Andover-Harvard collects on an all-inclusive basis the history and ecclesiastical records of Unitarian, Congregational, Friends, Mennonite and other free Churches. It covers on a selective basis the history and ecclesiastical records of American Protestant denominations.

Catholic Theology: Widener's unique collection on Catholic dogmatic and moral theology is kept up as much as funds are permitting.
In the field of Patristic studies, with its impact on so many other disciplines, the aim is a thorough coverage of editions of texts and studies.
Catholic Biblical studies are bought by Andover-Harvard Library, as this library is purchasing all relevant studies in this field regardless of the religious affiliation of the author.

Orthodox Catholics (Eastern Church): The responsibility in this field has been with Widener. With the exception of Biblical studies, liturgy and ritual, and Orthodox-Protestant relations, which would go to Andover-Harvard regardless of language or national origin, Widener is acquiring the major portion (historical, doctrinal and political) of the materials on the Orthodox Church.

Judaism: This field presents greater complexity. Andover-Harvard assumes responsibility for all works on the Old Testament and the Biblical period, including Jewish works. This would also include Essene material and work on the Dead Sea Scrolls. Post-Biblical Judaism is the responsibility of Widener, where there is a very strong collection that has recently been strengthened by the Friedman gift.

Bibles and Biblical Studies: Widener maintains a collection of standard editions in English and some editions of importance to philological studies. A few standard commentaries are kept in Widener. The field of Biblical texts, Biblical theology and Biblical criticism is covered by the Andover-Harvard Library.

The Non-Judeo-Christian Religions: It is very difficult to be precise in this broad field, though the major body of materials is kept at Widener.

Appendix III

Large supplementary collections are at the Peabody Museum Library on the primitive religions and at Yenching Library on the Oriental religions.

The book selection in areas such as the Philosophy of Religion, the relation of State-and-Church, Communism-and-Religion, etc., is done in conjunction with the selection of materials in related fields (philosophy, history, government, etc.).

370

CANADIAN DOCUMENTS

	Main	Law	Business	Medicine	Government	Science
I. Parliamentary Publications						
Statutes						
Annual statutes		X				
Special compilations		X				
Senate						
Debates	X					
Journals	X					
Standing committees — Proceedings						
Banking and commerce			X			
External relations	X					
Finance	X					
Human rights and fundamental freedoms	X					
Immigration and labor	X					
Legislation		X				
Natural resources	X					
Public health and welfare				X		
Railways, telegraphs and harbours			X			
Transport and communications			X			
House						
Debates	X					
Journals	X					
Standing committees — Proceedings						
Agriculture and colonization	X					
Atomic energy						X
Banking and commerce			X			
Civil Service Act		X				
Criminal Code		X				
Defense expenditures and estimates	X					
External affairs	X					
Immigration	X					
Industrial relations					X	
Mines, forests, waters						X
National defense	X					
Public accounts	X					
Railways, canals			X			
Social Security	X					

	Main	Law	Business	Medicine	Government	Science
Unemployment insurance	X					
War expenditure	X					
Royal Commissions	X					
Conferences (*e.g.* Federal-Provincial Conference, 1957)	X					
II. Departmental Publications						
Agriculture — annual report	X					
Economic Annalist: bimonthly review	X					
Atomic Energy Control Board — report	X					
Chief Electoral Officer — report	X					
Citizenship and Immigration — annual report	X					
Civil Service Commission — annual report	X					
Defense Production — report			X			
External Affairs — report	X					
Conference series	X					
Documents and White Papers	X					
External affairs, monthly	X					
Treaty series	X					
Finance — annual report	X					
Public accounts of Canada	X					
Fisheries — annual report						X
Fisheries Research Board—annual report						X
Insurance — report			X			
Judiciary		X				
Canada Law Reports		X				
Justice		X				
Restrictive Trade Practices Commission — reports		X				
Commissioner of Penitentiaries — annual report		X				
Labour — annual report	X					
Labour Gazette, monthly	X					
Labour Legislation — reports		X				
Unemployment Insurance Commission — reports		X				
Mines and Technical Surveys — annual report						X
Geological Survey of Canada						X
National Defense — annual report	X					
Bureau of Current Affairs NATO Countries Series	X					
National Health and Welfare — annual report				X		
Report series				X		
Canada's Health and Welfare, monthly				X		
Occupational Health Review, quarterly				X		

	Main	Law	Business	Medicine	Government	Science
National Library — annual report	X					
National Research Council — annual report	X					
Canadian Journal of Biochemistry and Physiology						X
Canadian Journal of Botany						X
Canadian Journal of Microbiology						X
Canadian Journal of Zoology						X
National Revenue — annual report	X					
Taxation statistics	X					
Income tax regulations		X				
Northern Affairs and National Resources — annual report	X					
Water resources papers					X	
Forestry — publications						X
Public Archives — publications	X					
Public Printing and Stationery — annual report	X					
Canada Gazette		X				
Public Works — annual report	X					
St. Lawrence Seaway Authority — annual report	X					
Secretary of State — annual report	X					
Tariff Board — reports			X			
Trade and Commerce — annual report			X			
Foreign Trade, fortnightly			X			
Dominion Bureau of Statistics — all publications			X			
Canada Year Book	X					
Canada, annual	X					
Canadian Statistical Review	X					
Census Division — all publications	X					
Health and Welfare Division				X		
Judicial Statistics		X				
Labour and Prices Division					X	
Transport — annual report			X		X	
Unemployment Insurance Commission					X	
Veterans Affairs — annual report	X					

APPENDIX V
AUTHORIZATION FOR BOOK PURCHASING

PURCHASE, SALE, AND ACCEPTANCE OF GIFTS OF LIBRARY MATERIALS

Section 6.05 of the By-Laws of the Board of Trustees provides that no agent, officer, or employee of the University shall make any contract, agreement, promise, or undertaking in the name of the University or on behalf of the University, except pursuant to authorization granted by the Board.

The following resolution was adopted by the Board upon the understanding that any expenditures made pursuant to the authorization must be either (i) within an approved budget, (ii) covered by a restricted fund for the purpose for which the expenditure is to be made, or (iii) specifically approved by the Controller. Accordingly, the authorization granted must be administered at all times within these limitations.

Resolution No. 31

Authorization Resolution for University Libraries

Resolved: That the Director, the Associate Directors, the Assistant Directors and the Chief Librarian of the Acquisition Division of the University Libraries be and each is hereby authorized and empowered in behalf of The Board of Trustees to execute purchase orders and purchase contracts not involving the expenditure of more than $10,000.00 for the purchase of books, journals, periodicals or other library materials, and bibliographic, binding, microfilming and other library services for the University Libraries; provided, however, that any purchase order or purchase contract for such materials or services involving the expenditure of more than $1,000.00 shall be entered into only by the Director of the University Libraries or, in his absence, an Associate Director of the University Libraries.

Further Resolved: That the order clerks of the Acquisition Division of the University Libraries be and each is hereby authorized and empowered on behalf of The Board of Trustees to execute purchase orders up to $100.00 in amount for the purchase of books, journals, and periodicals for the University Libraries.

Further Resolved: That the Director, the Associate Directors, the Assistant Directors, the Chief of the Acquisition Division and the Head Librarian of the Gift Department of the University Libraries be and each is hereby authorized and empowered on behalf of The Board of Trustees to sell unrestricted gifts of books, journals, periodicals, or other library

374

materials, or books, journals, periodicals or other library materials withdrawn from the collection of the University Libraries, which have been determined by the responsible curator or librarian not to be needed in the operation of the University Libraries, and in connection therewith, to execute any necessary documents of sale; provided, however, (1) that any documents of sale involving $100.00 or more in amount shall be executed only by the Director of University Libraries or, in his absence, an Associate Director of the University Libraries; and (2) that any documents of sale involving $10,000 or more shall be executed only by the Vice President for Business Affairs or the Business Manager.

Further Resolved: That the Director, the Associate Directors, the Assistant Directors, the Chief of the Acquisition Division and the Head of the Gift Department of the University Libraries be and each is hereby authorized and empowered on behalf of The Board of Trustees to accept and acknowledge receipt of gifts of books, journals, periodicals, manuscripts, personal papers, or other bibliographic materials to the University Libraries; provided, however, that any such gift with a condition of permanent retention or any other restriction upon the unconditional right of the University Libraries to retain, sell or exchange the gift shall be accepted and acknowledged only by the Director of the University Libraries.

Further Resolved: That the Director of the University Libraries is hereby authorized and empowered on behalf of The Board of Trustees to authorize and appoint firms or individuals to select and purchase books, journals, periodicals and other bibliographic materials for the account of the University Libraries up to $10,000.00 in amount, and advance funds to firms or individuals so authorized and appointed to effect such selection and purchase; provided, however, that no such authorization, appointment or funds advance involving the expenditure of more than $1,000.00 shall be made until it shall have been first approved as to fund availability by the Office of the Controller.

Further Resolved: That the Director, the Associate Directors, the Assistant Directors, and the Director of the Technical Information Service of the University Libraries be and each is hereby authorized and empowered on behalf of The Board of Trustees to enter into library materials loan and exchange agreements with other university libraries, non-profit organizations, and governmental agencies and enter into agreements with other university libraries, non-profit organizations, governmental agencies and private firms and individuals for the furnishing of lending and bibliographic services of the University Libraries; provided, however, that any such loan agreement, exchange agreement or agreement for the furnishing of library services shall provide for termination by the University Libraries at any time without notice and without liability.

APPENDIX VI
PURCHASE AGREEMENTS
(Stanford University Libraries)

EXHIBIT 1. INSTRUCTIONS TO A SERIALS VENDOR

1. The attached purchase order is for a serial publication. This subscription is to *begin* with the date or volume specified.

2. This order is to be serviced on an "until forbid" basis. On this basis you should supply us automatically each issue as it is published and continue to supply until a formal cancellation is sent to you.

3. Your invoicing in triplicate should be automatic. It should reach us well in advance of the expiration date so there will be no interruption of service. All *invoices* and *shipments* should be addressed to:

> Serial Department
> Stanford University Libraries
> Stanford, California 94305

4. Indexes and supplementary numbers are to be serviced automatically as part of this subscription.

EXHIBIT 2. ON-APPROVAL AGREEMENT FOR
SCIENTIFIC AND TECHNOLOGICAL PUBLICATIONS

The Stanford University Libraries hereby authorize the firm of _____ to send to the address given below scientific and technological publications of significant scholarly value in accordance with the following stipulations and conditions.

This agreement comprises the following:

> Section A: General conditions
> Section B: Types of material excluded
> Section C: Subjects excluded
> Section D: Subjects included (refer to Appendix A)
> Section E: Shipping instructions

Section A: General Conditions

1. This agreement covers the publications of universities, associations, academies, institutes, and other scientific and professional organizations, and trade presses. All languages in Western alphabets are to be included for the earth and biological sciences, but only English, and the German publications of Springer-Verlag, for other sciences and technology.

376

2. Books will be sent as soon as possible after publication, even if they have not yet been listed in the relevant bibliographies.

3. The Stanford University Libraries have the privilege of returning for credit to _____ any books sent under this agreement which are not wanted for the Libraries. The firm will credit the Libraries with the full price of such returned books. Returns will be made as promptly as possible.

4. The firm of _____ will clearly mark each title sent to the Stanford University Libraries in the weekly listing of the *Publishers' Weekly* and the *British National Bibliography* for books listed in these sources. These marked lists and all correspondence dealing with this agreement will be sent to:

> Head Librarian
> Order Department, Science and Technology Books
> Stanford University Libraries
> Stanford, California 94305

5. The staff of the Stanford University Libraries will check the marked lists, indicating supplementary selections. The relevant pages of the bibliographies will be xeroxed and sent to _____ to serve as orders for these books, which should be sent with subsequent blanket order shipments.

6. No item shall be sent of which the price exceeds $50.00. Any such item which seems desirable for inclusion will be so marked on the bibliography but will not be sent unless selected by one of the Stanford reviewers.

7. This agreement shall be in effect indefinitely, but may be cancelled by either party upon three months' notice to the other.

8. A separate multiple-copy (at least four copies) invoice should be inserted in each title.

Section B: Types of Material Excluded

1. Journals, periodicals, numbered bulletins, *except for the first issue,* which should be sent.

2. Terminal sets, i.e., multi-volume works to be published over a long period of time in a stated number of volumes. Examples are dictionaries, encyclopedias, collected papers and letters, collected works, etc. Standing orders for these will be entered as desired. *However, the first issue should be sent.*

3. Books for children or young people.

4. Books for students *below* the advanced undergraduate level.

5. Manuscripts, typescripts, and television, radio or motion picture scripts.

6. Maps and atlases.

7. Reprints without change, extracts, separates from larger works.

8. Anthologies, books of readings, selections from larger works by one or several authors. But *include symposia* if within other criteria.

9. Government publications, and publications of government associations (UN, UNESCO, FAO, OAS, etc.).

10. Instruction books for trades or professions; manuals for the operation and repair of machinery, equipment, or appliances, trade catalogs, supply catalogs.

11. Theses or dissertations for academic degrees. Dissertations published as treatises by established publishers and offered through the general book trade should be included if they fall within other criteria.

12. Sound recordings of any description.

13. Books from publishers included in blanket order and approval/purchase programs. [See Appendix II, pp. 366-7.]

Section C: Subjects Excluded

Publications on the following subjects from any source are to be excluded. Any that are wanted will be separately ordered.

1. Medicine, dentistry, related topics such as psychiatry and psychotherapy, veterinary medicine.

2. Agriculture, forestry, horticulture, animal husbandry, gardening.

3. Home economics, child care, family living.

4. Gymnastics, athletics, sports, games, hobbies.

5. Calendars, almanacs, university catalogs, schedules.

6. Lists of graduate degrees granted, lists of dissertations and theses, lists of courses of instruction.

7. Annual reports, presidents' messages and addresses, inaugural lectures of officers or faculty. Include lectures given on endowments (e.g., Godkin, West) only if of major scope and evident value.

Section D: Subjects Included

This agreement is designed to bring promptly to the University Libraries currently published works of scholarly value in the fields of science and technology relevant to Stanford's research and teaching programs. Certain subjects, specified in Section C, are to be omitted entirely or in part from this coverage, because they are selected by other procedures, or are collected only selectively. Subjects to be included in the dealer's selection are shown below [pp. 379-82].

Section E: Shipping Instructions

Library materials in the fields of science and technology are to be sent separately from books which are sent under the terms of other agreements. Shipments of materials are to be sent at convenient intervals (e.g., every few days or once a week; the Order Department will consult on this). They should be sent to:

> Order Department, Science and Technology Books
> Stanford University Libraries
> Stanford, California 94305

It is understood that the dealer will pay shipping costs and insurance. Shipments under the blanket order plan for universities should be labelled: "Blanket Order."

Shipments under the approval plan should be labelled: "Approval Order, Science and Technology Books."

For the University Libraries:

Signed:_____Date:_____

Typed Name:_____

Title:_____

For ———:

Signed:_____Date:_____

Typed Name:_____

Title:_____

Subjects Included in Trade Press and Foreign University Approval Agreement

Branner Geological Library

Ceramics	Mineralogy
Climatology	Oceanography
Crystallography	Paleobotany
Geology	Paleontology
Geophysics	Petrography
Marine Biology	Petroleum Engineering
Mineral Engineering	Soils and Soil Mechanics

Chemical Engineering Library
(Note: Material at all university levels and above desired)

Chemical Engineering	Process Dynamics
Fuel Cells	*Exclude Petroleum Chemistry*
Fluid and Solid Mechanics	

Computer Science Library

Include cybernetics, mathematical tables, and all categories in "Classification System for *Computing Reviews*," published in *Comprehensive Bibliography of Computing Literature*. New York, Association for Computing Machinery, 1967. pp. ix-x.

379

Appendix VI

Engineering Library
(Subdivisions of main subjects are *not* limitations, but extensions)

Aeronautics and Astronautics
  Astrophysics
  Bio-astronautics
  Celestial Mechanics
  Guidance
  Missiles and Rockets
Civil Engineering
  Construction
  Environmental Engineering
    Air and Water Pollution
  Hydraulic Engineering
  Ocean Engineering
  Transportation
Electrical Engineering and
Electronics
  Bio-medical Electronics
  Circuits
  Communication Systems
  Computer Technology
  Information Theory
  Radioscience
  Systems Theory and
    Techniques
Engineering Mechanics
  Experimental Mechanics
  Stress Analysis
  Structural Mechanics
Industrial Engineering
  Budgeting Systems
  Engineering Economy
  Management
  Production Planning

Materials Science
  Ceramics
  Crystals
  Metals
  Fatigue
Mechanical Engineering
  Automatic Control Systems
  Design
    Human Factors Engineering
  Graphics
  Heat Transfer
  Kinematics
  Thermodynamics
  Measurement
Nuclear Engineering
  Nuclear Reactor Design
  Nuclear Reactor Shielding
  Nuclear Reactor Theory
  Nuclear Power Systems
Operations Research
  Decision Theory
  Engineering Systems
  Mathematical Models
Bibliography and Reference
  Technical Dictionaries
  Multi-Lingual Dictionaries
  Bibliographies
General
  Social Consequences of
    Engineering
  Automation
  New Technology

Falconer Biology Library
  All phases of Biology

Mathematics-Statistics Library
  Mathematics
    General
      Logic and Foundations
      General Mathematical Systems
      Mathematical Recreations
      Mathematical Tables
      Bibliography

380

Algebra
 Set Theory
 Combinatorial Analysis
 Order, Lattices, Ordered Algebraic Structures
 Theory of Numbers
 Fields and Polynomials
 Algebraic Geometry
 Linear and Multilinear Algebra; Matrix Theory
 Associative and Non-Associative Rings and Algebras
 Category Theory and Homological Algebra
 Group Theory
 Topological Groups and Lie Theory
Analysis
 Calculus
 Functions of Real Variables
 Measure and Integration
 Functions of a Complex Variable
 Potential Theory
 Several Complex Variables
 Special Functions
 Ordinary Differential Equations
 Partial Differential Equations
 Finite Differences and Functional Equations
 Sequences, Series and Summability
 Approximations and Expansions
 Fourier Analysis
 Integral Transforms; Operational Calculus
 Integral Equations
 Functional Analysis
 Operator Theory
 Calculus of Variations; Optimal Control
 Automatic Control, Theory of
Geometry
 Convex Sets and Geometric Inequalities
 Differential Geometry
 General Topology
 Algebraic Topology
 Topology; Geometry of Manifolds
Analytic Mechanics, Mathematical Aspects of
 Mechanics of Particles and Systems
 Elasticity and Plasticity
 Fluid Mechanics; Acoustics
 Quantum Mechanics
Statistics
 Mathematical Methods
 Probability Theory

Frequency Distributions
Sampling Distributions
Estimation
Hypothesis Testing
Relationships
   Regression Analysis
   Correlation
   Ranking and Scaling Methods
Variance Analysis
Design of Experiments
Stochastic Theory and Time Series Analysis
Miscellaneous
   Nomograms and Graphic Methods
   Monte Carlo Methods
   Bibliography
   Machine Methods
Abstract or Mathematical Models
Adaptive Processes
Combinatorial Analysis
Control Processes
Game Theory
Markov Processes
Optimization Techniques
Queuing Theory

Physics Library

All areas of Physics on the upper division and graduate level, including:
   Mathematical Physics
   Plasma Physics
   Microwaves
   Electronics
   Laser and Maser Technology
   Biophysics

In addition, the following:
   Astronomy
   Astrophysics
   Meteorology
   History of Physics
   Biography of Physicists and Astronomers
   Philosophy of Science
   Science Dictionaries
   Mathematical and Physics Handbooks and Tables
   Society Publications: Symposia, Conferences, etc.
   Membership Lists

Appendix VI

EXHIBIT 3. BLANKET ORDER AGREEMENT

The Stanford University Libraries hereby authorize the firm of _____
to send to the address given below, on approval, all books of scholarly
value published in the German and English languages in East and West
Germany, Austria, and Switzerland, in accordance with the stipulations
and conditions set forth below.

A. *General Conditions of the Agreement*

1. Books will be sent as soon as possible after publication, even if they
have not been listed in the relevant bibliographies at that time.

2. The Stanford University Libraries have the privilege of returning
for credit any books sent under this agreement which are not wanted for
the Libraries; the firm will credit the Libraries with the full price of
such returned books.

3. Only books carrying 1968 or later imprints will be sent.

4. The Stanford University Libraries will send to the firm of _____
an initial supply of 500 of their multiple order forms to be used as specified below. The firm will notify the Order Department of the Stanford
University Libraries when approximately 100 forms remain so that a
new supply may be forwarded.

5. For every title shipped to Stanford the firm will type a multiple
order form furnished by the Libraries, retaining the copy marked "Purchase Order" for its own use; the remaining copies will be inserted in the
title. This order form must carry the price of the title to which it refers
in the space provided.

6. The firm will check each title sent in the *Deutsche Bibliographie:
Wochentliches Verzeichnis;* the *Oesterreichische Bibliographie* (semi-
monthly); or *Das Schweizer Buch* (semi-monthly) according to the
country of publication. These marked lists will be sent to the German
Curator, Stanford University Libraries, Stanford, California 94305 by
air mail. The Libraries will pay the subscription cost of these bibliographies when billed for them by the firm.

7. A second copy of each bibliography with every title marked which
has been sent, and which deals with recent (i.e., 1870+) history, political science, economics, sociology, education, and military and naval
science, will be forwarded to the West European Curator, Hoover Institution, Stanford University, Stanford, California 94305. From these lists
the Curator will select books for the Hoover Institution, and order them
through Hoover's regular acquisition system. The Hoover Institution
will pay for the subscription cost of the bibliographies.

8. The staff of the University Libraries will check the marked lists,
indicating supplementary selections to be included in later shipments.
The relevant pages of the bibliographies will be xeroxed and sent to the
firm to serve as orders.

9. No item shall be sent of which the price exceeds $50. Any which
seems desirable for inclusion will be so marked on the bibliography; but

it will not be sent unless it is selected by one of the Stanford reviewers.

10. The Stanford University Libraries, Order Department, should be notified when the total expenditure on materials through this arrangement has reached $10,000.

11. The original agreement will be effective for the calendar year 1968; but the agreement may be cancelled by either party upon three months' notice to the other.

12. Each shipment of books will be invoiced upon shipment. Two copies of each invoice should be sent by air mail to the Order Department and one copy enclosed in the shipment to which it refers. Invoices for blanket order shipments should be kept separate from invoices for books ordered by special individual purchase orders sent from Stanford. All invoices will be processed for payment promptly upon receipt of the books listed.

13. All shipments of books will be by surface mail, addressed as below, and labeled "_____ Blanket Order":

> Order Department
> Stanford University Libraries
> Stanford, California 94305
> USA

14. Shipments will be made at intervals of ten days to two weeks under normal circumstances, with due regard to postal regulations respecting size and weight of shipments.

B. Types of Material to Be Excluded

1. Serial publications: journals, bulletins, etc. The first volume only of a monograph series should be included if it falls within the subjects included, and if possible a prospectus of the series should be sent. *Subsequent volumes should not be sent on this blanket order; subscriptions will be placed for these series if wanted.*

2. Initial volumes of multi-volume sets of a general nature to be published over a long period of time should *not* be sent; but a prospectus of each such set should be sent for consideration and possible subscription. Monograph works published in several volumes *should* be included if they fall within the criteria for inclusion.

3. Books for children or young people.

4. Books for students below university level.

5. Manuscripts, typescripts, and television, radio, or motion picture scripts.

6. Maps and atlases.

7. Society and academy publications.

8. Government publications.

9. Reprints without change, extracts, separates from larger works, and translations into German from other languages.

10. Music scores.

11. Instruction books for trades or professions, manuals for the opera-

tion or repair of machinery, books on construction or repair of buildings or appliances, trade catalogs, supply catalogs.

12. Registers, directories, membership lists.
13. Theses or dissertations for academic degrees.
14. Sound recordings of any description.
15. Books published or distributed by the Wissenschaftliche Buchgesellschaft, Darmstadt. The latest yearly catalogs and latest announcements of WB are to be consulted.

C. Subjects to Be Included

1. German language and literature, including:
   Essays.
   Criticism.
   Scholarly bibliographies.
   Include new critical editions of German classics, including editions like the Hanser Klassiker (but *not Hanser Volksausgaben*) or Insel Klassiker (but *not Insel Ausgaben*).
   Exclude Bertelsmann and Knaur-Droemer classic editions.
2. Other humanities
   a. Linguistics and philology dealing with any language; but *omit* dictionaries. Include comparative, structural, socio- and psycholinguistics, child language.
   b. Theater and motion picture design, direction, and production; but *omit* scripts. Include history of the theater, motion picture and television from the production (not engineering) side.
   c. Biography falling within the included subject categories.
   d. Religion and theology, with emphasis on history and sociology of religion; the Reformation and the growth of humanism; history of missions, with special reference to Africa, Asia, and Latin America. *Omit* devotional works, prayer books, instructional works, catechisms, etc. *Omit* versions of the Bible.
   Include new works of well-known theologians, e.g., Rahner, Küng, Barth, Niemöller, etc.
   e. Philosophy. New works and new editions of older philosophers should be sent if they include new introductory or explanatory material, or substantial divergences from previous editions.
3. Social Sciences
   a. History. *For the following major areas of interest* there should be wide coverage; but materials of extremely local or specialized interest may be marked for attention by the Stanford reviewers:
   Western Europe, including British Isles, France, East and West Germany, Austria, Switzerland, Iberian Peninsula, Italy.
   The Slavic countries.
   The Balkan countries, including Byzantine history.
   The Far East (Japan, China, Korea).
   All Latin American countries.

All African countries, including Moslem North Africa.

For the following areas of minor interest works of substantial importance on the political, economic, and cultural life of the countries should be sent:

Southeast Asia (Burma, Thailand, Cambodia, Laos, Malay Peninsula, Vietnam, Singapore).

India and Pakistan.

Indonesia.

Philippines.

Australia.

Oceania.

The Near and Middle East.

Canada.

The Scandinavian and Baltic countries.

The Low countries.

b. Anthropology of all countries and races.

c. Economics; but *omit* techniques of business operation and management, and history of local businesses and industries. Economics of underdeveloped countries are of special interest. Land use from an economic standpoint should be included.

d. Political science and public administration, including political theory and administrative practice; international relations.

e. Sociology of all countries.

f. Psychology, with emphasis on experimental psychology. *Omit* psychiatry and popular accounts of cures, etc. Include scholarly works on parapsychology, extra-sensory perception, hypnotism, etc.

g. Geography of all countries, with emphasis on economic geography, human ecology, demographic studies, regional and national planning and land utilization.

h. Educational history and psychology in general; *omit* psychological tests, descriptions of national school systems, educational administration and practice.

D. Subjects to Be Excluded

Selections in these subjects will be made from the marked bibliographies when desired.

1. All fiction in any form: novels, short stories, poetry, drama.

2. Sciences and technological subjects; but include the general history of scientific thought and technological development.

3. Medicine, dentistry, and veterinary medicine.

4. Agriculture, forestry, horticulture, animal husbandry.

5. Fine arts and architecture; urban planning.

6. Archeology of all countries.

7. Domestic science, home economics, cookbooks, child-rearing, do-it-yourself books.

386

8. Law and international law; but include international relations (see C.3.d. — Political Science).

9. Educational practice, pedagogy, school administration, school construction, etc.

10. Gymnastics, sports and games, hobbies.

11. Astrology, fortune-telling, occultism.

12. Calendars and almanacs.

13. Business administration (see C.3.c — Economics).

14. Reference books, such as dictionaries, encyclopedias, both general and special, ready information books, etc.

All books and invoices are to be sent to the following address and labelled "＿＿＿ Blanket Order":

> Order Department
> Stanford University Libraries
> Stanford, California 94305
> USA

All marked bibliographies and prospectuses are to be sent to:

> German Language Curator
> Stanford University Libraries
> Stanford, California 94305
> USA

Second copies of marked bibliographies (history, political science, economics, sociology, education and military and naval science) are to be sent to:

> Hoover Institution
> Stanford University
> Stanford, California 94305
> USA

For the Stanford University Libraries:

Signed:＿＿＿＿＿＿＿＿＿＿＿＿＿＿＿＿＿＿Date:＿＿＿＿＿＿＿

Typed Name:＿＿＿＿＿＿＿＿＿＿＿＿＿＿＿＿＿＿＿＿＿＿＿＿＿

Title:＿＿＿＿＿＿＿＿＿＿＿＿＿＿＿＿＿＿＿＿＿＿＿＿＿＿＿＿＿

For ＿＿＿:

Signed:＿＿＿＿＿＿＿＿＿＿＿＿＿＿＿＿＿＿Date:＿＿＿＿＿＿＿

Typed Name:＿＿＿＿＿＿＿＿＿＿＿＿＿＿＿＿＿＿＿＿＿＿＿＿＿

Title:＿＿＿＿＿＿＿＿＿＿＿＿＿＿＿＿＿＿＿＿＿＿＿＿＿＿＿＿＿

EXHIBIT 4. EN BLOC AGREEMENT

THIS AGREEMENT, made and entered into as of the ＿＿＿ day of ＿＿＿, 19＿, by and between ＿＿＿ & co., a New York corporation, a majority of whose stock is owned by ＿＿＿, (hereinafter referred to as ＿＿＿), and THE BOARD OF TRUSTEES OF THE LELAND STANFORD JUNIOR UNIVERSITY,

387

a body having corporate powers under the laws of the State of California, (hereinafter referred to as "Stanford"),

WITNESSETH:

RECITALS:

A. ———, a dealer in art books with offices in New York City, desires to reduce substantially its inventory.

B. Stanford desires to purchase a substantial portion of the inventory of ——— upon the terms and conditions hereinafter set forth.

NOW, THEREFORE, for and in consideration of their mutual promises and for other valuable consideration, receipt whereof is hereby acknowledged, the parties hereto agree as follows:

1. Subject to the terms and conditions hereinafter set forth, ——— agrees to sell and Stanford agrees to purchase books from the inventory of ——— for a total amount of not less than One Hundred Thousand Dollars ($100,000), such total amount to be based upon the selling price of the books to Stanford, as hereinafter provided.

2. The inventory of books from which Stanford will make its selection is presently housed in the premises of ——— at ———, the ——— warehouse at ———, and in the residence of ——— in ———. Commencing as of the date of this agreement and continuing to and including ———, 19—, Stanford shall have the right to send one or more representatives to any or all of the above locations during normal business hours in order to make selections of the books which Stanford desires to purchase under this agreement. During this period ——— agrees that it will not enter into any contract or contracts with any other party or parties for the bulk sale of any portion of its inventory of books at any of the above locations, bulk sales being defined as any sale to any one customer in excess of 100 volumes. ——— affirms and acknowledges that there are no outstanding contracts for the bulk sale of any of such books.

3. During the period set forth in paragraph 2 above, Stanford representatives shall make tentative selections of inventory books to be purchased by Stanford under this agreement. Books tentatively selected by Stanford shall be placed on separate shelves by ——— until such time as Stanford shall notify ——— as to which of the tentatively selected books it desires to purchase. Stanford agrees to notify ——— of the titles of the tentatively selected inventory books it desires to purchase not later than ———, 19—.

4. The selling price of the books to be purchased by Stanford under this agreement shall be the list price less forty per cent (40%), and ——— agrees that all its inventory of books at any of the three locations set forth in paragraph 2 above shall be made available to Stanford at such discount. If the list price is not set forth on any inventory item,

_____ agrees to advise the Stanford representatives of the list price promptly upon request.

5. _____ agrees to provide Stanford with reasonable working space for several representatives at each of the locations set forth above during the period set forth in paragraph 2. _____ further agrees to permit Stanford to make photocopies of the title pages of any of the volumes tentatively selected by it. Stanford shall supply the photocopy machine and shall pay the costs thereof.

6. In the event that Stanford shall not select books from the inventory of _____ in the total amount of $100,000 (priced as provided in paragraph 4 above) by _____, 19___, it is agreed and understood that during the period commencing _____, 19___, and terminating _____, 19___, _____ will order art books as requested by Stanford and shall sell such books to Stanford at a price of twenty per cent (20%) below list price, such discount to apply to all orders, whether domestic or foreign. Stanford agrees to order a sufficient number of art books from _____ during such period to bring the total amount of its purchases to $100,000 (price at the applicable discounts as provided above, i.e., forty per cent (40%) on books in the inventory of _____ and twenty per cent (20%) on books specially ordered). Until such time as Stanford has purchased books in the total amount of $100,000, but in any event not later than _____, 19___, _____ agrees to give Stanford a first opportunity to purchase from new book lists of _____ prior to the public release of such lists and in this connection agrees to furnish such lists to Stanford not less than two weeks in advance of their public release.

7. _____ agrees to hold the books selected from its inventory by Stanford until receipt of written request by Stanford to ship the books to Stanford; provided, however, that Stanford agrees to request shipment not later than _____, 19___. Following receipt of the order to ship, _____, at its own expense, shall pack and crate the books in a secure manner and will deliver them to a common carrier for shipment to Stanford, attention Director of University Libraries, Stanford University, Stanford, California. Transportation charges shall be paid by _____. Title to the books shall vest in Stanford upon delivery of the books to a common carrier, and Stanford shall be responsible for arranging insurance coverage on the books following their delivery to a common carrier. _____ shall similarly pack and ship at its own expense any books specially ordered by Stanford pursuant to the provisions of paragraph 6 above.

8. Payment for the books purchased by Stanford under this agreement shall be made in four installments of Twenty-five Thousand Dollars ($25,000) each, the first installment to be paid within ten days following receipt of the books selected from the _____ inventory and the remaining installments to be payable yearly over a period of three (3) years commencing on the anniversary date of the payment of the first installment by Stanford. Any applicable sale or use taxes shall be

paid by Stanford. _____ shall prepare a list of all books selected by Stanford and shall furnish such list to Stanford together with an invoice at the time of the shipment of the books from New York.

9. _____ shall be responsible for compliance with the New York State Bulk Sales Act and shall furnish Stanford satisfactory evidence of such compliance in advance of the date of shipment of the inventory books from New York or, in the alternative, shall furnish Stanford with an opinion of an attorney authorized to practice law in New York that compliance with the New York State Bulk Sales Act is not required in connection with this transaction.

10. In the event of the destruction of a substantial portion of the inventory of _____ by reason of fire, flood, or other disaster prior to the shipment to Stanford of the inventory books, Stanford shall have the option of terminating this agreement upon the giving of written notice to _____ not more than sixty (60) days following such destruction.

11. This agreement shall not be assignable by either party without the express written consent of the other party. In the event of the transfer of the controlling interest in _____ & co. by _____ prior to the selection and shipment of the inventory books, Stanford shall have the right to terminate this agreement upon the giving of written notice to _____. Subject to the foregoing, this agreement shall be binding upon and inure to the benefit of the parties hereto, their successors and assigns.

12. _____ warrants that it has good title to the books to be sold to Stanford pursuant to this agreement and that such books are now and shall be delivered to Stanford free and clear of any security interest or other lien encumbrance.

13. The addresses of the parties for the giving of notice hereunder shall be as follows:

_____: _____ & Co.

New York, New York

Stanford: Director, Stanford University Libraries
Stanford University
Stanford, California

IN WITNESS WHEREOF, the parties hereto have executed this agreement in duplicate by proper persons thereunto duly authorized as of the day and year first hereinabove written.

By_____

Title_____

Approved as to form:

THE BOARD OF TRUSTEES OF THE
LELAND STANFORD JUNIOR UNIVERSITY

Approved as to
 fund availability:

By_____
Vice President for Business Affairs

390

APPENDIX VII
LIBRARY FACILITIES AND SERVICES
(EXCERPT FROM A UNIVERSITY'S *Administrative Guide*)

1. Bibliographical Services
   a. Major library units have reference librarians who are qualified to answer questions about particular University holdings or sources of publications.
   b. Extensive literature searches or bibliographical studies requiring hours of work normally cannot be undertaken. However, if special funds are available, staff can often be hired temporarily to undertake such assignments.
2. Eligibility for Using the Libraries
   a. The extent to which the resources and services of the libraries of the University may be used depends upon the type of association the individual has with the University. The libraries reserve the right to request the identification of users. Priority of use of each autonomous library is given to its own students or scholars.
   b. University students, faculty members, regular staff employees, and retired faculty and staff may use any of the libraries, subject only to the regulations of each library unit. Privileges for continuing graduate and undergraduate students are extended through the summer by the University Libraries upon presentation of a Spring Quarter registration card. Some autonomous libraries require current registration.
   c. The wives and husbands of University students, faculty, and staff may obtain a courtesy card for borrowing privileges from the Circulation Desk in the Main Library. The children of faculty and staff also may obtain a courtesy borrowing card if they are attending a senior high school, college, or university. Arrangements for courtesy borrowing privileges for family members at the autonomous libraries are made with the particular library.
   d. Scholars associated with the University have borrowing privileges at the libraries of the University without charge. Autonomous libraries may have slightly varying policies. This group includes:
      (1) Candidates for a higher degree who are teaching in the area; an authorization from the Graduate Study Office must be presented.
      (2) Master teachers assisting the School of Education in the teacher education program; identification is by means of lists sent from departments in the School of Education to the Main Library Circulation Division.

391

(3) Fellows of the Center for Advanced Study in the Behavioral Sciences; identification is by means of a list sent from the Center Director's office to the Main Library Circulation Division.

e. Certain categories of scholars may receive borrowing privileges at the libraries of the University without charge. This group includes:

(1) Visiting Scholars, postdoctoral fellows, etc., who are not required to register on an attendance permit basis; identification is by means of a courtesy card obtained from the Registrar's Office upon receipt of a written request from a department head.

(2) Medical School postdoctoral fellows, interns, and residents; identification is by means of a courtesy card obtained from the Dean's Office of the School of Medicine.

(3) Visiting Scholars from institutions outside the local area; identification is by means of a faculty card from their institution presented to the Main Library Circulation Division.

f. Scholars not associated with the University but who are affiliated with institutions in the local area may receive borrowing privileges at the University Libraries, with the exception of the Undergraduate Library, upon payment of an annual fee. Privileges are in accordance with particular regulations of the autonomous libraries.

g. All alumni of the University and individuals not otherwise qualified may request access to all libraries through the Main Library Circulation Division, or through the autonomous libraries, upon payment of an annual fee.

h. Industrial and commercial firms have access only by arrangement with the Medical Library, Library of Business, Law Library, Research Institution, or the Technical Information Service of the University Libraries. A fee is charged.

i. Access fees for library services sometimes are waived for non-profit organizations or organizations which, because of reciprocal benefits, are given free use of special subject collections. Policies and fees may be obtained from the Main Library and the autonomous libraries.

3. Borrowing Privileges

a. Nearly all books and other material in the University's libraries may be borrowed by those eligible. Copies of the printed Borrowing Regulations for the University Libraries are available upon request. Autonomous libraries have their own circulation rules which in general terms are identical to these regulations but may be different in some details.

b. Persons seeking a cataloged book that is unavailable at a particular time may request notification when the book is available. Upon request, the libraries recall books from persons who have had a book on extended loan.

c. A faculty member who needs material that is out on loan may request and be given the name of the borrower. The Library reserves the right to reveal to other readers the name of the person to whom a book is charged if such person fails to return the book after being requested to do so.

d. Any borrower intending to leave the local area for more than one week should either return all library materials charged to him or make arrangements with the library to insure prompt return of materials if needed.

e. Fees charged students for overdue books normally do not apply to faculty and staff unless the lending regulations of the particular library so state. A charge for lost books normally applies to all borrowers.

f. Borrowing privileges are subject to cancellation for cause. Privileges are non-transferable; borrowing for any unauthorized person constitutes grounds for withdrawing library privileges.

4. Carrel Assignments

a. Study carrels or individual desks in the Main Library and in the Research Institution are assigned by the circulation librarian in the particular library. Some carrels are available for assignment in departmental libraries.

b. These private study facilities are in such short supply that priority is given to faculty members or students working on a doctoral thesis or similar extended research. Carrels may have to be shared with another person.

5. Catalogs of University Library Holdings

a. A Union Catalog is maintained on the second floor of the Main Library. This card catalog lists nearly all publications held at the University with the exception of the holdings of the Undergraduate Library and the Linear Accelerator Center. A copy of the Undergraduate Library book catalog is available for reference at the Union Catalog.

b. The Union Catalog includes cards with general bibliographical data and locations for serial publications, but details of the holdings of periodicals and other serials are maintained in the Serials Record or in the Government Document Division in the Main Library or in the autonomous libraries.

c. Special catalogs, lists, or published sources provide references for many government documents and all manuscripts, archives, and sheet maps, technical reports, and other non-book materials.

d. A catalog for sound recordings is in the Archive of Recorded Sound, and a book catalog exists for sound recordings in the Undergraduate Library.

e. Most large microtext series are not individually cataloged. Instead, lists or bibliographies located at the Union Catalog or in reference collections serve as the index of individual books or other items in a series. Examples of microtext series are non-depository U.S. government documents, early English and American books and periodicals, U.S. presidential papers, Atomic Energy Commission technical reports, and the Human Relations Area Files.

    f. Each departmental and autonomous library has a catalog of its own holdings.

6. Course Reserve Services

    a. Books, periodicals, and other library materials may be placed on reserve when assigned by the faculty for courses of instruction. Reserve books to be used as required reading by undergraduates are provided in the Undergraduate Library or in the larger science libraries. Library materials for graduate courses are provided in the larger departmental libraries or in the Main Library Reference Room.

    b. To insure that books will be available for students, faculty members should have reserve lists in the hands of the appropriate library as follows:

        (1) Not later than the week of final exams of the preceding quarter when books are known to be in the library.

        (2) From four to six weeks before the week of final exams if the book is not in the library and purchase in the United States is required.

        (3) Two months or longer is required for books that must be purchased from foreign sources or for searching out-of-print titles. The time required should be verified with the library before class assignment.

        (4) At least two months for photographic reproduction of portions of a publication still under copyright since permission must be obtained for copying.

    c. Assignment of recordings, discs or magnetic tapes, can be handled through the Audio Library in the Undergraduate Library.

    d. Assignment of microtexts can be handled in the Microtext Reading Room, but the time required for the assignment should be discussed with the library because of the limited number of reading machines.

    e. Assignment of a rare book or manuscript should be discussed in advance with the Chief of the Division of Special Collections or the Manuscripts Librarian in the Main Library.

    f. Assignment of newspapers, maps, and other special materials should be discussed with the reference librarians in the Main Library.

7. Film Rentals

    a. The AV Office in the Main Library will arrange to borrow any motion picture film, film strip, or slide for the instructional or research use of any member of the faculty, staff, or for student groups.

b. A film bibliographical service is available in the AV Office, and previewing can be arranged at the Audio Library of the Undergraduate Library. Any charges incurred for film rental are borne by the individual or department requesting the loan and must be covered by a Purchase Requisition.

c. Projectors, screens, sound equipment, and operators are available if needed outside the library by arrangement with the Public Events Section in the Physical Plant Department. Requests for Equipment and operators should be made at least one day in advance on a Physical Plant Work Order.

8. Interlibrary Loan Service

a. The Interlibrary Loan Service facilitates the work of faculty and graduate students whose research requires short-term use of materials not locally available and which are not justifiable for library purchase. Undergraduates normally can borrow only the foreign newspapers available through the Center for Research Libraries in Chicago.

b. There is no charge for interlibrary borrowing except in the Medical Library and the Library of Business.

c. The individual for whom the book is borrowed must agree to observe fully any stipulations placed by the lending library on the duration of loan, place of use, or photocopying restrictions.

d. The Library will purchase in photocopy form material not available on interlibrary loan from another institution if such purchase is within acquisition policies and if funds are available.

e. No material will be borrowed which is in print or which is required reading for a course.

f. Except in the Faculties of Law, Business, and Medicine, members of the University who wish to purchase a photocopy of materials in another library for their personal use may arrange this through the Main Library Interlibrary Loan Service. The purchaser reimburses the Library upon receipt of the material.

9. Microtext Services

a. Microtexts include roll microfilm, microfiche, opaque Microprint, Microcards, and film strips. Most microtexts are located in the Microtext Reading Room in the Main Library basement.

b. Reading equipment for each type of microtext is available. There are two enlargement printers for all forms of transparencies. Enlargement prints are available at cost.

c. A few portable microfilm readers are available for faculty members who wish to read roll film in their studies or offices.

d. Some microtexts and readers are also available in the Undergraduate Library, Music Library, Education Library, Geology Library, Chemistry Library, and the Research Institution.

10. Photocopy Services

   a. Photocopy services are provided for students and faculty at locations in the Main Library, the Undergraduate Library, the Geology Library, the Biology Library, the Physics Library, the Food Research Institute, the Library of Business, and the Medical Library.

   b. Subject to copyright restrictions, library materials may be copied at nominal rates within a few minutes. Delayed service is available at all but the Medical Library at a discount. Users may deliver materials to be copied and return later to pick up completed orders. Charges are paid in cash or will be billed to University accounts when an Interdepartmental Request is submitted.

   c. Faculty and staff may telephone requests for photocopies of library materials to the Reference Desk in the Main Library, or requests may be sent to the Interlibrary Loan Service, Main Library. A nominal charge is added for bibliographical searching and obtaining the material. The photocopies are sent by interdepartmental mail unless a special messenger arrangement is made. An Interdepartmental Request must be submitted to cover charges for these services.

   d. Requests for enlargements, reductions, archival quality copies, reproductions suitable for publication, or special copies of library materials will be referred by the Library to the Photo-Reproduction Services Department. Charges incurred are billed to the individual or are covered by an Interdepartmental Request.

APPENDIX VIII
USE OF THE
HARVARD COLLEGE LIBRARY
BY VISITING READERS

The Harvard College Library exists primarily for the faculty and students of Harvard College and the Harvard Graduate School of Arts and Sciences, and more broadly speaking for all members of the University. However, it welcomes use by other scholars to the largest extent consistent with its primary purposes.

The Harvard College Library is comprised primarily of the collections in the Widener, Houghton, Lamont, and Fine Arts Libraries. In addition, there are a number of departmental libraries separately housed which are part of the College Library. Widener contains the central research collection; Houghton, the rare books and manuscripts; Lamont, books selected for course instruction as well as collateral reading for course work and recreational reading; and Fine Arts, the central collection in the fine arts for the whole of the University.

USE OF THE WIDENER LIBRARY

Alumni

Alumni of Harvard and Radcliffe may use books in the Library without fee. They may borrow books for outside use on payment of an annual fee of $50.00. An alumnus who does not make regular use of the Library but who wishes to borrow a book on a special occasion should apply for this privilege at the Reference Desk.

Scholars Residing Nearby

Other persons who reside in the vicinity and are engaged in serious work of a scholarly nature may be granted use of books in the Library without fee for one month in any one year. Application forms may be obtained at the Library Privileges Desk in Widener Library. Such persons wishing to borrow books, or to use the Library for more than one month, may do so for specified periods subject to the fees listed below.

$$3 \text{ months} - \$\ 75.00$$
$$6 \text{ months} - \$125.00$$
$$1 \text{ year} \quad\ - \$200.00$$

Graduate students at nearby universities should rely primarily on the resources of their own and public libraries. However, the College Library will entertain applications from doctoral candidates engaged in research for their dissertations on recommendation by their own librarians.

Appendix VIII

Visiting Scholars

Faculty members of other colleges and universities, and other qualified persons engaged in scholarly work, who come from outside the Boston area to do research are granted without fee the use of books within the Library for a period of three months. Such persons wishing to borrow books, or to remain longer than three months, may apply on the basis of the fees described above.

Graduate students at colleges and universities outside the Boston area are given use of books within the Library for a period of one month without fee. Those students wishing to borrow books, or to remain longer than one month, may apply on the basis of the fees described above.

Casual Use

Persons who wish, without applying for a formal card, to see a specific book not found in other libraries accessible to them should ask for this privilege at the Reference Desk.

Admission to the Book Stack

Access to the stack is not automatic, but this privilege is granted to visiting scholars and other qualified individuals who have received general library privileges, when circumstances justify it. It cannot, however, be granted to graduate students from other colleges and universities.

Stack Desks

During term time the demand for desks in the Stack by graduate students is such that it is seldom possible to assign them to visitors, but a limited number are usually available during the summer.

Borrowing for Outside Use

Books are usually lent for one month, but may be recalled after ten days for the use of another reader. The prompt return of books called in for use by others is essential. Books in demand may be limited to ten days at the time of circulation. The due date is stamped in the back of the book, and a fine of ten cents a day is charged for each volume overdue. A fine of $1.00 a day is charged for recalled books which are not returned. All persons, on leaving the building, are required to show their books at the Inspection Desk, and to open their bags and briefcases.

Hours

The Widener building is open during term time (late September to early June, except Christmas recess) Monday to Friday from 8:45 A.M. to 10:00 P.M. and Saturday from 8:45 A.M. to 5:30 P.M. During Summer School the hours are the same except that the Saturday closing hour is 5:00 P.M. At other times the Library is open Monday to Friday from 9:00 A.M. to 5:00 P.M. and Saturday from 9:00 A.M. to 1:00 P.M.

398

Appendix VIII

The Library is closed New Year's Day, Independence Day, Labor Day, Thanksgiving Day, and Christmas, and the afternoon of Christmas Eve. Access is restricted on Commencement Day.

Many departments or services have shorter hours. The Harvard University Archives (where Harvard dissertations may be consulted) is open Monday to Friday from 9:00 A.M. to 5:00 P.M. The delivery service at the Circulation Desk is available during the hours the Library is open. The Library and Circulation Desk are open, but nearly all special departments are closed on Washington's Birthday, Memorial Day, Columbus Day, and Veterans Day.

USE OF THE HOUGHTON LIBRARY

Any person with a serious interest may use the rare materials in the Houghton Library, unless restricted by terms of gift, upon identifying himself and filling out a registration card. It is desirable for persons unaffiliated with Harvard to bring letters of introduction and to write ahead stating what it is they wish to see. The hours of the Houghton Library are 9:00 A.M. to 5:00 P.M. Monday to Friday and 9:00 A.M. to 1:00 P.M. Saturday, except on the holidays noted above.

USE OF THE LAMONT LIBRARY

The Lamont Library is open to visitors only during the Summer School. The Summer School Catalogue should be consulted for details concerning the Library and other privileges available at that time on payment of a $50.00 fee.

USE OF THE DEPARTMENTAL LIBRARIES

The Harvard College Library also includes about forty smaller units, typically working collections for particular groups of students. Conditions of use by persons outside the department of instruction vary widely; further information is obtainable at the Widener Reference Desk.

In addition to these units of the College Library, there are within the University approximately thirty libraries of affiliated research institutions and graduate professional schools. Inquiry concerning the use of these should be made directly to the libraries concerned.

September 1967

APPENDIX IX
USE OF MANUSCRIPTS
BY VISITING SCHOLARS

REPORT OF THE
COMMITTEE ON THE USE OF MANUSCRIPTS BY VISITING SCHOLARS
SET UP BY THE ASSOCIATION OF RESEARCH LIBRARIES[1]

Your committee was asked to formulate a proposed policy on the preservation and use of unpublished manuscripts: the raw material of scholarship. In our deliberations, we have considered the problem in relation to three types of libraries; (1) public libraries, federal, state and local; (2) university and college libraries; and (3) independent privately endowed semi-public libraries such as the Huntington Library and the Morgan Library. Your chairman wrote to thirteen libraries in these categories and asked the librarians to comment on the problem and to send copies of all their forms and policy statements regarding the use of manuscripts in their libraries. The excellent report on "the arrangement and use of recent large manuscript collections" of an ad hoc committee set up by the American Historical Association was made available to us by the committee chairman, Thomas C. Cochran, of the University of Pennsylvania. All this material was circulated to your committee. . . . The following policies were formulated.

General Policy
Acquisition, Preservation and Use

It is the duty of every librarian to encourage the proper use and publication of manuscripts under his care. It is his responsibility to make them (or photographic reproductions of them) easily available to qualified investigators, and to take such steps as are necessary to insure their physical safety and to preserve them in as nearly a pristine condition as possible for the use of scholars now and in the future. He should be alive to opportunities to acquire manuscripts, remembering, however, that selfish competition between libraries may encourage the owner to have a fanciful idea as to the monetary value of his manuscripts and thus defeat the common cause of preservation for use, as is the case when an integral collection is broken up at sale and scattered to the four winds. The cause of scholarship is best served by the librarian building on strength in his own institution, and directing to their proper

[1] ARL *Minutes,* July 6-7, 1951. pp. 32–4.

home manuscripts which would fit into or supplement strong collections in other institutions. The librarian should make every effort to discourage restrictions being placed on the use of manuscripts, such as are sometimes requested by former owners, and in any case require a terminal date for restrictions, and wherever possible he should acquire publication rights along with physical possession.

Reading Room Rules

Some rules are necessary to regulate access to manuscripts and all investigators should be made acquainted with them. Most scholars are perfectly aware of the reasonable regulations and in sympathy with them. The following excellent reading room rules are largely adopted from the report of the Cochran Committee.

1. No smoking.
2. Use of ink shall be discouraged.
3. No marking of manuscripts and no writing of notes on top of manuscripts.
4. Existing order of manuscripts shall be carefully preserved.
5. Curator shall be notified of any manuscript apparently misplaced.
6. Extreme care shall be exercised in handling fragile material. (In the case of certain fragile or unusually precious manuscripts, the Librarian should be able to satisfy many investigators with photographic reproductions.)

With reference to the qualifications of prospective users, the librarian must be satisfied that they are trustworthy, intend to use the material for scholarly purposes, and are sufficiently trained to do so.

Freedom of Access

Librarians should give all qualified investigators complete freedom of access to manuscripts. Freedom of access includes the privileges of studying the manuscript or collection of manuscripts, of taking notes, of copying and of ordering photographic reproductions. Freedom of access does not include the right to publish. If a scholar requests the photographic reproduction of a large collection of manuscripts, such a request should be granted only when it comes with the sponsorship of another library, and the reproduction should be sent to that library with the understanding that it will take the responsibility of supervising the use of the reproductions, permitting freedom of access but referring requests to publish to the original library. All requests for photographic reproductions must be specific; if there is a question of selection and judgment as to what is to be reproduced the investigator must make his own selection or employ some one to do it, and not expect that service from the staff of the library. The scholar must be prepared to pay complete photographic costs, but these should be established on a reasonable cost basis. When the investigator plans to visit a library to study manuscripts, he should give the institution advance notice of his visit and his needs.

Each library should keep a complete record of the users of its manuscripts, the manuscripts used, and the purpose of each use. The primary object of this record is for the protection of scholars by enabling the librarian to inform them of other projects in their field, with a view to preventing two men working on the same project at the same time, with ultimate conflicts on publication plans. When questions of analogous use arise the librarian should make every effort to bring the scholars together in the belief that a conference or correspondence will cause apparent conflicts to disappear.

Right of Publication

Freedom of access does not include the right of publication. Publication is defined as:

1. Printing the text verbatim in whole or in such a substantial part as in effect to constitute the whole.
2. Paraphrasing the text to such an extent as to disclose the essential content of the manuscript.

There are two types of property rights in manuscripts:

1. *Common law literary property*, which vests in the author or his heirs or assigns. It is the obligation of the scholar or publisher and not the library to secure permission to publish from the owner of this right, and to assume any liabilities if it cannot be cleared.
2. *Physical possession*, which resides in the owner of the manuscript.

It is only this latter right which a library usually has at its disposal.

The right to publish must be specially requested from the librarian stating in specific terms the nature of the use, the name of the intended publisher, and place of publication. If possible, it is courteous of the author to present to the library a copy of his publication.

The right of publication should be granted by the librarian without reservation. The committee recognizes that university and college libraries have a special responsibility to their faculty and students, and often acquire manuscript material for publication by a faculty member or a student working for the doctor's degree, and will therefore be obliged in *exceptional circumstances* to assign priorities in the publication of the manuscripts. The exceptional need for exclusive publication rights should be carefully considered and limited in duration (not more than three years), because priorities contravene the principles of liberal publication which the committee endorses.

The committee recognizes that independent semi-public libraries operating on endowment income have a pre-eminent concern that their

402

manuscript material shall be given expert scholarly treatment and adequate publication, and may predicate their authorization for publication on these considerations.

It should be emphasized that restrictions on publication must not interfere with freedom of access, which should be, in effect, unlimited.

JAMES T. BABB, Chairman
FREDERICK B. ADAMS, JR.
FREDSON BOWERS
JULIAN P. BOYD
ROBERT A. MILLER
CONYERS READ

APPENDIX X
USE OF MS MATERIAL IN THE
HARVARD UNIVERSITY LIBRARY

The MSS in the Harvard University Library are divided into two main groups: Harvard Archives and MSS other than Harvard Archives.

HARVARD ARCHIVES
Voted by the President and Fellows 7 March 1938
The Harvard Archives are deposited in the Library for safe keeping, not primarily for reference, study, or use for which other MS collections are acquired. Though deposited in the Library, title to them does not rest with the Library.

The following rules shall be observed in connection with the use of Archive MSS:

(1) The President's papers more than fifty years old may be consulted after approval by the Librarian or his representative, who in case of doubt shall refer to the President. Quotations or publication shall not be approved without permission from the Corporation.

(2) The President's papers less than fifty years old shall be treated as confidential. In general the Corporation disapproves of their use for consultation or other purposes and authorizes the Librarian so to inform applicants for access to these papers. If the Librarian believes that a special exception is justified, he may refer the matter to the Corporation with a statement of the grounds for his recommendation. If the application concerns papers written by or to a person who is still alive, the Librarian shall, if practicable, ascertain such person's wishes before referring the application to the Corporation.

(3) Records of the Corporation and the Board of Overseers more than fifty years old may be consulted after approval by the Librarian or his representative, who in case of doubt shall refer the application to the Corporation or the Board of Overseers. Permission to quote or publish shall be given only after approval by the officers of the body concerned.

(4) Records of the Corporation and the Board of Overseers less than fifty years old may be consulted only after authorization by the body in question.

(5) Financial records for 1909 or earlier may be consulted after authorization by the Librarian or his representative, who in case of doubt shall refer the application to the Financial Vice-President

404

or the Treasurer. Permission to quote or publish shall be given only on the authorization of the Financial Vice-President or the Treasurer.

(6) Financial records after 1909 may be consulted only with the approval of the Financial Vice-President or the Treasurer.

(7) Departmental records for 1909 or earlier may be consulted after authorization by the Librarian or his representative, who in case of doubt shall refer the matter to the head of the department concerned. Quotation or publication shall be permitted only with the approval of the head of the department in question.

(8) Departmental records after 1909 may be consulted only after approval by the head of the department or division concerned.

(9) Archives not noted in the above groups may be consulted with the approval of the Librarian or his representative, who in case of doubt will refer applications to the President or to the officers of the University directly concerned.

(10) Personal papers which are in the College Archives but which concern neither the business of the University or the conduct of its officers may be treated by the Librarian as if they were MSS other than Harvard Archives.

MSS OTHER THAN HARVARD ARCHIVES
Voted by the President and Fellows 7 March 1938

(1) In controlling the consultation and use of these MSS the Library shall consider the following:

(2) The physical safety of the material that is presumably unique and irreplaceable.

(3) Restrictions necessary out of regard for the rights and susceptibilities of others.

(4) That to encourage or authorize the publication of MS material by unqualified persons is unfair to the persons who collected and preserved the material, and a disservice to scholarship. MS collections are not to be treated, for the sake of students or anyone else, as Christmas pies into which Jack Horners may stick their thumbs to pull out plums.

(5) Unpublished MSS, including personal letters, may not lawfully be published, even by the owner of the physical material, without the consent of the author or those who claim under him by assignment, devise, or descent.

(6) Although there is no further question of literary property in MS which has once been published, it is to be remembered that republication may infringe upon copyrights.

(7) For administrative purposes MSS are old or modern. A MS is classed as modern until it is at least fifty years old, and until the author and the persons referred to therein have died.

(8) In the absence of reasons to the contrary, it may be assumed that

the Library controls the literary property in old unpublished MSS to which it has legal title.

(9) In the absence of reasons to the contrary it is to be assumed that legal objections to the publication of modern MSS may be raised by persons interested unless it is clear that the right to publish has been vested in the Library.

(10) When the Library acquires manuscripts by gift or otherwise, it should, so far as practicable, establish a record concerning the Library's rights and duties with respect to consultation and publication. In dealing with persons who own the literary rights the Library should obtain, when acquiring MSS, either a release and assignment of all literary rights and property, or a statement in writing defining such restrictions as are intended to be imposed on the Library's power and discretion.

(11) Where literary property is lodged in the Library (or in the University or one of its departments) conditions with respect to royalties or other profits from publication may properly be imposed in the interest of the institution.

With the above considerations in mind, the Librarian or his representative *may* permit a properly qualified applicant to consult a MS after the applicant has filled out and signed, on the form provided . . . , a specific request for the consultation. This form shall state among other things that the applicant agrees that he will not publish now or later from the MS without making specific application, which must be approved by the Librarian or his representative.

The administrative interpretation of these rules, and authority to decide questions not clearly covered by them, is entrusted to the Librarian.

REVISION IN REGARD TO THESES AND PRIZE PAPERS

Voted by the President and Fellows 20 November 1951

VOTED: To establish the following revised regulations in regard to the use of manuscript theses and prize papers in the University Archives:

(1) When a thesis is accepted in partial fulfillment of the requirements for a degree, or a manuscript is successful in a prize competition, it shall become the physical property of the University, and it may be lent, or its use restricted, in any way the Director of the University Library sees fit.

(2) The literary rights, including those of publication, copying extracts, or closely paraphrasing from the manuscript, shall remain the property of the author, except that the University shall have the right to make available to the public and copyright any unpublished thesis or prize paper at any time after the expiration of five years from the time it was accepted. Every reader using one of these

manuscripts shall be required to sign a printed acknowledgement of the fact that all literary rights are so reserved.

(3) Special agreements concluded in the past between the Library and departments or divisions regarding the use of these accepted previous to the adoption of this vote shall not be abrogated by it.

(4) If an author wishes to lay more stringent restrictions upon the use of his thesis, he must obtain the endorsement of the head of the department under which the thesis was written and then make application to the Director of the Library.

APPENDIX XI
AUDIO SERVICES OF THE
J. HENRY MEYER MEMORIAL LIBRARY

GENERAL INFORMATION

The Audio Services of the Meyer Library are designed primarily to support the instructional program of the University. Facilities include an Audio Library of music and the spoken word, listening rooms, audiovisual equipment and related services. The Audio Services Office is located in the southeast corner of the ground floor, Room 172, Meyer Library, Stanford University.

The Audio Library and Its Collection

Emphasis has been placed on meeting curricular needs through assigned class use and individual listening. However, the Audio Library encourages use by students to broaden their appreciation of music and the spoken word. A collection of disc and tape recordings covering music, drama, poetry and other materials is available at the Audio Library Desk located in Room 160; the Library will include lectures and speeches as the faculty may request. Recordings do not circulate outside of the Audio Library, nor are they available for visual browsing since they are not arranged by composer, author or title. A catalog of the collection is available at the Audio Library desk.

Reservation of listening positions and recordings is limited to course requirements of faculty members of the University. Reservations should be made in advance; at least by 5:00 P.M. of the day prior to the day of use.

Purchase suggestions for recordings not now in the Audio Library may be directed to the librarian on duty at the Reference Information Desk, 2nd Floor, Meyer Library, or to the Head of the Audio Services, Room 172.

Audio Facilities

Audio Library Control Center. This center provides a variety of program channels, including three disc turntables, three tape decks and an FM tuner. Programs originating from the Audio Library Control Center may be received in Room 160, the three Group Listening Rooms, the Forum Room and the Seminar Rooms, all located on the ground floor of the Meyer Library.

A daily program of music and the spoken word is also transmitted to 332 carrels having audio outlets along the periphery of the upper three floors of the Meyer Library. Earphones for these may be charged out at the Loan Desk, 2nd Floor.

Audio Library (Room 160). Fifty individual listening positions are available in this room, with permanently attached earphones at each position to allow for stereophonic listening. Programs originate from the Audio Library Control Center in this room, although recordings from the Audio Library collection may be played with student control at certain local positions within the room.

Listening Rooms (Rooms 163, 173, and 177). Each of these rooms seats a maximum of nine persons for class use. Stereophonic listening is available in each room via wall-mounted loudspeakers with a choice of using a tape and disc console within the room, or receiving a program from the Audio Library Control Center.

Forum Room. This auditorium-type room is available for special occasions when a need arises for audio-visual facilities during the quarter. Seating in this room can accommodate 120 persons.

Seminar Rooms. Classes held in these rooms have access to all audio-visual facilities of the Meyer Library, including programs originating from the Audio Library Control Center.

Portable Equipment

Portable projection and audio equipment is available for class use in the Meyer Library. Such equipment may also be scheduled for use in conjunction with lectures and meetings held in the Forum Room or the Seminar Rooms. Requests for this service should be made to the Audio Services Office.

Equipment includes: a 16-mm projector, tape recorder (½ track type), 2″ x 2″ slide and 35-mm filmstrip projectors, and both opaque and overhead projectors. Portable projection screens are also available for use within the building.

Dubbing Facilities

Room 160 and the Group Listening Rooms provide all audio facilities for classroom functions. Personally-owned recordings or reproducing equipment may not be used in these rooms. However, the Audio Services Office can arrange for duplication of recordings when necessary for class use in the Meyer Library. There is no charge for duplication, but tapes become part of the permanent Audio Library collection.

To Whom Is It Available?

1. Upon presentation of a valid University identification card, any student, faculty member or staff member may make use of Audio Library facilities if a listening position is available. Priority is given to scheduled class functions.

2. Assignment of positions in Room 160, Audio Library, will be made only by the attendant on duty at the Control Desk. Unoccupied posi-

tions may not be used for general study purposes, but must remain free for use of audio materials.

3. All listening positions are reserved for persons using University-owned audio equipment. No personally owned recordings or any type of recording or reproducing equipment, including earphones, may be brought into the Audio Library or any of the group listening rooms. This is to prevent possible damage to University equipment.

4. The three Group Listening Rooms are assigned primarily for class-room use, as reserved by an instructor on a regular schedule or for a single occasion. However, requests for use of these rooms by student groups may be directed to the Head of Audio Services, Meyer Library. Such requests may be made at the Audio Services Office, Room 172, between 8:00 A.M.-5:00 P.M., Monday through Friday, at least one day prior to the requested day of use.

5. Lounge seating in the Audio Library which is not equipped for earphone listening is intended primarily for use by those persons using scores and librettos in connection with class assignments.

6. Individual students may not reserve recordings or listening positions in the Audio Library or in any of the Group Listening Rooms.

How to Obtain a Recording?

1. A catalog of the collection is available at the Audio Library desk. Recordings in the Audio Library collection are not available for visual browsing since they are not arranged by composer, author or title.

2. A borrower wishing to listen to recordings in Room 160 must fill out a circulation request slip at the Audio Library desk. Request slips must also be made for recordings used at consoles in the Group Listening Rooms when permission has been obtained to use those rooms. Use in either case may be dependent on prior reservations for class use.

3. Persons may borrow only one recording at a time. Where albums contain several records, a person must check out the entire album and be responsible for all records. No individual records will be charged from albums.

4. If several persons are listening to a recording which has been borrowed from the Audio Library desk and the original borrower finds it necessary to leave the building, one of those persons who wishes to continue to listen to the recording must recharge it at the Audio Library desk in his or her own name for such continued use. The individual to whom a recording or album is charged must be present during the entire period of use.

5. *Important:* Recordings should not be left on machines when leaving the room temporarily. Borrowers are responsible for recordings until properly returned to the Audio Library desk.

6. Every damaged or lost recording will be billed at replacement cost, plus a five-dollar processing fee to the person signing it out for room

use. Every recording in an album is considered as a separate item for this purpose.

7. No Audio Library recordings may be borrowed for use outside of the Meyer Library building.

Care of Equipment

1. Record or tape jackets should be kept in the appropriate slots in the listening tables while a person is listening to a recording. Recordings and their jackets must be returned to the Audio Library desk together.

2. After use, earphones in Room 160 should be returned to the proper hook beneath the listening table.

3. To avoid possible damage to electronic equipment, unauthorized persons will not be permitted behind the Audio Library desk at any time.

4. To prevent damage to audio equipment, all persons are asked not to place their feet on listening tables in the Audio Library.

5. Smoking is not permitted at any time in the Audio Library or any of the Group Listening Rooms.

INFORMATION FOR THE FACULTY

Reservations of Listening Facilities

Faculty members of the University may make reservations for class use of the Audio Library or the three Group Listening Rooms in conjunction with course requirements. It is necessary that these be made in advance: between the hours of 8:00 A.M. and 5:00 P.M., Monday-Friday, through the Office of the Head of Audio Services, Extension 4980, at least one day prior to the day of use.

Faculty members reserving any of the Group Listening Rooms are requested to obtain the necessary keys for these rooms from the Audio Library desk, Room 160, shortly before class use. At the close of the class period, the instructor should see that the room is secured, the power switch turned to the "Off" position on the console and the console locked if it has been used, and the keys returned to the Audio Library desk.

Audio Use of Seminar Rooms and Forum Room

Recordings from the Audio Library collection or personally owned recordings previously duplicated by Audio Services may be broadcast via loudspeaker for classroom use to any of the Seminar Rooms or to the Forum Room. Requests for this service should be made in advance as described under *Reservations of Listening Facilities*.

Faculty members desiring to use recordings for classroom functions within the Seminar Rooms or the Forum Room may request use of portable reproducing equipment available through the Audio Services Office. Arrangements for such class use should be made in advance of the class meeting as above.

411

Appendix XI

Duplication of Tapes for Classroom Use in the Meyer Library

1. To avoid possible damage to or loss of personally owned recordings, Audio Library personnel are not permitted to accept these for use on Audio Library equipment, or to hold them on a temporary basis in the collection. However, the Meyer Library Audio Services will duplicate such recordings without charge for classroom use in the Meyer Library. These will become part of the permanent Meyer Library collection to be made available for listening by all authorized users. A minimum of three full working days is required for duplication.

2. When duplicating a personally owned recording for classroom use in the Meyer Library, the Audio Services cannot provide an extra copy for the instructor.

3. The Audio Library will be pleased to include in its permanent collection faculty-requested lectures and speeches if these are available on tape.

4. Personal recording or duplicating equipment may not be used in either the Audio Library or the Group Listening Rooms. However, personal equipment and recordings may be used by faculty in the Seminar Rooms or the Forum Room in the Meyer Library.

September, 1967

APPENDIX XII
PRESERVATION AND STORAGE OF SOUND RECORDINGS[1]

An optimum compromise storage environment for . . . [phonodiscs] which is compatible with library operations would:

(1) Prevent fungal damage by not providing an environment suitable for fungal activity. This can be accomplished by:
   (a) Reducing fungal nutrients to a minimum by keeping discs clean and not using nutrient packaging materials for storage.
   (b) Reducing moisture on disc surface below amount required by fungi.
(2) Keep moisture content of disc environment at a satisfactorily low value which is, at the same time, not so low as to cause undesirable changes in certain materials. A moisture content in equilibrium with 50 per cent R.H. at 70° F seems to be satisfactory.
(3) Keep temperature reasonably constant and at as low a figure as is compatible with human activity.
(4) Deny access of ordinary sunlight or artificial lighting of the shorter wave lengths (such as certain mercury vapor fluorescent lights).
(5) Store all discs in the vertical attitude, keep them clean, do not use rough surfaced packaging materials, and do not permit sliding contact of disc surface with other surfaces.
(6) Provide a vapor and gas barrier between the disc and the ambient atmosphere. Inert gas purging of the package prior to closure is feasible in a large operation, but is probably not necessary as just prevention of the renewal of oxygen and atmospheric contaminants in the disc environment should reduce the attack by the agents to a tolerable level.

The extent to which these measures can be taken is, of course, dependent on the operation of the individual library. If possible it is, of course, desirable to air-condition completely the entire library and keep its environment dust free, at 50 ±10 per cent R.H. and 70±5° F. If this is not possible, the playback and packaging facility environments should meet these standards and the stacks should meet the temperature standards.

The technique of handling discs should be carefully supervised. Discs should be kept clean both for playback and storage. The techniques used

[1] A. G. Pickett and M. M. Lemcoe, *Preservation and Storage of Sound Recordings*. . . . Washington, Library of Congress, 1959. pp. 47–8, 61–2.

413

in the laboratory for this study were tedious but effective. Routine cleaning was accomplished by using two commercially available systems:

(1) Prior to playback or packaging: a sparingly applied detergent solution with an applicator of sheared acetate velvet fibres.

(2) During playback: a sparingly applied ethylene glycol solution with a brush and mohair applicator pad. . . .

The recommended procedure for storing magnetic tape is to:

(1) Use only metal reels with an unslotted hub of N.A.R.T.B. dimensions (10″ reel size). The flanges of these reels must be replaced if they are deformed out of plane.

(2) Package reels in sealed metal cans or sealed boxes of a material such as polyethylene/cardboard/foil/polyethylene laminate. The boxes should be stacked on edge in the shelves. Tape should not be packaged until it is in equilibrium with 70° F and 50 per cent R.H.

(3) Stack temperature should be maintained at a temperature of 70°±5° F for often used recordings, and storage in special vaults at 50±°5° F is recommended for seldom used and valuable recordings. Stack humidity should be kept at 50 per cent ±10 per cent R.H. if this is feasible.

(4) Playback and packaging rooms should be maintained dust free and at 70°±5° F and 50 per cent ±10 per cent R.H. Tapes exposed to other environments should be conditioned in the playback environment before playback.

(5) Stray external magnetic fields should not be permitted in the stack, playback and packaging environments. The maximum flux density permitted should be 10 gauss. It should be remembered that all current-bearing wires have associated magnetic fields. Ordinary electric circuits, if properly installed and balanced, will cause no trouble because the fields will "cancel out."

(6) Playback equipment should be maintained as recommended by the manufacturer. This includes cleaning, tape transport adjustment, and component demagnetization.

(7) A rewind and inspection deck, separate from playback facilities, should be used for packaging and inspection. Winding tension for $1\frac{1}{2}$ mil tape should be constant torque of 3–5 ounces at the hub of a 10-inch N.A.R.T.B. reel.

(8) The best tape presently available for storage purposes appears to be $1\frac{1}{2}$ mil Mylar base with some doubt existing as to the coating to base adhesion of this type of tape. Any of the tape manufacturers are presently capable of producing longer-lived tapes if there is sufficient demand for them and it is hoped that one or more of them will do so. Each of the major manufacturers pro-

414

duces good tape and each product seems to have a slight advantage over disadvantage in others. The competition in this market is enforcing rapid advances in tape construction and formulation which should result in tapes of superior potential longevity in the foreseeable future.

(9) Tape should be recorded at a maximum level below 2 per cent harmonic distortion (4 db below normal recording level is usually satisfactory). The first and last fifteen feet of the tape should not be used for program recording but should have a burst of 10 mil wavelength (approximately 750 cps at 7½ ips) signal at maximum recording level preceded and followed by several layers of blank tape for inspection purposes. Tape should be aged in the packaging room for six months prior to recording. Recorded tape which has been exposed to other than the prescribed environment should be conditioned in the packaging room for six weeks prior to packaging.

(10) Tape should be inspected once every two years measured from time of last playback and rewound so that the curvature of the base is opposite to the direction of the previous curvature. This inspection should consist of measurement of print-through caused by the toneburst at the end of the tape and a spot check at the tape end next to the hub for coating adhesion or delamination. It need not include playback.

The benefits of rewind are in reduction of creep induced curvature and print-through. The disadvantage is in exposing the surface to oxidative attack. The tape should be inspected and wound after each playback.

(11) Storage shelves should be of wood or a non-magnetizable metal free from vibration or shock. . . .

APPENDIX XIII
FLOOR PLANS

JOHN M. OLIN LIBRARY, WASHINGTON UNIVERSITY   **LEVEL ONE**

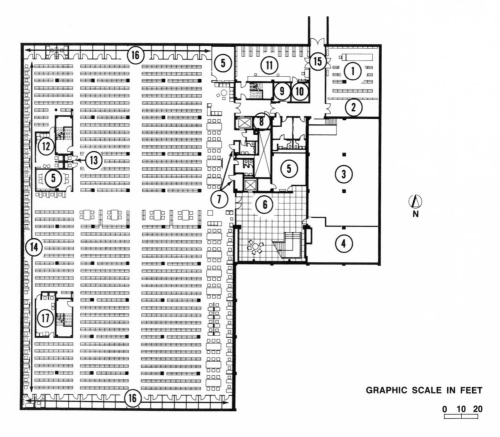

GRAPHIC SCALE IN FEET

0   10   20

1 Bibliographic Searching Department (Blanket Order Section and Searching)	**9** Refuse Deposit
2 Equipment Storage	**10** Supply Storage
3 Mechanical Equipment	**11** Shipping Room
4 Offices: Bibliographers, Systems staff	**12** Student Lounge
5 Seminar Room	**13** Typing Rooms
6 Lobby	**14** Carrels for Graduate Students
7 Maintenance Closets	**15** Receiving Tunnel
8 Incinerator	**16** Faculty Studies
	17 University Archives Office

Appendix XIII

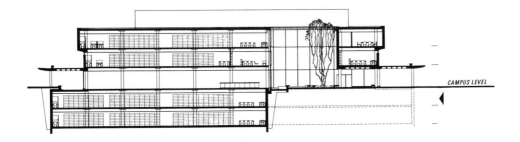

CAMPUS LEVEL

JOHN M. OLIN LIBRARY, WASHINGTON UNIVERSITY   **LEVEL TWO**

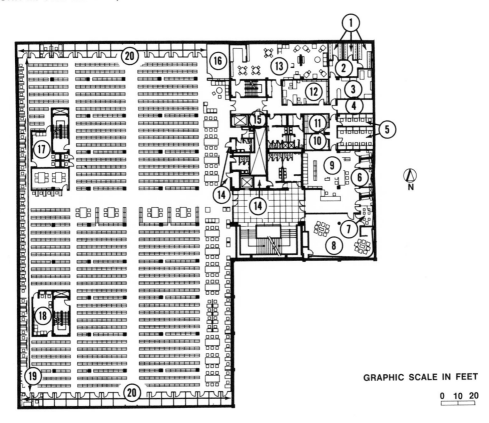

GRAPHIC SCALE IN FEET

0   10   20

1	Photo Darkrooms	
2	Microfilm Camera Room	
3	Photo Lab (Xerox Copy Service)	
4	Maintenance Storage	
5	Microtextual Material Reading Rooms	
6	Phono Listening Booths	
7	Projection Room	
8	Multipurpose Room	
9	Audio-Visual Public Service	
10	Audio-Visual Department Chief	

11	Audio-Visual Staff Workroom
12	Bindery Preparation
13	Staff Lounge
14	Maintenance Storage
15	Supply Storage
16	Seminar Room
17	Documents Staff Office
18	Student Lounge
19	Carrels for Graduate Students
20	Faculty Studies

Appendix XIII

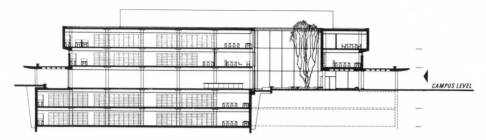

JOHN M. OLIN LIBRARY, WASHINGTON UNIVERSITY **LEVEL THREE**

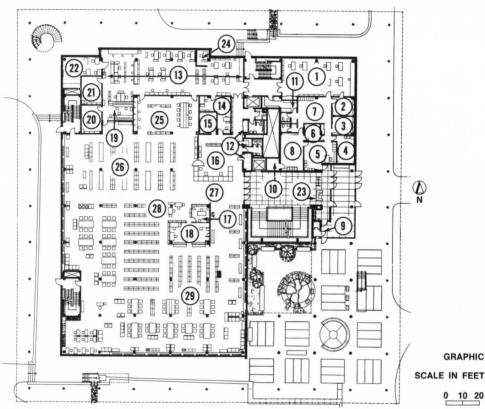

CAMPUS LEVEL

GRAPHIC

SCALE IN FEET

0   10   20

1 Office — Acquisitions Chief	**15** Office — Circulation Department Chief
2 Office — Assistant Director for Technical Services	**16** Circulation Staff Work Area
3 Office — Assistant Director for Readers Services	**17** Office — Reference Department Chief
4 Office — University Librarian	**18** Reference Department Staff Office
5 Administrative Office Reception Area	**19** Serials Records — Public Service
6 Office — Administrative Assistant	**20** Office — Serials Department Chief
7 Administrative Secretaries	**21** Office — Catalog Department Chief
8 Office — Director of Libraries	**22** Catalog Card Production Room
9 Outside Book Return	**23** Exit Control
10 Storage	**24** Office — Bibliographic Searching Department Chief
11 Central Xerox (for staff)	**25** Bibliography
12 Maintenance Closets	**26** Public Card Catalog
13 Technical Services Area	**27** Circulation Desk
14 Circulation Department Staff Office	**28** Reference Desk
	29 Periodicals

Appendix XIII

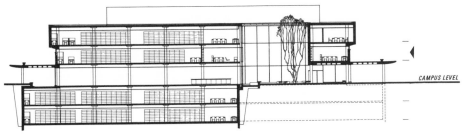

JOHN M. OLIN LIBRARY, WASHINGTON UNIVERSITY　　　　　**LEVEL FOUR**

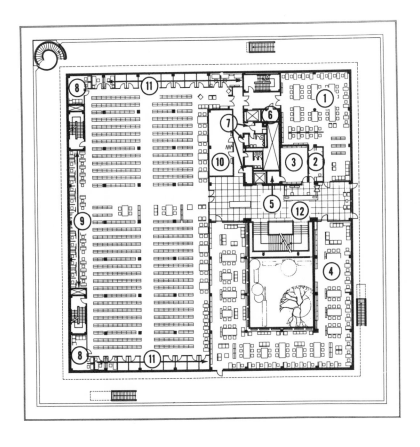

N

GRAPHIC

SCALE IN FEET

0　10　20

1 North Reserve Reading Room	**7** Maintenance
2 Office — Reserve Staff	**8** Student Lounge
3 Closed Reserve Stacks	**9** Carrels for Graduate Students
4 South Reserve Reading Room	**10** Classrooms
5 Keypunch Room (Circulation Control)	**11** Faculty Studies
6 Storage	**12** Reserve Desk

Appendix XIII

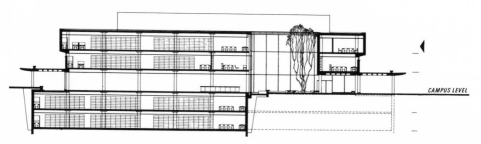

JOHN M. OLIN LIBRARY, WASHINGTON UNIVERSITY　　　　　　　**LEVEL FIVE**

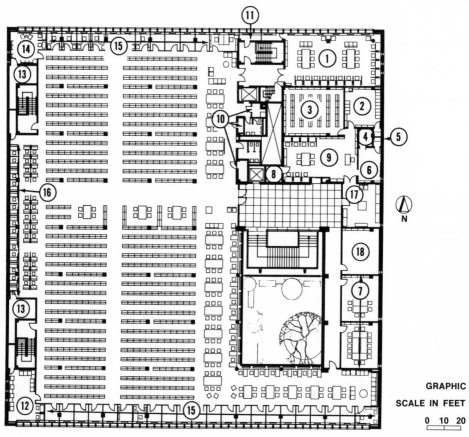

GRAPHIC

SCALE IN FEET

0　10　20

1 Manuscript Storage and Staff Work Area	**10** Maintenance
2 Rare Book Cataloging Staff	**11** Storage
3 Rare Book Stacks	**12** Student Lounge
4 Vault	**13** Mechanical Equipment and Storage
5 Storage	**14** East Asian Staff Office
6 Office — Rare Book Department Chief	**15** Faculty Studies
7 Seminar Rooms	**16** Carrels for Graduate Students
8 Storage	**17** Exhibit Area
9 Rare Book Reading Room	**18** Isador Mendle Memorial Room

Appendix XIII

JOHN M. OLIN LIBRARY,

CORNELL UNIVERSITY

LOWER LEVEL FLOOR PLAN

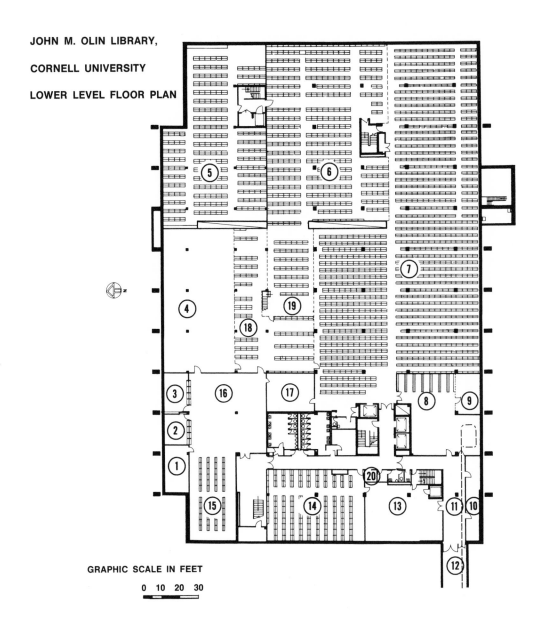

GRAPHIC SCALE IN FEET

0 10 20 30

1	Periodicals Reading Room	**16**	Spray Room	**29**	University Archives
2	Reference Reading Room	**17**	Catalog Department		Exhibit Room
3	Study	**18**	Catalog Librarian	**30**	University Archives
4	Rare Book Department	**19**	Serial Binding Librarian		Reading Room
5	Typing	**20**	Serial Binding Department	**31**	Lobby
6	Librarian, Rare Books	**21**	Central Serial	**32**	Check Out Desk
7	Curator, Rare Books		Record Department	**33**	New Books
8	Staff Workroom	**22**	Central Serial Librarian	**34**	Reference Department
9	Vault	**23**	Technical Services	**35**	Reference Department Librarian
10	Sculpture Court		Department	**36**	Reference Desks
11	Wason Collection	**24**	Acquisition Department	**37**	Gallery
	Reading Room		Librarian	**38**	Catalog and Bibliography
12	Curator, Wason Collection	**25**	Acquisition Department	**39**	Conveyor
13	Workroom	**26**	Machine Room	**40**	Circulation Desk
14	Wason Stack	**27**	Regional History Curator	**41**	Circulation Department
15	Conference	**28**	Regional History Office	**42**	Circulation Department Librarian

JOHN M. OLIN LIBRARY,

CORNELL UNIVERSITY

FIRST FLOOR PLAN

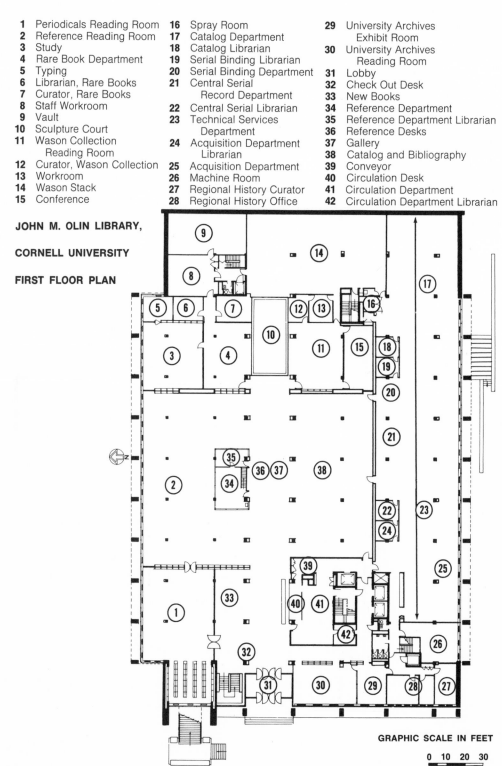

GRAPHIC SCALE IN FEET

0 10 20 30

Appendix XIII

1 Director
2 Administrative Assistant
3 Files
4 Conveyor
5 Utility Room
6 Storage
7 Staff Lounge
8 Faculty and Student Lounge
9 Sculpture Court

10 History of Science Collections
11 Icelandic Curator
12 Icelandic Stacks
13 Faculty Studies
14 Conference Room
15 Assistant Directors
16 General Office
17 Elevator Lobby
18 General Stacks

JOHN M. OLIN LIBRARY, CORNELL UNIVERSITY

SECOND FLOOR PLAN

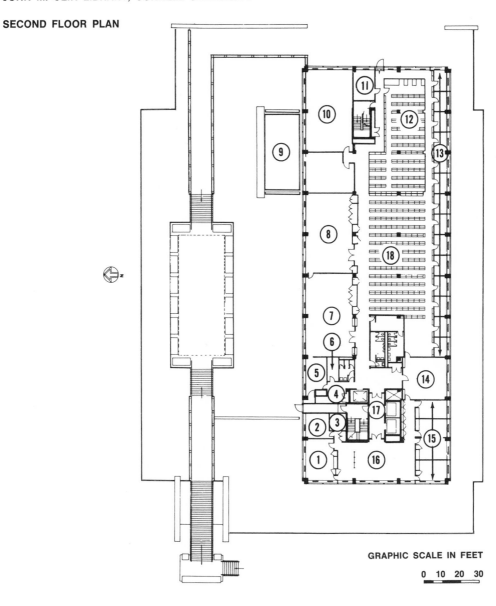

GRAPHIC SCALE IN FEET

0   10   20   30

Appendix XIII

1 Graduate Study
2 Faculty Study Rooms
3 Locked Carrels
4 Student Carrels
5 Graduate Study
6 Typing
7 Conference Room
8 Conveyor
9 Return Book Shelf
10 Stack
11 Oasis

JOHN M. OLIN LIBRARY, CORNELL UNIVERSITY
TYPICAL FLOOR PLAN 3rd, 4th, 5th and 6th FLOOR

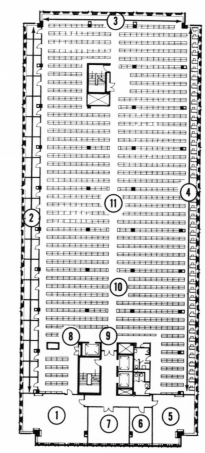

GRAPHIC SCALE IN FEET

0   10   20   30

Appendix XIII

1 Graduate Study
2 Conveyor
3 Student Carrels
4 Faculty Studies
5 Student Carrels
6 Graduate Studies
7 Conference Room
8 Return Book Shelf
9 Stack
10 Oasis

JOHN M. OLIN LIBRARY, CORNELL UNIVERSITY
SEVENTH FLOOR PLAN

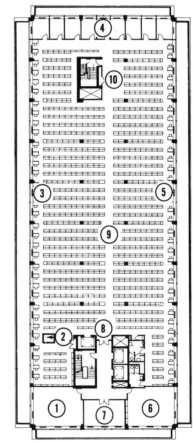

GRAPHIC SCALE IN FEET

0   10   20   30

INDEX

427

431

STATE UNIVERSITY OF NEW YORK · AT BUFFALO ·

THE
LOCKWOOD
MEMORIAL
LIBRARY
COLLECTION
OF
RARE BOOKS

RUTGERS
UNIVERSITY
LIBRARY

17 2 66

WILLIAM CHARVAT
American Fiction Collection

The Ohio State University Libraries

THE
BENJAMIN MARCH
ORIENTAL LIBRARY

COLUMBIA UNI
LIBRARI

GIFT OF
The Friends
The Columbia L

THE
William Hobart Royce
BALZAC
COLLECTION

SYRACUSE
UNIVERSITY

THE
UNIVERSITY
OF CHICAGO
LIBRARY

· THE · LIBRARY · OF · THE ·
The
E. DeGOLYER
COLLECTION
in the History of
SCIENCE AND
TECHNOLOGY
· UNIVERSITY · OF · OKLAHOMA ·

UNIVERSITY OF UTAH
LIBRARY ★ MUSIC

Gift of
DAVID AUSTIN SHAND, I

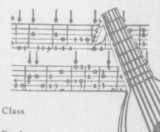

Class

Book